Your friend,

Delilae

Creating a Culture of Revolution

The Allan K. Wildman Group for the Study of Russian Politics, Society, and Culture in the Revolutionary Era has established its Historical Series to promote research into the history of the workers, peasants, and intelligentsia in Late Imperial and Soviet Russia. Deborah Pearl's study of revolutionary worker circles highlights an aspect of the revolutionary movement that till now has escaped attention: the songs, poems, revolutionary tales, and novels widely used by all revolutionary groups in their contact with workers from the 1860s inception of the revolutionary movement through the 1905 revolution (and beyond). Her analysis emphasizes the Populist origins of the circles and the extent to which, a few years later, Marxists and Populists widely shared the cultural artifacts they employed. Her combination of cultural analysis and historical narrative marks an important step in recreating the realities of the worker-intelligentsia interaction so crucial to Russia's early 20th-century revolutions.

CREATING A CULTURE OF REVOLUTION

WORKERS AND THE REVOLUTIONARY MOVEMENT IN LATE IMPERIAL RUSSIA

DEBORAH PEARL

Bloomington, Indiana, 2015

SLAVICA

Cover: N. I. Verkhoturov, *Propagandistka v rabochem kruzhke* (*Propagandist in the Workers' Circle*), 1908, oil on canvas, by permission from the Gosudarstvennyi tsentral'nyi muzei sovremennoi istorii Rossii (State Central Museum of the Contemporary History of Russia), Moscow.

Library of Congress Cataloging-in-Publication Data

Pearl, Deborah Lee.
   Creating a culture of revolution : workers and the revolutionary movement in late imperial Russia / Deborah Pearl.
      pages cm. -- (The Allan K. Wildman Group historical series ; 8)
Summary: "Creating a Culture of Revolution explores the subculture of radical workers within the Russian revolutionary movement in the period 1870-1905. The analysis focuses on the workers' circle as the key institution in this subculture and on the varieties of revolutionary literature used for propaganda"--Provided by publisher.
   Includes bibliographical references and index.
   ISBN 978-0-89357-422-2
1. Working class--Political activity--Russia--History--19th century.
2. Working class--Political activity--Russia--History--20th century. 3. Working class--Russia--Societies, etc.--History. 4. Radicals--Russia--History. 5. Revolutionaries--Russia--History. 6. Social movements--Russia--History. 7. Subculture--Russia--History. 8. Politics and literature--Russia--History. 9. Propaganda, Communist--Russia--History. 10. Russia--Politics and government--1801-1917. I. Title.
   HD8526.P39 2015
   947.08'2--dc23

2015030488

Slavica Publishers
Indiana University
1430 N. Willis Drive
Bloomington, IN 47404-2146
USA

[Tel.] 1-812-856-4186
[Toll-free] 1-877-SLAVICA
[Fax] 1-812-856-4187
[Email] slavica@indiana.edu
[www] http://www.slavica.com/

For my daughter Susanna (1989–2012)

Contents

Acknowledgments

The research which culminated in this book would not have been possible without the support and encouragement of my teachers and other scholars, as well as years of dialogue and debate with students and colleagues. I owe the greatest debt to my teacher, the late Reginald Zelnik, who supervised my dissertation research and was my guide as I embarked on my scholarly path. Lively conversations with the late Richard Stites, helpful advice from the late Allan Wildman, and the sustained interest and broad perspective of the late Nicholas Riasanovsky were all of inestimable importance. Gary Marker, Rochelle Ruthchild, and Michael Melancon read each of the chapters carefully and provided valuable critique and suggestions. I gratefully acknowledge the assistance of librarians and other staff at the following libraries and archives: the State Archive of the Russian Federation (GARF), Moscow; the Russian State Historical Archive (RGIA), St. Petersburg; the Russian State Library, Moscow; the National Library of Russia, St. Petersburg; the Library of the Russian Academy of Sciences, St. Petersburg; the Library of the University of California, Berkeley; the Hoover Institution Library and Archives, Stanford University; the New York Public Library; and the Library of Congress.

Many friends, family members, colleagues, and associates deserve thanks for their support and friendship over the years of this book's gestation. While too numerous to thank each individually, I would like to mention the following: Jim Borchert and the late Susan Borchert, Gregory Conerly, Lee Steinback Drake, Orah Goldman, Sally Goldstein and the late Ron Goldstein, Lynne Koplof, Gary Marker and Ann Brody, Barbara and Allan Peskin, Rochelle Ruthchild, Cynthia Scheinberg, Cindy Shairba, Lujuana Treadwell, Blanche and Jack Valancy, Beth and Scott Wachter, and Alice Webber and Stephen Tobias. I am grateful to Hans Raillard for technical assistance and to my editor, Vicki Polansky, for her help in preparing the manuscript for publication.

ℭ ℬ

I would like to thank the following editors and publishers for permission to reprint portions of previously published articles in chapters 2 and 3:

"Political Economy for Workers: A. N. Bakh's Tsar-Golod," *Slavic Review* 50, 4 (Winter 1991): 768–78. Reprinted with permission of the publisher, the Association for Slavic, East European and Eurasian Studies.

"Tsar and Religion in Russian Revolutionary Propaganda," *Russian History* 20, 1–4 (1993): 81–107. Reprinted with permission of Brill Publishers.

"From Worker to Revolutionary: The Making of Worker Narodovol'tsy," *Russian History* 23, 1 (1996): 11–26. Reprinted with permission of Brill Publishers.

Tales of Revolution: Workers and Propaganda Skazki *in the Late Nineteenth Century,*" The Carl Beck Papers, no. 1303, 1998. Reprinted with permission of The Carl Beck Papers.

"Narodnaia Volia and the Worker," in *Workers and Intelligentsia: Workers in Late Imperial Russia. Realities, Representations, Reflections*, ed. Reginald E. Zelnik, International and Area Studies, no. 101 (Berkeley: University of California, 1999).

Introduction

The Russian Revolution of 1917 was preceded by a half century of revolutionary activity within Russia. Despite tactical and ideological differences, the various groups which made up the Russian revolutionary movement were in agreement in placing great importance on propaganda as a means of educating and winning adherents among Russian workers and peasants, as well as among the intelligentsia. From the 1870s, when radicals from the intelligentsia first made contact on any scale with members of the Russian *narod*, or common people, to the 1905 Revolution, propaganda among urban workers was a major focus of the revolutionary movement, and the workers' *kruzhok*, or circle, was the key institution. Together with the circle, a literature of propaganda took shape: works composed, selected, or adapted to educate and radicalize workers, introducing concepts and explaining how the current society was organized, the need for revolution, and principles of the future socialist society. The group of radical workers who participated in the circles served as propagandists themselves among other workers in their workplaces and neighborhoods. They became organizers of strikes and May Day demonstrations. Around these activities a radical subculture grew up, linking these workers through bonds of common endeavor, outlook, and camaraderie, made all the stronger by the illegal nature of the movement and the harsh penalties for those involved.

This study has grown out of an attempt to understand the role of Russian workers in the revolutionary movement: how did Russian workers develop the revolutionary outlook and the level of political consciousness and organizational experience that made them the crucial political and social force in the revolutions of 1905 and 1917? To answer this question, I needed to turn away from the usual tropes and icons of the history of the revolutionary movement—the famous figures and parties, the theories and ideologies—and focus on Russian workers at the most elementary level of their lives and experiences. Thus the initial phase of my research revolved around mapping the workers' revolutionary movement, identifying members of workers' circles in key cities, determining to the extent possible their background, age, occupation, level of education, and putting faces on the movement.[1] The movement at the grassroots level deviated in some surprising ways from the shape I had expected: for one, it was characterized by unity of tactics and ideas, rather than factional antagonism and disputes. The much-heralded terrorism of the Russian revolutionary movement, moreover, was observed in theory, rather than practice. In reality, the revolutionary movement consisted overwhelmingly of propaganda in workers' circles. I next turned to an investigation of what I term a "culture of revolution," the subculture of radical workers, based in the workers' circles and given shape by a variegated literature of propaganda. Here I sought to clarify the mindset of this small but influential cohort of radical workers and found in works of propaganda literature—from tales to poems to novels—one of the few artifacts left to us from the movement and a new approach to understanding the worldview, ideas, and aspirations that underpinned the workers' revolutionary movement.[2]

This book offers an alternative reading of the revolutionary workers' movement, with circle activity and propaganda literature at the center of a developing "culture of revolution": the experiences, practices, outlooks, and values of workers at the grassroots level of the revolutionary movement. It begins with a close look at the *kruzhok*, or circle, the pedagogy employed by circle leaders (usually from the intelligentsia), and topics and methods of study, as elaborated over the course of the late 19th century. One noteworthy finding is the remarkable congruence of circle studies over this period. At this most basic level, the revolutionary movement was a unified one, rather than composed of competing factions. Even more surprising, during the 1880s and early 1890s the leading revolutionary trend was represented by the People's Will (Narodnaia Volia), long considered defunct after 1881 and usually associated exclusively with terrorism. The circle was also the venue

---

[1] See Deborah Lee Pearl, "Revolutionaries and Workers: A Study of Revolutionary Propaganda among Russian Workers, 1880–1892" (Ph.D. diss., University of California, Berkeley, 1984); Pearl, "Educating Workers for Revolution: Populist Propaganda in St. Petersburg, 1879–1882," *Russian History* 15, 2–4 (1988): 255–84, reprinted in *Articles on Russian and Soviet History 1500–1991*, ed. Alexander Dallin, 3: *Imperial Russian History II 1861–1917*, ed. Gary M. Hamburg (New York, 1991), 181–200; Pearl, "Tsar and Religion in Russian Revolutionary Propaganda," *Russian History* 20, 1–4 (1993): 81–107; Pearl, "From Worker to Revolutionary: The Making of Worker *Narodovol'tsy*," *Russian History* 23, 1–4 (1996): 11–26; Pearl, "Narodnaia Volia and the Worker," in *Workers and Intelligentsia in Late Imperial Russia: Realities, Representations, Reflections*, ed. Reginald E. Zelnik (Berkeley, CA, 1999), 55–75.

[2] See Deborah L. Pearl, "Political Economy for Workers: A. N. Bakh's *Tsar-Golod*," *Slavic Review* 50, 4 (Winter 1991): 768–78; Pearl, *Tales of Revolution: Workers and Propaganda Skazki in the Late Nineteenth Century*, The Carl Beck Papers in Russian and East European Studies, no. 1303 (Pittsburgh, 1998).

for relations between *intelligenty* (members of the intelligentsia; singular—*intelligent*) and workers, a meeting ground for interaction between these two disparate social groups. The major portion of the book is devoted to analysis of the "literature of propaganda" read and discussed by workers, which is, I argue, a key vehicle for understanding the views of radical workers. These works, only rarely touched on in the historical literature, may provide more accurate evidence of the ideas permeating the workers' movement than manifestos issued by revolutionary organizations or memoirs written decades later. This focus permits investigation of key questions: how did workers come into contact with revolutionary ideas, how did they react to them, and how were these ideas assimilated or modified? Circle participation and familiarity with the works of literature used for propaganda were central to a new identity as radical workers, members of a small but important subgroup in Russian society, found in major cities and industrial areas. This "culture of revolution" thus became a factor of influence in the urban lower-class milieu during a period of major social and economic change, as the Russian Empire began to undergo rapid industrialization and urbanization.

While the literature of propaganda that informed the milieu of radical workers is at the heart of this book, my focus on the workers' movement at the grassroots level and the subculture of radical workers contributes to reevaluation of the broader subject of the history of the Russian revolutionary movement in several significant ways. My perspective brings together two topics usually dealt with separately: the history of the revolutionary movement, a story of ideologies, parties, and well-known leaders; and the history of the Russian workers' movement, most commonly highlighting the evolution of the working class and the growth of a strike movement. For many years the history of the revolutionary movement was a subject of intense interest both in the USSR and in the West: in both cases, it was regarded as the prehistory of the Communist Party of the Soviet Union. In both Cold War camps, the Bolshevik victors of October, under the post-1917 banner of the Communist Party, were taken to be the only meaningful representatives and the culmination of the pre-1917 movement. This narrow perspective, however, leads to a distorted view of the movement and one that is surprisingly bland, populated with faceless "masses" of workers. My book, by contrast, shows the workers' movement in the revolutionary movement and takes a genealogical rather than a teleological approach. This strategy leads to several major shifts in our picture of the revolutionary movement, most significantly: 1) the centrality of propaganda among urban workers to the movement as a whole; 2) the importance of the People's Will Party as not just or even mostly a terrorist organization, but the dominant revolutionary party for a good decade and a half, from the end of the 1870s; and 3) the unitary nature of the movement, at least at the grassroots level of urban workers, as opposed to the time-honored presentation of the movement as a succession of opposing groups and parties: beginning with the People's Will vs. the Black Repartition, followed by populists vs. Marxists, and so on.

While interest in the Russian revolutionary movement declined markedly with the demise of the Soviet Union, there are nevertheless some signs of renewal and reconceptualization. Broader histories of Russia tend to maintain a very traditional view on the revolutionary movement; more specialized monographs and articles, on the other hand, reveal some new perspectives and areas of interest. The most widely used Russian history texts include brief discussions of the revolutionary movement of the late 19th century but do not show the close relationship between the revolutionary and workers' movements in this period. They do not discuss revolutionary propaganda among workers, the People's Will is identified only as a terrorist organization, and in some instances the prominence of Marxism is dated to the 1880s. In these respects, the most popular overviews of Russian history continue to repeat the traditional story of the revolutionary movement.[3] Russian historian N. A. Troitskii, a specialist in the history of the People's Will and the tsarist legal system, makes brief reference to the revolutionary movement in his survey *Rossiia v XIX veke: Kurs lektsii*. Although he does not deal with revolutionary propaganda in the 1880s, he makes the revisionist assertion that the People's Will was not mostly about terror and notes that this party was the first to organize worker propaganda on a national scale.[4]

The importance of the half century of propaganda among workers which lay the foundation for revolution has not been sufficiently appreciated. A number of excellent works have been published on the revolutions of

---

[3] See Nicholas V. Riasanovsky and Mark D. Steinberg, *A History of Russia*, 8th ed. (New York, 2011), 401–02, 406, 457; and Catherine Evtukhov et al., *A History of Russia: Peoples, Legends, Events, Forces* (Boston, 2004), 481–82, 445–49. Similarly, the collective volume *Russia: A History*, ed. Gregory L. Freeze, 2nd ed. (Oxford, 2002), identifies the populist movement of the 1870s only with focus on the peasantry, identifies the People's Will as "terrorists," and makes no mention of worker propaganda by revolutionary groups. The chapter on Russia at the turn of the century also refers to the People's Will as "terror-oriented" and, while mentioning new contacts with urban workers, deems this secondary to alliances with liberals (192, 206.) A closer look at the history of the movement would more accurately emphasize the importance of propaganda among various elements of the population: students, peasants, the military, and perhaps the most important, urban workers, whose movement overlapped with the revolutionary movement, as well as having its own perspective and identity.

[4] N. A. Troitskii, *Rossiia v XIX veke: Kurs lektsii* (Moscow, 1997), 263–65.

1905 and 1917.[5] While these revolutions themselves exerted a profound revolutionizing effect on workers, the prior existence of a revolutionary subculture among workers makes their crucial role during the revolutions easier to understand. Although understandably considered background to the "main event," major reference works on 1917 have little to say on the decades-long revolutionary movement.[6] The history of the Russian revolutionary movement has traditionally consisted of a formulaic recital: peasant-oriented populism and the "movement to the people" in the 1870s, the rise of terrorism in the form of the People's Will Party, the abrupt demise of the People's Will and the revolutionary movement after the assassination of Alexander II in 1881, followed by the 1880s—an era of "small deeds"—and then finally the resurrection of the workers' movement, now social democratic, in the mid-1890s, all presented as unarguable fact. This long-accepted analysis thus ignores the link between the workers' and revolutionary movements from the early 1870s, and mistakenly views the 1880s as a kind of "blank" period. This view is seen most glaringly in regard to the revolutionary milestone of 1 March 1881, presented as the culmination of the crisis of revolutionary populism and the prelude to the decline of the movement in the 1880s. This interpretation can be seen, for example, in the major works on the revolutionary movement by Yarmolinsky, Walicki, Wortman, Sedov, and Volk.[7] Franco Venturi, author of the most comprehensive Western treatment of revolutionary populism, ends his history abruptly with the assassination of the tsar and the execution of the perpetrators.[8] Nevertheless, Venturi's

---

[5] See, to name only a few of the valuable works on this subject, Gerald D. Surh, *1905 in St. Petersburg: Labor, Society and Revolution* (Stanford, CA, 1989); Robert Weinberg, *The Revolution of 1905 in Odessa: Blood on the Steps* (Bloomington, IN, 1993); Laura Engelstein, *Moscow, 1905: Working-Class Organization and Political Conflict* (Stanford, CA, 1982); Henry Reichman, *Railwaymen and Revolution: Russia, 1905* (Berkeley, CA, 1987); Diane Koenker, *Moscow Workers and the 1917 Revolution* (Princeton, NJ, 1981); S. A. Smith, *Red Petrograd: Revolution in the Factories, 1917–18* (Cambridge; 1983).

[6] See Edward Acton, V. Iu. Cherniaev, and William G. Rosenberg, eds., *Critical Companion to the Russian Revolution, 1914–1921* (Bloomington, IN, 1997); and Harold Shukman, ed., *The Blackwell Encyclopedia of the Russian Revolution* (Oxford, 1988).

[7] See Avrahm Yarmolinsky, "A Pyrrhic Victory," chap. 15 in *Road to Revolution: A Century of Russian Radicalism* (New York, 1962); Andrzej Walicki, *The Controversy over Capitalism: Studies in the Social Philosophy of the Russian Populists* (Oxford, 1969), 106; Richard Wortman, *The Crisis of Russian Populism* (London, 1967), 157; M. G. Sedov, *Geroicheskii period revoliutsionnogo narodnichestva: Iz istorii politicheskoi bor´by* (Moscow, 1966), chaps. 5 and 6; and S. S. Volk, *Narodnaia volia 1879–1882* (Moscow–Leningrad, 1966), 115–16.

[8] Franco Venturi, *Roots of Revolution: A History of the Populist and Socialist Movements in Nineteenth Century Russia*, trans. F. Haskell (New York, 1966).

magisterial *Roots of Revolution* remains an essential work for understanding the early chapters of the revolutionary movement, with emphasis on the populist ideologies that distinguished the Russian movement from socialist movements in the West. Venturi includes discussion of propaganda activities among both peasants and workers, as well as students, and provides a good starting point for studying the movement. Although, as noted, Venturi ends his history with the events of 1 March 1881, more recent research has begun to question the traditional description of the 1880s as a period of modest efforts, of decay and decline, which separated the peasant-oriented populism of the 1870s from the growth of a social democratic workers' movement in the 1890s. Norman Naimark, in *Terrorists and Social Democrats*, begins to fill in the map of the revolutionary 1880s, showing the great variety of organizations and activities, and the complex and fluid ideologies of the period. A second work to investigate this period is *The Revolutionary Movement in the 1880s* by Derek Offord. While both works make reference to propaganda among workers, this topic is not a focus of either work.[9]

In Soviet historiography, 1883 is an important date in the revolutionary almanac—in that year the first Russian Marxist group, which took the name Emancipation of Labor Group, was founded in Swiss emigration by Georgii Plekhanov, Pavel Aksel'rod, Vera Zasulich, and a couple of other members. At that point, as the Soviet version goes, the revolutionary movement became Marxist, and populism immediately becomes suspect. In fact, although the Marxist views and publications of the Group were read and debated by radical *intelligenty* in Russia, its connections with Russia were tenuous, and the groups calling themselves *narodovol'tsy* (adherents of the People's Will) dominated the field. Nevertheless, from that year Soviet histories of the movement focused on the working-class propaganda of groups known as social democratic (or, more accurately, proto–social democratic): those Petersburg groups associated with the names of Dmitrii Blagoev and Pavel Tochisskii in the 1880s and Mikhail Brusnev in the early 1890s. Two important histories of these groups are those by R. A. Kazakevich on the Tochisskii and Brusnev groups and by Iu. Z. Polevoi on Russian Marxist groups from 1883 through the early 1890s.[10] A more nuanced view of the movement was on display in Soviet works of the 1920s by V. I. Nevskii, S. N. Valk, and N. L. Sergievskii; a more recent

---

[9] Norman M. Naimark, *Terrorists and Social Democrats: The Russian Revolutionary Movement under Alexander III* (Cambridge, MA, 1983); Derek Offord, *The Russian Revolutionary Movement in the 1880s* (Cambridge, 1986).

[10] R. A. Kazakevich, *Sotsial-demokraticheskie organizatsii Peterburga kontsa 80-kh–nachala 90-kh godov: Kruzhki P. V. Tochisskogo i M. L. Brusneva* (Leningrad, 1960); Iu. Z. Polevoi, *Zarozhdenie marksizma v Rossii, 1883–1894 gg.* (Moscow, 1959).

work that provides information on a broader spectrum of groups involved in propaganda among workers was published by G. S. Zhuikov in 1975.[11]

Soviet-era histories of the Russian working class provide information on the development of industry in late 19th-century Russia, the growth of a working class and its many subgroups, and the rise of a labor movement marked by strike activity. L. M. Ivanov, editor of the compact and informative *Istoriia rabochego klassa Rossii 1861–1900 gg.*, includes consideration of revolutionary propaganda. He gives a positive evaluation of populist propaganda in the 1870s and refers to People's Will propaganda in the 1880s, where "in most cities there were no [social democratic groups]"; nevertheless, the populism of the People's Will is described as a declining trend.[12] The useful *Istoriia rabochikh Leningrada* also integrates discussion of the revolutionary movement as it relates to workers. The work's emphasis is on the physiognomy of the working class and especially the history of strikes at various factories. Mention of the revolutionary movement leaps from populist propaganda of the early 1870s to, from 1883, the rise of Marxism. The 1890s, in standard Soviet fashion, revolve around Lenin and the Union of Struggle and the opposing "economists."[13]

The relationship between workers and the revolutionary movement in the 1890s was treated by two American scholars in books published in the 1960s: *Social Democracy and the St. Petersburg Labor Movement: 1885–1897* by Richard Pipes and *The Making of a Workers' Revolution: Russian Social Democracy, 1891–1903* by Allan K. Wildman. Both books focus on the early stages of Social Democracy as a political movement in Russia and address the question of the relationship between the movement's two constitutive social groups, the revolutionary intelligentsia and politically conscious workers, to arrive at different conclusions. Pipes views Social Democracy and the labor movement in Petersburg as two separate movements that never managed to coalesce:

---

[11] V. I. Nevskii, "K istorii 'Partii russkikh sotsial-demokratov' (Blagoevskaia gruppa)," *Proletarskaia revoliutsiia*, no. 5 (1922): 297–302, and other works; S. N. Valk, "Posle 1 marta 1881 g.," *Krasnyi arkhiv*, no. 2 (45) (1931): 147–64, and other works; N. L. Sergievskii, *Partiia russkikh sotsial-demokratov: Gruppa Blagoeva* (Moscow–Leningrad, 1929), and other works; G. S. Zhuikov, *Peterburgskie marksisty i gruppa "Osvobozhdenie truda"* (Leningrad, 1975).

[12] L. M. Ivanov, ed., *Istoriia rabochego klassa Rossii 1861–1900 gg.* (Moscow, 1972), 171. Key worker radicals of the years around 1890 are said to be "separating from the common populist tendency into an independent proletarian-democratic trend" (176). See also the useful essays in L. M. Ivanov, ed., *Rossiiskii proletariat: Oblik, bor'ba, gegemoniia* (Moscow, 1970).

[13] V. S. Diakin, ed., *Istoriia rabochikh Leningrada*, 1: *1703–fevral' 1917* (Leningrad, 1972). The indispensable document collection for working-class history in this period is the multivolume *Rabochee dvizhenie v Rossii v XIX veke: Sbornik dokumentov i materialov*, ed. A. M. Pankratova and L. M. Ivanov, 4 vols. (Moscow–Leningrad, 1950–63).

although they sometimes cooperated, they represented groups with different motivations and goals. Pipes also emphasizes what he sees as the "unpolitical and sometimes decidedly antipolitical" nature of propaganda in the workers' circles of the early 1890s. Wildman argues for a more unified view of the movement and offers a more convincing interpretation of the complex inter-relationship between workers and *intelligenty*. In their assessment of circle propaganda both scholars are actually quite close. I have found, on the con-trary, more politicized circle studies and greater radicalism on the part of "advanced" workers.[14]

Recent years have seen the appearance of new topics and new approaches to the study of workers and the revolutionary movement. Our picture of the radical worker has been transformed by the research of the late Reginald Zelnik. In a series of books and articles, he brought the workers' movement to life by focusing on specific events, such as the Kreenholm strike of 1872, and individual workers, most notably Semen Kanatchikov. His research succeeds in illuminating the broader movement through the lens of concrete examples, bringing into focus the human dimension of the workers' movement.[15] Working-class culture and the culture of worker outliers who gave voice to the dreams and longing of workers are analyzed by Mark D. Steinberg, who has focused on worker-poets in the period after 1905, using their literary works as a key to workers' values and desires.[16] Articles by Zelnik, Steinberg, and other authors published in two collections continue to enlarge the field of research on Russian workers. *Workers and Intelligentsia in Late Imperial Russia,*

---

[14] Richard Pipes, *Social Democracy and the St. Petersburg Labor Movement: 1885–1897* (Cambridge, MA, 1963); see 13–14; Allan K. Wildman, *The Making of a Workers' Revolu-tion: Russian Social Democracy, 1891–1903* (Chicago, 1967).

[15] See, among other works by Reginald E. Zelnik: *Labor and Society in Tsarist Russia: The Factory Workers of St. Petersburg, 1855–1870* (Stanford, CA, 1971); Zelnik, "Russian Bebels: An Introduction to the Memoirs of Semen Kanatchikov and Matvei Fisher," pt. 1, *Russian Review* 35, 3 (July 1976): 249–89, and pt. 2, *Russian Review* 35, 4 (October 1976): 417–47; Zelnik, ed. and trans., *A Radical Worker in Tsarist Russia: The Autobiography of Semen Ivanovich Kanatchikov* (Stanford, CA; 1986); Zelnik, "'To the Unaccustomed Eye': Religion and Irreligion in the Experience of St. Petersburg Workers in the 1870s," *Russian History* 16, 2–4 (1989): 297–326; Zelnik, "On the Eve: An Inquiry into the Life Histories and Self-Awareness of Some Worker-Revolutionaries," in *Making Workers Soviet: Power, Class, and Identity*, ed. Lewis H. Siegelbaum and Ronald Grigor Suny (Ithaca, NY, 1994), 17–65; Zelnik, *Law and Disorder on the Narova River: The Kreenholm Strike of 1872* (Berkeley, CA, 1995).

[16] See Mark D. Steinberg, *Proletarian Imagination: Self, Modernity, and the Sacred in Russia, 1910–1925* (Ithaca, NY, 2002); and Steinberg, "'A Path of Thorns': The Spiritual Wounds and Wandering of Worker-Poets," in *Sacred Stories: Religion and Spirituality in Modern Russia*, ed. Steinberg and Heather J. Coleman (Bloomington, IN, 2007), 304–29.

edited by Zelnik, includes a number of papers presented at a conference in St. Petersburg in 1995 on the topic "Workers and Intelligentsia in Russia in the Late Nineteenth and Early Twentieth Centuries." Among the topics addressed are relations between workers and revolutionary parties, proletarian culture, and workers and the First World War. The other volume, *New Labor History: Worker Identity and Experience in Russia, 1840–1918*, edited by Michael Melancon and Alice K. Pate, includes studies of workers and religion by Page Herrlinger, Alice Pate on workers and post-1905 Social Democracy, and Michael Melancon on Petrograd factory committees in 1917.[17] The connection between workers and the Socialist Revolutionary Party, in the period from the late 1890s through the early 20th century, is examined by Christopher Rice in *Russian Workers and the Socialist Revolutionary Party through the Revolution of 1905–07*. Although the SRs are most commonly seen as heirs to the earlier populists, focused on terror on the one hand and propaganda among the peasantry on the other, Rice shows that in fact the main focus in the early 20th century was on propaganda among workers; the circle activity he describes, moreover, closely resembles that of the movement of the 1870s through 1890s.[18] Michael Melancon also emphasizes the role of Socialist Revolutionary propaganda among workers and, in a series of publications, highlights the fundamental unity of the workers' revolutionary movement. While theoretical disputes were publicized, local organizations worked together across the ideological spectrum.[19]

While research on Russian workers seeks to provide a more accurate picture of the workers' movement and to integrate this movement into the

---

[17] Reginald E. Zelnik, ed., *Workers and Intelligentsia in Late Imperial Russia: Realities, Representations, Reflections* (Berkeley, 1999); Michael Melancon and Alice K. Pate, eds., *New Labor History: Worker Identity and Experience in Russia, 1840–1918* (Bloomington, IN, 2002). A brief mention cannot do justice to the varied essays in these collections. See my review of the latter collection in *Canadian Slavonic Papers* 46, 1–2 (March–June 2004): 254–56.

[18] Christopher Rice, *Russian Workers and the Socialist-Revolutionary Party through the Revolution of 1906–07* (New York, 1988), 42–46.

[19] See, among other works, Michael Melancon, "The Socialist Revolutionaries from 1902 to 1907: Peasant and Workers' Party," *Russian History* 12, 1 (Spring 1985): 2–47; Melancon *"Stormy Petrels": The Socialist Revolutionaries in Russia's Labor Organizations 1905–1914*, The Carl Beck Papers in Russian and East European Studies, no. 703 (Pittsburgh, 1988); Melancon, "Athens or Babylon? The Birth of the Socialist Revolutionary and Social Democratic Parties in Saratov, 1890–1905," in *Politics and Society in Provincial Russia: Saratov, 1590–1917*, ed. Rex A. Wade and Scott J. Seregny (Columbus, OH, 1989), 73–112; Michael Melancon and Alice K. Pate, "Bakhtin contra Marx and Lenin: A Polyphonic Approach to Russia's Labor and Revolutionary Movements," *Russian History* 31, 4 (Winter 2004): 387–417.

broader Russian society, analysis of the Russian revolutionary movement
has tended in recent years to focus on terrorism, apparently assumed to be
the most noteworthy and certainly most sensational aspect of the movement.
Interest in this topic is undoubtedly linked to present-day concerns about
global terrorism. Among the most important recent works are studies of Dmitrii Karakozov, who made an unsuccessful attempt on the life of the tsar in
1866; of Vera Zasulich's shooting (not fatal) of the St. Petersburg governor in
1878; of the intriguing story of the double agent Sergei Degaev, prominent
in the People's Will in the early 1880s; and of the life of Aleksandr Ul'ianov,
Lenin's older brother, which ended on the gallows following a failed attempt
to assassinate Alexander III in 1887.[20] Perhaps the most prominent scholar
to address the subject of terror and the revolutionary movement has been
Anna Geifman. Geifman focuses in particular on the terrorist acts of the
early 20th century and argues that in this period the revolutionary terrorism
characteristic of earlier stages of the revolutionary movement underwent a
fundamental transformation, with an exponential growth in terrorist acts,
and, although engaged in by members of all radical parties, usually divorced
from any principles and distinguished by indiscriminate violence.[21] While
the above works offer thought-provoking theories of revolutionary terror and
fascinating new details on the actors involved, they engage the revolutionary
movement from a narrow focus that does little to aid understanding of the
workers' movement. In my period of focus—the late 19th century—terrorism
is not a major factor. Geifman may be correct in her analysis of the rather different terror—in ideology, personnel, and targets—of the early 20th century,
and the reasons for this posited shift should be more closely investigated. By
contrast, while O. V. Budnitskii, a contemporary Russian scholar, also focuses
on the early 20th century, he emphasizes the connection between terrorist acts
and political ideology. Like other historians of this topic, however, he does not
situate terrorism within the revolutionary movement as a whole or the workers' revolutionary movement in particular.[22]

---

[20] Claudia Verhoeven, *The Odd Man Karakozov: Imperial Russia, Modernity, and the Birth
of Terrorism* (Ithaca, NY, 2009); Ana Siljak, *Angel of Vengeance: The Girl Who Shot the
Governor of St. Petersburg and Sparked the Age of Assassination* (New York, 2008); Richard
Pipes, *The Degaev Affair: Terror and Treason in Tsarist Russia* (New Haven, 2003); Philip
Pomper, *Lenin's Brother: The Origins of the Russian Revolution* (New York, 2010).

[21] See Geifman's major work, *Thou Shalt Kill: Revolutionary Terrorism in Russia, 1894–
1917* (Princeton, NJ, 1993); and also Anna Geifman, *Entangled in Terror: The Azef Affair
and the Russian Revolution* (Wilmington, DE, 2000); and Geifman, *Death Orders: The
Vanguard of Modern Terrorism in Revolutionary Russia* (Santa Barbara, CA, 2010).

[22] O. V. Budnitskii, *Terrorizm v rossiiskom osvoboditel'nom dvizhenii: Ideologiia, etika,
psikhologiia (vtoraia polovina XIX–nachalo XX v.)* (Moscow, 2000). See also Budnitskii,

In the present book I examine the revolutionary movement from a different perspective, that of the workers' movement at the grass roots and the lived experience of those who participated in the movement. The key institution of the workers' circle comes in for examination in only a few of the previously mentioned works, and the literature of propaganda which comprises the major focus of my work is virtually ignored. Due to this neglect, a review of relevant scholarly work on revolutionary literature is brief. Soviet scholars led the way in this endeavor, in most cases focusing on a single work of literature.[23] Several of these scholars can be considered pathbreakers in the study of Russian revolutionary literature. V. G. Bazanov collected a number of key propaganda works of the populist 1870s, published with an introduction in the indispensable work *Agitatsionnaia literatura russkikh revoliutsionnykh narodnikov.*[24] V. F. Zakharina has also focused on literature of this period, examining both legal and illegal literature used for propaganda and contrasting literature of the early and later years of the 1870s.[25] N. S. Travushkin was the first scholar to explore the varied works of foreign literature in Russian translation that became part of the revolutionary repertoire.[26] Few Western scholars have engaged with this topic. One noteworthy exception is the essay by Reginald E.

Istoriia terrorizma v Rossii v dokumentakh, biografiiakh, issledovaniiakh, 2nd ed. (Rostov-na-Donu, 1996); Budnitskii, *Zhenshchiny-terroristki v Rossii* (Rostov-na-Donu, 1996). For another post-Soviet study of early 20th-century revolutionary terrorism, see K. V. Gusev, *Rytsari terrora* (Moscow, 1992).

[23] See, for example, M. M. Klevenskii, "Khudozhestvennaia literatura 70-kh godov na sluzhbe revoliutsii ('Skazka Kota-Murlyki')," *Literatura i marksizm,* no. 4 (1931): 117–25; and A. E. Larin, "Pamflet V. Libknekhta 'Pauki i mukhi' v Rossii nakanune i v gody pervoi russkoi revoliutsii," *Voprosy istochnikovedeniia i istoriografii* (Vladivostok) 4 (1975): 21–34.

[24] V. G. Bazanov, ed., *Agitatsionnaia literatura russkikh revoliutsionnykh narodnikov: Potaennye proizvedeniia 1873–1875 gg.* (Leningrad, 1970). See also V. G. Bazanov, *Ot fol'klora k narodnoi knige* (Leningrad, 1973); and Bazanov, *Russkie revoliutsionnye demokraty i narodoznanie* (Leningrad, 1974).

[25] V. F. Zakharina, *Golos revoliutsionnoi Rossii: Literatura revoliutsionnogo podpol'ia 70-kh godov XIX v. "Izdaniia dlia naroda"* (Moscow, 1971).

[26] N. S. Travushkin, "Zarubezhnaia khudozhestvennaia literatura v revoliutsionnoi Rossii (2-ia polovina XIX v.–nachalo XX v.)" (Doctoral diss., Astrakhanskii gosudarstvennyi pedagogicheskii institut im. S. M. Kirova, 1973); see, among other works, Travushkin, "Zarubezhnaia belletristika v russkom revoliutsionnom obikhode," in *Iz istorii russkoi i zarubezhnoi literatury* (Saratov, 1968), 79–98; Travushkin, "Zarubezhnyi utopicheskii roman v russkom revoliutsionnom dvizhenii kontsa XIX–nachala XX veka," *Uchenye Zapiski Astrakhanskogo gosudarstvennogo pedagogicheskogo instituta im. S. M. Kirova* (Astrakhan, 1969): 93–114.

Zelnik, "Weber into Tkachi: On a Russian Reading of Gerhart Hauptmann's Play *The Weavers.*"[27]

Creating a Culture of Revolution examines the literature of propaganda that comprised what can be thought of as a radical canon, made up of a variety of literary "genres" and forming a corpus of literature that shifted over time. I have chosen four genres that were widely popular: revolutionary tales, or *skazki*; pamphlets on political economy; revolutionary poetry and song; and foreign novels in translation. Taken together, they demonstrate the variety of works and genres. Each chapter examines the most widely used works of the genre in question, together with consideration of a number of lesser works. I analyze the form and content of the works and also present evidence on their use and reception. The broad time span—from the early 1870s to the 1905 Revolution—allows for chronological as well as geographical breadth. Our picture of the revolutionary movement derives primarily from St. Petersburg, and there is sound basis for this. From the 1860s through the 1917 Revolution new developments in the movement tended to appear first in the capital—the seat of government, location of prominent institutions of higher education, and home to the country's most extensive working class. The history of the revolutionary movement outside Petersburg, however, has been relatively neglected. I have attempted to broaden the picture, in the following chapters, in showing that revolutionary workers were not confined to Petersburg. A fuller picture of the revolutionary movement among workers must take into account trends and activities that mirrored and reinforced those of Petersburg, as well as those that displayed original responses to differing conditions.

Throughout this period, we see these literary works entwined with the key institution of the workers' circle. Investigation of the little-known revolutionary canon provides new insight into the culture of revolution. While the corpus of propaganda literature was for the most part created by members of the radical intelligentsia, validation by worker readers was necessary for lasting inclusion. What were the views and ideas presented and/or adopted by radical workers, and do they add up to a unified world view? I argue that these works led to an understanding of history, society, and the economic system. Concepts of politics were introduced, leading to a growing political awareness and what could be termed, to use a modern concept, a sense of citizenship. Questions of civic culture and the presence of a public sphere have drawn thoughtful commentary from scholars of late imperial Russia. Should the subculture of radical workers then be seen as part of a growing public sphere? In the period prior to the revolution of 1905 it is difficult to view

---

[27] Reginald E. Zelnik, "*Weber* into *Tkachi*: On a Russian Reading of Gerhart Hauptmann's Play *The Weavers*," in *Self and Story in Russian History*, ed. Laura Engelstein and Stephanie Sandler (Ithaca, NY, 2000), 217–41.

this separate and illegal movement in this light, and I will not be couching the discussion in these terms. It is, however, not unreasonable to think of the world of the radical worker as a kind of "alternative civic culture": it involved new associations and activities, with discussion of new ideas and literary works at its heart.[28]

The concept of "socialism" is essential to understanding the revolutionary movement as a whole. While I devote part of chapter 4 exclusively to the question of "what socialism meant to workers," socialism—as both an ideal and a European wide movement—is inextricably woven throughout the discussion of all the propaganda genres studied here. For many workers, it could be said that whatever they read and discussed in the circles: that was socialism. Such ideals as freedom, equality, and human rights were all as-

---

[28] Virtually all writings on the public sphere take as their point of departure Jürgen Habermas, *The Structural Transformation of the Public Sphere: An Inquiry into a Category of Bourgeois Society*, trans. Thomas Burger with the assistance of Frederick Lawrence (Cambridge, MA, 1989). See also Craig Calhoun, ed., *Habermas and the Public Sphere* (Cambridge, MA, 1992), which raises the issue of "public spheres" in the plural. Geoff Eley discusses "competing spheres" in "Nations, Publics, and Political Cultures: Placing Habermas in the Nineteenth Century" (306), and in Habermas's conclusion to the volume, "Further Reflections on the Public Sphere," he also concurs with the idea of multiple and competing spheres, including that of plebian culture. Applying the related concept of "civil society" to late imperial Russia has posed some difficulty. Scholars have identified elements contributing to the formation of a social sphere distinct from the state, but have hesitated to recognize its existence, compared to the societies of Western Europe. In the end Samuel Kassow concludes, a "public sphere was developing ... [and] did create a new sense of possibility"; Edith Clowes, Samuel D. Kassow, and James L. West, eds., *Between Tsar and People: Educated Society and the Quest for Public Identity in Late Imperial Russia* (Princeton, NJ, 1995), 371. As Alice Pate and Michael Melancon have shown, the public sphere became considerably more robust in the period following the revolution of 1905 through the outbreak of World War I. Both argue that in that period workers and workers' issues were part of a broader reform-oriented social spectrum. See Alice K. Pate, "Workers and *Obshchestvennost*': St. Petersburg, 1906–1914," *Revolutionary Russia* 15, 2 (2002): 53–71; and Michael Melancon, *The Lena Goldfields Massacre and the Crisis of the Late Tsarist State* (College Station, TX, 2006). Also relevant is Antonio Gramsci's concept of "hegemony," which he uses to explain the cultural domination of the ruling class that permeates society but opens the possibility of the development of the culture of the working class arising from an internal "struggle of political 'hegemonies'": "Consciousness of being part of a particular hegemonic force (that is to say, political consciousness) is the first stage towards a further progressive self-consciousness...."; Antonio Gramsci, *Selections from the Prison Notebooks*, ed. Quinton Hoare and Geoffrey Nowell Smith (New York, 1971), 333. Gramsci further analyzes the development of "subaltern" groups and elsewhere emphasizes the importance of such elements of "workers' democracy" as workshops and socialist clubs (336; David Forgacs, ed., *The Antonio Gramsci Reader: Selected Writings 1916–1935* [New York, 2000], 80–81)—a group into which the workers' circle fits nicely.

sociated with socialism and can be viewed as preconditions for a modern outlook and participation in politics. Just as significant, the revolutionary movement fanned the sense of injustice that fueled the revolutionary struggle. Socialism and revolution were the pillars of the movement. Participation in a clandestine movement, one revolving around workers' most longed for goals, could not help but elicit various strong emotions. The connection between emotions and revolutionary ideals is seen most directly in relation to poetry and song, and I note this relationship in chapter 4. Here and elsewhere I point to other elements that could well be subsumed under the heading of "emotions history."[29] (I do not however intend to engage in the theoretical issues surrounding this subfield to any significant degree.) All of these concepts and associations were represented by and conveyed through revolutionary literature and reinforced by circle study. Taken together, these ideas, embedded in the workers' movement, led to the creation of a "language of revolution" in which workers could express their understanding and goals of their movement and the hoped-for future society.

This study is based on a variety of sources: archival documents (including files of the tsarist police and judicial system), published collections of documents, journals of the early Soviet period, and relevant scholarly literature by Russian and Western historians. The works of propaganda literature themselves, often quite rare, are of central importance. Memoirs of participants in the movement are especially valuable, as they provide one of the main indications of reactions to this literature. Memoir evidence, however, is always subject to the well-known unreliability of memory. Moreover, a further caution is in order: how accurate are memoirs written after the October 1917 revolution and published in the Soviet Union under Communist Party auspices? Frederick C. Corney has published the most important study of this problem, pointing out common tropes in memoirs of 1917, often elicited by Istpart (the Party's Commission on the History of the October Revolution and the Russian Communist Party) questionnaires, or officially sponsored "evenings of remembrance."[30] While memoirs (as well as other sources) must be looked at with a critical eye, the period under investigation in this book deals with an earlier stage in the revolutionary movement, and in addition a

---

[29] For recent research in the field of history of emotions, see Susan J. Matt and Peter N. Stearns, eds., *Doing Emotions History* (Urbana, IL, 2014); Mark D. Steinberg and Valeria Sobol, eds., *Interpreting Emotions in Russia and Eastern Europe* (DeKalb, IL, 2001); Ian Plamper [Jan Plamper], Shamma Shakhadat [Schamma Schahadat], and Mark Eli [Mark Elie], eds., *Rossiiskaia imperiia chuvstv: Podkhody k kul'turnoi istorii emotsii* (Moscow, 2010).

[30] Frederick C. Corney, *Telling October: Memory and the Making of the Bolshevik Revolution* (Ithaca, NY, 2004).

number of memoirs that have survived predate the 1917 Revolution.[31] To the extent that their information is corroborated by other sources, we can accept it as accurate. Moreover, the information that we are concerned with—which works were read in workers' circles—was often not the most important for early Soviet authorities engaged in framing the story of the October Revolution.

The works selected for detailed examination virtually chose themselves. On the basis of extensive reading of memoirs, archival records, and document collections, in particular *Rabochee dvizhenie v Rossii*, certain works stood out by their repeated mention. Archival and other sources provide good information on the composition, publication, and distribution of illegal literature and on the number and size of editions. Specific works are frequently mentioned in memoirs and police reports, and illegal works seized during arrests were noted in judicial records. In this way the relative use and popularity of specific works can be estimated. Some withstood the test of time, even over decades; others proved ephemeral. The question of reception, how workers understood and reacted to these works, is perhaps the most elusive and intriguing. In a key article on cultural history, Alon Confino has referred to "the issue of reception, that ogre that awaits every cultural historian."[32] Most documents, even when naming works of literature, rarely record the reader's or listener's reaction. Nevertheless, we can provide some information on this important question. Where information on reception of this literature exists, I have included it. As noted above, the relative popularity of specific works can be inferred based on the frequency with which works are mentioned and reproduced, and I have attempted to assess workers' reactions to these works and to theorize as to the reasons for their popularity.

Finally, I would like to highlight several additional concepts important to the chapters that follow. The concepts of "culture" and "subculture" are basic to this analysis. When referring to the "culture of revolution," I have in mind Raymond Williams's reference to the "'social' definition of culture, in which

---

[31] To name some of the earlier memoirs: Vasilii Golubev (published 1906), V. V. Sviatlovskii (manuscript written c. 1912), K. M. Takhtarev (first edition published 1902), V. V. Bartenev (published 1908), M. S. Aleksandrov (Ol'minskii) (published 1906), and I. V. Babushkin (written in 1902)—all participants in the Petersburg movement of the late 1880s/early 1890s; P. V. Antonov, a prominent worker-*narodovolets* of the 1880s (written in 1906); M. A. Krol' (activist in the 1880s, memoirs published in New York). Reginald Zelnik has translated the memoirs of Vasilii Gerasimov, a participant in the Kreenholm strike of 1872 who penned his memoirs at the beginning of the 1880s, in his *Law and Disorder on the Narova River*, 270–95; see also Zelnik's introduction in that book, 10–11.

[32] Alon Confino, "Collective Memory and Cultural History: Problems of Method," *American Historical Review* 102, 5 (December 1997): 1395.

culture is a description of a particular way of life."[33] By any standard, the distinctive and to a great extent separate lives of radical workers—both within the Russian working class and the broader society—comprised a subculture, which has been defined as follows: "Subcultures must exhibit a distinctive enough shape and structure to make them identifiably different from their 'parent' culture. They must be focused around certain activities, values, certain uses of material artefacts, territorial spaces, etc. which significantly differentiate them from the wide culture."[34]

Another important concept is one that I call "revolutionary pedagogy." As we will see, radicals from the intelligentsia undertook revolutionary propaganda among workers with a dual goal: revolutionary as well as educational. Those involved in this "education for revolution,"[35] both workers and members of the intelligentsia, thought about the kinds of knowledge that workers needed to make sense of their world, and of history and their place in it. This stress on the importance of education in the circles calls to mind the "pedagogy of the oppressed" which Paulo Freire developed in Latin America roughly one century later. In the Russian workers' movement, circle discussion, often prompted by readings, led to dialogue between propagandists and circle members. In Freire's words, "Dialogue with the people is radically necessary to every authentic revolution."[36] Russian radicals had instinctively chosen this approach.

The concept of "experience" is relevant to this analysis in two different ways. First, this concept serves as a counterweight to the time-honored approach to the history of the Russian revolutionary movement, which focuses on theory and leaders from the intelligentsia. This book by contrast seeks to present the revolutionary movement at the grass roots and to convey the experiences of workers in the movement. In addition, as scholars have pointed out, "experience" is by no means a transparent concept that can be

---

[33] Raymond Williams's works demonstrate the importance of viewing history through the lens of culture. See "Towards a Sociology of Culture," chap. 1 in his *Culture* (Cambridge, 1981); and "The Analysis of Culture," chap. 2 in *The Long Revolution* (Westport, CT, 1975).

[34] See John Clarke et al., "Subcultures, Cultures and Class: A Theoretical Overview," in *Resistance Through Rituals: Youth Subcultures in Post-War Britain*, ed. Stuart Hall and Tony Jefferson (London, 1975), 13–14. See further on the concept of subculture Dick Hebdige, *Subculture: The Meaning of Style* (London, 1986).

[35] See Pearl, "Educating Workers for Revolution."

[36] Paulo Freire, *Pedagogy of the Oppressed* (New York, 2000), 128.

used uncritically.[37] Experiences gained through participation in the "culture of revolution" did not simply "happen" to radical workers, but shaped their identity as well. With this caveat in mind I seek to uncover the lives of radical workers in a basic sense—where they lived and worked, what circles and other activities they participated in, which works of literature they read—and then to attempt to recover from the sources the voices of these revolutionary workers.[38]

ෆ ๛

We now turn to analysis of the radical workers' "culture of revolution" and the special literature at its core. This monograph consists of five chapters: chapter 1, "Creating a Culture of Revolution," sets the scene for the analysis of propaganda literature that makes up the major portion of the book. It explores the workers' revolutionary subculture and in particular the workers' circle. Each of the next four chapters takes a close look at one genre of revolutionary literature. Chapter 2, "Tales of Revolution, examines the revolutionary tale or *skazka*. Chapter 3, "Political Economy for Workers," deals with the three major pamphlets on political economy. Chapter 4, "The Revolutionary Songbook: Poetry and Song," investigates the role of poetry and song in the movement from the 1870s to 1905. Chapter 5, "The Revolutionary Novel: Foreign Literature in Translation," explains the fascinating success of novels as revolutionary literature.

---

[37] Two important works useful for thinking about "experience" and the discipline of history are Joan Scott, "The Evidence of Experience," in *Practicing History: New Directions in Historical Writing after the Linguistic Turn*, ed. Gabrielle M. Spiegel (New York, 2005), 199–216; and Martin Jay, *Songs of Experience: Modern American and European Variations on a Universal Theme* (Berkeley, CA, 2005).

[38] Reginald Zelnik concludes his study of the memoirs of two radical workers with a reminder of the human experience that underlies broad historical currents: "The memoirs of Kanatchikov and Fisher are not the tales of super-human proletarian heroes. They each tell a human story of pain and vulnerability, but also of courage and resilience. Through them we can begin to visualize the real lives of some of Russia's revolutionary workers; we can see them as they were before they vanished into the amorphous granite of their giant monuments" (Zelnik, "Russian Bebels," pt. 2, 447).

Chapter 1

Creating a Culture of Revolution

> Clear awareness of the goal ... can only be
> achieved by means of intellectual and moral
> evolution. Reading books, lively discussion, and
> the example of developed people—these are the
> means of attaining this development. The goal of
> improving the workers' situation rests first of all
> on [workers] themselves.... Let that group of ...
> developed workers help their comrades emerge
> from the darkness of ignorance....
> —Proclamation confiscated from St. Petersburg
> worker N. D. Bogdanov, 28 November 1891[1]

In 1891 Nikolai Bogdanov, a young metalworker, was arrested and expelled from St. Petersburg for revolutionary activity. Police found that Bogdanov was at the center of a web of illegal activity. Among the evidence presented against him was the fact that he had recited to two female factory workers the poem "My Grievous Sin," a work of illegal verse first published in the 1870s.[2] Such propaganda activity was at the heart of the revolutionary workers' movement, often involving members of the radical intelligentsia, but carried out by such workers as Bogdanov as well. By 1891 activist workers in St. Petersburg were organized in a network of circles. In addition to circle study, they engaged in workplace propaganda and strike agitation, and organized demonstrations and the first May Day celebrations in the Russian Empire. How did workers become involved in the revolutionary movement? What were their experiences? What function did works of propaganda literature, such as the above poem, play in the workers' movement and in the creation of a new world view?

---

[1] Rossiiskii gosudarstvennyi istoricheskii arkhiv (RGIA) f. 1405, op. 92, d. 10979, ll. 9–9ob.

[2] Ibid., l. 39.

This chapter will provide the background for the analysis of the role and impact of propaganda literature that makes up the following four chapters. Chapter 1 is divided into three sections. The opening section consists of a snapshot of the workers' movement in St. Petersburg in 1891 and illustrates the web of relationships, practices, and beliefs that made up the subculture of radical workers, of what I term a "culture of revolution." As workers created a revolutionary subculture, they also constructed new identities for themselves. They came to see themselves as a distinctive group, with new values, institutions, traditions, and relationships. As Russia entered the modern age, the workers' revolutionary subculture served as a kind of alternative civic culture, something distinct from already existing cultures: the peasant/traditional, the official, and that of the intelligentsia. Radical workers were thus not "typical" or "representative" members of the Russian working class. In this regard, they bear comparison to the mid-19th-century Parisian workers whose voices are heard in Jacques Rancière's remarkable work, *Nights of Labor.*[3] Like their French counterparts, these Russian workers attempted to steal extra nighttime hours for study, in this case in the *kruzhok*. Still (and in contradistinction to the proletarian thinkers and writers portrayed by Rancière), this culture of radical workers was part of the broader working-class culture and the urban lower-class milieu. Its boundaries were always porous, overlapping with workplace, family, school, and neighborhood, as well as the broader revolutionary movement. Worker participants were not isolated in the *kruzhki*, but were involved in networks of connections both within and outside the movement. The world of radical workers was as much about experiences, processes, and practices as it was about ideas and ideologies. In the second section I provide an analysis of the key institution of the workers' revolutionary movement in the period from 1870 to 1905, the workers' *kruzhok* or circle. The circle provided a kind of political education, often led by propagandists from the intelligentsia, with attention given to programs of study aiming to inculcate a revolutionary curriculum. The third section addresses the subject of propaganda literature. A growing body of propaganda literature served as a means of transmission of revolutionary ideas; these were works composed for, read by, and often appropriated for use by workers. This "literature of revolution," made up of various "genres," comprised the scaffolding for revolutionary propaganda both within and outside the workers' circle. This literature has rarely been studied in any comprehensive way. The major part of this book presents an

---

[3] See Jacques Rancière, *Nights of Labor: The Workers' Dream in Nineteenth-Century France*, trans. John Drury (Philadelphia, 1989), translation of Jacques Rancière, *La nuit des prolétaires* (Paris, 1981). On Rancière's project of challenging traditional boundaries and concepts in working-class history, see his essays in Rancière, *Staging the People: The Proletarian and His Double*, trans. David Fernbach (London, 2011).

extended analysis of these works which served, I argue, as a narrative for
the revolutionary workers' movement and informed the thinking, goals, and
actions of its members.

The Subculture of Radical Workers: St. Petersburg, 1891

The experiences of St. Petersburg workers Nikolai Bogdanov and Vera
Karelina, both 21 years old in 1891, serve to illustrate this radical workers'
subculture.[4] By 1891 St. Petersburg boasted a city-wide network of *kruzhki* in
the various factory and working-class districts of the city. Representatives
of the districts made up the "central workers' circle," which was linked to a
group of *intelligenty*, mostly students at the Technological Institute and other
schools, who served as propagandists in the circles. (The organization of this
period is usually referred to in the literature as the Brusnev organization
or the Workers' Union.)[5] While most of these *intelligenty* and a number of
the workers identified themselves as social democrats, a group of radicals
calling themselves *narodovol'tsy* (People's Will adherents) were also active,
and their underground press provided much of the propaganda literature
of the time.[6] By 1891, there may have been as many as 50 circles in the city,

---

[4] The Petersburg workers' movement of this era is particularly well illuminated by two
important collections of workers' memoirs: K. M. Norinskii et al., *Ot gruppy Blagoeva k
"Soiuzu Bor'by" (1886–1894 gg.): Stat'i i vospominaniia K. M. Norinskogo, V. A. Shelgunova,
V. Nevskogo, M. Ol'minskogo. Materialy po delu M. I. Brusneva i Iu. V. Mel'nikova. Rechi
rabochikh 1 maia 1891 goda* (Rostov-na-Donu, 1921); and E. A. Korol'chuk, ed., *V nachale
puti: Vospominaniia peterburgskikh rabochikh 1872–1897 gg.* (Leningrad, 1975).

[5] See treatments in A. M. Orekhov, *Pervye marksisty v Rossii: Peterburgskii "rabochii
soiuz" 1887–1893 gg.* (Moscow, 1979); Kazakevich, *Sotsial-demokraticheskie organizatsii
Peterburga*; and Naimark, *Terrorists and Social Democrats*, chap. 7.

[6] See M. S. Aleksandrov [M. S. Ol'minskii], "'Gruppa narodovol'tsev' (1891–1894
gg.)," *Byloe*, no. 11 (November 1906): 1–27; and P. Kudelli, *Narodovol'tsy na pereput'i:
Delo lakhtinskoi tipografii* (Leningrad, 1926). In the historiography of the revolutionary
movement social democracy tends to be presented as the default ideological position,
with the continued presence of the People's Will ignored. The distinction between
"social democrats" and "*narodovol'tsy*" could be seen in student groups in Petersburg
in the early 1890s, but student propagandists seem to have mostly ignored this distinction in propaganda among workers. One key member of the group of student
tekhnologi (students at the St. Petersburg Technological Institute) even hesitated to
give that group the label "social democratic," and another member was closer to the
local *narodovol'tsy*. It appears most accurate to say that ideological tension was weak
in this period. See Vas. Golubev, "Stranichka iz istorii rabochego dvizheniia: Pamiati
N. V. Shelgunova," *Byloe*, no. 12 (December 1906): 111–12; L. B. Krasina [Nikitich], "Iz
perepiski L. B. Rasina za gody 1887–1895," in *Leonid Borisovich Krasin ("Nikitich"): Gody*

making a total of several hundred workers who can be considered active in the movement.[7]

Nikolai Bogdanov was one of these activists. In 1891, at a secret 1 May gathering of radical workers (the first in Russia), he gave a speech that expressed his political views, his hopes for the future, his identity as a radical worker, and the meaning the movement (workers' and socialist) held for him. Bogdanov exhorted his listeners to emulate the freer workers of Western Europe, who were not only able to celebrate 1 May openly, but had been successful in obtaining constitutions, freedom of the press and assembly, and other political rights, "which make it easier to struggle with the existing [capitalist] economic order." The ultimate goal is a society "in which there will be neither poor nor rich, and all will share happiness and prosperity [dovol'stvie] in equal measure," a society of "Freedom, Truth, and Brotherhood."[8] Bogdanov's speech points to a new identity for workers as political actors and citizens, represented most distinctively in identification with workers in the West, and also conveys a sense of the "social imaginary"[9] shared by this group of workers, the value system which they hoped to see embodied in an ideal society. This was certainly a new perspective for members of the Russian common people, or narod: one that differed both from that of earlier radical workers of the 1870s and 1880s (who with some exceptions identified themselves more specifically as participants in the broader revolutionary movement) and from that of radicals from the educated classes, whose ideas, conveyed to workers in propaganda circles and literature, were adapted as well as adopted by workers and often refashioned with new emphases for what workers saw as their own somewhat different needs. Bogdanov's words take on additional meaning when we examine the experiences, outlook, and lifestyle of the subculture to which he belonged: that of radical workers.

---

podpol'ia. Sbornik vospominanii, statei i dokumentov, ed. M. L. Liadov and S. M. Pozner (Moscow–Leningrad, 1928).

[7] See estimates in M. I. Brusnev, "Vozniknovenie pervykh sotsial-demokraticheskikh organizatsii: Vospominaniia," Proletarskaia revoliutsiia, no. 2 (14) (1923): 21–22; V. M. Karelina, "Na zare rabochego dvizheniia v S.-Peterburge," Krasnaia letopis', no. 4 (1922): 14; A. E. Karelin, "[Vospominaniia o rabochikh kruzhkakh Brusnevskoi organizatsii]," in Korol'chuk, V nachale puti, 246; M. Ol'minskii, "O vospominaniiakh N. D. Bogdanova," in Norinskii et al., Ot gruppy Blagoeva k "Soiuzu Bor'by," 44.

[8] Bogdanov's 1 May speech, reprinted in Orekhov, Pervye marksisty, 169–70.

[9] For a discussion of this concept, see Bronislaw Baczko, Les imaginaires sociaux: Mémoires et espoirs collectifs (Paris, 1984).

Bogdanov's biography resembles in many ways that of other workers of his cohort.[10] He grew up in St. Petersburg, where he attended a city primary school. At age 14 (1884) he became an apprentice metal craftsman (*slesar´*) in the workshops of the Warsaw Railroad. It was here that he first became aware of radical ideas, propounded by one of the "last of the Mohicans of Narodnaia Volia,"[11] as he put it, who began to suggest things to read, beginning with the poems of Nikolai Nekrasov and Turgenev's novel *Virgin Soil* (*Nov´*). In the mid-1880s Bogdanov, still in his teens, organized a self-education circle for workers. No *intelligenty* were involved, and reading material consisted of articles from old issues of the "thick" journals, such as *Sovremennik* (The Contemporary) and *Otechestvennye zapiski* (Fatherland Notes), purchased at the flea market. Bogdanov continued his formal education at the evening school run by the Imperial Russian Technical Society. Here he met others workers who had organized similar *kruzhki*, and in 1888 members of his circle considered themselves fortunate to obtain the professional services of a student propagandist, one of the local group of social democrats. As noted, by 1890 the circles were organized in a citywide network, and Bogdanov was a member of the central circle of activists. By this time he was working as a metal fitter at the Card (Kartochnaia) Factory in the Nevskii district.

Bogdanov's biography underscores the importance of the network of connections that supported his life choices and activities. For example, in 1891 he was sharing an apartment with another metal craftsman at the Card Factory, Aleksandr Filimonov, whom he had met at the evening classes at the Technical School. The role of Sunday schools and evening courses for workers (sponsored by the Imperial Russian Technical Society [Imperatorskoe russkoe tekhnicheskoe obshchestvo] or large enterprises such as the Baltic Shipbuilding Plant) illustrates the permeability of boundaries between workers involved in the movement and those outside. Teachers in the schools, often radicals themselves, lent a political slant to lessons in geography or literature,

---

[10] Sources of biographical information on Bogdanov include Ol'minskii, "O vospominaniiakh N. D. Bogdanova," 39–46, most of which was reprinted as N. D. Bogdanov, "Na zare sotsial-demokratii (Vospominaniia)," in Korol'chuk, *V nachale puti*, 225–36; "Bogdanov, Nikolai Dement'evich," in *Deiateli revoliutsionnogo dvizheniia v Rossii: Bio-bibliograficheskii slovar´* (hereafter *DRDR*), ed. V. Vilenskii-Sibiriakov et al., (Moscow, 1927–34), 5, vyp. 1, cols. 384–86; RGIA f. 1405, op. 92, d. 10979, 1891 g. V. V. Sviatlovskii, an employee of the St. Petersburg Public Library, had close contacts with the city's radical workers. He gives an appealing portrait of Bogdanov: a popular and beloved leader among the workers, he stood out as a good speaker ("rare at that time"), and "the soul of a whole series of circles." See V. V. Sviatlovskii, "Na zare rossiiskoi sotsial-demokratii," *Byloe*, no. 19 (1922): 145–46. (Sviatlovskii notes that his article was submitted to the journal about ten years earlier, but had been lost.)

[11] Ol'minskii, "O vospominaniiakh N. D. Bogdanova," 39.

and activist workers found the schools useful for inspecting likely recruits. Bogdanov noted that the Sunday and evening schools "lightened the work of the circles"[12] by providing a broad educational foundation.

The key institution in the life of the radical worker was the *kruzhok*, the essential site of identity formation as a "conscious" or radical worker. Besides providing a political and cultural education (and warmth and sociability), the *kruzhok* was also the arena for interaction with the intelligentsia, in the person of a student propagandist. Members of the group of Petersburg social democrats (made up primarily of students at the Technological Institute, the university, and other institutions of higher learning) attempted to follow an ambitious study program drawn up by Mikhail Brusnev in their circle instruction. Propagandists were to begin with topics in natural science, then move on to Darwin, theories of culture (including Engels's *Origin of the Family, Private Property, and the State*) and political economy, to peasants in Russia and the West, the working-class and labor movements, and culminate with study of socialism.[13]

Natural science was viewed as the foundation on which to ground thorough knowledge of social science. Treatment of scientific questions in the circles often had the effect of leading workers to question their religious faith. (While not mentioned by *intelligenty* as a specific goal, the passivity of the Russian *narod* was seen as stemming from the twin belief in the tsar and obedience to the church.) The teaching of Darwin's theory of evolution also represented a direct challenge to the story of creation presented by the church. Study of science may have had the function of bridging, in some way, the large gap in education between radical *intelligenty* and workers. Perhaps the propagandists, if only unconsciously, were attempting to aid the workers in achieving the worldview of the intelligentsia.[14] The topic of "history of culture" was represented in circle studies of this Petersburg organization

---

[12] Ibid., 45.

[13] This program is reprinted in full in Pankratova and Ivanov, *Rabochee dvizhenie v Rossii*, 3, ch. 2, 131–32. Frequent mention is made of the use of Engels's work for propaganda in this period, probably in the form of lectures by the propagandist or notes in Russian. A Russian translation was not published until 1896. See Korol'chuk, *V nachale puti*, 400 n. 5.

[14] For reactions of workers to science teaching in the circles, see Sviatlovskii, "Na zare Rossiiskoi sotsial-demokratii," 143; and Karelina, "Na zare rabochego dvizheniia v S.-Peterburge," 275. A pair of workers were emboldened by their knowledge to challenge the explanation of creation given by the priest at the evening class for workers (c. 1890) and were kicked out of school as a result. See K. Norinskii, "Moi vospominaniia," in Norinskii et al., *Ot gruppy Blagoeva k "Soiuzu Bor'by,"* 19. On the teaching of science in workers' circles of an earlier period, see Zelnik, "'To the Unaccustomed Eye,'" 297–326.

by two works: Iu. Lippert's *History of Culture* (translated from the German in 1894) and Engels's *Origin of the Family, Private Property, and the State*. How this work was used is explained by Vasilii Shelgunov: by showing how the family and the state gradually changed their forms under the influence of economic conditions, the worker's view that everything existing had been created by God was shaken.[15] Works on political economy and socialism were of course central to circle studies. Workers read articles on political economy and social criticism from the old "thick" journals—works by Chernyshevskii, Dobroliubov, Pisarev, Saltykov-Shchedrin, Nikolai Shelgunov. Here again circle studies could be viewed as giving workers the same ideological baggage acquired by the intelligentsia youth in the preceding two decades. Marx's *Kapital* was considered an essential work by the social democratic propagandists, and workers gave it respect, although few were able to read it for themselves. They assimilated some of Marx's ideas through lectures given by propagandists, who presented such concepts as wages and surplus value. Several popularizations of Marx's teachings also circulated, including works by Karl Kautsky and Gabriel Deville (both in translation) and a popular exposition of the chapter on surplus value composed and lithographed by student propagandist R. Klassen. Works by Lassalle were also widely used in circle studies of this period.[16]

Readings discussed in the circles included pamphlets on popular science and political economy, articles from the "thick" journals of the intelligentsia (including articles on Western workers and trade unions by the radically inclined publicist Nikolai Shelgunov, as well as older works by Chernyshevskii and Pisarev), and works of fiction both Russian and in translation—the novel *Spartacus* by the Italian author Raffaello Giovagnoli was very popular at this time. Works of illegal literature also circulated, including publications of the emigré social democratic Emancipation of Labor Group and the People's Will. The thirst for knowledge and the importance of books are recurring themes in the memoirs of these workers. Bogdanov worked to build up a good collection: when he was arrested in November 1891 the police seized a huge library of books which was, they told him, "completely unsuitable for a worker."[17]

---

[15] Vasilii Shelgunov, "Rabochie na puti k marksizmu," in Korol'chuk, *V nachale puti*, 344–45.

[16] See Sviatlovskii, "Na zare rossiiskoi sotsial-demokratii," 150; K. M. Takhtarev, *Rabochee dvizhenie v Peterburge (1893–1901)* (Leningrad, 1924), 24; V. Karelina, "Iz dalekogo proshlogo," in Liadov and Pozner, *Leonid Borisovich Krasin*, 88; K. Norinskii, "Dopolnenie k vospominaniiam," in Norinskii et al., *Ot gruppy Blagoeva k "Soiuzu Bor'by,"* 47.

[17] Ol'minskii, "O vospominaniiakh N. D. Bogdanova," 44. For a more detailed look at two specific workers' circles in the Petersburg organization, see 1) on the circle

While the initial choice of themes and readings was made by propagandists from the intelligentsia, based on their conception of what workers needed to know, what workers took from their readings was not necessarily what the *intelligenty* intended. Rather, a process of appropriation and adaptation went on, as workers created a new identity as "conscious" workers. Bogdanov and others learned of the history and activities of Western European workers and their parties, particularly the German Social Democratic Party, from newspapers and journal articles, and took them as their model, referring to them frequently in their discussions with other workers. They became familiar with the ideas of Marx and Lassalle but also read old populist brochures from the 1870s and People's Will publications.[18] The orientation of activists like Bogdanov could be termed "workerist," as well as socialist. As Bogdanov put it, in a manuscript seized at the time of his arrest, "The cause of the improvement of the workers' situation rests first of all on [workers] themselves."[19] Some workers called for the creation of a worker intelligentsia to replace the tutelary role of *intelligenty* from the upper classes.[20] In fact, one distinctive characteristic of the Petersburg workers' movement of 1890–91 was the dominant role of workers as organizers and propagandists. Police records

founded by Ivan Timofeev: V. V. Fomin, "Vospominaniia o podpol'noi rabote revoliu-tsionnykh kruzhkov na Baltiiskom zavode i ob umstvennykh techeniiakh vnutri kruzhkov za period s 1887 po 1893 god," in Korol'chuk, *V nachale puti*, 183, 187; Norinskii, "Dopolnenie k vospominaniiam," 47; Norinskii, "Kratkaia avtobiografiia," in Korol'chuk, *V nachale puti*, 293–94; and I. I. Egorov, "[Iz vospominanii o rabochikh kruzhkakh v Peterburge 1888–1892 goda]," in Korol'chuk, *V nachale puti*, 237–38; and 2) on the circle of textile workers organized by Fedor Afanas'ev: L. B. Krasin [Nikitich], ""Delo davno minuvshikh dnei (1887–1892)," 102–04; V. Karelina, "Leonid Borisovich—propagandist i organizator rabochikh kruzhkov," 87–88; M. I. Brusnev, "Pervye revoliutsionnye shagi L. Krasina," 68, all in Liadov and Pozner, *Leonid Boriso-vich Krasin*; and A. G. Boldyreva, "Minuvshie gody," in Korol'chuk, *V nachale puti*, 255, 258–59.

[18] Vera Karelina mentions that workers were reading *Kalendar' Narodnoi Voli* [People's Will Calendar] (Geneva, 1883). What seems to have particularly interested them were the portraits of Zheliabov, Perovskaia, and other heroes and martyrs of the movement included in this "almanac." (This was the only issue published.) See V. Karelina, "Vos-pominaniia o podpol'nykh rabochikh kruzhkakh Brusnevskoi organizatsii" (1889–1892 gg.), in Korol'chuk, *V nachale puti*, 286.

[19] RGIA f. 1405, op. 92, d. 10979, l. 8.

[20] See the case of Andrei/Matvei Fisher, discussed in Zelnik, "Russian Bebels," pt. 2, 417–47. Eric Hobsbawm comments on the attraction of British workers to socialism: "The working classes were ... interested in the new ideology not for itself, but only as part of a package that included the struggle for a better life—i.e., through something like the labour movement. Men did not become freethinkers but 'worker freethinkers'...." See Hobsbawm, *Workers: Worlds of Labor* (New York, 1984), 43.

reveal the propaganda activity of Bogdanov's friend Aleksandr Filimonov. A worker at the Obukhov plant met Filimonov at the Vargunov Sunday school. They frequently walked to school together and, according to the testimony of this worker, Filimonov conversed with him on the abysmal situation of Russian workers compared to that of workers in Western Europe, who had united to show governments their strength and had won freedom of speech and assembly, so that they could better defend their rights. Russian workers needed to achieve not only a shorter working day and higher wages but such political rights as a constitution and the right to vote. Filimonov, at least under police questioning, took pains to point out that "he sympathized with the workers', not the revolutionary movement, and that he would like to see the Government take measures to improve the material situation of workers and to allow workers to hold meetings and form associations and various producers' enterprises."[21]

Realistic in their appraisal of their actual strength, Bogdanov and his fellow activists saw themselves most specifically as "conscious" workers, with a responsibility toward the mass of the working class. (Brusnev referred to such politicized workers as "Russian Bebels.")[22] Bogdanov defined their task as follows:

> In order for our activity to be as fruitful as possible, we must strive to the utmost to develop ourselves and others both intellectually and morally and to work more energetically, so that those around us will regard us as intelligent, honest, and capable, and will trust us and see us as examples to follow.[23]

They were to serve as role models, to present new values appropriate for the movement and for a better life.[24] Bogdanov became a lifelong propagandist, devoting himself to teaching and organizing for decades. A worker who met him in 1891 recalled that Bogdanov even developed a kind of theory of geo-

---

[21] RGIA f. 1405, op. 92, d. 10979, ll. 39–40, 43ob., 44. Filimonov's views clearly show the influence of Lassalle's works, and indeed, among items seized by police in the Bogdanov/Filimonov apartment was a manuscript synopsis of volume 1 of Lassalle's works, written in Filimonov's hand (ibid., l. 36.) For more on Filimonov's background, see ibid., ll. 6–7ob.

[22] Brusnev, "Vozniknovenie," 19–20.

[23] Proclamation composed by Bogdanov, reprinted in Orekhov, *Pervye marksisty*, 175.

[24] On the image of the "conscious" worker, see also Takhtarev, *Rabochee dvizhenie*, 34, 37; I. V. Babushkin, *Vospominaniia I. V. Babushkina, 1893–1900 gg.* (Moscow, 1955), 39; Boldyreva, "Minuvshie gody," 256.

metric progression of propaganda: if every propagandized worker would in turn reach one other worker per year, the workers' party would reach an enormous size within several decades, and the workers would win their rights.[25]

The presence of women workers was a new development in the revolutionary movement at this time. Bogdanov was an early mentor to Vera Karelina, who went on to become a noted activist herself. Her experiences call into question the usual representation of the Russian revolutionary worker as a male worker. Karelina was a ward of the Imperial Foundling Home in St. Petersburg, raised by a peasant foster mother and sent to work at a Petersburg maternity hospital in 1884.[26] Her early interest in books and ideas was encouraged by *kursistki*, student midwife trainees she met at the hospital. In 1890, when she was 20, she began working as a weaver at the New Cotton Spinning Factory, located on the Obvodnyi Canal. Through male friends (also former wards, now working at a textile factory in the Narva district) she met a worker at the Warsaw Railroad repair shops who often read her Nekrasov's poems and other literary works. He in turn introduced her to Nikolai Bogdanov. (Greinart, the railroad worker, had attended Technical School classes with Bogdanov.) Bogdanov guided Karelina's further intellectual and political development, which included the reading of Chernyshevskii's *What Is to Be Done?* and works by Pisarev and Uspenskii.

In 1890 Karelina joined a *kruzhok* of textile workers organized by the weaver Fedor Afanas'ev, one of the most respected workers in the movement. The circle included one other female worker, Anna Gavrilova (Boldyreva), with whom Karelina became close. This circle was part of the citywide network already mentioned. Studies were led by a young student, Leonid Krasin, who, as Karelina notes in her memoirs, spoke particularly about economic questions. Vera and her new friend Anna soon organized a circle of women workers, including textile workers and workers at the Foundling Home. Bogdanov came up with a propagandist: Mikhail Aleksandrov (Ol'minskii)— at this time a member of the Petersburg Gruppa Narodovol'tsev (Group of Narodovol'tsy).[27] Most of the women in this circle married men from the

---

[25] A. Fisher, *V Rossii i v Anglii: Nabliudeniia i vospominaniia peterburgskogo rachochego (1890–1921 gg.)* (Moscow, 1922), 13.

[26] On Karelina, see Karelina, "Na zare rabochego dvizheniia v S.-Peterburge"; Karelina, "Vospominaniia o podpol'nykh rabochikh kruzhkakh"; Karelina, "Iz dalekogo proshlogo," 81–92; and Rose L. Glickman, *Russian Factory Women: Workplace and Society, 1880–1914* (Berkeley, CA, 1984), 173–80.

[27] Both Krasin and Ol'minskii were later prominent Bolsheviks.

group of Petersburg activists,[28] including Vera herself, who married Aleksei Karelin, a lithographer and circle comrade of Nikolai Bogdanov. In 1890–91, Karelina was also a member of the central workers' circle.

Karelina's memoirs, with their evocation of working-class Petersburg, the consistent noting of location, street, and district, allow us to map the boundaries of the subculture of radical workers, as they carved out a new kind of public space. These boundaries were not fixed but overlapped with neighborhood, workplace, networks of friends and family (and in Karelina's case, ties from the Foundling Home). Her memoirs include telling descriptions of the communal apartments set up by radical workers, in which male and female workers found new ways of living together which fit their image of the "conscious" worker striving toward a better future society. The residents of one communal apartment, used as a meeting place by the central workers' circle, illustrate typical connections: the inhabitants included A. Karelin (later Vera's husband), leading activist Gavriil Mefodiev and his wife, an unidentified seamstress, and the wife of a worker exiled from the capital, with her two children.[29]

When police surveillance made this apartment unsafe, Karelina helped set up the next communal apartment. Banking on stereotypes of lower-class women, Vera and Anna Gavrilova found a small apartment "in a bad neighborhood" (v zlachnom meste): the large building also contained two houses of prostitution. This was perfect for conspiracy: the doorman was sympathetic, and the police turned a blind eye to the comings and goings of various male visitors. Vera describes the set up: in one room a party would be going on, people "sang, played the accordion, danced, and in the other [room] serious conversations were held, propaganda." Radicals looked over possible new recruits in the first room—"if they weren't suitable, they weren't invited again, but if they turned out to be 'ours' they soon passed through to the other, back room." Karelina depicts the "purity" of relations between these young men and women as a subject of wonder: male comrades often stayed late, and if the distance home was too far, they would spend the night on the floor. Moral responsibility was an important principle for "conscious workers." Karelina recalls one comrade who seduced a young woman but did not want to marry her, claiming financial hardship: "we collected money for him and celebrated a wedding."[30]

To be a "conscious" worker required more than reading and espousing radical ideas: it called for a certain lifestyle, one embodying the revolutionary

---

[28] Karelina, "Na zare rabochego dvizheniia," 13.

[29] Ibid., 15.

[30] Ibid.

socialist ideals of equality, camaraderie, and solidarity. Vera describes the next apartment, on the Vyborg Side, where she lived with three other young women and several male workers, in idyllic tones perhaps colored by the nostalgia of hindsight: "We truly lived as a commune: we contributed money to a common fund, had a common kitchen, laundry, and library. Everyone did housework, and we had no quarrels or disagreements about these matters."[31]

Bogdanov, Karelina, and the other members of the community of radical Petersburg workers were engaged in creating revolutionary tradition, culture, and values. The chapters that follow will expand our picture of the complex process by which ideas picked up from reading or transmitted by intelligentsia propagandists were appropriated by workers, but a few points can be noted here. By 1890 the Petersburg workers' movement had a history dating back to the 1870s and was aware of this history. Older workers still survived who provided links to earlier phases of the movement, and earlier populist literature circulated. There were no clear divisions between "populists" and "Marxists," contrary to the usual impression of rigid ideological distinctions asserted in the historiography, where the default position for this period is usually stated to be social democratic. In actuality, while the Petersburg movement of the early 1890s had a new social democratic flavoring, older elements of Russian socialism overlapped, coincided, and merged. The bottom line: determining workers' ideological affiliation may not be of primary importance. Two events from the spring of 1891 illustrate the process of creation of a radical workers' culture: the delegation to the writer Nikolai Shelgunov, and the celebration of 1 May. (In both cases, it is not clear where the initial idea originated, but workers enthusiastically embraced and were the major actors in each event.) Shelgunov was well known to the workers who were members of the *kruzhki* for his articles on Western European workers and their labor movements (for example, "The Proletariat in France and England" ["Proletariat vo Frantsii i v Anglii"]). When the writer became gravely ill, the suggestion was made to send a delegation to express their sympathy on behalf of Petersburg workers. This idea was eagerly taken up by members of the central workers' circle, who composed an address, which was presented by several workers, probably including Bogdanov. Shelgunov was apparently greatly moved—he had no idea that workers read his articles. When the writer died several weeks later (April 1891), members of the central circle insisted, over objections from the *intelligenty*, that workers participate in Shelgunov's funeral. A sizable group of workers (70–100) joined students and other members of the public in the funeral procession, which took on the character of a political demonstration. Leading the way was a group of workers bearing a wreath inscribed "To

---

[31] Ibid., 18.

one who has pointed out the way to freedom and brotherhood—from the Petersburg workers."[32]

The Petersburg central workers' circle also took the initiative in organizing the first May First celebration in Russia. (The date had been designated as an international labor holiday at the International Socialist Congress held in Paris in 1889.) Since a public demonstration was impossible under Russian conditions, plans were made for a secret meeting in the woods outside the city. About 200 workers attended, as well as three of the social democratic *intelligenty* involved with the circles. As noted above, Bogdanov was one of the speakers. All the speeches were given by workers, one extemporaneously, others, memoir accounts insist, with only stylistic correction by the students.[33] Among the common themes of these speeches are the oppressed situation of Russian workers, compared to that of workers in the West; a sense of solidarity with workers elsewhere; and the role of the "developed" or politicized workers like themselves. Although not mentioned by name, the speeches show familiarity with the ideas of Marx and Lassalle. While the intelligentsia were certainly one source of knowledge, workers made the ideas their own, informing them with their own experience. They had their own sense of their place in a revolutionary tradition, which public figures they held to be significant, which holidays to celebrate.

The distinctive feature of the Petersburg movement in 1890–91 was the role of workers as organizers and propagandists. Karelina takes pains to emphasize "the purely worker character of [our] organization."[34] Workers like Bogdanov organized their own circles and engaged in informal propaganda in their workplaces. At the time of his arrest (November 1891), Bogdanov was

---

[32] This address is reprinted in Pankratova and Ivanov, *Rabochee dvizhenie v Rossii*, 3, ch. 2, 129–30. It was signed by 66 workers (Kazakevich, *Sotsial-demokraticheskie organizatsii Peterburga*, 162). On the Shelgunov demonstration and funeral, see also Brusnev, "Vozniknovenie," 25–26; Golubev, "Stranichka," 118–20; Kazakevich, *Sotsial-demokraticheskie organizatsii Peterburga*, 161–65; Orekhov, *Pervye marksisty*, 77–80.

[33] Eyewitness accounts of the May 1st celebration vary in regard to some of the factual details. See Brusnev, "Vozniknovenie," 27–28; Ol'minskii, "O vospominaniiakh N. D. Bogdanova," 43–44; Orekhkov, *Pervye marksisty*, 86–88; S. N. Valk, "Materialy k istorii pervogo maia v Rossii," *Krasnaia letopis'*, no. 4 (1922): 250–74; V. V. Sviatlovskii, "K istorii pervogo maia (1890–1893 g.)," *Byloe*, no. 16 (1921): 167–73. The St. Petersburg Group of Supporters of the People's Will hectographed and distributed four speeches in 1891, with a second edition in 1892. This is only one of the examples of the ways in which the press of the People's Will was crucial to the success of propaganda activity. The same speeches were also published by the Emancipation of Labor Group in 1892, with a foreword by Plekhanov and the address to Shelgunov. In their published form, the speeches were widely used as a work of propaganda literature.

[34] Karelina, "Na zare rabochego dvizheniia v S.-Peterburge," 18.

found to be continuing his work of political education among women workers at his factory. As seen above, the vehicle in this case was a popular illegal poem from the 1870s which so impressed one of his female listeners that she made her own copy.[35]

One question which calls for further investigation is the effect of participation in the movement on workers' family and personal lives. Karelina's memoirs address this issue in somewhat greater detail than those of other workers. Karelina notes that workers' wives were often opposed to their husbands' involvement, or jealous of their relations with Karelina and other younger women. Male workers sometimes asked Vera to speak to their wives and help change their attitudes. Families also made arrest more difficult—the police would allow pleading wives and wailing children to visit workers in jail, hoping to weaken their resolve.[36]

To conclude this brief snapshot of the subculture of radical workers, we must keep in mind that we cannot view participants apart from other inhabitants of the broader urban lower-class milieu: their families, neighbors, co-workers, fellow students at evening classes. A complete reconstruction of the world of radical workers would need to take into account other factors in their surroundings and draw on recent research on such topics as the new commercial culture, the mass press and growing popular literacy, the influence of temperance and religious societies, and the developing and modernizing life of urban Russia.[37] These radical workers can be seen as creating a new kind of civic culture, as they forged a new identity for themselves as political actors. For those who were part of it, the movement represented not just an ideology, but values and a way of life. Looking back on her early years, Vera Karelina seems to dwell with particular fondness on life in the communal apartments: their friendship, "purity," shared endeavors, and the fun they had—a setting in which principles and life were one. Vera recalls that they'd "get up in the morning and, instead of a prayer, they'd break into a chorus of 'Stenka Razin.'"[38] In rereading the sources with an eye to the meaning of the

---

[35] See RGIA f. 1405, op. 92, d. 10979, ll. 33, 38–39.

[36] Karelina, "Vospominaniia o podpol'nykh rabochikh kruzhkakh," 283–85.

[37] See, for example, Jeffrey Brooks, *When Russia Learned to Read: Literacy and Popular Literature, 1861–1917* (Princeton, NJ, 1985); Stephen P. Frank and Mark D. Steinberg, eds., *Culture in Flux: Lower-Class Values, Practices, and Resistance in Late Imperial Russia* (Princeton, NJ, 1994); Catriona Kelly and David Shepherd, eds., *Constructing Russian Culture in the Age of Revolution, 1881–1940* (Oxford, 1998); Page Herrlinger, *Working Souls: Russian Orthodoxy and Factory Labor in St. Petersburg 1881–1914* (Bloomington, IN, 2007).

[38] Karelina, "Na zare rabochego dvizheniia v S.-Peterburge," 18.

movement in its own terms, rather than solely as a foreshadowing of 1917, we may get closer to understanding the values of the revolutionary and socialist movement for Russian workers and its significance for Russian history.[39]

The Kruzhok

The workers' circle, or *kruzhok*, was the key institution of the workers' revolutionary movement. Consisting of a small number of workers and led most often by a member of the revolutionary intelligentsia, typically a student, the circle provided a kind of cultural and political education that was meant to enlighten and revolutionize. Hundreds of circles were scattered throughout the cities and industrial centers of the Russian Empire, displaying remarkable similarity in their activities and creating a network whose filaments were linked by contacts between circles. Such groupings were strictly illegal, but

---

[39] Note on the later careers of Nikolai Bogdanov and Vera Karelina: Both of these workers continued their careers as organizers among workers following their initial arrests in the early 1890s. Exiled from the capital, Bogdanov worked as a social democratic propagandist in Voronezh (where he spent most of the next two and a half decades), Khar'kov, and Ivanovo-Voznesensk, punctuated by several arrests. A veteran of the Voronezh workers' movement, M. Zhabko, credited Bogdanov with the initial organization of workers' circles in that town in 1893: "As a worker, he knew our milieu, customs, and mores well. He knew what approach to take with workers and was met with warm sympathy in their milieu" (M. Zhabko, *Iz dalekogo proshlogo: Vospominaniia starogo rabochego* [Moscow–Leningrad, 1930], 57). In Khar'kov, he also helped found a legal society of metalworkers in 1898. From 1902–08 he was a member of the united Social Democratic committee in Voronezh and president of the metalworkers' union. In around 1908 he joined the Mensheviks. The 1917 revolution found Bogdanov in Voronezh, where he was a member of the local Menshevik committee, president of the metalworkers' union, and also a member of the city duma and town council. The biographical dictionary *Deiateli revoliutsionnogo dvizheniia v Rossii* notes two arrests, in 1919 and 1924, and states that he ceased political and public activity after 1919 due to poor health. He died in Moscow in 1929. See "Bogdanov, Nikolai Dement'evich," 5: col. 385. Vera Karelina returned to St. Petersburg from exile in 1896, in time to participate in the textile strike of that year. She pursued her organizing efforts among female textile workers through 1905, working with the Union of Struggle and other social democratic groups. In 1903–04 she created womens' groups within Father Gapon's Assembly of Russian Factory Workers and, clearly expecting violence, organized a battalion of female medics (*sanitarki*) for Bloody Sunday. Karelina was arrested after 9 January, but was released that summer and elected to the St. Petersburg Soviet. After 1905 she continued to be active in workers' cooperatives and unions. Karelina married Aleksei Karelin, a lithographer active in St. Petersburg *kruzhki* from the 1880s and a fellow member of the central workers' circle in 1890–91. They had at least two children. On the activities of Karelina and her husband in 1905, see Surh, *1905 in St. Petersburg*, 116–25; Glickman, *Russian Factory Women*, 184–86, 194–95; and notes to Karelina, "Vospominaniia o podpol'nykh rabochikh kruzhkakh," 405–06.

workers would generally receive lesser penalties than members of the intelligentsia, who might spend years in prison or exile. For membership alone,
without other criminal activity, workers were often sent back to their village
or a provincial town away from the major centers.[40]

The fairly well-organized circle network active in St. Petersburg in 1891,
depicted above, arose on the foundation of 20 years of circle organization in
that city. As previously noted, the revolutionary workers' movement was not
confined to the capital. From the 1860s through the 1917 Revolution, however,
new developments tended to appear first in St. Petersburg; they were then
frequently adopted throughout the empire. A brief chronological survey will
highlight the evolving relationship between workers and the revolutionary
movement from the 1870s through the 1890s, with emphasis on Petersburg.

The role of workers in the revolutionary movement was a major topic of
debate and an essential component of program statements by revolutionary
groups throughout the last few decades of the 19th century. While the perception of workers and interpretation of their role underwent important
shifts, the nature of propaganda activity among workers remained relatively
unchanged. The ideology of the Russian revolutionary movement of the
1870s, when workers' circles first appeared in appreciable numbers, was
known as *narodnichestvo*, or populism, an anarchist brand of socialism. As
populists (*narodniki*) they viewed the "people" (*narod*), the mass of Russia's
peasant population, as the most important component of the revolution that
would overthrow the tsarist regime, to be followed by the reconstruction of
Russian society on a socialist basis. Populists viewed workers as members of
the *narod* who happened to be working in cities and industrial areas (and were
thus accessible to the propagandists). This perspective guided members of the
revolutionary intelligentsia in their perception of workers and in the views
presented in propaganda.[41] The first major initiative in making contact with
urban workers was taken in the early 1870s by members of the Petersburg
Chaikovskii circle, who began meeting and leading lessons with small groups
of workers.[42] Similar propaganda activities were carried out in Odessa through

---

[40] Nikolai Troitskii presents statistics, including sentences, on trials of revolutionaries
in the 1870s and 1880s. These figures give an incomplete view of the penalties meeted
out, however, as many cases were decided "by administrative order" and never came
to trial. See N. A. Troitskii, *"Narodnaia volia" pered tsarskim sudom* (Saratov, 1971); and
Troitskii, *Tsarskie sudy protiv revoliutsionnoi Rossii* (Saratov, 1976).

[41] On the ideology of revolutionary populism, see the documents reprinted in S. N.
Valk et al., eds., *Revoliutsionnoe narodnichestvo 70-kh godov XIX veka: Sbornik dokumentov
i materialov*, 2 vols. (Moscow, 1964–65), 1, ch. 1: 19–201.

[42] The circle that came to be known as the "Chaikovskii circle" was originally founded
by Mark Andreevich Natanson, a Petersburg medical student, in 1871. Upon his

the South Russian Union of Workers founded by Evgenii Zaslavskii, and in Moscow by members of the All-Russian Social Revolutionary Organization. By the late 1870s an organization made up entirely of workers, the Northern Union of Russian Workers, was carrying out propaganda and organizing work in Petersburg. These were only the most significant of the workers' circles that began to appear in cities throughout the empire, as well as the capitals.[43]

The link between socialist radicals and urban workers was strengthened during the period 1879–82, when the two revolutionary "parties," the People's Will (Narodnaia Volia) and the Black Repartition (Chernyi Peredel), dominated the revolutionary scene. These parties had emerged from a schism in the nominally unified Land and Freedom Party (Zemlia i Volia), and each claimed the heritage of the preceding populist movement. As populists (narodniki) they continued to view the "people" (narod) as the most important component of the revolution that would overthrow the tsarist regime and as the foundation of the postrevolutionary society. The People's Will, however, was most noted for its new tactic of terrorism directed against government figures, whereas the Black Repartition continued to proclaim its allegiance to peaceful propaganda among the peasantry. The stated goals of the two parties, however, contained a paradox. Both parties now found themselves devoting much energy to propaganda among urban workers, an activity virtually unmentioned in the polemic surrounding the split in the movement. This propaganda activity has been overshadowed by the dramatic terrorist exploits of the People's Will, culminating in the assassination of Alexander II on 1 March 1881.[44] It was arguably more significant, however, for the growth of the revolutionary movement. Many radicals, from both parties, began to regard workers as a social group distinct from the rural peasantry and propaganda activity as a form of political education that would prepare

---

arrest only months later, a leading role was taken by Nikolai Vasil'evich Chaikovskii. Natanson went on to further revolutionary activity, punctuated by arrests, escape, and exile. In the early 20th century he was a member of the Central Committee of the Socialist Revolutionary Party and later a leader of the Left SR movement. On his early revolutionary years, see Venturi, *Roots of Revolution*, 472.

[43] On workers' circles of the 1870s, see Venturi, "The Working Class Movement," chap. 19 in *Roots of Revolution*; B. S. Itenberg, *Dvizhenie revoliutsionnogo narodnichestva: Narodnicheskie kruzhki i 'khozhdenie v narod' v 70-kh godakh XIX v.* (Moscow, 1965), 186–93; Reginald E. Zelnik, "Populists and Workers: The First Encounter between Populist Students and Industrial Workers in St. Petersburg, 1871–74," *Soviet Studies* 24, 2 (October 1972): 251–69; Itenberg, *Iuzhno-rossiiskii soiuz rabochikh: Vozniknovenie i deiatel'nost'* (Moscow, 1974); O. D. Sokolov, *Na zare rabochego dvizheniia v Rossii*, 2nd ed. (Moscow, 1978); E. A. Korol'chuk, *"Severnyi soiuz russkikh rabochikh" i revoliutsionnoe rabochee dvizhenie 70-kh godov XIX v. v Peterburge*, ed. K. G. Sharikov (Leningrad, 1971).

[44] See Venturi, *Roots of Revolution*, chaps. 21 and 22.

workers for a future revolution in Russia. Seen through the prism of worker propaganda, the traditional dichotomy between the parties loses much of its sharpness.[45] During the period 1879–82 Russian radicals developed forms of circle organization, a revolutionary curriculum, and a body of propaganda literature that were to serve as a model for propaganda activity throughout the 1880s and 1890s. Ideological differences were not without significance, but had little effect on propaganda, which was in fact the main revolutionary activity. Organizational work in Petersburg, where both parties had their centers, was especially vibrant. The People's Will had a special Workers' Group to oversee propaganda, and a network of workers' circles linked working-class quarters throughout the city. For a brief period groups affiliated with both parties were also active in other cities and towns, although the Black Repartition soon ended its existence as a coherent party.

In the standard historiographical treatment, the People's Will disappeared from the scene following the assassination of Alexander II and the execution of key members of that party; the 1880s are labeled the era of "small deeds," when the revolutionary movement virtually went into hibernation.[46] In fact, revolutionary activity continued through the decade under the banner of the People's Will, in particular propaganda among workers. The party now took on a broader and more decentralized form, and groups of radicals calling themselves *narodovol'tsy* (adherents of the People's Will), both workers and intelligentsia, continued to engage in propaganda and organizing activity throughout the 1880s. In addition, there were smaller groups, sometimes off-shoots of the old Black Repartition, calling themselves *narodniki*, as well as a few noteworthy groups in Petersburg who, inspired by the German and other labor movements, called themselves social democrats.[47] One could refer to a "revolutionary ideology of the 1880s" which combined aspects of the older populism with the more Western and worker-oriented philosophy of Marx and Lassalle. It appears, however, that during this period ideological distinctions were of minor importance in workers' circles.[48]

---

[45] For the official program documents of People's Will and Black Repartition, see Valk et al., *Revoliutsionnoe narodnichestvo*, 2: 137–58, 170–200.

[46] Venturi ends his magisterial treatment of the first phase of the Russian revolutionary movement on 1 March 1881. See also a major Soviet-era study, Volk's *Narodnaia Volia 1879–1882*, which ends shortly thereafter.

[47] For the program of the Party of the Russian Social Democrats (1884) (also known as the "Blagoev group"), see "Draft Program of the Russian Social Democrats" ("Proekt programmy russkikh sotsial-demokratov"), reprinted in "Programma pervogo v Rossii s.-d. kruzhka," ed. B. Nikolaevskii, *Byloe*, no. 13 (July 1918): 43–48.

[48] To give only one example, I. I. Popov, a member of the Petersburg People's Will Workers' Group in the early 1880s, writes of close relations with the group calling itself

By 1890, as we have seen, a network of workers' circles existed in Petersburg, united in a city-wide organization usually known as the "Brusnev group" (after one of the key figures, a student at the Technological Institute) or the Petersburg "Workers' Union" (Rabochii Soiuz). While *narodovol'tsy* were still present in Petersburg (and elsewhere), it appears that many of these workers identified themselves as social democrats, to a great extent based on their studies in the circles. The history of the labor movement in the West was a major circle theme; readings included the Communist Manifesto, popularizations of *Capital*, and publications of the Emancipation of Labor Group, among others. While we certainly see influence from student *intelligenty* in this direction, it is not surprising that these workers saw in their Western European counterparts their aspirations and goal, and a party that put the working class at center stage. The organization assumed the two-part division typical of city workers' organizations in the 1890s: an organization of *intelligenty* in charge of propaganda in the circles, and a workers' organization uniting the various circles, headed by what was known as the Central Workers' Circle, consisting of worker-representatives from working-class districts or important plants. At the same time, the Petersburg Group of Narodovol'tsy, which was active until the mid-1890s, had a printing operation that furnished illegal literature and also had worker contacts.[49] By the mid-1890s the Petersburg social democrats were known as the Petersburg Union of Struggle for the Liberation of the Working Class (Soiuz bor'by za osvobozhdenie rabochego klassa). Similar Unions of Struggle were organized in Moscow and Kiev.[50] At the same time, the tactic of "propaganda," which had come to mean circle study, had been joined by that of "agitation," referring to strike and labor agitation among broad numbers of workers. Even so, circles continued to be central to the workers' movement

---

the Social Democrats. According to Popov, "circles of workers and even propagandists" were frequently transferred between the groups, and they shared such basic principles as the belief that "the cause of liberation of the working class must be carried out by the workers and laborers themselves." See I. I. Popov, "Revoliutsionnye organizatsii v Peterburge v 1882–1885 gg.," in *Narodovol'tsy posle 1-go marta 1881 goda: Sbornik statei i materialov, sostavlennyi uchastnikami narodovol'cheskogo dvizheniia*, ed. A. Dikovskaia-Iakimova (Moscow, 1928), 58–59.

[49] On the Petersburg "Workers Union," see Orekhov, *Pervye marksisty*. On the Group of Narodovol'tsy, see Kudelli, *Narodovol'tsy na pereput'i*.

[50] On the Petersburg Union of Struggle, see the memoirs in Korol'chuk, *V nachale puti*: I. V. Babushkin, "[Iz vospominanii]," 304–31; V. A. Shelgunov, "Vladimir Il'ich v Peterburge," 347–50 and "Iz dalekogo proshlogo Il'icha," 350–51; I. I. Iakovlev, "Vospominaniia o V. I. Lenine i peterburgskom 'Soiuze bor'by,'" 352–61; G. M. Fisher, "Ob Il'iche," 362–65; A. P. Il'in, "V. I. Ul'ianov v rabochikh kruzhkakh Peterburga v epokhu 'Soiuza bor'by za osvobozhdenie rabochego klassa,'" 366–71; and F. I. Bodrov, "Moe pervoe znakomstvo s Il'ichem," 376–78.

into the 20th century (a topic deserving of more attention), by which point
the revolutionary movement was divided into parties representing two major
ideological currents: the Socialist Revolutionaries, heirs of the earlier populist
movement; and the Social Democrats, who identified with the Marxist
orientation of Western European socialists.

cs so

What were the major aspects of the workers' circle, its personnel, programs
of study, and readings? The circle underwent remarkably little change over
time. From the beginning, those workers involved in the circles tended
to be the more skilled, urbanized, and educated. The memoir accounts of
Petersburg workers of the early 1890s allow for some analysis of that cohort
of circle workers. About 200–300 workers were involved in the circles of this
period,[51] thus comprising only a tiny portion of the Petersburg working-class
population, which numbered about 143,000 in 1890.[52] (Keep in mind that these
census figures almost certainly underestimate the actual number of workers in
the capital, as they do not include migrant workers and perhaps miss workers
in small shops as well.) Most of the circle participants (whose occupations can
be identified) were employed at large metal or machine industry plants. Their
backgrounds varied: many were born in the provinces, some from peasant
families. Others came from families of workers, and a few from other social
groups. St. Petersburg workers had a much higher level of literacy than Russian
workers as a whole,[53] and the circle workers were an extremely well-educated
group. Almost all at some point attended one of the evening or Sunday
schools for workers or one of the schools attached to the large plants. Love of
books and a thirst for knowledge are recurrent motifs in these workers' own
recollections of their personal development. While thus not typical members
of the Petersburg working class, they played a major role in the development
of a workers' movement. While skilled workers predominated from the
1870s, textile and other workers were also members of circles. By the 1890s,

---

[51] Brusnev, "Vozniknovenie," 21–22; Golubev, "Stranichka," 113. This profile is based
on analysis of 92 specific workers (82 men and 10 women) mentioned in the memoir
literature as participants in the circle movement of this period.

[52] Diakin, *Istoriia rabochikh Leningrada*, 1: 127–28, 180–81—based on the 1890 census,
within the city limits.

[53] Literacy rates were 77.6 percent for male workers and 40.8 percent for female,
compared to 59.9 percent and 34.9 percent in the country as a whole, according to the
1897 census. See ibid., 184–85.

the presence of women workers was a striking development.[54] This picture holds true for other parts of the empire as well. In the south, railroad workers, especially from the repair and machine shops, played a major role; artisans and artels of construction workers were also active in such southern cities as Odessa.

While workers frequently organized and led their own circles, most propaganda activity began on the initiative of radical *intelligenty*. In 1880, at the peak of their propaganda activity in St. Petersburg, the People's Will and the Black Repartition drew their propagandists predominantly from the student milieu. Some of these young radicals devoted themselves almost exclusively to propaganda work: in their minds, propaganda among individual workers came to be identified as the very essence of the revolutionary movement, in much the same way that earlier populist youth, especially during the "movement to the people," had identified the revolution with their work among the peasantry. Two such young propagandists were Ivan Kakovskii and Ivan Orlov, both of whom were instrumental in setting up the People's Will Workers' Group and in formulating the curriculum and methodology for student leaders of workers' circles. Kakovskii, a Petersburg University student, joined the People's Will and became involved in organizing workers soon after he arrived in Petersburg from Kiev in 1879. A visitor described the passion and enthusiasm with which Kakovskii, although seriously ill, spoke of "the great role that the working class could play in the Russian revolutionary movement, the powerful, though still hidden strength this class possessed, the shining victories that awaited us in the future."[55] Orlov had been engaged in the education of workers, teaching reading and other basic subjects with the goal of "raising [their] intellectual level," before his involvement in the revolutionary movement. Even his purely "cultural" work, as he termed it (in testimony) had, however, definite political goals. He hoped such instruction would make workers receptive to socialist ideas, and he envisioned a broad plan to attain this goal, beginning with the organization of workers in study circles, the formation of mutual aid funds (*kassy*), and the eventual linkage of circles into one organization. In 1880–81, as a recognized authority in this field, Orlov aided both organizations—People's Will and Black Repartition—

---

[54] Although women from the intelligentsia participated in the revolutionary movement in other ways, sources for this period mention hardly any women as directly involved in propaganda with workers. Sof´ia Perovskaia, one of the People's Will leaders, was a notable exception. See Sergei Ivanov, "Iz vospominanii o 1881 gode," *Byloe*, no. 4 (1906): 233. On the difficulty experienced by one would-be propagandist, Neonila Salova, see N. Salova, "Pamiati Kokovskogo," *Byloe* (Rostov-na-Donu), vyp. 2 (1906): 85.

[55] M. A. Krol´, *Stranitsy moei zhizni* (New York, 1944), 27; see also [Salova], "Pamiati Kokovskogo," 83–84, 87.

in their propaganda activities, though he apparently refrained from becoming a member of either party.[56]

Aleksei Bakh, a prominent People's Will activist in southern and provincial towns in the 1880s, was representative of the changing emphasis of the revolutionary movement. Bakh was the author of the popular illegal brochure *Tsar Hunger* (*Tsar'-golod*, 1883), an exposition of political economy aimed at workers, the direct fruit of his propaganda in workers' study circles. As a member of the Kiev Organization of the People's Will party, Bakh trained two subgroups of propagandists, who in turn supervised workers' circles. For Bakh, propaganda and organizing activity, including among workers, was the most important task of the revolutionary movement.[57] One could go further: various participants in the movement, particularly in the 1880s, claimed that propaganda among workers was the revolutionary movement. The *narodovolets* Vasilii Sukhomlin, an active revolutionary in the south, later wrote: "Work in the provinces consisted mainly in the organization of 'local workers' groups,' which always included in their program mass agitational work among the factory population and in surrounding villages." Similarly, an early member of the Petersburg social democrats of the mid-1880s, Prince Viacheslav Kugushev, a student at the Forestry Institute, wrote that "the basic task of the group was the organization of workers' circles and systematic propaganda in them."[58]

Many of the propagandists involved with the Petersburg workers' organization of the early 1890s were students at the Technological Institute, and their practical training at various local factories facilitated contact with workers. Their goals were clear. Mikhail Brusnev later wrote that "we, social democrats, went to the workers with the goal of preparing them to be devoted and conscious leaders of the workers' movement, because the basis of our view on the labor movement was that 'the liberation of the workers must be the task of the workers themselves.'" The German Social Democratic Party served as a model: "Bebel was our ideal, and we wanted to make of our worker-listeners future Russian Bebels."[59] It should be noted, however, that the question of who created the organization, workers or *intelligenty*, lacks a

---

[56] Testimony of Ivan Orlov in Valk et al., *Revoliutsionnoe narodnichestvo*, 2: 159–61.

[57] See A. N. Bakh, *Zapiski narodovol'tsa*, 2nd ed. (Leningrad, 1931), 176, 180–83.

[58] V. I. Sukhomlin, "Iz epokhi upadka partii 'Narodnaia Volia,'" (ch. 4), *Katorga i ssylka*, no. 7–8 (28–29) (1926): 99; "Vyderzhki iz pis'ma Viach. A. Kugusheva k V. G. Kharitonovu," supplement to V. Kharitonov, "Iz vospominanii uchastnika gruppy Blagoeva," *Proletarskaia revoliutsiia*, no. 8 (79) (1928): 65.

[59] Brusnev, "Vozniknovenie," 19–20; see also Golubev, "Stranichka," 111. University student Vasilii Golubev recalled the years around 1890 as a period when one segment

clearcut answer. Several activist workers claim a reverse direction of influence. Vera Karelina emphasizes the "purely worker" character of the organization, its growth due to organizing work by workers, although with the aid of the *intelligenty*. According to Shelgunov, the workers looked on the intelligentsia propagandists as (mere) educators.[60]

Radicals who gravitated toward worker propaganda took their mission quite seriously. Throughout the late 19th century, propagandists put major effort into devising appropriate programs of study. While studies were not identical among workers' circles, certain basic assumptions were commonly held. (When workers led circles, they typically picked up on some of the standard readings, topics, and discussion questions.) By 1881, the People's Will flagship organization in Petersburg was successful in creating an organization for propaganda among workers which in its size, scope, and level of complexity transcended all the previous efforts of the 1870s. Activities of the Workers' Group were supervised by an "agitational group" which included some of the party's foremost revolutionaries, among them Andrei Zheliabov and Sof'ia Perovskaia, important members of the People's Will's Executive Committee (the party's core group of leaders). Each member of the agitational group supervised the training of a group of propagandists, usually students.[61] The development of what might be termed a revolutionary pedagogy was of special interest to members of the group, who worked at developing an appropriate curriculum for workers' circles. In this curriculum, rudiments of elementary education formed a basis for presentation of broader concepts of, for example, political economy and explicitly political themes. In his circle of students, Ivan Kakovskii gave practical advice on how to interest workers in political topics and on methods to use in leading circles. He composed a curriculum for elementary subjects which was used by one of the student propagandists:

> [I]n *history*, the program recommended stressing the negative aspects of the [Russian] political system and influencing opinions in the direction of negation of monarchy and in favor of popular self-government. To this end, special attention would be given to periods

---

of the radical intelligentsia found in propaganda of socialism among workers an answer to the question of "what is to be done?" ("Stranichka," 106).

[60] Karelina, "Na zare rabochego dvizheniia v S.-Peterburge," 18; V. A. Shelgunov, "Vospominaniia V. A. Shelgunova," in Norinskii et al., *Ot gruppy Blagoeva k "Soiuzu Bor'by,"* 58. See also Fisher, *V Rossii i v Anglii*, 15–16.

[61] "Delo o prestupnoi propagande v srede s.-peterburgskikh rabochikh (1881 god)," *Byloe*, no. 1 (13) (January 1907): 290; "Pokazaniia pervo-martovtsev," *Byloe*, no. 4–5 (1918): 241; "Pamiati Grinevitskogo," *Byloe* (Rostov-na-Donu), vyp. 1 (1906): 7.

marked by a strong upsurge of the popular spirit: the Time of Troubles, the rebellions of Sten´ka Razin and Pugachev, etc. *Arithmetic* problems should make use of such concepts as wages, profit, etc.[62]

Another "program for studies with workers," composed by the non-party activist Ivan Orlov and approved by both People's Will and Black Repartition, recommended beginning with lessons in arithmetic, geography, and other basic subjects, as the first stage in preparing workers for revolution.[63] The less tangible aspects of the propagandist's role were highlighted by Petr Tellalov, another talented propagandist, who headed the People's Will workers' organization during the fall of 1881. At his training sessions for student propagandists, Tellalov liked to emphasize the importance of the propagandist's moral qualities: the personal impression made by the propagandist was as important as the material he discussed. A good propagandist must appeal to workers not only with his ideas, but with his "personal qualities."[64]

The Petersburg "Blagoev group" of the mid-1880s took the name "Party of the Russian Social Democrats," explicitly linking themselves to the socialists of Western Europe. Systematic studies were carried on in accordance with programs worked out in advance, which varied depending on the "preliminary preparation of [workers'] groups and embraced cycles of knowledge ranging from the rudiments of natural science to the history of culture, political economy, and the fundamental principles of Marxism."[65] Copies of such a program were seized by police when a group member was arrested. Although covering many of the same topics, this program is far more detailed than those used by *narodovol´tsy* of the early 1880s. While not as ambitious as implied by the above description (a program beginning with natural science), the program is quite thorough in providing the kind of "knowledge" that the group considered necessary for Russian workers: knowledge of their circumstances, as well as information on workers and workers' movements in the West, Russian history with emphasis on the peasant movement, European history with emphasis on

---

[62] "Iz zakliucheniia prokurora," in Valk et al., *Revoliutsionnoe narodnichestvo*, 2: 273–74.

[63] "Iz pokazanii I. G. Orlova o propagande sredi peterburgskikh rabochikh," in ibid., 260 and 384 n. 140.

[64] Testimony of Anton Boreisha, quoted in I. I. Mindlina, "Deiatel´nost´ revoliutsionnykh narodnikov sredi rabochikh Peterburga i Moskvy (1879–1882 gg.)," *Uchenye zapiski 1-go Moskovskogo pedagogicheskogo instituta inostrannykh iazykov* 34 (1965): 199. On Tellalov, see E. I. Iakovenko, *Petr Abramovich Tellalov* (Moscow, 1930); and V. N. Figner, *Zapechatlennyi trud* (Moscow, 1964), 1: 315. For more on propaganda activity by the People's Will and Black Repartition, see Pearl, "Educating Workers for Revolution."

[65] "Vyderzhki iz pis´ma Viach. A. Kugusheva," 165.

popular liberation movements, and various theories of socialism and political economy.[66] Georgii Lavrov, another group member, went into detail on the nature of circle studies in his testimony after arrest (although he insisted this was all hypothetical):

> [F]irst, present to the workers the basic principles of political economy in its separate aspects, then acquaint them with the situation of workers in Western Europe and Russia, explaining to them the historical course of the workers' movements, as well as their value, and finally clarify to them the essence of socialism, presenting the goals and tendencies of the two revolutionary parties, "Narodnaia Volia" and the "Social Democrats," and indicating that the needs and desires of workers are included in the program of the latter party.[67]

A similar program of study served as a template for propagandists in the Petersburg workers' organization of 1891. The ten-point program began with 1) reading, writing, and arithmetic; and went on to 2) natural science; 3) Darwin's theory; 4) history of culture; 5) political economy; 6) life and history of peasants in Russia and Western Europe; 7) condition of the working class in Russia and Western Europe; 8) history of social movements in Europe and Russia; 9) economic politics and socialism; and 10) a program-minimum of demands for the present time.[68] One can infer that this program was the subject of much debate, since almost all the *intelligenty* who wrote memoirs felt the need to either justify or criticize it. Practically speaking, the average circle was relatively short-lived; there was rarely time to complete such a thorough course of study. Some felt the program was too academic; it seemed that the group was involved in purely "cultural" and not revolutionary work. Brusnev was apparently responding to criticism of this type in a letter he wrote to an associate in 1892:

> [Y]ou know quite well that I was never a peaceful cultural worker. I think you know that I have always been a revolutionary; however, I

---

[66] See Gosudarstvennyi arkhiv Rossiiskoi Federatsii (GARF) f. 102 (DP—Departament Politsii), 3 d-vo, d. 91, l. 13; the document referred to seems to be the untitled document reprinted in *Krasnaia letopis'*, no. 7 (1923): 275–84. See Sergievskii, *Partiia russkikh sotsial-demokratov*, 139–41; and N. L. Sergievskii, introduction to *Rabochii: Gazeta partii russkikh sotsial-demokratov (blagoevtsev) 1885 g.*, ed. Sergievskii (Leningrad, 1928), 5.

[67] GARF f. 102, 3 d-vo, d. 467, 36ob.–37. Detailed lectures were seized from Lavrov. See above file and RGIA f. 1405, op. 87, d. 10268, ll. 94–96.

[68] The program is reprinted in full in Pankratova and Ivanov, *Rabochee dvizhenie v Rossii*, 3, ch. 2, 131–32.

never preached banging one's head against a wall, but advised laying in a stock of more effective tools.... What kind of activity does all this point to? Indignation, unification, instruction and organization of the only revolutionary class, the working class [is the only way to assist progress].[69]

The full program, however, was intended only for circles of the most advanced workers. There was in practice a "program-minimum" for less advanced workers. One propagandist describes an abbreviated course, typical of those actually accomplished in the circles:

brief information on political economy (the theory of Marx on value and surplus value), information on the labor movement in the West, a survey of the history of culture (the origin of classes, the significance of economics in history), the history of the revolutionary movement in Russia, the French Revolution, on state structure in the West, and other topics.[70]

As can be seen, throughout this period propagandists had a distinctive program in mind, starting with elementary education, even literacy, often including geography and natural science, but especially emphasizing the conditions of peasants and workers, popular uprisings, revolutions, and labor movements in the West and in Russia.[71]

---

[69] RGIA f. 1405, op. 93, d. 10547, ll. 304ob.–05. Sviatlovskii also found a principled justification for this approach: "We looked upon socialism as a world outlook formulated by the task of life.... From this followed the depth of our formulation of propaganda work, beginning with natural science and, where necessary, with literacy" (Sviatlovskii, "Na zare Rossiiskoi sotsial-demokratii," 152).

[70] Brusnev, "Vozniknovenie," 21; V. B_____ [V. V. Bartenev], "Vospominaniia peterburzhtsa o vtoroi polovine 80-kh godov," *Minuvshie gody*, no. 10–11 (1908): 196.

[71] See I. I. Popov's unusually detailed description of circle studies carried out by members of the Petersburg Narodnaia Volia Workers' Group, "Revoliutsionnye organizatsii," 55–57. On the Petersburg circle around the Baltic plant worker Ivan Timofeev in the early 1890s, see Norinskii, "Moi vospominaniia," 10–11; Fomin, "Vospominaniia o podpol'noi rabote," 188–90; Egorov, "[Iz vospominanii o rabochikh kruzhkakh]," 237–38; Norinskii, "Kratkaia avtobiografiia," 293–94. See also the experience of Moscow worker M. P. Petrov, "Moi vospominaniia," in *Na zare rabochego dvizheniia v Moskve: Vospominaniia uchastnikov moskovskogo rabochego soiuza (1893–95 gg.). Dokumenty*, ed. S. I. Mitskevich (Moscow, 1922), 188; Ekaterinoslav worker A. Smirnov (1890s), "Vospominaniia o 1-om kruzhke s.-d. raabochei partii g. Ekaterinoslava v 1894 g.," in *Istoriia ekaterinoslavskoi sotsial-demokraticheskoi organizatsii 1889–1903: Vospominaniia,*

Cß ℬ

Throughout the history of the Russian revolutionary movement, there were often two major competing ideological currents: People's Will/Black Repartition, for example, or populist/Marxist. While most histories of the movement emphasize ideological distinctions, it appears that such distinctions had much less presence in the workers' movement than among the radical intelligentsia, while not being completely absent. As we have seen above, the study program of the Blagoev group/Party of Russian Social Democrats included discussion of the difference between Narodnaia Volia and the social democrats, and why the latter was the better choice for workers. From my reading of the evidence, however, I find the usual picture of antagonism between ideological enemies to be overdrawn, especially in relation to the workers' movement. As we have seen, the People's Will and Black Repartition groups of 1879–81 tended to ignore the peasantry, in contradiction to program statements, and to follow nearly identical lessons in workers' circles. While negotiations for cooperation in this area never reached formal agreement, circles of workers were often transferred from a Black Repartition to a People's Will propagandist and vice versa, and publications of the two parties were passed back and forth.[72] Some propagandists kept a foot in both camps—Ivan Orlov is a good example. For these radicals, propaganda among workers, the process of education and development of political consciousness, seems to have been an end in itself, a priority more important than the theoretical differences between parties.

There was one major distinction, however, between the above two parties: the acceptance on the part of the People's Will of terror as a political tactic (more often seen in theory than in practice) and the summons in party program documents to prepare for violent revolution.[73] How did Petersburg workers perceive the differences between the two parties? Most sources emphasize that party differences were deliberately downplayed in propaganda among workers, and workers were often unaware of the party affiliation of their propagandists. According to Vasilii Pankratov, one of the few workers of the time to have written memoirs, workers did not pay attention

---

dokumenty, literaturnye i khudozhestvennye materialy, ed. M. A. Rubach (Ekaterinoslav, 1923), 11–16.

[72] V. S. Pankratov, "Iz deiatel'nosti sredi rabochikh v 1880–1884 gg.," *Byloe,* no. 3 (1906): 244.

[73] See the "Program of the Executive Committee" ("Programma Ispolnitel'nogo Komiteta") (of the People's Will Party) and the "Program of Worker-Members of the 'People's Will' Party" ("Programma rabochikh-chlenov partii 'Narodnoi voli'"), reprinted in Valk et al., *Revoliutsionnoe narodnichestvo,* 2: 170–74 and 184–91.

to the theoretical differences between *chernoperedel'tsy* and *narodovol'tsy*, but accepted propagandists from either group, as long as they were interested in working with workers and brought them revolutionary literature. Workers felt the existence of two groups was natural. As they put it: "Even husband and wife don't agree on everything, but they still live and work together and raise children"; "even fingers on one hand are not the same, but all are useful."[74] Pankratov, in his recollections, stresses the participation of "conscious" workers in what they saw as a workers' as well as a revolutionary movement. Radicalized workers had a general "revolutionary" rather than a party identity. If Pankratov is to be believed, the propagandists in turn were often viewed by them as undifferentiated "illegal *intelligenty*," rather than, or as well as, members of the People's Will or Black Repartition parties. There is some evidence that the People's Will was identified by at least some workers with terrorist acts. In his postarrest testimony, Ivan Orlov, for example, described his chagrin at repeatedly finding himself in the situation of criticizing some terrorist exploit of the People's Will to workers who admired it:

> [I] explained to the workers that the political organization of a particular society was the result of certain economic relations, that however much we tried to change political relations, economic relations would remain the same until a significant part of the masses realized the necessity of changing them.... But it seems that my words were not successful in cooling the workers' terrorist ardor ... [S]ome time [later] ... another revolutionary, a terrorist, would come to them and begin to prove the necessity of such activity; the workers responded to his preaching thus: "See, this one's giving matters a push, but that one (indicating me) cares more for ideas.... It's better to accomplish something."[75]

Overall, however, cooperation was the rule. An important interaction between seemingly opposing groups is seen in mid-1880s Petersburg, when the Narodnaia Volia Workers' Group was close to two other socialist groups: the Party of Russian Social Democrats and the Polish party "Proletariat."[76]

---

[74] V. S. Pankratov, *Vospominaniia: Kak prikhodilos' rabotat' sredi rabochikh v 1880–1884 gg.* (Moscow, 1923), 11; Pankratov, "Iz deiatel'nosti sredi rabochikh," 239.

[75] "Iz pokazanii I. G. Orlova o propagande sredi peterburgskikh rabochikh" (27 May 1881), in *Revoliutsionnoe narodnichestvo*, 2: 262 (document no. 73).

[76] I. I. Popov, "Venedikt Arsen'evich Bodaev," *Katorga i ssylka*, no. 9 (106) (1933): 148; I. I. Popov, *Minuvshee i perezhitoe: Vospominaniia za 50 let*, 1: *Detstvo i gody bor'by*, 2nd ed. (Leningrad, 1924), 91. On the the Polish party "Proletariat," see Norman M. Naimark, *The History of the "Proletariat": The Emergence of Marxism in the Kingdom of Poland, 1870–1887* (Boulder, CO, 1979).

The Social Democrats shared such basic principles with the Workers' Group as the belief that "the cause of liberation of the working class must be carried out by the workers and laborers themselves" and recognition of the need for a minimum of political rights.[77] The two groups worked closely in the area of propaganda among workers; members of Blagoev's group distributed publications hectographed by the Workers' Group, and the latter distributed issues of the Social Democrats' newspaper for workers, *Rabochii* (The Worker).[78] Nikolai Borodin, a social democrat from the Blagoev group, recalled that while on the level of theory lines were beginning to be drawn between the adherents of the two revolutionary ideologies, there was a major area on which both agreed:

> the necessity for political development of the masses and the preparation of conscious revolutionary activists. The *narodovol'tsy* also had a group involved primarily in propaganda among workers; our group was always in contact with it and even shared literature.[79]

The letters sent by the Petersburg Social Democrats in early 1885 to the emigré leaders of both revolutionary camps testify even more conclusively than retrospective memoirs to the close relations between members of the two revolutionary organizations in Petersburg. The Social Democrats had already begun negotiations with the People's Will Workers' Group and, as they wrote to the Emancipation of Labor Group (the first Russian Marxist theorists, headed by Plekhanov and Aksel'rod), "in our views on activity among workers there is absolutely no difference [between us], and the workers' group of 'the People's Will' completely agrees to carry on the cause jointly, both as to funds, and in relation to libraries."[80]

By the mid-1890s, the nature of propaganda among workers was an issue in the increased rivalry between the Petersburg Social Democrats and *narodovol'tsy*. Debates were organized in the spring of 1894 by representatives of the SD propagandists and members of the newly resurgent Group of Narodovol'tsy to give worker activists the opportunity to clarify their stand

---

[77] I. I. Popov, "Revoliutsionnye organizatsii," 58–59.

[78] Ibid., 59; I. I. Popov, *Minuvshee i perezhitoe*, 100; I. I. Popov, "Fedor Vasil'evich Olesinov," *Katorga i ssylka*, no. 5–6 (114–15) (1934): 228.

[79] N. D. Borodin, *Idealy i deistvitel'nost': Sorok let zhizni i raboty riadovogo russkogo intelligenta (1879–1919)* (Berlin, 1930), 12.

[80] Nikolaevskii, "Programma pervogo v Rossii s.-d. kruzhka," 50; see also B. N___skii [B. Nikolaevskii], "K istorii 'Partii russkikh sotsial-demokratov' v 1884–86 g.," *Katorga i ssylka*, no. 5 (54) (1929): 65.

on the rival ideologies. In the eyes of the workers, the Social Democrats stood for gradual education and broad, many-sided knowledge for workers. The *narodovol'tsy*, on the other hand, apparently limited their circle lectures to the history of political struggle, or even engaged in purely political agitation, calling on workers to overthrow the autocracy. Although the debates produced no real resolution, the majority of workers present favored the Social Democrats, although it was decided that *narodovol'tsy* propagandists were to be allowed in the circles "under supervision."[81]

The association with terror was perhaps the People's Will's most distinctive aspect, and at times terror was a topic of discussion, both among *intelligenty*, where in the 1880s the topic of "economic and factory terror" was sometimes hotly debated, and by workers, who sometimes supported the idea of assassinating hated police officials.[82] Theoretical support for terrorist acts made little difference, however, in the work of circle propagandists on a day-to-day level, and most workers connected with circles in the orbit of a local People's Will organization paid it no attention.[83] Rather than viewing circles as divided by ideological conflict, the workers' revolutionary movement is more accurately seen as a unified revolutionary—or revolutionary and workers'—

---

[81] K. M. Norinskii, *Pod nadzorom politsii: Vospominaniia* (Moscow, 1974), 39–42; Takhtarev, *Rabochee dvizhenie*, 29–35; Zelnik, "Russian Bebels," pt. 2, 427–28; V. A. Shelgunov, "Vospominaniia V. A. Shelgunova," 56; Fisher, *V Rossii i v Anglii*, 24. It should be noted, however, that the Petersburg social democrats and the Group of Narodovol'ltsy drew closer together at this time, in great part because of their shared interest in propaganda among workers. See Kudelli, *Narodovol'tsy na pereput'i*, 13.

[82] The South-Russian Workers Union (Kiev, 1880–81), a populist (but non-People's Will) organization founded by Elizaveta Koval'skaia and Nikolai Shchedrin, preached the doctrine of "economic terror." See Elizaveta Koval'skaia, *Iuzhno-russkii rabochii soiuz, 1880–1881* (Moscow, 1926), 10, 14–15. The Party of the Young People's Will, which took shape in a period of crisis of leadership, frequently debated the topic of "agrarian and factory terror." See I. I. Popov, "Revoliutsionnye organizatsii," 68–69; "Programma organizatsii 'Molodoi partii' Narodnoi voli"; O. A. Saikin, "Iz istorii narodovol'cheskogo dvizheniia," *Sovetskie arkhivy*, no. 3 (1969): 65. On workers, see Pankratov, "Iz deiatel'nosti sredi rabochikh," 251. According to Pankratov, some workers called for the assassination of police chief Sudeikin (*Vospominaniia*, 42–43). See also [G. Novopolin], "Poslednie usiliia: Iz revoliutsionnogo proshlogo Ekaterinoslavshchiny," *Puti revoliutsii*, no. 2–3 (5–6) (1926): 51; P. Peshekerov, "Rabochii narodovolets G. G. Rudometov," *Katorga i ssylka*, no. 11 (60) (1929): 167.

[83] In reference to the Petersburg Workers' Union of the early 1890s, one worker writes: "What was our political orientation? We were not yet called SD circles. We were simply a *kruzhok*, with a definite revolutionary inclination—[towards] workers." Another worker recalled that circle members at the Baltic Plant were simply known as *kruzhkovtsy* [circle members] (Egorov, "[Iz vospominanii o rabochikh kruzhkakh]," 238–39). See also Fomin, "Vospominaniia o podpol'noi rabote," 181.

movement. Two basic points were at the foundation of the whole movement: it was revolutionary and socialist. Circle life throughout this period and throughout the empire was remarkably uniform. Workers received the same political education, one that created the sensibility of workers and worker Bolsheviks who found themselves in critical roles during and after 1917.

03   80

The circles also had a historical dimension, manifested in remarkable continuity over time. Workers who became radicalized in the 1880s often traced their interest in the movement to early workplace contact with one of the "last of the Mohicans" of the People's Will, as Nikolai Bogdanov put it (above). *Narodovol´tsy* were not replaced by social democrats, a view propagated by social democrats at the turn of the century,[84] as well as by Soviet-era historians, as if one group of workers was succeeded by another. Rather, the movement of the 1880s and into the 1890s was characterized by shadings, overlappings, and an ideological mixture of ideas as successive circles formed, reconstituted, and evolved.[85] A closer look at the sources reveals a number of examples of continuity of workers' circles. In St. Petersburg, to give one example, the circle headed by worker Ivan Krutov in the mid-1880s included workers from the Putilov and Baltic plants, as well as the Port. By the late 1880s the circle had had a succession of seven propagandists (whose views were those of "*narodovol´tsy* of the 1880s"), one of whom noted that he had been introduced to the circle by Aleksei Peterson, an older worker with revolutionary experience dating

---

[84] Note the rather awkward presentation of movement history in specific cities presented in reports on activities in major centers prepared by the Union of Russian Social Democrats in 1900. While the pamphlet *Workers' Movement in Khar´kov* begins by claiming no link between current social democratic circles and earlier propaganda efforts by *narodovol´tsy*, later reference is made to "remnants of People's Will circles," and a parallel report on the workers' movement in Odessa and Nikolaev notes the decline in People's Will circles after 1881 but then makes reference to circles that were the "weak successors" of these *narodovol´tsy*. See Izd. Soiuza russkikh sotsial-demokratov, *Rabochee dvizhenie v Khar´kove* (Geneva, September 1900), 1–3; and Izd. Soiuza russkikh sotsial-demokratov, *Iz rabochego dvizheniia v Odesse i Nikolaeve* (Geneva, July 1900), 5–7.

[85] Robert Service has noted that even among such leading Russian Marxist theorists as Lenin, Trotskii, and the Menshevik P. P. Maslov it is impossible to fully disentangle the populist and Marxist strands of their thought. See Robert Service, "Russian Populism and Russian Marxism: Two Skeins Entangled," in *Russian Thought and Society 1800–1917: Essays in Honour of Eugene Lampert*, ed. Roger Bartlett (Keele, UK, 1984), 220–42.

back to the early 1870s.[86] There were other veterans of the Petersburg workers' movement of the early 1870s who continued to be active. These included Karl Ivanainen, first propagandized by the *chaikovtsy* in 1873 and over the next eight years involved in the movement in Petersburg, Odessa, and Moscow, between periods of imprisonment and exile; Baltic Plant worker Login Zhelabin, who had known worker-*pervomartovets* (1 March conspirator) Timofei Mikhailov; and Vasilii Buianov, who had been arrested in 1881 for revolutionary activity. Nil Vasil'ev, who may have been propagandized by the Nechaev or Chaikovskii circles, was about 50 years old when he joined Tochisskii's Association in the mid-1880s.[87] Of workers in Kiev in 1879–80 organizer Mikhail Popov wrote, "Among Kiev workers links with revolutionaries were never lost"; when *narodovol'tsy* created a workers' organization in Odessa at that time, an ongoing network of circles dating from the South Russian Union of Workers served as the foundation.[88] The police recognized this continuity and often voiced their frustration:

> Attempts to disseminate revolutionary teachings and anti-government agitation among the working population in Petersburg … have followed continuously one after another since the mid-70s. When one group of agitators were arrested and prosecuted, other like-minded ones continued the cause of worker propaganda, which was something like a preparatory school for those beginning [revolutionary activity].[89]

In addition to continuity of the workers' movement in individual cities, a broader geographical continuity was maintained when workers from the capitals were exiled to provincial cities, or departed to escape arrest, thus spreading the movement to more locations in the provinces. In this way, by the 1890s the workers' movement had a history, and also a martyrology. Workers

---

[86] B_____[Bartenev], "Vospominaniia peterburzhtsa," 175, 190–91. Peterson, identified by Bartenev only as A. N. P____son, was active in the movement from the early 1870s, when he worked at the Patronnyi (Cartridge) Plant. He was one of the organizers of the Northern Union of Russian Workers. After exile in Siberia, he returned to Petersburg in 1886, worked at the Izhorsk plant in Kolpino and then at the Baltic Shipbuilding Plant. See Korol'chuk, *"Severnyi soiuz russkikh rabochikh,"* 304.

[87] On Ivanainen, see "Ivanainen (Ivanain), Karl Adamovich," in *DRDR* 2, vyp. 2, cols. 479–81. For Zhelabin, see Norinskii, "Dopolnenie k vospominaniiam," 50. On Buianov, see *DRDR* 5, vyp. 1, col. 576. On Vasil'ev, see A. Breitfus, "Tochisskii i ego kruzhok," *Krasnaia letopis',* no. 7 (1923): 328, 330, 336; GARF f. 102, 3 d-vo, d. 1112, vol. 1, l. 51ob.

[88] M. R. Popov, "Iz moego proshlogo," *Minuvshie gody,* no. 2 (February 1908): 182; Figner, *Zapechatlennyi trud,* 1: 292.

[89] *Obzor vazhneishikh doznanii* 3 (1 January–1 May 1882), 52.

recalled their association with prominent worker activists of earlier times, and the revolutionaries of the People's Will "heroic" period were revered.[90]

⋈ ⋊

The *kruzhki* were the essential integument that bound the workers' movement together, and taking a circle-oriented perspective allows us a new way of looking at the revolutionary movement as a whole. By the late 1890s and early 20th century, the workers' circle was no longer the only institution around which radical workers organized. The first May Day celebrations, although clandestine, had taken place, an era of street demonstrations was on the horizon, and strikes were becoming more organized and politicized. This period is associated in the historiography of the movement with the transition to the tactic of "agitation," after the much debated brochure "On Agitation," by Arkadii Kremer and Iulii Tsederbaum (Martov).[91] There was a sense that the workers' revolutionary movement was beginning to outgrow the circles that had been the primary vehicle for propaganda among workers since the 1870s. (Interestingly, it was often the circle veterans who wanted to continue the emphasis on "propaganda.")[92] While other foci for revolutionary activity appeared, however, the circle remained central into the early 20th century, and propaganda literature remained key, including the works created and used in earlier decades. The circles nurtured a committed group of activists who went on to play leadership roles in strikes and organizing activity. During the massive textile strike in Petersburg in May–June 1896 a number of leading workers (including Babushkin and Shelgunov) from the generation of the late 1880s–early 1890s, together with newer recruits, continued circle propaganda

---

[90] Timofei Mikhailov, one of the *pervomartovtsy*, was long remembered by the workers who knew him. The assassination of Alexander II and the execution of the key conspirators had the effect of raising the prestige of the People's Will among workers, as well as others. According to one source, workers who had known Zheliabov, Perovskaia, and Mikhailov wanted to free them, but this idea was not realized. The illegally published *Almanac of the People's Will* (*Kalendar' Narodnoi Voli*; Geneva, 1883) circulated among workers. Among literature confiscated when a member of the Blagoev group was arrested was a biography of Perovskaia and an essay, "Khalturin's Stay in the Winter Palace," reprinted from the *Kalendar'*. See V. Kharitonov, "Iz vospominanii uchastnika gruppy Blagoeva," *Proletarskaia revoliutsiia*, no. 8 (79) (1928): 155.

[91] On the debate over agitation and the origins of the Petersburg Union of Struggle for the Emancipation of the Working Class, see V. A. Shelgunov, "Vospominaniia V. A. Shelgunova," 57–58; V. A. Shelgunov, "Rabochie na puti k marksizmu," 348–50; and Babushkin, *Vospominaniia I. V. Babushkina*, 61–71. See also the excellent discussion in Wildman, *Making of a Workers' Revolution*, chaps. 2 and 3.

[92] See Babushkin, *Vospominaniia I. V. Babushkina*, 64.

and factory agitation. The leaflet campaign carried out by the Union of Struggle did much to prepare the ground for the textile strike. During the strike, many Petersburg workers made contact with politically conscious workers and *intelligenty* for the first time. Circles continued to flourish even during the strike, and members raised money for the striking textile workers and played an active role in strike agitation, speaking at meetings and distributing quantities of propaganda literature.[93]

Propaganda Literature

While the *kruzhok* was the key institution of the workers' revolutionary movement, central to membership in the subculture of radical workers, the literature of propaganda was the vehicle for the ideas that gave the movement its meaning. This literature circulated both within and outside the workers' circles and was critical to the workers' understanding of the movement's ideas. The chapters that follow are devoted to a close analysis of this literature and its role in the movement, providing a key to understanding the ideas that informed the movement and the views that were presented to and by radical workers.

From the early 1870s, literature played an important role in propaganda among workers. The Petersburg Chaikovskii circle had a "literary committee" that wrote leaflets considered suitable for propaganda.[94] (The leaflets were printed on the group's press in Geneva and were then smuggled into Russia.) Program statements referred to the complementary activities of "propaganda" and "agitation." The official journal of the Black Repartition Party, for example, noted that "oral and written propaganda must introduce into the people's consciousness the idea of a socialist revolution with all its implications and consequences."[95] As a whole, this worker propaganda literature can be viewed

---

[93] The strike affected almost all the textile factories in Petersburg, with close to 16,000 workers involved. See Diakin, *Istoriia rabochikh Leningrada*, 1: 206. See Wildman, *Making of a Workers' Revolution*, chap. 3. For details on propaganda activity during the strike, see GARF f. 102, 3 d-vo, d. 580, vol. 1; GARF f. 124, op. 5, d. 2 (1896), vol. 2; GARF f. 102, 7 d-vo, d. 319.

[94] On the Chaikovskii circle "literary committee," see Peter Kropotkin, *Memoirs of a Revolutionist* (New York, 1968), 324; and N. A. Charushin, *O dalekom proshlom: Iz vospominanii o revoliutsionnom dvizhenii 70-kh godov XIX veka*, 2nd ed. (Moscow, 1973), 137, 192.

[95] *Chernyi Peredel*, no. 2 (September 1880), reprinted in Petrogradskoe biuro komissii po istorii Oktiabr'skoi revoliutsii i Rossiiskoi Kommunisticheskoi Partii, *Chernyi Peredel: Organ sotsialistov-federalistov, 1880–1881 g.* (Moscow–Petrograd, 1923), 192. Pavel Aksel'rod, a leader of Black Repartition and by all accounts an extremely tal-

as a corpus with shifting and overlapping layers. Certain works and genres are associated with specific periods of the movement, but some works remained popular for decades. For example, revolutionary *skazki*, tales modeled on the traditional Russian folktale but with radical content, are associated with the 1870s; some poems composed in the 1870s were popular for decades, as were certain "tendentious" novels. The book or pamphlet was also an object, a physical representation of the revolutionary movement. The appearance, format, the "look" of the work all helped create an association with the movement.[96] Illegal literature was so closely linked with revolutionary activity that a propagandist said of one circle that the workers were eager for any kind of tendentious or illegal literature—specifics seemed irrelevant.[97] Workers often complained of a dearth of literature: attempts to smuggle literature from abroad were difficult to arrange and not always successful; handwritten or hectographed works were time-consuming to produce. On their own initiative some workers searched second-hand stores and flea markets for back issues of the old "thick" journals, with their informative articles on Russian politics and society accessible to those who could read the "aesopian" language of these legally published journals.[98]

What did literature mean to radical workers? Recent works on reading and popular culture make clear the complexity of this question and the difficulty of finding simple answers to the relationship between a radical worker and a piece of revolutionary literature. Roger Chartier, one of the most prominent scholars in this field, introduces the useful concept of appropriation: what the author intends and what the reader makes of a given text is not necessarily obvious: "creative invention lies at the very heart of the reception process." Revolutionary literature cannot be taken as a transparent transmission from writer to worker reader. In reference to early modern European culture, Chartier

---

ented propagandist, had written of the power of propaganda to transform popular movements and have a powerful moral and intellectual effect on the development of popular thought and feelings. See [Aksel'rod], "Perekhodnyi moment," *Obshchina*, nos. 8 and 9 (November and December 1878), quoted in O. V. Aptekman, introduction to *Chernyi Peredel*, 99–100; O. K. Bulanova, "'Chernyi Peredel' (vospominaniia)," in *Gruppa "Osvobozhdenie Truda": Sbornik* 1 (1924): 117; and O. V. Aptekman, *Obshchestvo "Zemlia i Volia" 70-kh gg.: Po lichnym vospominaniiam*, 2nd ed. (Petrograd, 1924), 101.

[96] Roger Chartier maintains, "In print writings ... the format of the book, its page layout, the ways the text is divided, and the typographical conventions all have an 'expressive function' and contribute to the construction of meaning"; Chartier, *On the Edge of the Cliff: History, Language, and Practices* (Baltimore, 1997), 82.

[97] N. Volkov [I. I. Mainov], "Narodovol'cheskaia propaganda sredi moskovskikh rabochikh v 1881 g.," *Byloe*, no. 2 (1906): 180.

[98] See Fomin, "Vospominaniia o podpol'noi rabote," 183.

writes: "the texts, the words ... aimed at shaping the thought and conduct of the common people" were often "less than totally efficacious.... Such practices always created uses and representations not necessarily in accordance with the desire of those who produced the discourses."[99] Moreover, context, the way in which a propaganda brochure was encountered, matters: a book is always situated "within a network of cultural and social practices that give it meaning. Reading ... is an activity, individual or collective, produced on each occasion by a form of sociability."[100] Chartier also notes that the process of reading is fluid, circulating between groups and crossing social boundaries, and revolutionary literature in particular served as a vehicle linking two disparate social groups: radicals from the educated classes and workers. It is important to note that propaganda literature linked the oral and the written. Workers who were illiterate or poorly literate could hear works read aloud, as they often were in the circles, accompanied by discussion led by the propagandist. This common circumstance serves to illustrate Chartier's point that oral and written culture overlap, rather than representing successive stages of development.[101] It should be kept in mind as well that literacy was growing, especially among young male workers in major cities such as Petersburg, and, although rarely mentioned in workers' memoirs, workers were exposed to a variety of genres of popular literature as well: tales of bandits and detectives, of exotic peoples and superstition unmasked.[102] These new kinds of popular works were part of the context in which propaganda literature was read.

The question of *reception* of this literature is key, and also one of the most difficult to answer. (Recall Alon Confino's frustration with the issue of reception, "that ogre that waits every cultural historian.")[103] Most sources do not record responses to specific works; more often works are merely named, but this information can be telling. By noting the presence of specific works— in memoirs, as well as lists of literature seized at arrest and other official documents—we get a sense of which works were most popular, which were

---

[99] Roger Chartier, "Texts, Printing, Readings," in *The New Cultural History*, ed. Lynn Hunt (Berkeley, CA, 1989), 171; Chartier, *The Cultural Uses of Print in Early Modern France* (Princeton, NJ, 1987), 7.

[100] Chartier, *Cultural Uses of Print*, 183.

[101] Chartier, "Texts, Printing, Readings," 169–70. On the importance of reading aloud, Chartier writes, "Thanks to the various social situations in which reading aloud occurred, there existed in pre-revolutionary societies a culture dependent on writing, even among people incapable of producing or reading a written text" (*Cultural Uses of Print*, 5).

[102] See Brooks, *When Russia Learned to Read*.

[103] Confino, "Collective Memory," 1395.

most frequently read by workers and used in propaganda. Wherever possible, I have tried to include workers' reactions to specific works of literature, which are sometimes noted in memoirs. In his studies of literacy and popular culture in England, David Vincent calls literacy "a crucial element in the system of values by which social groups define themselves or are subject to definition by those in power over them" and makes the broad claim that "the encounter with books produced a fundamental change in the mind of the reader."[104] This was certainly true of Russia's radical workers. Reading illegal literature was a basic activity that indicated participation, at some level, in the revolutionary movement. Beyond that, love of books and a thirst for education and knowledge are recurrent motifs in workers' own recollections of their personal and revolutionary development. Many years later, some of these politically active workers could still recall the first piece of illegal literature they read. As Ivan Babushkin tells it, an SR [sic—probably People's Will] leaflet he was shown by a fellow worker turned him into an "antigovernment element" almost on the spot, ready to sacrifice anything for the cause.[105] If workers did not think of the future historian's need for detailed information on their reactions to revolutionary literature, we must nevertheless keep in mind the link between these works and their audience. As Jonathan Rose emphasizes in his study of the intellectual life of the British working classes, "Texts do nothing by themselves. The work is performed by the reader, using the text as a tool."[106]

Both legal and illegal works of literature were used in propaganda. Legal works, including works of Russian literature (among them those by Gleb Uspenskii, Nekrasov, and Turgenev) and foreign works in translation, carried no penalty and were frequently used in initial contact with workers new to the movement. These works, often labeled "tendentious" by the authorities, could include Russian works highlighting the condition of the *narod* or foreign novels with plots revolving around revolutions or revolts. Some propagandists felt

---

[104] David Vincent, *Literacy and Popular Culture: England 1750–1914* (Cambridge, 1989), 4, 9.

[105] Babushkin, *Vospominaniia I. V. Babushkina*, 25.

[106] Jonathan Rose, *The Intellectual Life of the British Working Classes* (New Haven, 2001), 15. Rose also stresses the importance of *intertextuality*: "our understanding of a text is shaped by everything else we have read." (41.) He quotes a British worker who "proclaimed that Bunyan, Burns, Shelley, Byron, Aeschuylus, Dante, Schiller, and *Les Miserables* 'all helped to rouse and nourish in me a passionate hatred of oppression and an exalting hope of the coming of a new era'" (48). It appears that radical literature had a similar cumulative effect on Russian workers.

strongly that illegal literature was too risky and should be avoided whenever possible. Pavel Tochisskii was especially adamant in this view.[107]

Circle studies and propaganda literature reinforced each other. As we have seen, circle study topics included peasant revolts, European revolutions, and Western socialist and labor movements. Newspapers were among the types of legal literature used in propaganda. *Russkie Vedomosti* (Russian News) and other newspapers frequently published correspondence on labor movements in the West and served as a source for knowledge and discussion, while raising the aspirations of Russian workers for their movement. For the circle members, the Western European labor movement became a subject of burning interest. They read the brief newspaper accounts of May Day celebrations and strikes with great joy. This tactic was a successful one—reading of the victories of Western workers "automatically raised the spirits of the listeners."[108] (Revolutionary organizations sometimes published illegal newspapers for workers as well.) As noted, through discussion and reading aloud, oral and written propaganda were closely linked. For the worker with little education, the focus of some groups on basic literacy, as well as elements of geography and science, provided the broader educational groundwork for revolutionary literature and a new worldview. These works of literature provided new knowledge and ideas: they recounted Russian and European history, explained the Russian political and economic system and analyzed the exploitation of workers and peasants, all the while emphasizing that this situation was not divinely ordained, but was created by human actors and could be remade. Workers' circles and city organizations often collected libraries of appropriate literature, of which they were often quite proud. These libraries in turn often served as a focus for organization and for attracting new members.[109]

---

[107] Breitfus, "Tochiskii," 329; RGIA f. 1405, op. 89, d. 11129, l. 103ob. See the list of frequently read works in 1880–81 in Pankratov, "Iz deiatel'nosti sredi rabochikh," 252–53; and works recommended by the Petersburg Social Democrats, *Krasnaia letopis'*, no. 7 (1923): 275.

[108] See workers V. Fomin and I. Egorov on the profound impact on circle workers of news of the achievements of the Western labor movement: Fomin, "Vospominaniia o podpol'noi rabote," 188; and Egorov, ""[Iz vospominanii o rabochikh kruzhkakh]," 238–39.

[109] The Tochisskii organization had an extensive library which was perhaps even more central to its activities than workers' circle studies. See Breitfus, "Tochisskii," 330. On the library used by Khar'kov workers and students in 1879, see also V. V. Shirokova, "Vozniknovenie narodovol'cheskoi organizatsii v Khar'kove," in *Iz istorii obshchestvennoi mysli i obshchestvennogo dvizheniia v Rossii*, ed. M. S. Persov (Saratov, 1964), 80–83; on an illegal library in Kiev at the same time, see A. I. Bychkov, "Delo o revoliutsionnykh kruzhkakh v Kieve v 1879, 1880 i 1881 gg.," *Letopis' revoliutsii*, no.

ೞ   ಭ

What kinds of literature did workers discuss in the circles and circulate among themselves in their workplace or residence? While works of legal literature— from Russian classics to the leading newspaper *Russkie Vedomosti*—were frequently used in propaganda, it was revolutionary literature that set the tone for the movement, works that circulated clandestinely and represented one of the elements that made circle meetings liable to criminal prosecution. In the chapters that follow I view revolutionary literature as a corpus of works, with genres shifting over the decades from the 1870s to the revolution of 1905. I have chosen four of the major "genres" of revolutionary literature: revolutionary tales (*skazki*), pamphlets on political economy, revolutionary poetry and song, and works of foreign literature in translation. (Of these four genres, the first three were illegal; the last was made up of works that were, at least initially, legally published.) Illegal literature, with all the revolutionary virtues of radical speech, spoke to workers directly, without the veil of aesopian language, and needed relatively little interpretation, compared to works of legal literature. It was these works that workers later remembered, that comprised the link between workers and radicals from the intelligentsia, and workers and the broader revolutionary movement. Each chapter examines the most widely used works of their respective genres and shows the ways in which they were linked with the circles and the subculture of radical workers. Through this detailed analysis, we can see the variety of forms, language, and ideas these works expressed. This literature thus gives us a new perspective from which to understand the worldview of radical workers, their experience in the revolutionary movement, and the meaning this movement held for them.

2 (7) (1924): 57. See Takhtarev's detailed list of typical selections in a circle library (c. 1893–94) in *Rabochee dvizhenie*, 29–30.

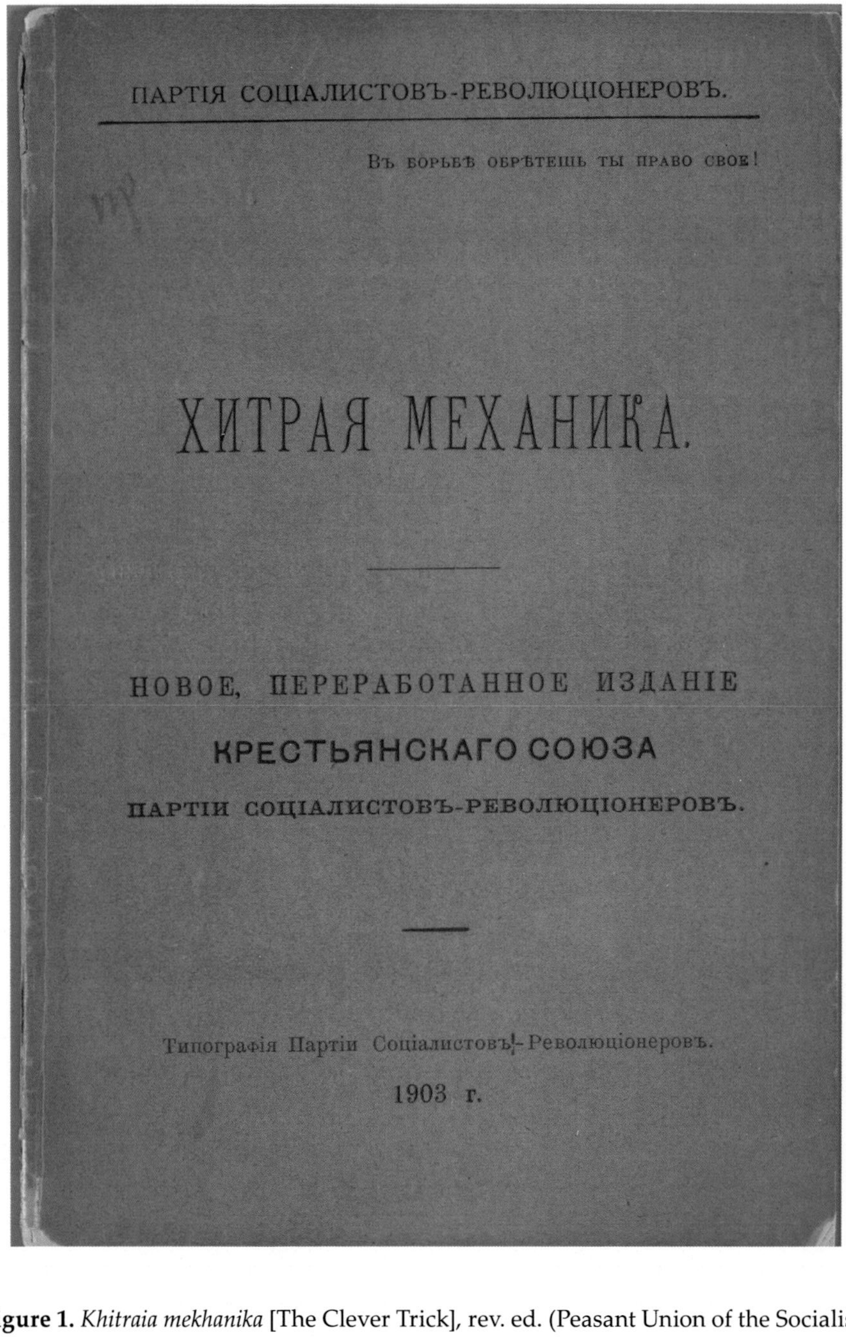

Figure 1. *Khitraia mekhanika* [The Clever Trick], rev. ed. (Peasant Union of the Socialist Revolutionary Party, 1903). RRL 21.719, Houghton Library, Harvard University.

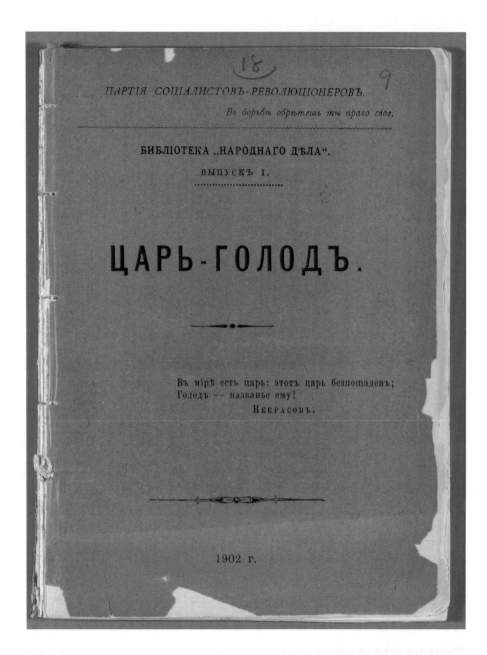

ПАРТІЯ СОЦІАЛИСТОВЪ-РЕВОЛЮЦІОНЕРОВЪ.

Въ борьбѣ обрѣтешь ты право свое.

БИБЛІОТЕКА „НАРОДНАГО ДѢЛА".

ВЫПУСКЪ I.

ЦАРЬ-ГОЛОДЪ.

Въ мірѣ есть царь: этотъ царь безпощаденъ;
Голодъ — названье ему!

НЕКРАСОВЪ.

1902 г.

Figure 2. *Tsar-golod* [Tsar Hunger] (Socialist Revolutionary Party, 1902). RRL l.42, Houghton Library, Harvard University.

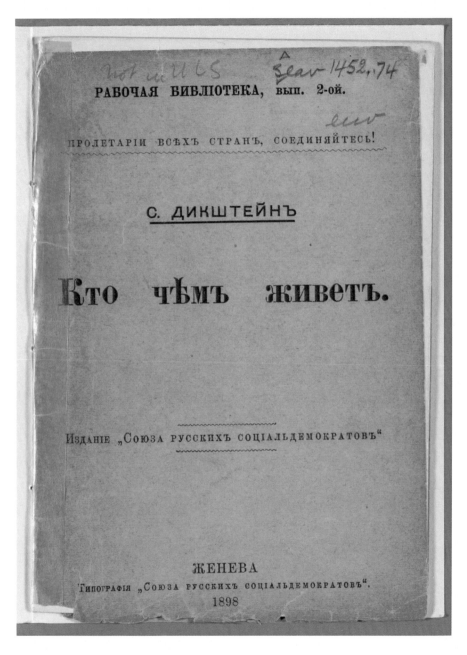

ПРОЛЕТАРІИ ВСѢХЪ СТРАНЪ, СОЕДИНЯЙТЕСЬ!

С. ДИКШТЕЙНЪ

Кто чѣмъ живетъ.

Изданіе „Союза русскихъ соціальдемократовъ"

ЖЕНЕВА

Типографія „Союза русскихъ соціальдемократовъ".

1898

Figure 3. S. Dikshtein, *Kto chem zhivet* [Who Lives By What] (Union of Russian Social Democrats, 1898). RRL 4.121, Houghton Library, Harvard University.

Chapter 2

Tales of Revolution: Propaganda *Skazki*

> This story you should read,
> And to its words pay heed!"
> —Epigraph to *Where Is It Better? A Tale of Four Brothers and Their Adventures*[1]

The dawning of radical consciousness is a key episode in the published autobiographies of Russian worker-revolutionaries. Frequently, this moment of epiphany is linked with the reading of some work of underground, illegal literature. Such is the case with Petr Moiseenko, an active participant in the revolutionary and labor movements from the 1870s, best known as one of the instigators of the Morozov strike of 1885.[2] In his *Memoirs of an Old Revolutionary* he states at the outset: "I must begin my memoirs from the time when illegal brochures first came my way: 'The Tale of Four Brothers,' 'The Clever Trick,' 'The Tale of a Kopeck,' and the 'Revolutionary Songbook.' From that time my awakening from the old religious teachings began."[3] Moiseenko

---

[1] "Skazku etu chitai, /Da na us sebe motai!" *Gde luchshe? Skazka o chetyrekh brat'iakh i ob ikh prikliucheniiakh*, in Bazanov, *Agitatsionnaia literatura*, 267.

[2] On the strike at the Morozov textile factory in Orekhovo-Zuevo (Ivanovo-Voznesensk industrial region) in January 1885, see: 1) document nos. 1–71 in Pankratova and Ivanov, *Rabochee dvizhenie v Rossii*, 3, ch. 1, 123–302; 2) P. A. Moiseenko, "Iz vospominanii P. A. Moiseenko," in P. A. Alekseev et al., *Rabochee dvizhenie v Rossii v opisanii samykh rabochikh: Ot 70-kh do 90-kh godov* (Moscow, 1933), 131–73; and 3) N. I. Tolokonskii, *Orekhovo-Zuevskaia stachka 1885 g.* (Leningrad, 1956). A number of studies were issued commemorating the centenary of the strike, among them N. A. Ivanov et al., eds., *Morozovskaia stachka 1885 g. i rabochie tsentral'nogo promyshlennogo raiona Rossii v kontse XIX–nachale XX v.: Tezisy vystuplenii uchastnikov XV zonal'noi mezhvuzovskoi nauchnoi konferentsii, posviashchennoi 100-letiiu Morozovskoi stachki* (Moscow, 1984); V. Ia. Laverychev and A. M. Solov'eva, *Boevoi pochin rossiiskogo proletariata: K 100-letiiu Morozovskoi stachki 1885 g.* (Moscow, 1985); and N. I. Mekhontsev, comp., *Probuzhdenie: K 100-letiiu Morozovskoi stachki* (Moscow, 1984).

[3] P. A. Moiseenko, *Vospominaniia starogo revoliutsionera* (Moscow, 1966), 15. Moiseenko dates this event to the early 1870s, but mid-1870s is probably more accurate, given the publication dates of these works.

was at that time a young weaver at a provincial textile factory. A friend's brother apparently obtained these booklets at the fair in Nizhnii Novgorod. As Moiseenko and his friend began to study them, their disbelief grew: the contents seemed to be truthful, yet were so at variance with what they had been taught. Since the two young men were "quite religious," they sought clarification at a nearby monastery, an adventure which only led to further disillusionment and, as Moiseenko tells it, loss of faith. What were these booklets, and what role did they play in the revolutionary movement? How could "tales" like those named above, published anonymously and illegally, become a catalyst for a complete rethinking of received beliefs, including previously held religious beliefs, or even lead a young worker to embark on the path of revolution?

In investigating the revolutionary tale and other genres of propaganda literature, I take a new approach to the study of the revolutionary workers' movement, one that proposes to explore hitherto "unknown" or disregarded layers of this movement's history. We begin with the *skazka*, a genre associated with the revolutionary propaganda of the 1870s. To those familiar with the standard history of the movement, the narrative of the 1870s seems a familiar one: peasant-oriented populism, the movement "to go to the people," the turn to terrorism at the end of the decade, culminating in the assassination of Tsar Alexander II on 1 March 1881. The personalities, activities, and ideology of this period seem to have been thoroughly investigated. During the Soviet period, revolutionary populism was viewed ideologically, as a negative foil to subsequently triumphant Marxism/communism. This perspective underpinned the periodization and parameters limiting the scholarship of Soviet-era historians. The populist 1870s was a relative "safe" subject for scholarly investigation, as the period predated the appearance of Marxism in the Russian revolutionary movement. The scholarly achievements of the early Soviet period, however, came to a halt in the mid-1930s, as the study of Russian populism (with its association with terrorist acts) was shut down in the Stalin period. Research on the revolutionary populist movement was revived in the 1960s with a new flowering of research. It is thus not surprising that two of the most important scholars of propaganda literature, V. G. Bazanov and V. F. Zakharina, deal precisely with this period.[4] Their traditional emphasis on

---

[4] The 1920s saw an outpouring of scholarship on the revolutionary movement of the 1860s–80s: memoirs, document collections, journals devoted to the revolutionary past, and numerous articles. Among the scholars who laid the groundwork for study of the revolutionary movement were B. P. Koz'min, Sh. M. Levin, A. A. Shilov, R. M. Kantor, and V. I. Nevskii. Prominent scholars of revolutionary populism who published during the second, post-Thaw wave of scholarship include B. S. Itenberg, V. A. Tvardovskaia, and S. S. Volk, whose works are noted below. The most important works by

the peasant orientation of the *narodniki* (populists) of the time, and their fairly narrow chronological focus, however, obscure the broader picture. While the long-accepted narrative of populist propaganda in the 1870s highlights the seeming failure to reach the peasantry with revolutionary ideas, a more accurate picture shows that the *skazka* had a history that extended far beyond the decade of the 1870s and that the revolutionary tale served as an integral part of successful propaganda among urban workers.

Sources for this chapter include official documents from archives of the tsarist secret police and the Ministry of Justice, in addition to works of propaganda literature. Memoirs of participants in the movement are also indispensable and serve a dual purpose. They provide factual information: the what, where, and when of underground groups, for example, or the titles of works in a circle's library. Such information can often be corroborated by comparing several memoirs, as well as comparison to government sources. They also convey the experience of life as a radical worker, recollected at a certain distance of time. Many of the memoirs trace the pattern of a life story and follow the trajectory, whether consciously or not, of a journey from darkness to enlightenment. The memoirs are thus important for the stories they tell of the experiences of radical workers and for the way in which the stories are told, to a greater or lesser extent, through the tropes of this particular genre, that of radical workers' memoirs. The reader of Moiseenko's memoirs is struck by the way he often uses revolutionary literature to elaborate on the events of his life. Although Moiseenko himself does not remark on this inter-twining of literature and experience, the manner in which he narrates his life story underlines the significance of propaganda literature for the workers' movement.

Of the various genres of propaganda literature, the revolutionary *skazka* or tale (modeled on the traditional folktale but with a revolutionary content and moral) was often the vehicle for a worker's first encounter with illegal literature and revolutionary thought. As we attempt to understand workers' reception and appropriation of these and other works, as opposed to the intentions and understanding of propagandists from the intelligentsia, we must bear in mind the context in which workers first learned of or read (or heard) these works. Illegal works differed from the legal works to which workers were also exposed in the circles in several very basic ways. Freed from the strictures of censorship, *skazki* and other works of illegal literature could bluntly expose and criticize the existing social and political order, not sparing the upper classes, the church, even the tsar himself; they could call for revolution and describe the desired socialist society. As proscribed works,

---

Bazanov and Zakharina are Bazanov, *Agitatsionnaia literatura*; and Zakharina, *Golos revoliutsionnoi Rossii*.

with harsh penalties attached for possession, they often held the allure of the forbidden, creating bonds of conspiratorial comradeship between those who read and passed them on. Some workers seem to have perceived these works as containing secret knowledge that would shed light on the reasons for their harsh existence and answer the question of what could be done. One worker writes that as a teenage worker at a Moscow factory in the mid-1890s he began reading some works of legal but "tendentious" literature with other young workers: "We heard that there were still other books—underground, uncensored, in which was written the whole truth about workers and which showed workers what it was necessary to do to improve their situation. We very much wanted to read such books; although we knew that people were imprisoned and persecuted for them, we searched for them everywhere." Some time later a radical worker was hired at the factory. After some months, having sworn them to secrecy he assembled ten or so of the young workers in the cemetery (a setting that no doubt heightened their sense of the fateful nature of the gathering) on a Sunday morning: "and for the first time we heard underground books.... We, holding our breath and with sinking hearts, heard these pamphlets; we were fearful, but at the same time we understood the real truth." The meeting continued until evening: "After that our eyes were opened and we began to think about things in a new way."[5] (A number of similar examples could be given. To some extent, it does not appear to matter which work of illegal literature workers heard or read; the first such contact made an indelible impression. The booklet itself sometimes seems to be a talismanic object.)[6]

CR   BO

The decade of the 1870s was marked by the appearance of a revolutionary *movement* in Russia, as distinct from individual thinkers or circles of radical-minded students and other *intelligenty*. It was moreover the period when radical *intelligenty* first made contact on a significant scale with peasants and workers, members of the *narod*, or common people. Revolutionary tales, or

---

[5] Volynkin, "Iz vospominanii rabochego," in Mitskevich, *Na zare rabochego dvizheniia v Moskve*, 210.

[6] For other examples, see Babushkin, *Vospominaniia I. V. Babushkina*, 24–25; A. I. Shapovalov, *Po doroge k marksizmu: Vospominaniia rabochego revoliutsionera* (Moscow, 1922), 62–63; and A. V. Shotman, *Zapiski starogo bol'shevika* (Leningrad, 1963), 27. Reginald Zelnik, describing propaganda among workers in St. Petersburg in the early 1870s, similarly notes the "exalted atmosphere" student propagandists "created at the secret, illegal, politically charged 'studies' ... they arranged for their pupils" ("'To the Unaccustomed Eye,'" 315).

skazki, were modeled after the traditional folktale, but were written with a didactic purpose and a revolutionary moral.[7] These works bore colorful titles that conjured up tales of the supernatural, the wisdom of popular sayings, or the sacred truth of religious tracts: *The Clever Trick (Khitraia mekhanika), The Tale of a Kopeck (Skazka o kopeika), Out of the Frying Pan into the Fire (Iz ognia da v polymia!), On Truth and Falsehood (O pravde i krivde).* The best known of this genre, including those mentioned above, are part of a group of pamphlets associated with the peasant-oriented populism of that period, beginning with the Chaikovskii circle and encompassing the movement "to the people." They were composed in the early to mid-1870s and first printed on the presses of revolutionary groups at the time: the Chaikovskii circle and *Rabotnik* presses in Geneva, the *Vpered!* presses in London and Zurich.[8]

The members of the Chaikovskii circle were among the first to confront the issues involved in propaganda and organizing activities among the *narod.* An idealistic group of young men and women, students and other *intelligenty,* their views on propaganda among workers and their methods were reflected in the activities of subsequent groups; many members were involved in later phases of the rapidly evolving revolutionary populist movement of the 1870s. The group, known as the *chaikovtsy* after Nikolai Chaikovskii, an early member,[9] was active in St. Petersburg in 1871–74. Members devoted themselves first to the distribution of hard-to-obtain political and social literature to students (referred to as the *knizhnoe delo*—"cause of the book"). Then, as individual members began to meet and carry on educational work with local workers, the group's emphasis shifted to propaganda among this sector of the population, seen by many members as likely emissaries to the peasantry, a first step toward revolution. Branches sprang up in Moscow, Odessa, Kiev, and other cities as well. Views on propaganda were hammered out in the group's "literary committee," which selected and composed works they felt would be

---

[7] On the Russian folktale, or *skazka,* see Jack V. Haney, *An Introduction to the Russian Folktale* (Armonk, NY, 1999); W. E. H. [William E. Harkins], "Folktales," in *Handbook of Russian Literature* (New Haven, 1985), 147–48.

[8] Petr Lavrov and Mikhail Bakunin were the two most influential theorists for the populist radicals of the 1870s, although their ideas were modified and adapted. The publishing activities of émigrés in both camps were critical for the success of the movement in Russia. Lavrov's journal *Vpered!* performed a unifying function for the scattered radical groups in Russia—although Lavrov's ideas were by no means accepted uncritically. A group of Bakuninist émigrés (Z. K. Ralli and others) published *Rabotnik,* a journal for workers, and other literature on their press in Switzerland.

[9] In judicial proceedings, such as the trial of the "193," for example, the government referred to the group as the *chaikovtsy.* As noted above (chap. 1, n. 42), the group's original founder was Mark Andreevich Natanson.

suitable for the intended audience of peasants and workers.[10] Unlike the works distributed earlier, the publications for the popular audience would have to bypass the censor; the group set up a press in Switzerland and embarked on illegal publishing activity.[11]

The selection of the *skazka* form reveals some assumptions about the type of literature that would appeal to the Russian peasant or member of the *narod*: the brochures resemble the type of cheap, *lubochnaia* literature with which they were already familiar.[12] These were narrative works, they told a story (largely through dialogue or conversation), and the language was a "folksy," presumed peasant style, frequently studded with sayings and popular idioms. Were peasants in fact the audience for these works? For the most part, revolutionary populists of the 1870s did not make a clear distinction between peasants and urban workers. While many if not most populists envisioned their audience as a peasant one, at the same time, they carried on significant propaganda among urban workers, and this did not contradict their conception of the

---

[10] On the "literary committee," see the memoirs of Petr Kropotkin: P. A. Kropotkin, *Zapiski revoliutsionera* (Moscow, 1966), 286–87. Kropotkin also wrote a kind of manifesto for the group, "Dolzhny li my zaniat'sia rassmotreniem budushchego stroia?", which was the subject of much debate. It is worth noting, in contradistinction to the constant emphasis in the historiography on the "peasant only" focus of the populists of the 1870s, that this document regularly uses the phrase "peasants and urban workers"— clearly two distinct groups that were the focus of attention for the *chaikovtsy*. For this important document, see Valk et al., *Revoliutsionnoe narodnichestvo*, 1: 55–118.

[11] The Chaikovskii Circle is one of the most intensively studied revolutionary groups of the late 19th century. For additional information, see Venturi, *Roots of Revolution*; Itenberg, *Dvizhenie revoliutsionnogo narodnichestva*; and Zelnik, "Populists and Workers." A number of *chaikovtsy* wrote memoirs. Those by Prince P. A. Kropotkin, L. E. Shishko, N. A. Charushin, and S. S. Sinegub are particularly interesting. See L. E. Shishko, *Sergei Mikhailovich Kravchinskii i kruzhok chaikovtsev: Iz vospominanii i zametok starogo narodnika* (St. Petersburg, 1906); S. Sinegub, "Vospominaniia chaikovtsa," *Byloe*, no. 8 (1906): 39–80; no. 9 (1906): 90–128; no. 10 (1906): 31–77; and Charushin, *O dalekom proshlom*.

[12] The *lubok* was a cheap popular print; the term *lubochnaia* was applied to cheaply printed pamphlet literature aimed at the lower-class customer. See the entries "Lubok" and "Lubochnaya literatura" in Terras, *Handbook of Russian Literataure*, 266–67; also Brooks, "The Literature of the Lubok," chap. 3 in *When Russia Learned to Read*. V. F. Zakharina suggests that Bervi-Flerovskii may have encouraged use of the form (*Golos revoliutsionnoi Rossii*, 58). V. V. Bervi—pseudonym Flerovskii—author of two important radical works, *Polozhenie rabochego klassa v Rossiii* (1869) and *Azbuka sotsial'nykh nauk* (1871), was close to the Chaikovskii circle. See "Bervi (psevdonim Flerovskii), Vil'gel'm Vil'gel'movich (Vasilii Vasil'evich)," in *DRDR* 2, vyp. 1, cols. 106–09; and Itenberg, *Dvizhenie revoliutsionnogo narodnichestva*, 92–100.

narod, the lower-class working people as a whole.[13] Urban workers were often viewed as members of the *narod* who were temporarily living and working in the city. *The Clever Trick*, arguably the most famous of these tales, seems geared to this particular contingent of the popular whole, beginning with the words, "There's a fellow at our factory...."[14]

Some of these *skazki* continued to circulate and provoke discussion in *kruzhki* of radical workers through the 1880s and 1890s and, in some cases, even into the 20th century. Tsarist police and judicial records attest to the persistent popularity of a small number of such works, which were used for propaganda among workers by *narodovol'tsy*, social democrats, and socialist revolutionaries. Close study of propaganda among workers in the 1880s and the first half of the 1890s indicates that three of these works from the 1870s were particularly successful: 1) *The Clever Trick* (*Khitraia mekhanika*), written by the economist V. E. Varzar and originally published on the *Vpered!* press in 1874;[15] 2) *The Tale of Four Brothers* (*Gde luchshe? Skazka o chetyrekh brat'iakh i ob ikh prikliucheniiakh*—usually known as *Skazka o chetyrekh brat'iakh*), written by Lev Tikhomirov, with a revised and more revolutionary ending by Petr Kropotkin (both members of the "literary committee" of the Chaikovskii circle), and printed by the *chaikovtsy* in 1873; and 3) less well known, but (according to my evidence) still rather popular, *On Truth and Falsehood* (*O pravde i krivde*) by S. M. Stepniak-Kravchinskii, printed on the *Rabotnik* press in 1875. (Kravchinskii had also been a member of the "literary committee" of the *chaikovtsy*.) These three pamphlets went through numerous editions in various formats: printed, hectographed, lithographed, and handwritten, by groups in various cities and towns of the Russian Empire. In the initial, printed editions of the 1870s, pains were taken to mask their true identity with misleading covers, false publication information (including censorship approval), and sometimes with other titles. (*On Truth and Falsehood*, for example, had an expanded title that suggested a religious tract: *Sermon on Good Friday of the Right Reverend Tikhon Zadonskii, Bishop of Voronezh. On Truth and Falsehood* [*Slovo na velikii piatok preosviashchennogo Tikhona Zadonskogo, episkopa Voronezhskogo. O pravde i krivde*]. Another pamphlet was given the ambiguous title *Out of the Frying Pan*

---

[13] See Venturi, *Roots of Revolution*, 489; Yarmolinsky, *Road to Revolution*, 169, 174; V. A. Tvardovskaia, *Sotsialisticheskaia mysl' Rossii na rubezhe 1870–1880 gg.* (Moscow, 1969), 68.

[14] As noted, the most sustained analysis of propaganda literature to date has focused on the populist movement of the 1870s. See Zakharina, *Golos revoliutsionnoi Rossii*; and Bazanov, *Agitatsionnaia literatura*.

[15] *The Clever Trick*, while one of the works associated with the populist *skazki* of the 1870s, more properly belongs with the genre of pamphlets on political economy, considered in chapter 3.

*and Into the Fire! Or, Here's a Fine Kettle of Fish! Not a Fairy Tale, But an Actual
True Story of Our Time [Iz ognia da v polymia! ili Vot tebe babushka i Iur'ev den'! Ne
skazka, a byl'-pobyval'shchina iz nashikh dnei].*)

By the 1880s, the *skazka* was just one genre in a growing corpus of propaganda literature, alongside poetry, lessons in political economy, biographies
of the heroic martyrs of the People's Will, translated novels such as *Emma*
by the German Lassallean Jean Baptiste von Schweitzer, and other forms. In
recollections by intelligentsia propagandists from this period, *skazki* are frequently mentioned in listings of literature used for propaganda, usually with
an almost formulaic collective reference, for example: "We read the workers
... the brochures of the seventies"; "not to mention the old popular brochures
'The Clever Trick,' 'Tale of Four Brothers,' etc."; "Of course we also used the
popular-agitational revolutionary literature of that time, for example, 'The
Clever Trick.'"[16] Numerous references to and evidence of the use of these
tales exist, as well as commentary on their popularity with workers. (Some of
the more educated and politicized workers may not have been satisfied with
them, but they tended in any case to read the same works of "tendentious"
literature being read by young members of the intelligentsia at the time.)[17]

The appeal of the *skazki* to an audience of urban workers raises several
questions for further investigation: How did this peasant-oriented literature
transfer to workers? What was the role of the propagandist in this process? Is
the peasant/worker distinction even an important one? We also need to know
more about other kinds of literature that workers were familiar with: What
was the circulation and readership of the cheap publications of *lubochnaia*
literature and, toward the end of the century, the newer popular newspapers
and illustrated magazines?[18] Workers also read religious literature and were
exposed to other kinds of works in schools.

How was the revolutionary tale told, and what ideas did it present? Perhaps
the most popular was *The Tale of Four Brothers*, a story that led Moiseenko
to question his beliefs about the world and society. This tale was composed
by Lev Tikhomirov, a member of the Moscow affiliate of the St. Petersburg

---

[16] I. I. Popov, "Revoliutsionnye organizatsii," 57; Tereshkovich, "Neskol'ko slov po
povodu vospominanii Gotsa," 112, and P. K. Peshekerov, "Propaganda narodovol'tsev
sredi rabochikh v Rostove," both in Iakimova-Dikovskaia et al., *Narodovol'tsy posle 1-go
marta 1881 goda*, 125.

[17] See, for example, G. V. Plekhanov, *Russkii rabochii v revoliutsionnom dvizhenii: Po
lichnym vospominaniiam* (Leningrad, 1940), 27–28; see works seized when the worker
Vasilii Pankratov was arrested, in Pankratov, *Vospominaniia*, 25, 28.

[18] See the excellent discussion of popular literature in Brooks, *When Russia Learned to
Read*; see also Louise McReynolds, *The News Under Russia's Old Regime: The Development
of a Mass-Circulation Press* (Princeton, NJ, 1991).

chaikovtsy and a medical student at Moscow University.[19] Members of the group's literary committee, however, found his ending to be too pessimistic; the task of rewriting the conclusion in its published form was undertaken by Kropotkin. Although the tale was originally used for propaganda among both workers and peasants in the 1870s, it stood the test of time. Archival and memoir materials show that it continued to be used among urban workers through the 1880s and into the 1890s. It was reproduced and distributed by local *narodovol'tsy* in Moscow, Odessa, Kishinev, St. Petersburg, and elsewhere; 85 copies were seized when police discovered the press that the People's Will had managed to set up in Taganrog in 1886. This *skazka* was also read avidly by workers associated with the early social democratic Tochisskii group in St. Petersburg in the mid-1880s, and it continued to circulate among social democratic workers in the capital in the early 1890s.[20]

Beginning with the title and opening lines, the reader/listener is drawn by the story form to learn about the brothers and their adventures. The un-named narrator's "I" intrudes into the story only twice, once in the first paragraph. "No one knows when exactly, but not very long ago; no one knows where, but they say that once upon a time in Mother Russia there lived four brothers." They lived in the "dense" forest (*dremuchii les*) of fairy tales and "had never seen another human face." "How did they turn up in the forest?" the narrator asks, "I must confess, I never heard anything about that."[21] One day the brothers get lost chasing a bear and end up on a mountaintop from

---

[19] Lev Tikhomirov (1852–1923) was a major figure in the revolutionary movement of the 1870s and 1880s. He spent several years in prison and stood trial in the "Trial of the 193" in 1877. Tikhomirov was a member of the Executive Committee of the People's Will and continued to direct party affairs from exile in Switzerland. Following a personal crisis, he abjured his years of revolutionary activity and was pardoned by Tsar Alexander III in 1888. He returned to Russia a committed monarchist. See Lev Tikhomirov, *Vospominaniia* (1927; Moscow, 2003); Venturi, *Roots of Revolution*, 642–43; Offord, *The Russian Revolutionary Movement*, 30–33; and Naimark, *Terrorists and Social Democrats*, 103–04.

[20] A few examples: "Delo o prestupnoi propagande," 292; S. I. Mitskevich, "Moskovskie revoliutsionnye kruzhki vtoroi poloviny 1870-kh godov," *Katorga i ssylka*, no. 4 (11) (1924): 58–59; M. I. Drei, "Zametki o rabochem dvizhenii v Odesse v 1880–1881 gg.," *Katorga i ssylka*, no. 5 (12) (1924): 76; GARF f. 102, 7 d-vo, 1884 g., d. 573, l. 18ob. (Kishinev). On the People's Will press in Taganrog, see GARF f. 102, 7 d-vo, d. 42, chast' 3, l. 8ob.; Breitfus, "Tochisskii i ego kruzhok," 330; Norinskii, "Dopolnenie k vospominaniiam," 48 (St. Petersburg, early 1890s).

[21] *Gde luchshe? Skazka o chetyrekh brat'iakh i ob ikh prikliucheniiakh*, reprinted in Bazanov, *Agitatsionnaia literatura*, 267. For a complete translation of this tale as reprinted above, see Pearl, *Tales of Revolution*, 12–47. Page references to the Russian version will be given in text.

which they see an inhabited valley spread out below them. Surely life must be wonderful for such a large group of people living together. Their curiosity aroused, they decide to leave their beloved forest home. "Bowing in all four directions," the brothers set out on the quest so central to folktales—but in this case with four, rather than the usual three brothers, parting to travel to the north, south, east, and west. The action that takes place in this introduction as well as in the incidents that follow is heavily embellished with detail. Long passages are presented in the form of conversations or dialogue, with use of colloquial language and appropriate folk sayings or proverbs, the repository of popular wisdom.

The oldest brother, Ivan, goes north and begins his adventures among peasants engaged in back-breaking field work, while the well-dressed landowner yells orders and then goes off in his carriage. "Do you like that man so much that you do all his work for him?" Ivan asks. (The brothers' naiveté allows them to pose basic questions that get at the root of the relations of power and exploitation in the peasants' lives.) The landholding arrangement and the concept of profit are explained. In the end, the peasants explain, they are forced to work for the landowner out of fear of military reprisals. This section of the tale also includes Ivan's conversation with a landowner in a different village, where he figures out the rule of thumb that the rich can throw their weight around and the poor have to put up with it; a conversation in a tavern that explains why the tsar's emancipation was a disaster for the peasants; and an incident in which Ivan overhears the headman[22] and the butcher plotting to get livestock from the peasants of another locale by collecting taxes early and forcing them to sell their cows. Ivan reveals the conspiracy, but the peasants are afraid to fight those in power. The policeman soon arrives, summoned by the headman. He arrests Ivan as an instigator; Ivan is jailed and soon sentenced for rebellion to Siberia.

Each set of adventures in the tale includes multiple incidents and touches on several different topics, with emphasis on the oppressiveness and wrong-doing of the rich and powerful: landowners, village police, merchants, priests, mediators, factory owners and foremen, even the tsar. The second brother, Stepan, travels south, hoping to figure out why peasants let the rich rob them. He finds himself at a village meeting, where the mediator[23] is trying to get the peasants to agree to move to a piece of land that is sandy, rocky, and completely unsuitable for cultivation. The peasants refuse: they'll die

---

[22] *Starshina*—headman or official elected by the peasants of a *volost'*, a local administrative unit or canton composed of several peasant communes.

[23] *Mirovoi posrednik* (sing.)—peace mediator or arbitrator designated by the government from among local nobles to resolve disputes between peasants and landowners following emancipation.

either way. Soldiers are summoned and a bloody conflict ensues. The soldiers, of course, are peasants too; tragically, one soldier shoots an old man who happens to be his father. Stepan goes to other villages and tries to rouse the peasants to fight back against their oppressors. The *narod* must stop being its own enemy; all the villages, all of Russia, must rise at the same time. The upshot of Stepan's experiences: the peasants of the first village are forcibly relocated to the unsuitable land; Stepan is arrested, jailed, and sentenced to Siberian exile.

Dem'ian, the third brother, experiences and investigates the plight of the worker in an urban setting. As he witnesses the dishonest ways in which manufacturers make a profit at the workers' expense, he begins to ask, "'How do people get rich?'" It appears that factory owners steal their wealth from the poor, just as the landowners do. Dem'ian is enlightened by some "knowledgeable people" (an oblique reference to radical *intelligenty*), who provide a brief history lesson: "There was a time long ago when there were no landowners in Rus'; there were free peasants, and all the land belonged to them. At that time there weren't tsars yet" (284). His informants go on to explain that when the Tatars conquered Rus' they put the Moscow Grand Prince in charge, and he became the tsar. Over time the tsar gave his nobles power over the peasants, the peasants' land, and finally the peasants themselves. Although the peasants are now free, the landowners still have the land. Again in this section of the tale there is a vignette of peasants forced to sell their livestock to pay taxes, this time with a priest exhorting them to do their duty and "render unto Caesar." Dem'ian's arrest follows.

Luka, the youngest brother, explores the true nature of the church more thoroughly. He decides to go to a monastery to see "how good people live." He suffers total disillusionment at the corruption and venality he finds. The "tears" of the wonder-working icon are mechanically produced; the holy relics are made of wax; and the "cures" are faked. Luka tries to tell the people who come to the monastery on pilgrimage about this trickery; arrest and Siberian exile are the foregone conclusion. The last section of the tale takes place at the boundary between Russia and Siberia; several parties of convicts meet, and the brothers are reunited. They review their findings: there is no place good for the poor. But the day will come, Ivan prophesies, when the narod, sleeping like the "bewitched hero of the fairy tale," will awaken in all its strength and avenge itself on its enemies, whom he enumerates. He ends on a utopian note: "Happy will be that wonderful time, when there will be no evil on the earth, no injustice, no oppression, no violence." The earth, forest, and meadows will belong to the peasants, the factories in the towns to workers; there will be no tsars, landowners, or other oppressors. The concluding lines of the tale call for justice and vengeance in an apocalyptic uprising. That night the brothers escape and go forth to spread the word throughout Russia, calling the peasants to a "bloody feast." At long last the people will heed the call, and then Mother Russia will roar like the sea and drown all her enemies "in her powerful waves" (294–95).[24]

What made the *Tale of Four Brothers* an effective work of propaganda? At this point in the analysis, we must engage in some speculation. Although the tale is frequently mentioned in memoir literature and other sources, I have not come across an explicit discussion by a worker or propagandist of its impact. (Moiseenko does, however, include a detail in his memoirs that underlines the significance this tale had for him. He and other worker radicals were quite inventive in their propaganda techniques at the New Cotton-Spinning Factory in St. Petersburg in 1877; they included in their repertoire improvisational performances of *Tale of Four Brothers*.)[25] What comes through most strongly in this illegal work, its core, is the revelation of the real situation of the *narod*. The tale explicitly draws back the curtain of official explanation to reveal the pervasive exploitation and oppression of the common people and to name those responsible. The booklet points the finger at the people's enemies: the landowners, priests, bosses, merchants, police, mediators, even the tsar himself. It claims to present the truth. Throughout, the theme of strength in unity is emphasized. Once the *narod* realize their power, all villages, the whole land will combine forces: they will then be strong enough to destroy their oppressors. The means and goals of the popular uprising are treated only briefly in the conclusion: violent popular revolution, and a society where the land and factories are held in common, by the workers. (The term *socialism* is not used. Some of the other tales go into much more detail on the nature of the desired society.) The form of this work also has much in common with that of other works in this genre: much of the tale is told in dialogue form, with numerous questions and answers. In this way, it served the function of teaching workers how to carry on discussions with other workers, how to answer basic questions.

A look at two other frequently read *skazki* from the cycle of tales of the 1870s will give a fuller picture of this genre of revolutionary literature. "The Tale of a Kopeck" and "Of Truth and Falsehood" were also products of the Literary Committee of the Chaikovskii Circle, both written by one of the most prolific authors of tales, Sergei Mikhailovich Kravchinskii (who later wrote under the pen name Stepniak). Kravchinskii was one of the most colorful revolutionaries of the age. For this radical, revolution meant action, and the varied facets of

---

[24] *Skazka o chetyrekh brat´iakh*, 294–95. As noted above, the conclusion, with its inspiring call to arms and promise of a new future life, was penned by Kropotkin.

[25] Moiseenko, *Vospominaniia starogo revoliutsionera*, 20–21.

the movement were reflected in his exploits. He joined the Chaikovskii Circle as a graduate of the Artillery Academy in St. Petersburg and enjoyed leading studies with workers. He went on to engage in propaganda among peasants as a participant in the "movement to the people," fought in the uprising of Balkan Slavs against the Ottoman Empire that preceded the Russo-Turkish War, and was imprisoned for his role in a revolt in southern Italy. Back in Russia, he became a key figure in Land and Freedom and dramatized the turn to terror of a faction of the broader movement when he assassinated the hated head of the Third Section, General N. V. Mezentsov. He managed to flee abroad, where he continued to pursue his literary interests by writing for and about the Russian revolutionary movement and attempting to gain Western support for the cause.[26] Like Kropotkin, his fellow member of the Literary Committee, Kravchinskii went on to devote his life to a future society of equality and justice but did not neglect the importance of educating workers (and others) to understand the true workings of their society and the possibility of change.

Like other *skazki*, The *Tale of a Kopeck* minces no words in naming the oppressors of the *narod*. The tale begins: "How free and easy (*privol'noe*) life would be in Rus', brothers, if only we didn't have nobles, priests, and pot-bellied merchants."[27] And who thought up these oppressors of the *muzhik* [peasant—colloquial]? Who but the Devil. Ever since, the peasant was never left alone; "he was cut sharply by priests, nobles, and merchants. They cut him not with a knife, not with a sharp sword, but with a copper kopeck" (241). The tale is divided into three parts. In the first, we witness the great difficulties the muzhik endures to get a kopeck. After addressing a plea for assistance to "Damp Mother Earth," the peasant digs and digs until he finally finds a kopeck. (During this process he is addressed by a birch tree, a bird, and a fish, who ask why he is so dirty, disheveled, and worn out.) On the way home, he is waylaid by the priest, who gets him to hand over the kopeck. When the peasant returns home, he tells his wife that he gave away the kopeck "for the heavenly kingdom." Meanwhile, the priest has plans for the peasant's kopeck. He orders his sacristan (who does a bit of trade on the side) to buy him a suckling pig, and for his trouble, he'll give him the pig's tail. The sacristan takes the kopeck to a local trader, who goes to the peasant, shows him the kopeck, and demands a suckling pig, a hive of honey, and the skin of a wolf. "Good thing I've rested up from work," the peasant says, and sets

---

[26] On Kravchinskii, see *DRDR* 2, vyp. 2, cols. 671–74; Shishko, *Sergei Mikhailovich Kravchinskii*; Evgeniia Taratuta, *S. M. Stepniak-Kravchinskii—revoliutsioner i pisatel'* (Moscow, 1973). Stepniak-Kravchinskii's most famous work was *Underground Russia: Revolutionary Profiles and Sketches from Life* (New York, 1883).

[27] *Skazka o kopeike*, in Bazanov, *Agitatsionnaia literatura*, 241. This tale was printed by the *chaikovtsy* in Geneva in 1874.

out to fulfill the tasks. He begins by giving the trader the pig he'd been saving for a holiday—"Well, maybe when my little son is grown … we'll be able to celebrate the holiday the way it should be" (243). In detail, the tale follows the obedient peasant as he accomplishes his tasks, including a dramatic fight with a bear over the honey. Having killed the bear, he brings the bearskin with the honey to the merchant—who berates him for bringing him the skin of a bear, instead of a wolf and demands his trousers in recompense. The peasant hurries off, trouserless, to bring the kopeck to the noble to pay the arrears from last year's rental (*obrok*) of the pond. Arriving at the nobleman's mansion, he respectfully removes his cap and waits at the gate. As luck would have it, the nobleman's wife catches sight of the peasant without his pants and faints dead away! The noble berates the peasant, relieves him of his kopeck, and asks him to take a note to the village policeman. The note, of course, calls for the policeman to punish the peasant for his act of disrespect, with which the policeman duly complies, beating the peasant and and swearing at him. The fate of the peasant and his kopeck gets more and more complicated—the noble gambles away the kopeck, and the peasant is forced to work for the winner, fixing a dam under very dangerous circumstances, nearly drowning in the attempt. He figures that God will preserve him—without the peasant, where would He get the candle and incense for the church service (247)? Eventually, the peasant sees the light: with all his work, the same kopeck keeps coming back, and he keeps giving it away.

"I won't give anyone my kopeck!" the peasant decides, and thus begins part 2 of the tale. He refuses to give the kopeck to the priest, who runs to the noble, shouting "The peasant has rebelled" (*Muzhik vzbuntovalsia*). The peasant procedes to insult the noble, who orders the policeman to arrest him. Arriving at the peasant's hut, the policeman, spooked at the idea of a peasant in flagrant disobedience, thinks he's under attack—his adversaries (laughably) turn out to be farm animals. The officer writes to the Governor, and, with the help of a regiment of soldiers, the peasant is captured, jailed, and sentenced to 25,000 [sic] lashes. Moreover, the regiment will be quartered at his house until he gives up the kopeck, which he has hidden in his legging. Feeding the regiment will be his ruin. The peasant buries the kopeck in the woods and ruminates mournfully: "Without the kopeck—you might as well lie down in the grave, but with the kopeck—you might as well drown yourself in the river!" (253). With a sigh he once again invokes "Damp Mother Earth": "Teach me, an ignorant one, how to live.…"

The peasant falls asleep and dreams—something is rolling toward him— it's his very own kopeck! "Come with me," the kopeck says, and after a difficult journey, our peasant is flying through the air on a giant bird, an old man with a white beard his guide. In part 3, the muzhik is shown a vision of how society could be. With each scene, he is given an explanation by the old man. In the first scene the peasant sees people working together on the harvest. The old man illustrates the virtues of cooperative work with examples (for example, an old man who decides his wife is not doing her share; the resultant discord leads him to the conclusion that all should share equally). The old man recommends work as an *artel* (a workers' cooperative); workers should "love one another like brothers" (256). A cooperatively run market place is presented in the second scene—there are no bosses. The peasant wonders how this could work, and again the old man responds with a story of two shepherds, each stealing sheep from the other; no one gains. The final scene shows a spacious room with a round table covered with a bejeweled red cloth with gold tassels—"Is this a tavern or theater?" the peasant asks. What he sees, it turns out, are representatives of the people deciding to build a railroad. This is how it will be, the old man assures him, when "the kingdom of brotherly love, justice, and truth will reign on earth" (265).

The time has not yet come, however. The old man predicts storm and suffering, rivers of blood. He calls on the peasant to go out to the villages and towns, roads and markets, and preach what he has just seen. Even if he has to suffer, he must be strong, since "the Son of Man suffered and was crucified for the same thing that you will suffer for" (264). Then the peasant awakes, his resolve is reinforced by his observation of animal behavior (birds coming to the defense of a bird chased by a hawk; a flock of cattle defending the herd collectively against a predatory wolf), and he begins to spread the word, calling on the people to rise against the evildoers and preach the truth to their brothers, as the apostles did. "All of Mother Russia will rise; no hostile force can stand against her!" (266). The tale concludes that thus will the "kingdom of truth and love" reign on earth.

Each of the three parts of "Tale of a Kopeck" is devoted to a different theme. The first focuses on exploitation, showing why the peasant will never "make it." His hardearned money will always be taken by the priest, the noble, and others, and the authorities, here personified by the policeman; the governor will support them. The kopeck also underlines the new importance of the money economy. Exploitation of the narod has survived the demise of serfdom, and still holds sway in the capitalist economy. The second part brings up the way to throw off the yoke of exploitation—by resistance, as the peasant "mounts a *bunt* [rebellion]," throwing the authorities into consternation. The peasant's dream in part 3 shows elements of the future society—a socialist one, although the word "socialism" is not used (perhaps because the word was a foreign one?). Kravchinskii included in this tale a number of elements which he hoped would appeal to his audience. As is true of other tales, this one is quite lengthy (25 small-print pages in Bazanov's reprint), and the key points are enclosed

in an extended story, with dialogue, folk sayings, and many examples. There
are suspenseful episodes, such as the peasant's dramatic struggle with the
bear and his death-defying success in repairing the dam. There are humorous
elements as well: for example, when the trouserless peasant shocks the noble's
wife (who, following the death of her husband, loses no time in taking up with
a young officer); or when the policeman mistakes the barnyard animals for
an attack by the rebellious peasant. The problems are familiar ones, such as
the arrears the peasant owes. The pedagogical purpose of the tale is fulfilled
by the many varied examples, which elaborate on the basic themes and could
also serve as a model for explaining to others. A radicalized worker could
remember how the Old Man explained the workings of the new society to
the peasant protagonist of the tale; one could mock the unworthy nobles by
making fun of their decadent lifestyle. The tale's perspective on religion is
particularly interesting. The money-grubbing priest has a major role as one
of the peasant's worst exploiters. When the peasant finally refuses to play his
subservient role any longer and hand over his kopeck to the priest, he relates
a threatening story, recounting to the priest the tale of a priest who, for his
greediness, could not be buried. Yet the peasant's dream concludes with the
old man calling on the peasant to follow the example of Christ's suffering,
and the peasant calls on others to spread the word of truth as did the apostles.
A distinction is made here between the official religion of church and priest,
and the true religion of Christ and the apostles, a dichotomy which seems to
reflect the popular anticlericalism that, according to some sources, was common among peasants by the late 19th century.[28]

Another popular tale, *On Truth and Falsehood*, also by Kravchinskii, mounts
an even more powerful attack on religion.[29] The tale opens with a "reverie"
(*duma*) on Truth (*Pravda*) and Falsehood (*Krivda*), which are pictured as locked
in eternal struggle: "Falsehood rules throughout the world.... You can go to
the villages: the whole *narod* is laboring at backbreaking work.... Or go to the
towns—here too thousands of the people suffer from morning to night, as if
in hell, and die of hunger." These powerful concepts, Truth and Falsehood,
are personified: the latter lives in palaces and is dressed in brocade and gold,
the former is ragged, hungry, homeless. Nevertheless, Truth is the stronger,
and pursues Falsehood as the bright falcon chases the crow. The narrator
now turns to his audience, addressing the reader or listener in the familiar

---

[28] See Pearl, "Tsar and Religion," 94–102; Zelnik, "'To the Unaccustomed Eye,'" 322–23.

[29] Ironically, this illegal brochure was made up to look like a religious tract, with the
full title spelled out as *A Good Friday Word from the Right Reverend Tikhon Zadonskii,
Bishop of Voronezh. On Truth and Falsehood.*" See Bazanov, *Agitatsionnaia literatura*, 481–
82n; B. S. Itenberg et al., eds., *Svodnyi katalog russkoi nelegal'noi i zapreshchennoi pechati
XIX veka: Knigi i periodicheskie izdaniia*, 2nd ed. (Moscow, 1981–82), 2: 98 (no. 1771).

form: "Listen to what I'm about to tell you," and you'll understand the whole story of Truth and Falsehood (101–02). The story begins again: "From time immemorial Falsehood held sway on earth..." The *narod* is strong as a *bogatyr*, the hero of the old epics—so how did the people become enslaved by a small handful of people, who control all the wealth? The tale hammers home its answer: the *narod* cannot use its strength against its oppressors, because it is bound by three chains: those of the priests, the nobles, and the merchants.

The major part of the tale reads as a history lesson, covering a broad chronological sweep as it explicates the three chains in chronological order. In an apparent attempt to create a sense of history, the author makes a point of referring to specific dates and events, frequently telling the reader how many years ago events happened—it seems clear that developments are occurring at an increasingly fast pace. (For the listener without a formal education, this may have been a novel way to view the past, and one that emphasized its changing character). The first chain is the "priestly chain" (*tsep' popovskaia*), referring to the power that priests have over the people, and it is the most terrible of the three. This power is rooted "deep in the human heart—it is faith in God" (103). The writer goes on to discuss the history of religion in pagan days, explaining that for "three thousand years" the working people were enslaved by the priests. All this is changed, however, with the coming of Jesus, who reveals the lies of the priests and other oppressors and teaches that all people are equal and are brothers. His apostles spread the Gospel, and people flock to hear about the kingdom to come of truth, equality, and love. After this brief period of light, however, Falsehood returns. Christianity spreads, but with the conversion of the Emperor Constantine in the year 330, priests once again gain the upper hand. The brochure proceeds to bring into the picture the experiences of various Christian lands, including the conversion of "the Russian people" under Prince Vladimir in 988. Finally, the first break in the priestly chain came "250 years ago." Without using the term, the author here describes the Reformation. The Russian Raskol, he writes, had many similarities—the old books, crossing oneself with two fingers—these were not the real issues but were symbols, "like a banner for soldiers" (110).

With the priestly chain broken, the power of the nobles, the second chain, grew. Their power was based on the surviving remnants of the priestly lies—that kings received their power from God. Still, their power was not as strong: "priests held the peoples in slavery for thousands of years. ...it took less than 200 years to reveal the falsehood of the power of the tsar and landowners." The first to rise against the power of "tsars" and landowners were the French, "the most intelligent of foreign peoples." The author notes the date—1789—as is his practice, and the fact that this was "only 86 years ago" (111, 112). The enslavement caused by the third chain, that of the merchants, has now gained prominence. These "traitors" were allies of the *narod* during their fight against serfdom—but it's clear that the task of liberation was left incomplete. The people got rid of power over their persons, but did not gain control of the land or of capital (a word that no doubt was accompanied by the propagandist's explanation). Now an uprising against the rich is necessary. The booklet explains that the rich also rule in other countries: even in countries with representative government, representatives are chosen from the rich. This is due to the people's ignorance, the author explains. But breaking the third chain should be even less difficult, as the rich have less moral authority on which to base their power than did the priests, or rulers and landowners. The account moves toward the present, as the author notes the formation of a "union" 12 years ago by an unnamed small group of "simple workers"— possibly a reference to the creation of the First International. Today, this union has "several million" members. On a more apocalyptic note, the author prophesies the coming of the Last Judgment, "when there will be on earth neither poor nor rich, neither lords nor slaves, neither bosses nor subordinates (117). The kingdom of truth and love preached by Jesus Christ, and for which he suffered, will soon arrive.

In the concluding section the narrator asks, "How do I know that now the people will be freed from all their suffering?" Now the root of all suffering is clear: it is poverty, described as a witch sucking the people's blood. Popular ignorance is called poverty's daughter. The narrator briefly notes the basic principles of the future economic order: there will be no individual ownership of land or factories, which will be owned in common by artels of their workers. He goes on to discuss the nature of work, including the importance of machines, in the new economy, a socialist one—although again, as in "On Truth and Falsehood," the word "socialist" is not used. The booklet closes with an exhortation—the people need to fight, need to free themselves from the rich. Turning to the reader, who is addressed in the familiar form: "'But how am I supposed to do this?—you who are reading or listening to this book ask me. Am I supposed to pick up an ax and go after the exploiters?" The answer emphasizes the use of reason, as opposed to physical violence. The reader needs to make his tongue an ax, to cut down falsehood. Readers must spread the word, spread the struggle against falsehood, and this voice will grow louder and louder: "soon the Russian people will hear it, awake from their age-long sleep, and then woe to their evildoers!" (123).

With *Of Truth and Falsehood*, we can see some of the range of variation within the *skazka* form. The tale addresses the reader personally—"Listen here, I'll tell you..." (102)—and concludes with reference to "those who are reading or listening to this book" (122). The basic image is easily grasped: falsehood has bound the narod with three chains, which must be broken. Although other tales refer to religion and the priesthood, *Of Truth and Falsehood* is the one that deals most directly with this chain, the hardest to break. At the core of the tale is a history of religion—what it is, how it evolved. Rather than presenting Christianity as evil, the tale makes clear that the teachings of Jesus represent the truth, but were unfortunately suppressed by the priesthood. The emphasis on the teachings of Jesus as congruent with the principles of the desired future society recurs in other tales from the 1870s as well. (V. G. Bazanov maintains that the propagandists did not actually hold these beliefs, but were using religion to appeal to popular psychology.)[30] In addition to the importance placed on what was seen as true Christianity, in another aspect the tale modifies the received view on the target audience of these propagandists. Rather than focusing solely on issues relevant to the peasantry, much attention is given to towns as well. This tale also stands out for its emphasis on history and its attempt to impart a historical perspective with the use of dates and specific events, many dealing with other European countries: the Roman Church, the Reformation, the French Revolution. While the populists of the 1870s are usually sharply distinguished from Marxists, the influence of a Marxist perspective, with which the intelligentsia of the time was familiar, can be seen, although terms such as bourgeoisie and proletariat, capitalism and socialism, are not used. The "merchants" and "the rich" represent the current enemy, and the collective organization of work in the future society is briefly noted. The tale closes with the practical suggestion for action on the part of the tale's audience: to take what they have learned from this tale, and to spread the word.

CR RO

One main function of propaganda literature was to present a critique of the current social order. *Skazki* fulfilled that goal by presenting an analysis of the ways in which peasants and workers were exploited by Russia's dominant classes. Revolutionaries hoped in this way to dispel the misconception that things were "just that way." Rather, there were reasons: there were those who benefited from the people's labor, those who were to blame. Without the need to use the façade of Aesopian language to bypass the censor, illegal literature was tailor-made to name the oppressors. Its bluntness in this regard may have both shocked and intrigued workers who had never before encountered published literature or members of the educated classes who used this "forbidden" language. As we have seen, the *skazki* tended to present the same list of oppressors, especially the priests, the landowners (*pomeshchiki*), with

---

[30] V. G. Bazanov, introduction to *Agitatsionnaia literatura*, 13.

whom the tsar was often linked, and the merchants. (Sometimes the list was expanded to include the "bosses" and government officials.)

Encouraging uneducated members of the common people to assimilate this new perspective would not be easy, propagandists from the revolutionary intelligentsia knew. Their challenging and essential task was to change what seemed to be the basic world view of Russian peasants and workers in such a way as to make a revolutionary movement possible. Revolutionary propaganda typically called for the overthrow of Russia's autocratic government with the tsar at its head, after which society would be recreated on a new socialist basis. Of necessity, the literature that bore this message was produced and circulated illegally, as it transgressed the principal tenets of tsarist censorship. This message, moreover, collided with what seemed to be central beliefs of peasants and workers: 1) faith in the tsar as a benevolent ruler, the "Little Father" of the *narod*, and 2) the related, much noted religious faith of the Russian peasants, who most often referred to themselves as "Christians" or "Orthodox." Both of these beliefs were deemed to be responsible for what Russian radicals saw as the passivity and fatalism of the common people— qualities that needed to be transformed into activism and the awareness of a need for fundamental social change. This goal was a particular focus of propaganda in the 1870s, as we have seen in the treatment of these issues in the above three *skazki*. By the later decades of the 19th century, rumors about people called "socialists" (or "revolutionaries" or "students") had reached many workers in the cities, and even peasant villages. Significantly, these "socialists" were most commonly identified, in tones ranging from disgust to scandalized interest, as people who did not recognize the authority of God or the tsar.[31]

For those who have studied the Russian peasantry of the 19th century, faith in the tsar has appeared as a basic axiom of popular belief. It was this belief system that Russian radicals encountered in their propaganda among urban workers beginning in the 1870s. The "myth of the tsar," as Daniel Field has termed it,[32] expressed a view of the political system and an explanation for social ills: the tsar is a benevolent ruler, the "loving father" (*tsar´-batiushka*) of his trusting people; he wants only the best for them and would be shocked to know how they are being exploited by landowners, government officials, and other members of the upper classes. The noblemen and officials, however, keep this knowledge from him—they are the evil ones, responsible for serfdom

---

[31] See, for example, the memoirs of M. P. Petrov, a Moscow boilermaker. Rumors circulated at his factory (c. 1880) "that people known as socialists had appeared who didn't believe in God, had killed the tsar, and want to live without the authorities" ("Moi vospominaniia," 184).

[32] See Daniel Field, *Rebels in the Name of the Tsar* (Boston, 1976).

and other hardships suffered by the peasants. This myth found expression throughout centuries of Russian history. Peasant uprisings were often carried out in the name of the "true" tsar; the one on the throne, promulgator of harsh decrees, must be an imposter. Similarly, some peasants voiced their dissatisfaction with the emancipation legislation of 1861 by claiming that the nobles had hidden the real emancipation charter; peasants who believed in the tsar would wait for the "second freedom." Scholars have debated the meaning of peasants' ostensible belief in the tsar as a "loving father": should this "popular monarchism" be seen as a sign of ignorance and naiveté? Or rather were the peasants cunning and manipulative in their use of the myth, as Field suggests? David Moon, in his extensive study of Russian peasants, finds that they were knowledgeable about the terms of emancipation and other pertinent legislation and made use of the myth in a rational way to achieve their goals.[33]

This faith in the tsar, with whatever degree of sincerity it was held by members of the lower classes in Russia, posed an obvious obstacle for the cause of revolution. Revolutionaries also blamed this faith in the tsar's good will for the passivity of the common people, their lack of willingness to work for change (leaving aside the chaotic peasant revolts). Ekaterina Koval'skaia, for example, noted the problems of monarchism and passivity that she and Nikolai Shchedrin, founders of the South-Russian Workers' Union in Kiev (1880–81), faced in their organizing activity. The mass meetings organized by the Union drew many workers without previous contact with the revolutionary movement:

> After listening to us attentively, many [workers] told us that every-thing would somehow happen without them. Each conceived of this differently, depending on his level of development. The most advanced thought that some kind of revolutionary committee would take the land from the landowners and give it to the peasants. Others said that the tsar, having destroyed serfdom, was now struggling with the nobles to take land from them and give it to the *narod*....[34]

---

[33] For a detailed discussion of the "myth of the tsar" and its political uses, see Field, *Rebels*; David Moon, *Russian Peasants and Tsarist Legislation on the Eve of Reform: Interaction between Peasants and Officialdom, 1825–1855* (London, 1992), 174–76, 181; and Moon, *The Russian Peasantry, 1600–1930: The World the Peasants Made* (London, 1999), 271–79. On the figure of the tsar in folklore, see Maureen Perrie, "Folklore as Evidence of Peasant *Mentalité*: Social Attitudes and Values in Russian Popular Culture," *Russian Review* 48, 2 (April 1989): 127–29, 133–34, 141.

[34] Koval'skaia, *Iuzhno-russkiii rabochii soiuz*, 28–29.

Koval'skaia and Shchedrin concluded that a fundamental change in outlook
was a precondition for successful participation of workers in the revolutionary
movement. In an effort to combat entrenched attitudes, revolutionary leaders
devoted considerable attention in their official publications to the importance
of destroying the common people's faith in the tsar. This can be seen, for example, in the special "newspapers" for workers published by the populist
parties of the early 1880s, the People's Will and Black Repartition. Their publications *Rabochaia Gazeta* (The Workers' Newspaper) and *Zerno* (The Seed)
respectively highlighted articles and stories that addressed these issues directly. Sof'ia Perovskaia, a leading member of the Executive Committee of the
People's Will and most commonly identified with her roles as regicide and
revolutionary martyr, took a keen interest in propaganda among workers, an
activity in which she participated. She regarded destruction of popular faith
in the tsar as a key task of *Rabochaia Gazeta*.[35] Early Russian Social Democratic
groups took a similar approach. *Rabochii*, the newspaper of the St. Petersburg
Blagoev group, attempted to dispel the perceived passivity of the *narod* and
provide the "essential knowledge" that would encourage workers to act to
change their situation.[36]

Propagandists soon learned that the direct approach, beginning
propaganda among workers as yet unfamiliar with the revolutionary movement with attacks on the tsar (or on religion), was likely to be met by hostility
and suspicion. Activists, whether intelligentsia or workers themselves, were
often frustrated by the untutored political outlook of the average worker,
characterized by "devotion to the tsar, loyalty to the authorities, and respect
for the foremen and employers."[37] As one worker-activist noted, attacks on
God, the priesthood, or the tsar were ineffective methods of propaganda,
and might even win the propagandist a beating.[38] A popular saying summed
up this attitude: "Break the china, but don't touch the samovar!"[39] (In other
words, attacks on factory owners, landowners, and government officials

---

[35] A. Kornilova-Moroz, *Sof'ia L'vovna Perovskaia: Chlen ispolnitel'nogo komiteta partii
"Narodnaia volia"* (Moscow, 1930), 36. On *Rabochaia Gazeta* and *Zerno*, see Pearl,
"Educating Workers for Revolution," 273–79.

[36] See the lead article in *Rabochii*, no. 1 (1885), reprinted in *Rabochii: Gazeta partii russkikh
sotsial-demokratov (blagoevtsev) 1885 g.*, ed. N. L. Sergievskii (Leningrad, 1928), 21–29.

[37] I. Polonskii, "Iz zhizni partiinoi organizatsii (1898–1900 gg.)," in Rubach, *Istoriia
ekaterinoslavskoi sotsial-demokraticheskoi organizatsii*, 139.

[38] Pankratov, "Iz deiatel'nosti sredi rabochikh," 255.

[39] See Moiseenko, *Vospominaniia starogo revoliutsionera*, 24: "Posudu bei, a samovara ne
trogai"; and Zelnik, *A Radical Worker in Tsarist Russia*, 96: "You can break the cup, but
never touch the samovar!"

were acceptable—but not the tsar.) Propagandists thus usually began their discussions on issues close to the workers' day-to-day lives: conditions at the factory, cuts in pay, or fines.

Once the workers had been drawn into the movement, however, propaganda became much more explicit. Destroying the myth of the tsar was one important goal of the orally transmitted "lessons" presented in workers' circles, in which propagandists often lectured on Russian history, emphasizing the harsh policies of the tsars and their responsibility for serfdom. They pointed out the tsars' support for the landowners and the fact that ministers and bureaucrats were only carrying out the tsars' orders. Illegal literature provided another important vehicle for dissemination of revolutionary ideas. Only in this way could the "tsar-batiushka" be directly attacked or criticized before a working-class audience.

As we have seen, *skazki* frequently served as vehicles for social critique. In *The Tale of Four Brothers* Dem'ian becomes a factory worker and experiences the exploitation of workers at first hand. In the "history lesson" he receives from some "knowledgeable people" he is presented with information on the rise of the tsarist autocracy: the tsar is shown to be responsible for serfdom. Another tale, *Out of the Frying Pan and Into the Fire!* (also by Stepniak-Kravchinskii), focuses on the emancipation and the extent to which it disappointed the peasants, who failed to receive all the land to which they felt entitled and who had been obliged to pay for their freedom. The key event of emancipation provided fertile soil for the "myth of the tsar" to flourish: some claimed that the nobles and officials were to blame for this miscarriage of justice, not the tsar. This tale, however, emphasized the tsar's responsibility for the emancipation settlement: the peasants were still serfs, gone "from the bondage of whips to the bondage of hunger."[40] In *Tale of Four Brothers* and *On Truth and Falsehood*, for example, lessons in history, both factual information and a perspective involving change through time, were an important strategy in the propagandist's attempt to shake popular faith in the tsar.

Surviving documents and memoirs show that workers who became involved in the revolutionary movement ultimately lost the traditional faith in the tsar. By 1905, most commentators agree, blind faith in the tsar was dead among the Russian common people as a whole. The reasons for the death of the myth and the precise timing are still questions for investigation. Among the factors affecting urban workers we can see a crucial trajectory of events stretching from the Emancipation in 1861 through the assassination of Alexander II in 1881, various labor disputes, the famine of 1891–92, and the Khodynka Field catastrophe that marked the accession of Nicholas II to

---

[40] S. M. Stepniak-Kravchinskii, *Iz ognia da v polymia! Ili Vot tebe babushka i Iur'ev den'!"* reprinted in Bazanov, *Agitatsionnaia literatura*, 129.

the critical massacre on "Bloody Sunday" in 1905, with which that year of revolution began. On 9 January 1905, St. Petersburg workers, accompanied by wives and children, marched expectantly with banners and icons to the Winter Palace to petition the tsar for better economic and working conditions and civil rights. The answering rifle volleys and hundreds of casualties toppled the myth of the "Loving Father," not just among Petersburg workers but, as news spread, around the country. As one witness of the events leading up to Bloody Sunday put it, it was "the last day of faith in the tsar."[41] By the early 20th century, the workers' own experiences, in the new urban environment and in the factory setting, created a situation where traditional faith in the tsar was being put to the test. Propagandists, workers' circles, and revolutionary organizations were also part of this setting, posing questions that challenged unexamined beliefs.

Popular faith in the tsar was closely linked with religious faith, as seen in the pairing of God and tsar in folk sayings: "Only God and the tsar know," "God's will, the tsar's power," and many others.[42] As we have seen, the attitude of passivity and fatalism engendered by the belief that everything was "in God's hands," that the existing society and institutions were validated by political as well as religious authority, was considered by Russian radicals to be a major impediment to instilling a revolutionary outlook among peasants and workers.[43] Almost all "conscious" or "developed" workers, i.e., those

---

[41] V. Livshits, "Poslednii den' very v tsaria," *Proletarskaia revoliutsiia*, no. 1 (24) (1924): 276–79. Walter Sablinsky notes that Petersburg workers held the tsar personally responsible for the massacre: "The most significant effect of Bloody Sunday was this dramatic change in the attitude of the heretofore loyal lower classes." Walter Sablinsky, *The Road to Bloody Sunday* (Princeton, NJ, 1976), 275. Maureen Perrie concludes that even if Bloody Sunday "did not instantaneously destroy popular monarchism, ... the government proved unable to capitalize on it subsequently." Maureen Perrie, "Popular Monarchism: The Myth of the Ruler from Ivan the Terrible to Stalin," in *Reinterpreting Russia*, ed. Geoffrey A. Hosking and Robert Service (London, 1999), 156–69. For eyewitness accounts of the workers' mood in Petersburg, the nature of faith in the tsar on the eve of 1905, and the Gapon movement that organized the procession, see Livshits, "Poslednii den' very v tsaria"; A. Artamonov, *Ot derevni do katorgi: Vospominaniia* (Moscow–Leningrad, 1925), 19–23; V. F. G., *Za Nevskoi zastavoi: Zapiski rabochego Alekseia Buzinova* (Moscow–Leningrad, 1930), 32–41. See also Gerald Surh's analysis in his *1905 in St. Petersburg*, 155–67; and his "Petersburg's First Mass Labor Organization: The Assembly of Russian Workers and Father Gapon: Part II," *Russian Review* 40, 4 (October 1981): 436–41.

[42] Quoted in Michael Cherniavsky, *Tsar and People: Studies in Russian Myths* (New York, 1969), 191. Cherniavsky argues that such proverbs reflected the "personal and collective identity" of the Russian people (228).

[43] See the comments by Kazimierz Dobrowolski, "Peasant Traditional Culture," in *Peasants and Peasant Societies*, ed. Teodor Shanin, 2nd ed. (Oxford, 1987), 270–71:

most affected by and active in the revolutionary movement and socialist propaganda, seem to have lost this faith, and some became openly hostile to religion. This association between socialism, or more broadly radical views, and rejection of religion seems to have been grasped intuitively by the "man or woman in the street" in Russia's working-class neighborhoods. The word "godless" (*bezbozhnyi*), for example, was the most common epithet attached to the word "socialist" by ordinary workers.[44]

Clearly, the issue of religion posed a vexing and complex problem for revolutionary propaganda. Yet it was apparently largely one of tactics, since, for most members of the revolutionary intelligentsia, religion does not seem to have been an important personal issue. From the 1860s, the Russian radical tradition had a strong atheist and materialist bent. If religion is mentioned in memoirs at all, it is usually to note that the standard readings of radical students—Chernyshevskii, Pisarev, Lavrov, Darwin, and others—put an end to any personal religious faith the writer might have had. The broader European socialist tradition, both Marxist and anarchist strands,[45] was also characterized overall by atheism and hostility to institutionalized religion. This does not mean, however, as Jay Bergman has pointed out, that the figure of Jesus or the example of the early Christians did not have symbolic, ethical, or historical significance. Andrei Zheliabov, on trial in 1881 for the assassination of Alexander II, declared that while he rejected the Orthodox Church, he accepted the teachings of Jesus Christ.[46] The issue of openly antireligious propaganda, judging from memoirs and publications of revolutionary organizations, was subjected to less explicit discussion than that of faith in the tsar. Many, fearing to offend the sensibilities of peasants or workers, advised avoiding the subject of religion altogether. Petr Kropotkin, during his period

---

"[R]eligious beliefs ... played an important part in the preservation of traditional values."

[44] See Shapovalov, *Po doroge k marksizmu*, 20, 35; K. Mironov, *Iz vospominanii rabochego* (Moscow, 1906), 21; K. M. Norinskii, "Na svoikh khlebakh," in Rubach, *Istoriia ekaterinoslavskoi sotsial-demokraticheskoi organizatsii*, 32.

[45] The anarchist component of Russian populism, beginning with the influence of Kropotkin and Bakunin, is not always sufficiently acknowledged. For Bakunin's negative evaluation of both God and church, see the excerpt from *God and the State*, in *Russian Philosophy*, ed. James Edie et al. (Chicago, 1965), 1: 415–23. See also George L. Kline, "The Anarchist Critique: Bakunin and Tolstoy," chap. 1 in *Religious and Anti-Religious Thought in Russia* (Chicago, 1968).

[46] Noted in S. I. Mitskevich, *Na grani dvukh epokh: Ot narodnichestva k marksizmu* (Moscow, 1937), 26. See also Jay Bergman, "The Image of Jesus in the Russian Revolutionary Movement: The Case of Russian Marxism," *International Review of Social History* 35, 2 (August 1990): 220–48.

in the Chaikovskii circle, argued that peasants were "shocked, and at the very least not attracted to someone who says that there is no god, that the soul is not immortal."[47] Some propagandists did attempt to use the presumed religious faith of the peasant in revolutionary propaganda, but most opted to criticize priests and the Orthodox Church, rather than deny God.

For the worker in the process of developing a radical political perspective, by contrast, the question of religion was much more important. Religion is mentioned in virtually all of the workers' memoirs of this period, and loss of religious faith is a recurrent motif in the autobiographies of workers who became active in the movement, a kind of precondition for assimilation of a revolutionary outlook, part of the process by which they shed the mental structures and beliefs of the peasant village.[48] In F. N. Samoilov's description of his childhood in a poor village not far from Ivanovo-Voznesensk, for example, religious beliefs are intertwined with superstitions and bound up with the cycle of the agricultural year: veneration of saints, the weather, protecting the cattle from wolves, feast days—all are part of a seamless web of belief and custom. Peasant political views were "primitive": they believed that "without God the world would not exist; without the tsar the earth would be lacking in direction [ne pravitsia]."[49] A similar outlook characterized the lower-class urban milieu. One worker, describing his youth as a Petersburg metal worker, noted: "Everything around instilled [the belief that] 'everything is from God,' 'without God you'll never get anywhere,' and for a long time this religious narcotic possessed me too." He adds that "the books that came my way following my arrival from the village were about the saints, and especially various church sermons."[50]

Governmental authorities, not surprisingly, tried to nourish the traditional religious outlook of the lower classes, hoping thereby to produce God-fearing, obedient citizens who respected authority and were not prone to labor organization or strikes as a means of winning improved conditions in

---

[47] D. M. Odinets, "V kruzhke 'chaikovtsev,'" in *Nikolai Vasil'evich Chaikovskii: Religioznye i obshchestvennye iskaniia*, ed. A. A. Titov (Paris, 1929), 83. Scholarly analysis of the question of religion and propaganda has focused on the early to mid-1870s, particularly the activity of the Chaikovskii cicle and the movement "to the people." See especially the study by Reginald Zelnik, "'To the Unaccustomed Eye,'" 297–326; and B. S. Itenberg, "Revoliutsionnye narodniki i voprosy religii (Iz istorii 'khozhdenie v narod')," *Voprosy istorii religii i ateizma: Sbornik statei*, no. 11 (1963): 293–305.

[48] For a detailed description and discussion, see Zelnik, *A Radical Worker*.

[49] F. N. Samoilov, *Po sledam minuvshego*, 2nd ed. (Leningrad, 1948), 13; see also 12–17.

[50] A. M. Buiko, *Put' rabochego: Vospominaniia putilovtsa* (Leningrad, 1964), 19–20. For an especially interesting (if derogatory) account of religion in the Petersburg working-class milieu, see Shapavalov, *Po doroge k marksizmu*, 12–13.

the workplace. Lessons in religion, usually taught by priests, were included in the officially approved curriculum of elementary schools, both urban and rural, and in the evening and Sunday schools often attended by workers, and employers sometimes brought religion to the factory in the form of occasional services and sermons, or religious "conversations" for workers.[51] The Orthodox Church also carried on missionary work among workers. One of the more successful missionaries was the charismatic priest John of Kronstadt, who attracted many Petersburg workers to his sermons. Other priests founded temperance societies for workers.[52]

Religious sectarianism also flourished among urban workers in the late 19th century, following its earlier development among peasants first in Ukraine, and then in certain regions of Great Russia. The urban dimension of sectarianism had until recently[53] received little attention from scholars of the Russian working class, but workers' memoirs frequently note the presence of adherents of evangelical and Protestant beliefs, known at the time as *shtundisty* and *pashkovtsy*, among workers.[54] The sectarian protest against the established church, together with the perceived commitment to community, equality, and social justice, periodically led radicals (especially in the late 1870s and early 1880s) to consider focusing their propaganda efforts on sectarians and Old Believers.[55] While such efforts were usually unsuccessful, some kind of

---

[51] See Brooks, *When Russia Learned To Read*, 49–50; Ben Eklof, *Russian Peasant Schools: Officialdom, Village Culture, and Popular Pedagogy, 1861–1914* (Berkeley, CA, 1986), 53–54; Zelnik, *A Radical Worker*, 13; Zhabko, *Iz dalekogo proshlogo*, 29.

[52] On John of Kronstadt, see the biography by Nadieszda Kizenko, *A Prodigal Saint: Father John of Kronstadt and the Russian People* (University Park, PA, 2000). See also V. Sergeevich, *Zavod—kuznitsa revoliutsii: Rabochii o starom i novom zhit'e byt'e* (Moscow, 1929), 50–51; Mironov, "Iz vospominanii rabochego," 7–8; Buiko, *Put' rabochego*, 21; and Shapovalov, *Po doroge k marksizmu*, 27–30. As a teenage worker in the late 1880s, Shapovalov was very observant. He joined and recruited other young workers to a temperance society.

[53] For a nuanced study of the complex relationship between workers and the church, see Herrlinger, *Working Souls*.

[54] *Shtundizm* and *pashkovstvo* were umbrella terms for various dissenting/sectarian currents. For more information on sectarianism, see the following sources: A. I. Klibanov, *History of Religious Sectarianism in Russia (1860s–1917)*, trans. Ethel Dunn, ed. Stephen Dunn (Oxford, 1982); S. Stepniak [Kravchinskii], *The Russian Peasantry: Their Agrarian Condition, Social Life and Religion* (New York, 1888), 339–74; V. Zel'tser, "Iz istorii sektantstva v rabochei srede. (Sektanty v g. Nikolaeve v 1890–1900 gg.—po neopublikovannym materialam)," *Voinstvuiushchii ateizm*, no. 4 (1931): 29–46.

[55] For example, see S. Lion's comments on propaganda among worker-*shtundisty* in Odessa in 1877–78: they "held to 'pure' Gospel teachings, rejecting icons, priests, and

association was often made between sectarians and socialists in the working-class milieu.[56]

Although some politically active workers tried, at least for a time, to combine religion and socialism, the majority of workers who were drawn into the movement through socialist propaganda lost their previous religious faith. Disillusionment with religion was an important turning point in the process of rejecting their inherited outlook and beginning to formulate a new one. Contact with radical, socialist workers and/or illegal literature was the common starting point for this process. In some cases workers were impressed by explanations of natural phenomena that excluded God or the supernatural. In others, disillusionment was accelerated by incidents in which icons failed to give proof of divine will—icons were broken or were objects of discord, and God did not intervene to punish the guilty.[57] Petr Moiseenko, with whom this chapter began, relates the faith-shattering consequences of a visit to a monastery undertaken with hopes of clarifying questions about the world raised by the first illegal pamphlets he encountered. In an experience that echoes that of Luka, the youngest of the four brothers of the tale, Moiseenko was repelled by the venality and immorality of the monks: "All [my] faith was lost, not just in monks and priests, but in God too. If God is so powerful, why doesn't he do something about all this? And if he's powerless, he doesn't exist."[58] (Here, as elsewhere in Moiseenko's memoirs, we see a close parallel between his account of his revelatory experience and a trope common to the memoirs of radical workers, in this case that of loss of religious faith.) This rejection of religion, as much as any other aspect of radicalism, set circle members and other active workers apart from the majority. The average worker tended to be suspicious of "godless socialists," and often reacted to their godlessness with hostility. Women, in particular, reacted with suspicion, or so the memoirs suggest, because they tended to be both more religious than men and more difficult to draw into the revolutionary movement. "All workers affected by propaganda first wanted to break with religion," one memoirist recalled; he remembered

---

the rituals of the Orthodox Church." S. E. Lion, "Ot propagandy k terroru," *Katorga i ssylka*, no. 5 (12) (1924): 19–20.

[56] On an unsuccessful propaganda effort in Elizavetgrad in the early 1880s, see Pankratov, *Vospominaniia*, 84–87. Anna Boldyreva, a textile worker active in the Petersburg movement in the 1890s, was called "pashkovka" and "studentka" by other workers (Boldyreva, "Minuvshie gody," 256).

[57] See the experiences of the following workers: Samoilov, *Po sledam minuvshego*, 41–44; Mironov, *Iz vospominanii rabochego*, 8–9; Buiko, *Put' rabochego*, 22; Petrov, "Moi vospominaniia," 183.

[58] Moiseenko, *Vospominaniia starogo revoliutsionera*, 15–16.

many emotional scenes between such workers and members of their families, especially their mothers.[59] Still, there were exceptions. The views of those women (small in numbers) who became involved in the movement do not appear to have differed from those of "conscious" male workers.[60]

What was it about involvement in the revolutionary movement and exposure to propaganda that led most committed workers to reject religion? Propagandists sometimes differed in their approaches to religion, a divergence seen most clearly in comparing worker propagandists with those from the intelligentsia. Different propaganda was directed to different audiences, for example, politicized workers as opposed to those with no previous contact with radical ideas. Those workers who became committed to the socialist and revolutionary movement not surprisingly credited the *kruzhok*, the workers' circle, with an immense transformative power. F. N. Samoilov, a young peasant working in a textile factory in Ivanovo-Voznesensk in the early 20th century, voiced the views of others like him in his comments on the workers' circle he joined: "Circle studies opened before me a new world, one whose existence had been unknown to me before joining the organization."[61] Passage to this "new world" required, for many workers, a parting with the old one.

In general, propagandists addressing uneducated and unpoliticized workers took care not to offend the religious sensibilities of their listeners. As one Ekaterinoslav worker involved in circles in the 1880s put it, "workers reacted skeptically to propagandists: they were especially fearful when they began to talk to them about the tsar, God, and lying priests."[62] The discussion simply went nowhere if the propagandist brought up these subjects; if raised by the workers, on the other hand, the topics were acceptable.[63] Instead of responding with declarations that God did not exist or criticizing religion in general, propagandists from the intelligentsia used two different approaches, both in the literature and in discussions. Most frequently, criticism was directed at priests and at the Orthodox Church as an institution upholding the unjust social order. Sometimes, as we have seen in the *skazki*, the true values of Christianity, those of Jesus Christ and the early Christians, were

---

[59] Mironov, *Iz vospominanii rabochego*, 21–22. See also Zhabko, *Iz dalekogo proshlogo*, 34–35; Prokof'ev, "Iz perezhitogo," 111; and Muralova, "Iz proshlogo," 154.

[60] See, for example, the memoirs of Vera Karelina on the early 1890s, "Na zare rabochego dvizheniia v S.-Peterburge," 18.

[61] Samoilov, *Po sledam minuvshego*, 44.

[62] G. Knifutov, "Vospominaniia," in Rubach, *Istoriia ekaterinoslavskoi sotsial-demokraticheskoi organizatsii*, 67.

[63] M. Liadov, "Kak zarodilas' Moskovskaia rabochaia organizatsiia," in Mitskevich, *Na zare rabochego dvizheniia v Moskve*, 58.

contrasted with the hypocrisy and corruption of the contemporary church; by implication, these values did not contradict the essence of socialism.

In attacks on the priesthood, propagandists drew on an existing ambivalence toward priests in peasant culture. Priests had long been subjected to complaints and criticism and were the target of mockery in some satirical folktales.[64] As we have seen, revolutionary *skazki* commonly included the priest in a list of oppressors and exploiters of the common people, along with nobles, merchants, policemen, and the tsar. In *Tale of a Kopeck* a peasant earns a kopeck with great difficulty, only to have it taken away successively by the nobleman, merchant, and priest—three enemies of the people. The experiences of Luka, the youngest of the brothers in the *Tale of Four Brothers*, reveal the true nature of the church—its greed, hypocrisy, and lack of spirituality. Visiting a monastery, Luka witnesses monks swearing and fighting over the collection money, a group of monks and nuns having a drunken party, and miraculous icons that are fakes. *On Truth and Falsehood* sketches the history of Christianity in Russia. True Christian values are contrasted with the hypocrisy and corruption of the power structure:

> Christ taught that all men should be equal, like brothers. But how can people be equal when tsars, nobles, and officials rule over the people like a herd of livestock? Christ taught that all people must love one another like brothers. But can there be love when tsars, their nobles, and officials rob the people and make them do their will by force?[65]

If propagandists from the intelligentsia tended to treat religious issues cautiously, worker-activists involved in propaganda with workers as yet untouched by propaganda did at times use religious ideas and sources as a way to get workers to question the social and political order. Petr Antonov, a leading worker-*narodovolets* of the early 1880s, relates in his autobiography that he first began propaganda of socialist ideas in the 1870s, before he knew much about the theory of socialism himself. He used the Gospels as a propaganda aid: "[I]n my opinion they [were] the teachings of socialism, if you left out their mystical side."[66] E. I. Nemchinov, a worker active in the Moscow "Workers' Union" of the mid-1890s, noted the difficulty of propaganda among average workers, who had trouble understanding the "language of the intelligentsia":

---

[64] See Perrie, "Folklore as Evidence," 124–26.

[65] *O pravde i krivde*, 105.

[66] "Avtobiografiia P. L. Antonova," *Golos minuvshego*, no. 2 (1923): 85. According to Vera Figner's introduction, Antonov wrote this autobiographical statement in 1906, at her request.

"cadres of interpreters, of semi-intelligentsia workers" were needed to assist in the circle work. Like Antonov, Nemchinov often found it helpful to refer to passages in the Gospels during propaganda. Workers, he would explain, are only asking for what is theirs:

> [A]t the beginning, when Christians lived in a Christian way, they held their property in common, worked in common, and never lacked for anything.... [D]o you think the tsar, the nobles, and the rich care about us? No, and if not, then we have no reason to work for them; so let's figure out how to ... shake them off and advance to a society like that of early Christianity.[67]

While religion, though often touched on in workers' circles, was not usually a formal part of the curriculum, propagandists found that natural science afforded them a very effective, though indirect way to demystify faith. Topics ranged from the origins of the universe, astronomy, and meteorology (including explanations of such phenomena as eclipses and thunder) to geology and the age of the earth, physics and chemistry, and Darwin's theories. A telling example of the effect of bringing natural science into circle studies, and of the mutual interrelations of propagandist and workers, is presented in the memoirs of the young propagandist Mikhail Drei. During 1880 and 1881 Drei, a law student at Odessa's New Russia University and an active member of the local People's Will organization, met regularly with a circle of young carpenters living in the Moldavanka district. Recalling their meetings, he later wrote:

> One aspect of our discussions puzzled me for a long time.
> When I spoke with them about socialism, the commune, the future order, they made very appropriate remarks and listened with interest. But they became especially animated when our conversations turned to the topics of the origin of species, the phases of the moon, eclipses of the sun, the origin of the world, etc.
> Then they would immediately be all ears, trying not to miss a single word, asking questions and suggesting topics they would like to discuss.
> At first I thought this was a case of what Goethe called "disinterested curiosity," that my carpenters were simply interested in the wonders of the world and that our conversations didn't have any relation to politics and socialism.

---

[67] E. I. Nemchinov, "Vospominaniia starogo rabochego," in Mitskevich, *Na zare rabochego dvizheniia v Moskve*, 162.

But I became convinced that this was not the case. In the peasant's mind the whole social order with the tsar at its summit is so closely bound up with his superstitions that the one cannot be subjected to criticism without the other being shaken. The three whales on which the earth rests and the tsar with his whole order form one monolith, and it is impossible to destroy the political and social views of the peasants and workers and leave their faith in the three whales untouched. Workers listened to my presentation of Darwin with strained attention. This not only explained to them the riddles of the world—for them it was also politics.[68]

Although Drei refers to workers beginning to doubt their superstitious belief in the "three whales," rather than in specific Orthodox Christian teachings, he clearly sees an impact on the workers' outlook as a whole—a combination of religion, superstition, and faith in the tsar which cannot be easily disentangled. The authorities grasped this point as well. The prosecutor's report on the activity of Drei and other Odessa activists noted that propagandists would give lectures on natural science in workers' circles: "on the pretext of explaining natural phenomena attacks were usually made on the religious convictions of the *narod*."[69] As Reginald Zelnik has noted, the teaching of science was an effective element of the worker propaganda of the Petersburg Chaikovskii circle of the early 1870s;[70] it remained an important component of the circle curriculum at least through 1900.

How are we to understand the workers' interest in science and religion and the effects of circle propaganda? Here, as in other questions of "what workers thought," the evidence provided by workers' memoirs is invaluable. Mironov, a Moscow worker of the 1890s, connects his first encounters with "conscious" workers, his religious doubts, and his reading of new literature, including a book on astronomy. His experiences, he wished to emphasize, were shared by many workers: "I would like to show how closely linked propaganda of socialism and religious questions often were for workers."[71] For the workers attracted to circle studies (and it should be emphasized that the circle was not merely a venue for education but, as the workers were well aware, constituted an illegal association, linked with the revolutionary movement), science, politics, and socialism were not compartmentalized. Knowledge was a whole,

---

[68] Drei, "Zametki o rabochem dvizhenii," 76.

[69] RGIA f. 1405, op. 521, d. 410, ll. 66–67; and Pankratova and Ivanov, *Rabochee dvizhenie v Rossii*, 2, ch. 2, 497–98.

[70] See Zelnik, "'To the Unaccustomed Eye,'" especially 319–23.

[71] Mironov, *Iz vospominanii rabochego*, 9.

and it underpinned a way of looking at the world. New information, scientific and other, that showed that old beliefs were wrong led to a new "world view." As workers noted, the study of scientific questions in circles often had the effect of shaking the workers' religious faith. Scientific answers to "questions about the universe awakened the worker's mind, aroused his curiosity, and impelled him to seek answers to the questions that troubled him not in the priest's sermon, but in books."[72]

This new secular and scientific world view was, for many workers, reinforced by studies at evening and Sunday schools for workers which existed in Petersburg and other major cities by the 1880s. Classes on physics, geology, geography, astronomy, and other relevant topics were taught in these schools as well, usually by teachers with the desire to impart a modern, secular outlook to their worker pupils, and often sympathetic to the revolutionary movement as well. A second possible source of reinforcement for this new, unreligious outlook might have been the popular fiction circulating among the urban lower classes of this period. Jeffrey Brooks, in his study of this literature, analyzes the promotion of scientific and secular thinking and the scorn for superstition as an important theme of these works.[73] Although little mention is made of such works in the memoirs of worker-revolutionaries, Brooks suggests that these ideas can be taken as part of the common intellectual currency in the milieu of the urban lower classes.[74]

Under the impact of the city, the factory, and the introduction of new ideas, many workers searched for a new understanding to replace the values and beliefs of the peasant world. While not the only new influence, revolutionary propaganda, particularly in the workers' circle and exemplified by the revolutionary *skazki*, was a form of education and had the effect of fostering a new perspective on the world, bolstered by new knowledge: a secular viewpoint, modern concepts of political systems, a sense that traditional hardships and exploitation did not have to be endured fatalistically. Revolutionary propaganda that showed the tsar as the chief exploiter of the common people, rather than a semidivine figure; literature that pierced the façade of sanctity that covered hypocritical priests and oppressive church institutions; scientific discussions that presented an alternative explanation of the natural world: all contributed to a new outlook and sense of power that made possible a revolutionary movement among Russia's workers. All of these were points that propagandists wanted to convey to workers, and the *skazka* form seemed an ideal vehicle.

---

[72] Boldyreva, "Minuvshie gody," 258.

[73] See Brooks, "Science and Superstition," chap. 7 in *When Russia Learned to Read.*

[74] For fuller discussion of the above issues, see Pearl, "Tsar and Religion," 81–107.

ᘓ   ᘔ

The questions of the effectiveness, popularity, and reception of revolutionary literature are important ones. Various kinds of evidence suggest answers to these questions. We can gauge the use and popularity of *skazki* in various ways, keeping in mind that comprehensive figures on publication and dissemination do not exist, due to the peculiarities of illegal literature: copies were not only printed, but were hectographed and handwritten; they were ephemeral in physical format, frequently destroyed and hidden; people lied in an attempt to avoid penalties for possession of or association with illegal literature; and in memoirs written decades later, specific titles were often forgotten.

Nevertheless, we do have evidence which reveals the presence, numbers, and relative popularity of various *skazki*. The data and examples that follow indicate the scope, both geographically and chronologically, of the use of this literature. A major source, the magisterial *Svodnyi katalog russkoi nelegal'noi i zapreshchennoi pechati XIX veka*,[75] compiled from the widest possible variety of published and unpublished sources, is an unparalleled reference work in this regard. It notes, for example, initial press runs in the 1870s of 15,000 copies for *Tale of Four Brothers*; 5000 copies of *Tale of a Kopeck*; and 10,000 copies of *On Truth and Falsehood*.[76] Various lithographed and hectographed editions were produced as well, some of which may have escaped researchers' attention.

Official government documents provide additional evidence on *skazki* and their use. When persons or apartments of suspected radicals were searched, police kept careful lists of all works of illegal literature by title and quantity— all of this might contribute to an assessment of guilt.[77] (As to works of legal literature, these were not of interest to the police and were not noted, a lacuna which makes it difficult to view illegal literature in the broader context of all kinds of literature read.) Reference to specific titles, whether in contemporary police documents or retrospectively in memoirs, can be taken as a sign of acceptance of those works into the evolving revolutionary canon. Some works were seized in suspiciously large quantities, a reliable sign of propaganda activity. Some titles appear only once or twice; others are mentioned repeatedly. In this way, the relative popularity among the worker readers can be evaluated. One can assume that the ones that left little trace were not

---

[75] In addition to publishing information, *Svodnyi katalog* also notes Russian libraries and archives whose collections include these works.

[76] See Itenberg et al., *Svodnyi katalog*, 2: 109 (no. 1847); 2: 101 (no. 1791); and 2: 98 (no. 1771074).

[77] This evidence appears in Department of Police files on various groups, and in Ministry of Justice documents relating to evidence, trials, and sentencing.

found to be effective by propagandists involved with the workers' movement. When police cracked down on the People's Will press in Taganrog in 1885, they seized 85 copies of *Tale of Four Brothers*, apparently printed at the press. In another instance, during a search of premises belonging to a circle in Kazan' in the mid-1880s, police found a "primitive press" and uncovered hundreds of copies of the brochure *On Truth and Falsehood*.[78]

Memoirs provide a different kind of evidence, although, as always with memoirs, recollections of past experiences can be faulty or incomplete. Some memoirs do include information on publication and reproduction of specific works, but beyond this they convey information on reception and context. Recent works of scholarship have been quite critical and skeptical of workers' memoirs published post-1917, during Soviet times.[79] On this and other questions, however, corroborating evidence is often found in sources outside this post-1917 body of memoir literature—including government documents, memoirs published before 1917, and memoirs by non-Bolsheviks. *The Tale of Four Brothers* and other *skazki* were distributed to workers (by both members of the radical intelligentsia and other workers), read in workers' circles, included in (underground) libraries for workers, hectographed by local circles, and mentioned in records of literature seized during arrests (often in surprising quantities). Workers' memoirs make clear that the initial encounter with a piece of radical literature produced a powerful effect. Years later, workers such as Petr Moiseenko could often remember the precise work that first opened their eyes. Frequently, this work was a *skazka*. Nikolai Bogdanov, who, as we have seen, was a key member of the Brusnev organization in St. Petersburg in the early 1890s), recalled that his first introduction to illegal literature came in 1885, when, as a teenage apprentice at the Warsaw Railroad Repair Shops, an older worker, one of the "'last of the Mohicans' of the People's Will," suddenly disappeared, leaving him with the *Tale of Four*

---

[78] GARF f. 102, 7 d-vo, d. 42, ch. 3, l. 8; Itenberg et al., *Svodnyi katalog*, 2: 31 (no. 98); and *Obzor vazhneisheikh doznanii proizvodivshikhsia v zhandarmskikh upravleniiakh Imperii po gosudarstvennym prestupleniiam* (Department of Police, St. Petersburg), 11: 98.

[79] See especially Frederick C. Corney's important work *Telling October*. Sheila Fitzpatrick refers to "built-in bias" and comments on some of the pitfalls involved in relying on memoirs of worker-revolutionaries for evidence of workers' consciousness or *mentalité*: "To be a 'conscious' worker meant, among other things, knowing what kind of *mentalité* workers were expected to have." Sheila Fitzpatrick, "New Perspectives on the Civil War," in *Party, State, and Society in the Russian Civil War: Explorations in Social History*, ed. Diane P. Koenker, William G. Rosenberg, and Ronald Grigor Suny (Bloomington, IN, 1989), 11. Nonetheless, workers' memoirs should not, for that reason, be discounted. Read carefully, they are an invaluable source for any attempt to understand the lives and outlook of worker radicals and the broader working-class milieu.

Brothers and other illegal literature. This unexpected bequest was apparently instrumental in leading Bogdanov to begin to undertake some propaganda himself.[80] Vasilii Shelgunov, another young worker later prominent in the St. Petersburg movement, was also a teenage worker in the 1880s. He recalls that he received his first illegal works from a fellow student at the evening school for workers which he attended. The first mentioned is the *Good Friday Sermon of Tikhon Zadonskii*. (Interestingly, the pamphlet, better known as *On Truth and Falsehood*, is often referred to by this "masking" title, which headed the original Chaikovskii edition.) Shelgunov's father was quite upset with his son's choice of reading material: his father swore and said, "You read too much and they'll hang you."[81]

Written by the educated members of the radical intelligentsia for the (seemingly straightforward if dangerous) purpose of promoting revolution, in the hands of workers these same brochures could take on unintended shades of meaning, representing a connection with revolution in a much more concrete fashion. As *skazki* and other kinds of literature were appropriated by workers, their ideas underwent a subtle transformation. What did the revolutionary brochure mean in the hands of a newly literate or poorly literate worker? The context was important: *skazki* were often encountered in the context of circle studies, which involved a relationship with the propagandist, usually a member of the educated classes. Mikhail Drei, who gave his circle of carpenters *The Tale of Four Brothers*, among other works, found, as we have seen, that the circle studies gave him new insight into the worldview of the workers. Politically active workers who carried out their own propaganda work used *Four Brothers* as well.[82] Consciously or not, propagandists may have been influenced in their choice of the *skazka* by the type of reading material that was common in the lower-class milieu, the so-called *lubochnaia* literature, an offshoot of the popular print known as the *lubok*. Although works of nonfiction were also used in propaganda, the familiar format of the tale may have facilitated assimilation of new ideas.[83]

---

[80] Ol'minskii, "O vospominaniiakh N. D. Bogdanova," 39.

[81] V. A. Shelgunov, "Vospominaniia V. A. Shelgunova," 54.

[82] See Bogdanov, above. For an example of the use of *Four Brothers* in worker-led propaganda in Khar'kov in 1884, see A. M. Katrenko, *V bor'be za probuzhdenie narodnoi revoliutsii: Iz istorii revoliutsionno-demokraticheskogo dvizheniia na Ukraine v 80-kh–nachale 90-kh godov XIX v.* (Kiev, 1988), 72–73.

[83] Some activist workers mention their early reading of this popular literary form. See M. P. Petrov, *Moi vospominaniia*, 183; Shapovalov, *Po doroge k marksizmu*, 11. See also Brooks, "The Literature of the Lubok," chap. 3 in *When Russia Learned to Read*; and "Lubochnaya literatura" and "Lubok" in Terras, *Handbook of Russian Literature*, 266–67.

Hectographing[84] as a way to reproduce literature for propaganda was a basic circle activity (if members could get the necessary components). Grigorii Borziakov organized a circle of gymnasium students in Odessa in the 1880s that had apparently begun propaganda among workers. He recalls that they hectographed illegal literature, including *Four Brothers* and *The Clever Trick*, in repeated editions. Revolutionary circles also created libraries, sometimes for their members and sometimes for workers. The Tochisskii circle, one of the early proto-Social Democratic groups in Russia (Petersburg, mid-1880s), had an illegal library that included 10 to 15 copies of *Four Brothers*, which the group hectographed themselves, and 3 to 5 copies of *On Truth and Falsehood*. Andrei Breitfus, a former student and founding member of the group also known as the Association of St. Petersburg Workingmen, noted that the workers read this literature with great eagerness.[85] Memoirs of the Moscow People's Will group of 1883–85, in which future SR leader M. R. Gots played a leading role, had a library of legal and illegal literature for workers, including "the old popular brochures," such as *Four Brothers*.[86]

Of all the *skazki*, *The Tale of Four Brothers* seems to have been the most archetypal—everyone seems to remember that title. The titles of other *skazki* appear frequently in the sources as well. *The Tale of a Kopeck*, one of the titles noted by Moiseenko as figuring in his intellectual awakening, was widely used in the 1870s and 1880s. Influential theorist Petr Lavrov, who followed the Russian movement with intense interest from exile in Switzerland, noted that this brochure circulated widely—even though its "literary quality" was, in his judgment, inferior to that of *Four Brothers*.[87] It was used in propaganda among workers by populists during the mid-1870s in Kiev, Ivanovo-Voznesensk, and elsewhere. Radicals involved with the ostensibly opposing parties of Black Repartition and the People's Will equally made use of this work.[88] *On Truth*

---

[84] The hectograph, invented in Russia, was a printing process using ink and a gelatin pad to reproduce copies. Many illegal groups made use of this method: it was not difficult to obtain components and was less likely to attract attention than a press.

[85] Borziakov makes several references in his memoirs to propaganda among workers, without providing detail: Gr. Borziakov, "Revoliutsionnaia molodezh' v Odesse v 1882–1884 gg.," *Katorga i ssylka*, no. 8–9 (1929): 146, 150; Breitfus, "Tochisskii," 327–30.

[86] Tereshkovich, "Neskol'ko slov," 111–12.

[87] P. L. Lavrov, *Narodniki-propagandisty 1873–78 godov* (St. Petersburg, 1907), 138.

[88] See V. V. Kallash, ed., *Protsess 50-ti* (Moscow, 1906), 13, 78; Pankratova and Ivanov, *Rabochee dvizhenie v Rossii*, 2, ch. 2, 113; Mindlina, "Deiatel'nost' revoliutsionnykh narodnikov," 198; and E. R. Ol'khovskii, "K istorii "Chernogo Peredela" (1879–1881 gg.)," in *Obshchestvennoe dvizhenie v poreformennoi Rossii* (Moscow, 1965), 148; Mitskevich, "Moskovskie revoliutsionnye kruzhki," 58–59.

and Falsehood, which, as we have seen, first appeared in the 1870s, seems to have undergone something of a revival in the 1880s. It is mentioned in connection with People's Will groups engaged in or aspiring to propaganda among workers in Kiev and Odessa in the early 1880s, by a group of radical Jewish students in Kishenev in 1884, and by the People's Will group that set up the Taganrog press in 1886.[89] The first groups calling themselves Social Democrats, active in St. Petersburg in the 1880s, also made use of this work. Vasilii Shelgunov recalled that the *Good Friday Sermon of Tikhon Zadonskii* (as this work was persistently referred to) was the first illegal work that he read (in the mid-1880s).[90] Although information on the effects of these brochures is frustratingly scarce, there are occasional brief references: for example, Lidiia Loiko, an active propagandist in Kazan' in 1879, recalled that *The Tale of Four Brothers* "called forth so many questions that the discussion continued until the next day."[91] (I have not come across specific titles mentioned by workers in a negative light.)

Official sources frequently include information on how propaganda *skazki* were used. Documents from the period of the "movement to the people," particularly those connected with the major trials of the era, known as the "Trial of the 193" and the "Trial of the 50," uniformly associated with propaganda among peasants, actually include many examples of propaganda among workers. In particular, they show the close link between oral propaganda and the use of literature, including the *skazki* analyzed above and others. One propagandist, for example, a student at the St. Petersburg Technological Institute, made the acquaintance of workers at a tailoring workshop in the provinces. He first offered to teach them to read and write, and to read religious works. After the apprentices got used to him he read them various brochures (including *Four Brothers* and *Truth and Falsehood*), then led them into a discussion of the hard life of workers and the way their labor was exploited by the rich. "So they would live better, it was necessary to destroy the government and officials, and after that all would be equal." He gave

---

[89] Kiev, Zalkind and Zabello group (1883): RGIA f. 1405, op. 83, d. 11101, l. 114ob.; Odessa, Borziakov group: GARF f. 112, op. 1, d. 619, l. 217ob.; Kishinev (1884): GARF f. 102, 7 d-vo, d. 573, l. 18; Taganrog: GARF f. 102, DP, 7 d-vo, d. 42, ch. 3, l. 9.

[90] Blagoev group: RGIA f. 1405, op. 521, d. 428, l. 25; Dmitrii Ignatov and others, Petersburg: RGIA f. 1405, op. 88, d. 10026, l. 7ob.; Tochisskii organization illegal library: Breitfus, "Tochisskii," 330; Shelgunov, "Vospominaniia," 54.

[91] Lidiia Loiko, *Ot "Zemli i Voli" k VKP(b): 1877–1928. Vospominaniia* (Moscow–Leningrad, 1929), 37. See also V. Ia. Bogucharskii, *Aktivnoe narodnichestvo semidesiatykh godov* (Moscow, 1912), 226. Sofiia Bardina (Trial of the 50) undertook discussions in workers' dormitories in Moscow in the mid-1870s: her reading of *The Tale of Four Brothers* was deemed a great success.

out radical literature and told them to pass the booklets on to others. The close connection between propaganda and the revolutionary movement was emphasized by Kravchinskii: "Revolution always calls for a strong organization, which can be created only by means of propaganda, either socialist or purely revolutionary."[92]

The revolutionary tale, of all genres of propaganda literature the one that seems the most elementary and naïve, continued to be chosen, although less and less frequently, by those composing underground literature at least into the early 20th century. Two of these later *skazki—Falsehood Goes on Strike* (*Stachka lzhi*) and *Dream on the Eve of May First* (*Son pod Pervoe Maia*)—were used in propaganda among urban workers in 1898–1900. Both were written by Ekaterina Kuskova, at that time a Social Democrat, and published (without indicating the author) by the Union of Russian Social Democrats Abroad in 1898.[93] In the first, subtitled, *a fairy tale*, Falsehood is depicted as an old woman who now repents of past misdeeds and wants to do something good for humankind. A worker explains to her the concept of going on strike, and suddenly everyone starts speaking the truth, up to the tsar himself. Workers demand and obtain their rights, and Falsehood dies. The second tale ends on a more pessimistic note. This "true tale" (*skazka-pravda*) as it is called, tells a more realistic story of workers planning for a secret May First celebration. A Belgian worker contrasts the public May First demonstrations in his own country, and the central character has a dream in which he is transported to Belgium and sees at first hand how workers live in this freer Western country. He is rudely awakened, however, by the police who have come to arrest him; the compromising May First proclamations are in plain view. These two tales were used in propaganda among workers by Social Democrats in Kiev, Moscow, Ekaterinoslav, and Ivanovo-Voznesensk.[94]

The revolutionary year of 1917, following the overthrow of Tsar Nicholas II and the regime of the Romanovs, was marked by an outpouring of political literature, now freed from the bonds of censorship. Among the many kinds of works published by the socialist parties the *skazka* figured once again—now

---

[92] V. V. Kallash, ed., *Protsess 193-kh* (Moscow, 1906), 31–32; Kravchinskii is quoted in Kallash's foreword (v).

[93] See Itenberg et al., *Svodnyi katalog*, 1: 150 (nos. 856, 857, 858); 1: 174 (no. 1010); 3: 15 (no. 119). On Kuskova, see Barbara T. Norton, "The Making of a Female Marxist: E. D. Kuskova's Conversion to Russian Social Democracy," *International Review of Social History* 34, 2 (1989): 227–47.

[94] See GARF f. OODP [Osobyi otdel Departamenta politsii], d. 5, ch. 6, l. 3/1898, ll. 178, 182, 189; GARF f. 58 MGZhU [Moskovskoe gubernskoe zhandarmskoe upravlenie], op. 1, d. 40/49, l. 136; Pankratova and Ivanov, *Rabochee dvizhenie v Rossii*, 4, ch. 2 (1898–1900): 65, 372, 385, 509, 678.

calling not only for revolution, but contributing to the debate over the nature of the revolution and its outcome. Elizabeth Jones Hemenway has demonstrated how *skazki* "contributed to the construction of revolutionary culture in 1917 by rewriting the Russian foundation narrative." She has traced the evolution of the tales of 1917, beginning with those published in the immediate aftermath of the tsar's abdication, which mocked and defamed the tsar and the royal family in a carnivalesque inversion of the old order. By contrast *skazki* of the October period, from Bolshevik and other political perspectives, depict the socialist "band of brothers" now in the midst of fratricidal internal struggle.[95]

Viewing the workers' revolutionary movement through the lens of the *skazka* affords a new and different perspective on the underground subculture of radical workers. The revolutionary tale was a major genre in the political literature that, over decades, exposed Russian workers to radical ideas. It also aided in the formation of a revolutionary identity among those workers who became involved in the movement. In a familiar format, the *skazka* presented new knowledge and a new way to make sense of society, opposed to the teachings of official Russia: the government and government-sponsored cultural/educational activities, the Orthodox Church. Because illegal, the authors could avoid the oblique hints of Aesopian language used to circumvent the censorship. While the explanation of the propagandist was especially necessary for a "revolutionary" interpretation, illegal pamphlets could be and were read by workers on their own. In their plain language, they could tell the truth (from the perspective of the revolutionary movement) about society, point the finger in the face of the people's oppressors, use shockingly strong language, literally curse those in authority. These works had the power of free speech and embodied the ideals of the revolutionary movement. Workers were well aware of the risks involved in mere physical contact with these little booklets. To possess, read, or circulate them was grounds for punishment and exile. (Workers, however, unlike members of the intelligentsia, often tried to "play dumb" and denied testimony or material evidence linking them to these works. For example, Moscow workers arrested in 1875 made the following excuses to accusations: they "saw they were bad books and burned them"; they "didn't have time" to read the book; someone "forced him" to take the book, but since he was "completely illiterate" the whole thing was pointless.)[96] From the early stages of the existence of a body of propaganda literature, the *skazka* was a major component. It continued to play a role, revealing, in the

---

[95] See Elizabeth Jones Hemenway, "Nicholas in Hell: Rewriting the Tsarist Narrative in the Revolutionary *Skazki* of 1917," *The Russian Review* 60, 2 (April 2001): 189; and Hemenway, "Mother Russia and the Crisis of the Russian National Family: The Puzzle of Gender in Revolutionary Russia," *Nationalities Papers* 25, 1 (1997): 103–21.

[96] Kallash, *Protsess 50-ti*, 7.

guise of a tale, the exploitation of the *narod* at different levels, identifying the causes and culprits, and calling for revolutionary change. This distinctive genre, the *skazka*, seems to have derived some of its power from the narrative story line, intended to draw the reader into the adventures of its characters, who were common people like themselves. The tales may also have served as a link with the real or imagined past of the *narod*, immortalized in the numerous tales workers had heard and read since childhood.

Chapter 3

Political Economy for Workers

> There's a tsar in the world, a merciless tsar;
> His name is—hunger![1]

These lines, taken from Nikolai Nekrasov's poem "The Railroad" ("Zheleznaia doroga," 1864), serve as the epigraph for one of the most popular works of Russian revolutionary propaganda literature of the late 19th century, the pamphlet *Tsar Hunger* (*Tsar-golod*) by Aleksei Nikolaevich Bakh, a People's Will activist of the early 1880s. Nekrasov's poem vividly depicts the cost in human suffering of the construction of the Moscow to St. Petersburg railroad. As with other works by Nekrasov, one of the most popular poets of the time, the poem arouses the reader's sympathy for Russian common folk and outrage at their plight. Bakh, when faced with the task of devising lessons for workers' propaganda circles, picked up the striking image of Tsar Hunger, driving workers to labor and often to death, and used it as a recurring theme, while transforming the message. Bakh's brochure, a dissection and analysis of the capitalist system, leaves behind the world of poetry for that of cold reality. The author's purpose is not simply to inspire sympathy for the people's suffering but rather to lead his worker audience to understand the economic system that exploited them and to recognize the urgent need for revolution.

The ultimate goal of the revolutionary movement was the reorganization of society on a socialist basis. Before making the argument for a socialist society, however, radicals felt it was necessary to unmask the true workings of contemporary capitalist society, with its inherent injustice for working people. In the 1880s the question addressed by *Tsar Hunger,* that of the economic organization of society, came to the fore as the key issue in propaganda among workers. Radicals felt the need to compose works of propaganda (of necessity illegal) to address economic questions. *Tsar Hunger* was one of a group of three works of popular economic analysis that retained their popularity in the workers' revolutionary movement for decades. The other two were *The Clever*

---

[1] N. A. Nekrasov, "Zheleznaia doroga," in *Stikhotvoreniia. Komu na Rusi zhit' khorosho* (Moscow, 1969), 38–43.

Trick (*Khitraia mekhanika*), published in the 1870s, and *Who Lives By What?* (*Kto chem zhivet?*, 1885), a Russian translation of a work by a Polish socialist. This chapter will focus on expositions of political economy for workers, exemplified by these three brochures, which stand out as the most successful works in this genre. Why did radical propagandists consider this an important topic? How did they feel their analyses should be presented? How were these brochures used, and why did they appeal to workers? Use of these three works in propaganda was especially pronounced in the 1880s, the period following the assassination of Tsar Alexander II on 1 March 1881. Beyond their titles, these important works are little known; their frequent use in propaganda among workers in the 1880s calls for closer examination of a decade in the history of the revolutionary movement that has received much less scholarly attention than either the revolutionary populism of the 1870s or the social democratic and labor movements of the 1890s. In this chapter I present an analysis of this distinctive genre, created by radical *intelligenty* who strove to adapt the discipline of political economy to the needs of revolutionary propaganda among workers. I pair this analysis with a reconstruction of the workers' movement influenced by this genre. A closer look at these pamphlets and the context in which they were used leads us to a clearer picture of this decade, when the People's Will Party continued its revolutionary work and fostered a noteworthy cohort of worker-revolutionaries.

෬ ෩

The Russian revolutionary movement of the 1880s is the story of the People's Will Party after 1 March, a little-known chapter. In most treatments by historians the party is known solely for its terrorist exploits and is identified with its Executive Committee, which planned and carried out the assassination of Alexander II and other acts. Following 1 March, the story goes, the party's ringleaders were executed, arrested, and imprisoned, or escaped abroad, and the party virtually ceased to exist. The 1880s are seen as something of a hiatus in the movement, an "era of small deeds," such as zemstvo activity.[2] (An important exception to this received interpretation is provided by Norman M. Naimark in a detailed survey of the spectrum of revolutionary activity in this period.)[3] In fact, after 1 March the People's Will underwent organizational

---

[2] See treatments of the People's Will in Venturi, *Roots of Revolution*; Philip Pomper, *The Russian Revolutionary Intelligentsia* (New York, 1970); Shukman, *The Blackwell Encyclopedia of the Russian Revolution*, 59; Volk, *Narodnaia Volia 1879–1882*; and Sedov, *Geroicheskii period*.

[3] See Naimark, *Terrorists and Social Democrats*. Naimark's important work surveys the many facets of the revolutionary movement and challenges the usual portrayal. His

changes and entered a period of tactical and ideological revision. Strict leadership by the Executive Committee ended, and the party became broader and more decentralized, with groups and organizations calling themselves *narodovol'tsy* (adherents of the People's Will) scattered throughout Russia's cities and provincial towns. The terrorist activities for which the People's Will had achieved notoriety were of minor importance in this period, as organizing and propaganda, particularly among workers, absorbed the energies of most members, among them Aleksei Bakh, a leading provincial activist. An important aspect of this period was the role of worker-*narodovol'tsy* in the movement, as the numbers of workers' circles and radicalized workers continued to grow. Attention to the 1880s thus brings out more clearly the workers' role in what many of them saw as a workers', as well as revolutionary movement, and highlights the degree of worker agency in the movement.

Stepan Khalturin, famous for his role in the workers' movement of the 1870s, is the earliest and best-known of the worker-*narodovol'tsy*. A skilled mechanic from a well-off peasant family, Khalturin came to St. Petersburg in the early 1870s, became involved in the revolutionary movement through the Chaikovskii circle, and went on to become one of the leading organizers of Petersburg workers and a founder of the Northern Union of Russian Workers (1878), an organization by and for workers with a program showing the influence of labor movements in the West and advocating political rights, as well as improved conditions for workers.[4] As the Populist movement began to split over the tactic of political assassination, Khalturin and other worker activists were initially quite critical of this approach. The increased police surveillance and repression that resulted threatened their organizing efforts, rendering workers vulnerable to arrest. By early 1880, however, arrests had destroyed the Northern Union, and Khalturin came to believe that only the death of Alexander II would bring the political freedom necessary for the development

---

research shows the persistence and continuity of the movement in the 1880s, as well as the complex and mixed nature of revolutionary ideology and organization. Although he situates the workers' movement in his broader picture, the topic of revolutionary propaganda among workers is not examined in detail. A similar picture is presented by Derek Offord in *The Russian Revolutionary Movement*, with even less attention to workers, however.

[4] On Khalturin's activities in the period and the Northern Union, see Venturi, *Roots of Revolution*, chap. 19, especially 542–43; and Korol'chuk, "*Severnyi soiuz russkikh rabochikh*," 76–92. Soviet historians routinely emphasized "social democratic" features of the Northern Union's program, of which Khalturin was one of the main authors, in contradistinction to populist ideology of the time. See, for example, Iu. Z. Polevoi, *Stepan Khalturin: K 100-letiiu "Severnogo soiuza russkikh rabochikh"* (Moscow, 1979), 64–68.

of a workers' movement.[5] He began working closely with the People's Will, even volunteering to seek employment as a workman at the Winter Palace in order to plant dynamite for an explosion targeted at Alexander II. (The explosion took place in February 1880; although there were a number of victims, the tsar was not among them.) When the Executive Committee of the People's Will finally achieved its goal of assassinating Alexander II on 1 March 1881, radicals took note of what did and did not happen as a result: the hoped-for popular uprising did not occur, the government granted no political concessions, and, on the other hand, arrests and repression continued. For Khalturin, the lessons of 1 March included increased commitment to political assassination, termed "terrorism" in the language of the day, as a revolutionary tactic. A broad organization of workers seemed impossible under the existing circumstances. Khalturin's subsequent activities are less well known. Suffering from tuberculosis and forced to leave St. Petersburg to avoid arrest, Khalturin relocated to Moscow, where he once again became involved in organizing workers and for several months in 1881 headed the People's Will Workers' Organization in that city.[6] Khalturin then went south to Odessa, again with the intention of organizing workers. Here, however, he apparently found that the police activities of Major General Strel'nikov (given broad powers to combat the revolutionary movement in the southern region of the empire) posed an "insuperable obstacle" to such activity.[7] He became involved in plans by the Executive Committee for Strel'nikov's assassination and was executed (22 March 1882), along with one other, for carrying it out.

Franco Venturi, in his classic history of the revolutionary movement up to 1 March 1881, emphasizes the conflicting forces influencing radicalized workers of this period, the potential conflict between activity directed toward the creation and strengthening of a working-class movement, and the demands of the revolutionary movement:

> Politically, Khalturin was the most typical example of the specifically working-class mentality, which was forming among the more qualified

---

[5] Plekhanov, *Russkii rabochii*, 90–92.

[6] On Khalturin's activities in Moscow, see N. Volkov [I. I. Mainov], "Narodovol'cheskaia propaganda sredi moskovskikh rabochikh v 1881 g.," *Byloe*, no. 2 (1906): 181–82; Polevoi, *Stepan Khalturin*, 86–89; Pankratov, *Vospominaniia*, 44; Volk, *Narodnaia Volia*, 294. Khalturin's devotion to workers and his commitment to building a strong workers' movement are seen in both his activities and in descriptions of Khalturin by contemporaries. See, for example, Plekhanov, *Russkii rabochii*, 85–89. Khalturin himself left no memoirs or other writings (Polevoi, *Stepan Khalturin*, 43).

[7] A. M. Rubach, ed., "Ubiistvo gen. Strel'nikova i kazn' Khalturina i Zhelvakova," *Letopis' revoliutsii*, no. 2 (7) (1924): 189.

and best educated workers in St. Petersburg. Yet, at the same time he was the real symbol of the absorption of the finest of this type into the Populist ranks.... His story, indeed, contains all the drama implicit in this first stage of the Russian working class movement—torn between an awareness of the specific interests of the workers and growing political and revolutionary consciousness.[8]

It may be, however, that Khalturin saw no conflict between his identity as a worker and his actions, of the most extreme kind, in his identity as a revolutionary. Khalturin's story, and that of other radical workers, helps us see the interlinked relationship between the workers' movement and the broader revolutionary movement.

The revolutionary careers of other worker *narodovol'tsy* parallel that of Khalturin in some respects: paramount concern for and involvement in organizing and propaganda activities among workers; support for terror and the use of force in the revolutionary struggle and sometimes personal participation in such activities; and a period spent in the "underground," with an assumed identity and frequent travel from one town to another. These workers played a particularly important role in the development of the revolutionary and workers' movements in the 1880s, especially in the southern region of the Russian Empire. Our picture of the movement, based primarily on evidence from the northern capitals, St. Petersburg and Moscow, begins to look somewhat different when we turn to the South—the major cities of Kiev, Khar'kov, and Odessa, and provincial towns such as Rostov-on-Don, Taganrog, Novocherkassk, Poltava, Ekaterinoslav, and others.[9] In the South, with its lower level of industrialization, the movement was based to a lesser extent on factory workers; on the other hand, one of the most important components was made up of workers at the railroad repair shops, and a

---

[8] Venturi, *Roots of Revolution*, 543.

[9] Most published work on the Russian workers' movement, particularly works in English, has focused on the revolutionary movement in St. Petersburg. See, for example, Reginald Zelnik's "Russian Bebels" and his translation of Semen Kanatchikov's memoir, *A Radical Worker*; Pipes, *Social Democracy*; Wildman, *Making of a Workers' Revolution* (the latter emphasizes developments in St. Petersburg). (The works by Naimark and Offord noted above are an exception.) Among Soviet-era memoir collections, see Korol'chuk, *V nachale puti*; and E. R. Ol'khovskii, ed., *Avangard: Vospominaniia i dokumenty piterskikh rabochikh 1890-kh godov* (Leningrad, 1990). This predominant focus on Petersburg is justified, because shifts and developments often happened first in the capital city. However, memoirs published in such journals as *Proletarskaia revoliutsiia* and *Katorga i ssylka* in the 1920s and early 1930s, and memoirs published in provincial journals and collections, as well as archival sources, do provide material allowing us to broaden this geographical focus.

series of workers' circles expanded along the growing rail network. Artisanal and migrant workers (for example, artels of carpenters) were also involved. "Illegals," professional revolutionaries, both intelligentsia and workers, also had a greater presence in the South. This is partly due to the fact that many who began their revolutionary activity in St. Petersburg or Moscow went south at the point when, facing arrest, they were forced to go underground.[10]

Vasilii Pankratov, one of the few workers of this period to have left memoirs, was an important southern worker *narodovolets* of the early 1880s. He first bcame involved in the workers' movement in St. Petersburg in around 1880. At the time, he was a young, skilled metalworker, employed first at the Baltic and later the Semiannikov plant. Pankratov claims that workers of the time did not pay much attention to theoretical differences between the two revolutionary organizations, People's Will or Black Repartition. In his depiction, radicalized workers had a general "revolutionary" rather than a party identity; they saw the movement as a *workers'* as well as a revolutionary movement.[11] Pankratov's political identity appears to have become more closely tied to the People's Will from fall 1881, when he was forced to leave Petersburg to avoid probable arrest. He went to Moscow already something of a professional revolutionary, with the explicit intention of trying to organize Moscow workers. After a short time he moved further south, helping to organize workers around the People's Will banner in Rostov-on-Don, Khar'kov, Elizavetgrad, and other towns.

Although Pankratov's memoirs emphasize his peaceful activities as an organizer and propagandist among workers, as a member of the party's "fighting detachment" he also participated in such activities as attempts to rob the post to provide funds for party activities, and police documents noted that he "put up armed resistance" upon his arrest in Kiev in 1884.[12] Pankratov's memoirs present a volatile picture of the working-class milieu:

---

[10] V. I. Nevskii, whose research of the 1920s and early 1930s presents important guide-posts for a reconstruction of the revolutionary movement, was one of the few Soviet historians to stress the importance of the People's Will, particularly its role in worker propaganda and in the south. He writes that, "at the dawn of the workers' movement … there were worker-*narodovol'tsy*." V. I. Nevskii, introduction to "Rabochii Sbornik," *Krasnaia letopis'*, no. 4 (1922): 340. Elsewhere he notes the influence of the group of Rostov worker-*narodovol'tsy* mentioned below "on the development of the workers' movement in the whole south of Russia on the 1880s." See Nevskii, foreword to "'Rabochii'—rostovskii zhurnal 1883 goda," *Literaturnoe nasledstvo*, no. 2 (1932): 76. See also S. N. Valk's discussion of People's Will and worker-revolutionaries, "Molodaia partiia Narodnoi Voli," *Problemy marksizma*, no. 1 (3) (1930): 95–100.

[11] Pankratov, *Vospominaniia*, 11; Pankratov, "Iz deiatel'nosti sredi rabochikh," 239.

[12] See S. N. Valk, ed., "P. L. Antonov v Petropavlovskoi kreposti," *Krasnyi arkhiv*, no. 31 (1928): 115 n. 5; and GARF f. 102, 7 d-vo, d. 293, l. 26. Pankratov was sentenced to 20 years' imprisonment, a punishment meted out to the most dangerous revolutionaries.

this was a period of economic crisis and unemployment; of beatings of foremen and workers rioting in protest against intolerable conditions. He describes spies infiltrating factories and workers' circles; persecution by Petersburg Police Chief Sudeikin, who tried to get workers to turn informant; and workers with plans to assassinate hated police officials. This information serves as a kind of subtext in the memoirs, a partial explanation of a question Pankratov mentions but does not discuss in detail: why workers like himself turned to terrorism, at least in theory. For some workers, their circumstances and police persecution, combined with the new knowledge provided by the revolutionary movement, fed a desire to fight back. According to Pankratov, the People's Will did not, as was sometimes alleged, turn leading workers into terrorists: "worker-terrorists were created by the conditions themselves."[13]

Pankratov crossed paths in Khar'kov in 1883 with another worker-radical who, like him, had been forced by police surveillance and impending arrest to give up a settled existence for life as a peripatetic revolutionary. This worker was Petr Antonov, one of the most well-known worker-members of the People's Will and also a member of the "fighting detachment." Antonov, also a skilled metalworker, was born in Nikolaev and spent his life before his arrest in 1885 in various southern cities and industrial centers, working in railroad repair shops and factories in Odessa and in Poltava and Khar'kov provinces.[14] By 1882 Antonov was a valued member of the party and worked closely with Vera Figner, the last leading member of the Executive Committee still at large in Russia. In 1882–83 he was employed in the repair shops at the Liubotin depot of the Khar'kov-Nikolaevsk railroad and helped organize a circle of railroad workers there. According to one worker questioned by the police, the workers involved in the Liubotin circle stood out from their fellows by their good behavior, their love of reading, and the fact that they did not drink. A number also developed into good propagandists.[15] Following the arrest of the Liubotin circle in 1883, Antonov was forced to go underground. In 1885 he was arrested; the indictment listed a number of illegal and sometimes violent activities, including membership in the People's Will, living with false papers,

---

See his account in V. S. Pankratov, *Zhizn' v Shlissel'burgskoi kreposti 1884–1898* (1902; Petrograd, 1922).

[13] Pankratov, "Iz deiatel'nosti sredi rabochikh," 255.

[14] See Antonov, "Avtobiografiia," 85. This interesting memoir, which includes a detailed description of his childhood, was written by Antonov in 1906 at the request of Vera Figner. See Figner's introduction to Antonov, "Avtobiografiia," 77–78.

[15] On the Liubotin circle, see V. I. Sukhomlin, "Narodovol'cheskaia rabochaia organizatsiia na st. Liubotin, Khar'kovo-Nikolaevskoi zh. d.," *Puti revoliutsii*, no. 5–6 (8–9) (1927): 33–36, 40; RGIA f. 1405, op. 83, d. 11181; Antonov, "Avtobiografiia," 86–87.

storing explosives, and the 'assassination' of a worker-spy. His death sentence was commuted to life in prison; he spent 18 years in the Shlissel'burg fortress in St. Petersburg until released in 1905.[16]

In addition to notable individuals like Pankratov and Antonov, there were also important groups of worker *narodovol'tsy* which functioned with a great deal of autonomy and guided workers' movements in specific towns or industrial centers, again, especially in the southern region. Pankratov and Antonov each worked for a time with one such group of workers in Rostov-on-Don. The town's rapidly growing working class included factory workers, laborers connected with river trade and traffic, and workers at the railroad repair shops of the Vladikavkaz Railroad.[17] Movement participation was highest among the latter group. Intelligentsia members of the local People's Will group, mostly students, were the first to organize systematic propaganda. They led circle discussions and guided reading of legal and illegal literature: the goal was "the political education of workers."[18] One propagandist later explained that they did not want to turn workers into *intelligenty* or to transform them into terrorists, but rather to prepare them to carry out propaganda in the workplace among the general working population, something that propagandists from the intelligentsia would be unable to do.[19] In 1883 the Rostov worker-*narodovol'tsy* even managed to put out a hectographed journal, *Rabochii*, written entirely by workers and addressed to a worker audience. The single issue included articles on political economy.[20]

While local People's Will groups composed of students and other members of the intelligentsia were typically swept away by arrests after only a brief existence, workers' groups usually benefitted from a much greater

---

[16] See "Antonov, Petr Leont'evich," in *DRDR* 3, vyp. 1, col. 95. On Antonov, see also A. N. Makarevskii, "Rabochii-narodovolets P. L. Antonov: Vospominaniia," *Katorga i ssylka*, no. 5 (12) (1924): 272–81.

[17] On Rostov and its working class, see Peshekerov, "Propaganda narodovol'tsev," 116–17; and Pankratov, *Vospominaniia*, 66. According to S. N. Valk, there were 5,229 workers at 77 enterprises (Valk, afterword to "'Rabochii'—rostovskii zhurnal," 96).

[18] G. N—in [G. Novopolin], "Iz zhizni rabochikh narodovol'cheskikh kruzhkov: Pamiati Andreia Karpenko," *Katorga i ssylka*, no. 8–9 (1929): 205.

[19] Peshekerov, "Propaganda narodovol'tsev," 123–24. On the content of propaganda among Rostov workers in this period, see also "Dobruskina, Genrieta Nikolaevna" [autobiography], in *Entsiklopedicheskii slovar' Russkogo bibliograficheskogo instituta Granat*, 7th ed., supplement to vol. 40 (Moscow, n.d.), col. 124; reprinted in *Deiateli SSSR i revoliutsionnogo dvizheniia Rossii: Entsiklopedicheskii slovar' Granat* [reprint of supplements to vols. 40 and 41 of *Granat*, 7th ed.] (Moscow, 1989), 176 (col. 124).

[20] On this journal, see "'Rabochii'—rostovskii zhurnal"; 75–100; and Pankratov, "Iz deiatel'nosti sredi rabochikh," 250.

degree of continuity. The authorities often found it more difficult to penetrate workers' organizations, often composed of close-knit groups of neighbors and co-workers; in addition, they considered upper-class radicals more of a threat to the stability of the regime.[21] In Khar'kov, a major center of People's Will activity in the 1880s, a group of radical workers managed to keep a network of circles going, engaged in organizing work among broader strata of the working class, and escaped arrest for nearly a decade, until 1889. The Khar'kov workers' organization was similar to that in Rostov in its relative independence of local intelligentsia radicals. The core group of activists (which included several tailors, skilled workers from the railroad repair shops, and local factory workers) took on greater coherence in the mid-1880s with the merger of two previously existing groups of workers, one identifying themselves as *narodovol'tsy,* and the others calling themselves *narodniki* (a spin-off of earlier Black Repartition organizing efforts). Ideological distinctions, however, were less important than the common work of organizing Khar'kov workers. Group members were in close contact with the Khar'kov organization of *narodovol'tsy* and recruited its members (for the most part, students at Khar'kov University and the Veterinary Institute) as propagandists to lead studies in the more advanced circles. Worker-activists sometimes led circles of less knowledgeable workers themselves.[22]

This little-known generation of radical workers helped shape the Russian revolutionary and workers' movements. To some extent, their participation may have kept the movement from developing an exclusively top-down attitude in relation to workers. Revolutionaries from the working class, however, would always maintain a distinctive identity. The new political culture of the worker revolutionary involved a rejection of old views and the substitution of

---

[21] See, for example, the government's presentation of its case against the Khar'kov "Russian revolutionary group of workers" discussed here. The workers' activity is not seen as particularly revolutionary, with most blame (and harsher punishments) meted out to *intelligenty* associated with the case. The workers are termed "passive victims" of these "leaders." See RGIA f. 1405, op. 90, d. 10847, especially ll. 102–03. See also L. V. Freifel'd, "Zapozdalaia popravka," *Katorga i ssylka,* no. 4 (113) (1934): 124.

[22] See I. Veden'ev, "V Khar'kovskikh revoliutsionnykh kruzhkakh 1882–1889 gg.," *Letopis' revoliutsii,* no. 5 (1923): 102–03; V. Denisenko, "Khar'kovskaia gruppa partii 'Narodnoi Voli' 1885–1887 gg.," in *Narodovol'tsy 80-kh i 90-kh godov,* ed. A. V. Iakimova-Dikovskaia et al. (Moscow, 1929), 131; "Opyt programmy russkoi sotsial'no-revoliutsionnoi gruppy rabochikh," in V. I. Nevskii, *Ot "Zemli i Voli" k gruppe "Osvobozhdenie Truda"* (Moscow, 1930), 501–03. On the *narodniki* and *narodnichestvo* of the 1880s, a current deserving further study, see the works of N. L. Sergievskii: "Narodnichestvo 80-kh godov," in *Istoriko-revoliutsionnyi sbornik,* ed. V. I. Nevskii (Moscow–Leningrad, 1926), 3: 148–241 (article and supplementary documents); and "'Chernyi Peredel' i narodniki 80-kh godov," *Katorga i ssylka,* no. 1 (74) (1931): 7–58.

a different world outlook and set of political beliefs.[23] For those forced to give up their legal identity and "go underground," it called for divorce from the old working-class milieu, an often peripatetic life, a new community, and a new role among workers. With their strong commitment to overthrow of the government and construction of a new society, it is not surprising that they gravitated to the most radical and uncompromising strand of the revolutionary movement of their day, and the one identified with active combat against the tsarist regime.[24]

This new outlook and a new, one might say modern, set of political beliefs were the result of participation in workers' circles, of oral propaganda and discussions with radical students and other members of the intelligentsia, and the specific works of literature, often illegal, which figured in circle studies and were also passed around among workers. Political economy was a central topic in workers' circles during the 1880s (and later). If a local group felt the need to answer the demand for propaganda literature by printing something themselves, the choice often fell on one of these three key titles in the genre of political economy for workers. (The investment of time and energy required to set up a press, acquire type, and carry out the work of production without being detected—not to mention the extreme illegality of such an undertaking—lent a certain prestige to any group that managed to successfully carry out this endeavor. Having a press really "put a group on the map.") *The Clever Trick* was printed in quantity on a press set up in 1883 by a circle headed by Nikolai Iordan, a student at the Khar'kov Veterinary Institute; copies were also hectographed by a circle of gymnasium students in Odessa in 1884. The Moscow People's Will circle headed by Mikhail Gots (later a noted SR) had intentions of printing this brochure, and Dmitrii Blagoev's early Social Democratic group in St. Petersburg chose *The Clever Trick* as their first publication.[25] *Tsar Hunger* was printed by People's Will groups in Kazan'

---

[23] See Pearl, "Tsar and Religion," 81–107.

[24] For a more extensive treatment of worker *narodovol'tsy* and of the significance of terrorism for such workers, see Pearl, "From Worker to Revolutionary," 11–26.

[25] Khar'kov group: RGIA f. 1405, op. 85, d. 10943, l. 29ob. Iordan's Khar'kov circle may have preferred a *narodnik* identification, as opposed to People's Will; documents relating to their case refer to the "circle of worker *narodniki*." Members of the circle were arrested in January 1884. On the Odessa circle, organized by the central People's Will organization in Odessa, see the memoirs of the leading figure, Borziakov, "Revoliutsionnaia molodezh' v Odesse," 135. See also GARF f. 112 (OPPS), op. 1, d. 619. On Moscow in the period 1883–85, see K. M. Tereshkovich, "Neskol'ko slov," 113. There is some disagreement on whether the brochure was actually printed. See B. I. Nikolaevskii, "Programma pervogo v Rossii s.-d. kruzhka," *Byloe*, no. 7 (13) (1918): 41–42; S. A. Ovsiannikova, *Gruppa Blagoeva: Iz istorii rasprostraneniia marksizma*

and Tobolsk, as well as by Blagoev's group. Tochisskii's Social Democratic group hectographed copies for their workers' library.[26] A number of groups in the 1880s and 1890s—*narodovol'tsy* as well as social democrats—obtained copies of *Who Lives By What?*, published abroad by the Emancipation of Labor Group and later by the Free Press Fund. It was also hectographed, including by *narodovol'tsy* engaged in worker propaganda in Petersburg in the mid-1880s. A Yiddish translation appeared in 1887.[27]

Vasilii Pankratov and the other radical workers discussed above were influenced by these and other works of political economy. While Pankratov's memoirs make little mention of literature (in general memoir references to literature are sparse), in 1906 he could still recall the appearance of a new edition of *The Clever Trick* in 1881 as a special event.[28] Political economy, undoubtedly with the help of these brochures, was a key topic of study and discussion in the Rostov circle, and propagandists in Kharkov circles read chapters from Marx's *Capital*, as well as the more popular explication provided in *Tsar Hunger*.[29] In analyzing these brochures, we need to keep in mind that workers often took from them knowledge and impressions that went beyond what the authors intended. For example, A. S. Shapovalov, a Petersburg worker in the mid-1890s, later recalled the strong impression made by the first work of illegal literature he encountered, which happened to be *The Clever Trick*. He gave the booklet high marks for the clarity with which it explained the system of taxes through which the government robbed the peasants. But the illustrations, "which represented the tsar, generals, and ministers as the major thieves, and the tsaristsa as a prostitute with a crown on her head," made

v Rossii (Moscow, 1959), 53–54; Sergievskii, *Partiia russkikh sotsial-demokratov*, 44–45; Sergievskii, introduction to *"Rabochii,"* 8.

[26] M. E. Berezin et al., "Vospominaniia iz zhizni narodnicheskikh kruzhkov v Kazani (1875–1892 gg.)," *Katorga i ssylka*, no. 10 (71) (1930): 125; *Obzor vazhneishikh doznanii*, 13 (1888): 35–37; GARF f. 102, 3 d-vo, 1893, d. 467, 10ob., 25ob.; GARF f. 102, 3 d-vo, 1893, d. 91, 13osb.; Breitfus, "Tochiskii i ego kruzhok," 330.

[27] See, for example, Iu. M. Steklov, *Bortsy z sotsializm: Ocherki iz istorii obshchestvennykh i revoliutsionnykh dvizhenii v Rossii* (Moscow, 1918), 263–64; RGIA f. 1405, op. 88, d. 10026 (1887), ll. 6ob.–7. Police found 100 copies of *Kto chem zhivet?*" marked "izd. Rabochei arteli 1885," in a workers' apartment. See J. Frankel, "Roots of 'Jewish Socialism' (1881–1892): From 'Populism' to 'Cosmopolitanism'?" in *Imperial Russia, 1700–1917: State, Society, Opposition. Essays in Honor of Marc Raeff*, ed. Ezra Mendelsohn and Marshall S. Shatz (DeKalb, IL, 1988), 255.

[28] Pankratov, "Iz deiatel'nosti sredi rabochikh," 238.

[29] G. N—in, "Iz zhizni rabochikh," 208; Veden'ev, "V Khar'kovskikh revoliutsionnykh kruzhkakh," 102; L. V. Freifel'd, "Iz zhizni narodovol'cheskikh organizatsii kontsa 80-kh godov," in Iakimova-Dikovskaia et al., *Narodovol'tsy 80-kh i 90-kh godov*, 146.

an extraordinary impression. Whenever his mother left the room, he would feast his eyes on the "fairly crudely drawn pictures," which fascinated him: he "was especially impressed that the author was not afraid to portray the tsar as a thief and by doing so tell the truth about a personage that up to then most people had considered holy and whom the priests taught should be respected as God on earth."[30] In this rare description of a worker's reaction to a specific work of propaganda literature, we see the impact made by the brochure itself as an object. Not only was the booklet itself illegal, the illustrations daringly depicted the forbidden and mocked the sacred. This example serves to illustrate Roger Chartier's argument on the importance of a book's appearance, and the way it is used by readers, as well as its intellectual content.[31]

The discipline known in the 19th century as political economy is defined in one Russian source as "the science studying those social relationships of people arising from their economic activity."[32] Political economy, as it evolved from the writings of Smith, Malthus, and Ricardo through the 19th century, was the intellectual aspect of the European Industrial Revolution, central to the analysis of the new economic and social relations of a modernizing society. Presented as "science," these professedly neutral writings were used to justify the limitations and exploitative elements of industrial capitalism. Ricardo's "Iron Law of Wages," for example, explained why workers' wages would always be low; there could be no more hope of changing this than of modifying the law of gravity. The assumptions of political economy, however, were soon challenged by others (including Owen, Fourier, Blanc, Proudhon, and Marx and Engels) who, countering capitalism with socialism, criticized the new economic regime and proposed a society based on a new order. From the 1860s, political economy was considered a basic subject for well-read members of the radical intelligentsia, who showed great interest in all the standard Western works, as well as those of Russian writers. Study

---

[30] Shapovalov, *Po doroge k marksizmu*, 62–63. Further information on this edition of *The Clever Trick* is lacking.

[31] See Chartier, *On the Edge of the Cliff*, 82: "In print writings … the format of the book, its page layout, the ways the text is divided, and the typographical conventions all have an 'expressive function' and contribute to the construction of meaning.… By giving structure to the unconscious in reading (or listening), they support the work of interpretation. Thus both the imposition and the appropriation of the meaning of a text depend on material form whose modalities and treatment, long held to be without significance, delimit the intended or possible ways to comprehend the text."

[32] M. Sobolev, "Politicheskaia ekonomiia," in F. A. Brokgauz and I. A. Efron, *Entsiklopedicheskii slovar'* (St. Petersburg, 1898), 24: 305. Compare the definition in *Encyclopedia Britannica*: J. K. L. [John Kells Ingram], "Political Economy," in *Encyclopedia Britannica*, 9th ed. (New York, 1885), 19: 346–47.

circles of radical gymnasium and university students throughout Russia followed a generally accepted "countercurriculum" in their readings outside the officially approved course of study. The best known study guides were the "Odessa" and "Cheliabinsk" catalogs, as they were known: lengthy lists of recommended reading that circulated illegally. Works by Adam Smith and Ricardo, Nikolai Chernyskevskii's edited translation of John Stuart Mill's *Principles of Political Economy*, the first volume of Marx's *Capital*, and articles by such Russian popularizers of Marx as Nikolai Ziber are among those included.[33]

Students and others involved in revolutionary propaganda considered knowledge of political economy, the analysis and criticism of the capitalist system produced by the best minds of the day, essential to convey to workers. The primary vehicle was the workers' circle, in which popularized versions of the critique of political economy in Russian were read and discussed, with helpful commentary by the propagandist. Ivan Popov, a graduate of the Petersburg Teachers' Institute and member of the People's Will workers' group in 1882–84, put his teaching experience to work as a leader of workers' study sessions. He writes: "We … took as our point of departure the tenets of scientific socialism, with K. Marx and N. G. Chernyshevskii's *Notes* as the foundation. If the workers turned out to be … sufficiently developed people, we … introduced them to the history of literature, the basis of political economy, the situation of the working class and the peasantry here in Russia and abroad."[34] When one of the members of Blagoev's social democratic group was arrested in 1886, police seized from his apartment nine copies of a hectographed work entitled *Introduction to History and Political Economy*—apparently a program used for propaganda. The first lecture for "prepared" workers (actually covering enough material for several sessions) included the topic of political economy. Beginning with the "'political economy' of Karl Marx," this section also includes *Wage Labor and Capital* by Marx, Chernyshevskii's *Notes on Mill*, and Johann Most's *Capital and Labor*, as well as *The Clever Trick*.[35] Political

---

[33] See *Katalog sistematicheskogo chteniia* [Odessa catalog], 2nd ed. (Odessa, 1883), 27–28; and *Sistematicheskii ukazatel' luchshikh knig i zhurnal'nykh statei (1856–1883 g.)* [Cheliabinsk catalog] (Cheliabinsk, 1883), 13–15.

[34] I. I. Popov, "Revoliutsionnye organizatsii," 55–57.

[35] GARF f. 102, 3 d-vo, d. 91, l. 13; RGIA f. 1405, op. 87, 1886, d. 10143, l. 65. N. K. Sergievskii, a historian of the revolutionary movement writing in the early Soviet period, makes a fairly convincing case for identifying this document with a program partially reprinted in the journal *Krasnaia letopis'*, no. 7 (1923): 275–84 (Sergievskii, *Partiia russkikh sotsial-demokratov*, 139–41). He implies that he saw the whole document in the archives, although he gives no citation. While the identification is thus not absolutely certain, I conclude from internal evidence that a good case can be made for its having originated in the group of Petersburg Social Democrats.

economy was one of the ten points in the detailed program drawn up for propagandists from the Brusnev group (of Petersburg social democrats, in the early 1890s).[36] An abbreviated version of the "Brusnev program" was used in one of the circles, made up of metal workers at the Baltic shipbuilding and mechanical plant on Vasilievskii Island. According to one of the members, workers found political economy, which apparently entailed reading *Capital*, the most difficult subject. A copy of the tome circulated among the workers, but they found it hard to make headway with this difficult text. The workers themselves devised a method for attacking this subject, by taking turns at questions and answers.[37]

The historiography of the Russian revolutionary movement tends to emphasize conflict and contrast between competing ideological currents: People's Will vs. Black Repartition, later Populist vs. Marxist. While often the subject of heated debate among radical *intelligenty* (in cities where groups of more than one tendency existed), such distinctions were much less marked when it came to circle studies with workers, at least until the 1890s. As noted above, programs of study were virtually identical, whether drawn up by groups calling themselves *narodovol'tsy* or social democrats. Terrorism was not a topic debated in workers' circles (although some workers did associate the People's Will with terror), and circles of all shades in the late 19th century made use of Marx or Marxist concepts in the teaching of political economy. In the 1880s *narodovol'tsy* read *Capital* and other Marxist works in student circles and presented these ideas in workers' circles as well. According to one activist of the early 1880s, workers in his group were familiar with the contents of the first volume of *Capital* (as expounded in the works of the Russian economist Nikolai Ziber) and the *Communist Manifesto*.[38] Throughout the late 19th century, we come across radicals who were drawn to the movement primarily from a desire to work with and teach workers. This motivation, which could almost be called pedagogical, seemed, in the case of this cohort of propagandists, to override other aspects of revolutionary activity and may in part account for this striking uniformity of programs for use in workers' circles. In any case, the radicalizing effect of the study of political economy was recognized by all, including police and government officials. In presenting its case against

---

[36] This program is reprinted in full in Pankratova and Ivanov, *Rabochee dvizhenie v Rossii*, 3, ch. 2, 131–32.

[37] Norinskii, "Moi vospominaniia," 10–11; Fomin, "Vospominaniia o podpol'noi rabote," 189–90.

[38] See M. Ol'minskii, "Davnie sviazi," in Norinskii et al., *Ot gruppy Blagoeva k "Soiuzu Bor'by,"* 68; M. V. Bramson, "Otryvki iz vospominanii (1883–1886 gg.)," in Dikovskaia-Iakimova, *Narodovol'tsy posle 1-go marta*, 86; Valk, "Molodaia partiia," 98.

the Odessa People's Will group in the early 1880s, the government described methods of propaganda activity in detail, noting the presentation of basic principles of political economy, and the form it took:

> When presenting historical events and the laws of political economy, the forms of state government in Western Europe were portrayed in glowing outlines, while the deficiencies of our state and social order were pointed out and hostility toward the rich and the upper classes was instilled.... [T]heir precarious economic situation was explained to the workers, the immediate cause of which was explained as the high taxes. The only way out would be an open uprising against the government.[39]

Propagandists often found workers to be quite interested in economic questions and workers' immediate situation. One *narodovolets* of the early 1880s recollected: "From personal experience we knew that political questions interested workers less ... than questions of economics."[40] How did revolutionaries from the intelligentsia approach the task of presenting political economy to workers, popularizing Marx and other theorists they were reading and discussing in their own circles in a way that would be accessible to workers? This kind of literature called for a more straightforward style than that of the *skazki*. These works revealed the system of exploitation that bound workers and more generally the lower classes to their impoverished position in society. Radicals assumed that an understanding of how the economy worked to benefit the upper classes would lead workers to the desired goal of revolution and the construction of a new, socialist society. As such, these works were illegal ones, with the usual penalties for possession. The three works of political economy most frequently used in propaganda among workers were *The Clever Trick, Tsar Hunger,* and *Who Lives By What?*

The first of the brochures chronologically was *The Clever Trick* (*Khitraia mekhanika*) by V. E. Varzar. The word *mekhanika* also has the sense of a mechanism, a system for doing something—in this case, exploitation of the *narod*. Although usually listed as one of the series of "*skazki*" of the 1870s, together with the *Tale of Four Brothers* and *Tale of a Kopeck*, this work is not in fact a *skazka*, lacking the distinguishing elements of the traditional tale. The booklet's title is intriguing and (perhaps purposely) ambiguous. To a casual eye, it might appear to be one of the numerous chapbooks for the *narod*. (As

---

[39] RGIA f. 1405, op. 521, d. 410, ll. 66ob.–67; and Pankratova and Ivanov, *Rabochee dvizhenie v Rossii,* 2, ch. 2, 497–98.

[40] I. I. Popov, "Revoliutsionnye organizatsii," 55.

with others, the booklet, although published illegally, was provided with false publication information and censorship approval.) One worker was able to use this ambiguity to his advantage. On trial in 1876, he claimed that he merely borrowed the book to read, thinking it would have something to do with mechanics (*po mekhanicheskoi chasti*) [!] and could not even understand the five pages he read.[41] The brochure was first printed in 1874 on the *Vpered!* press in Zurich.[42] *Vpered!*, the most important illegal periodical of the 1870s, was edited by Petr Lavrovich Lavrov, who, from his base in European emigration, had enormous influence on the revolutionary movement of the 1870s. The ideological formulation of Russian populism, or *narodnichestvo*, owed much to Lavrov, who exercised his influence through the journal *Vpered!* and other writings. He urged the young members of the intelligentsia to confront their own position of privilege and their role in the exploitation of the people, contending that a long period of propaganda among the *narod* was the necessary precondition to revolution.[43] On the theoretical spectrum of the revolutionary movement, the antipode to Lavrov's gradualist position was held by Mikhail Bakunin, the noted anarchist who believed in the creative power of destruction.[44] Impatient with Lavrov's long-term gradual path to revolution, Bakunin that felt all the conditions for a peasant uprising were at hand—a spark was all it would take to produce a revolutionary conflagration in the countryside. In the debates that ensued among activists in Russia, many proclaimed themselves the adherents of one or the other of these figures.

Vasilii Egorovich Varzar (1851–1940), while a student at the St. Petersburg Technological Institute in the early 1870s, was a member of a circle of *lavristy* (supporters of Lavrov's views). The circle's main activity, in addition to distributing radical literature and attempting to organize workers' circles, was providing support for Lavrov's journal in Switzerland, sending articles and

---

[41] *Vpered!* 15 October 1876, col. 636.

[42] According to Boris Sapir, the place of publication should be London. Boris Sapir, ed., *"Vpered!" 1873–1877: Materialy iz arkhiva Valeriana Nikolaevicha Smirnova* (Dordrecht, Netherlands, 1974), 381 n. 91.

[43] Four volumes of *Vpered!* were published in Zurich and London between 1873 and 1876. A reprint was issued in 1974: *Vpered! Neperiodicheskoe obozrenie* (The Hague, 1974). *Vpered!* was published as a newspaper in London (1874–76). On Lavrov, see Philip Pomper, *Peter Lavrov and the Russian Revolutionary Movement* (Chicago, 1972); Andrzej Walicki, *A History of Russian Thought from the Enlightenment to Marxism* (Stanford, CA, 1979), 235–44; B. S. Itenberg, *P. L. Lavrov v russkom revoliutsionnnom dvizhenii* (Moscow, 1988); and Venturi, "Bakunin and Lavrov," chap. 17 in *Roots of Revolution*.

[44] On Bakunin, see Aileen Kelly, *Mikhail Bakunin: A Study in the Psychology and Politics of Utopianism* (New Haven, 1987); N. M. Pirumova, *Bakunin* (Moscow, 1970); and Mikhail Bakunin, *Statism and Anarchy*, trans. and ed. Marshall S. Shatz (Cambridge, 1990).

correspondence for *Vpered!*, and arranging for smuggling the journal into Russia and getting it distributed.[45] In 1873 Varzar himself was sent with an exhibit to the Vienna World Exhibit by the Technological Institute. In Zurich he met Lavrov and his close collaborator V. N. Smirnov, who together ran the *Vpered!* press. Inspired, as he tells it, by Tikhomirov's *Tale of Four Brothers*, Varzar decided to write something similar for the *Vpered!* press. The result was *The Clever Trick*, first printed in Zurich in 1874.[46] Varzar participated in the movement "to the people" with two months as a village "mower,"[47] but his years as an active revolutionary came to an end with graduation. A respected statistician for over half a century, he held positions in various government departments both before and after the 1917 revolution. He was first employed as a zemstvo economist and statistician in Chernigov province, and then served in the Ministries of Finance and of Trade and Industry, where he produced the first basic works in the field of Russian industrial statistics. In the Soviet period Varzar, a noted and respected leader in his field, continued his statistical research and was engaged in teaching advanced courses as well.[48]

Referring to *The Clever Trick*, Varzar later wrote that "my first literary work as an economist ... was a lively exposition in popular form, without any falsification under the guise of 'popular language' and without special literary effects—considered necessary at the time—of the theory of direct and indirect taxes, as a form of exploitation by the ruling class."[49] This understated categorization, however, does not capture the full range of topics, the persuasive arguments, or account for the widespread appeal of this work of propaganda literature.

Interestingly, for a work of propaganda literature composed during the (presumably) peasant-focused populism of the 1870s, *The Clever Trick* from its first words draws the attention of its audience to the working-class milieu: "There's a fellow at our factory..." The narrator tells of his extremely important and informative conversations with the worker in question, one Stepan, and

---

[45] I. G. Kuliabko-Koretskii, *Iz davnikh let: Vospominaniia lavrista* (Moscow, 1931), 114.

[46] V. E. Varzar, "Vospominaniia starogo statistika," *Donskoi statisticheskii vestnik (Organ Donskogo statisticheskogo biuro)* (Rostov-na-Donu) 3, 7–9 (1924): 7.

[47] Kuliabko-Koretskii, *Iz davnikh let*, 114.

[48] See biographical entries on Varzar in *Entsiklopedicheskii slovar' Russkogo bibliograficheskogo instituta Granat*, 7th ed., 7, col. 602; *Bol'shaia Sovetskaia entsiklopediia* (Moscow, 1927), 8, cols. 798–99; and *Bol'shaia Sovetskaia Entsiklopediia*, 3rd ed. (Moscow, 1971), 4, 301. See also Varzar's interesting memoirs, "Vospominaniia starogo statistika," in which he details the employment difficulties caused by the label of "untrustworthiness" that shadowed him during years of government reaction in the 1880s and 1890s.

[49] Varzar, "Vospominaniia starogo statistika," 7.

the brochure begins with a description of the latter's personality, expressed in admiring and colloquial detail. Stepan is "goodhearted, even affectionate, when dealing with his fellow worker; but if he gets into a skirmish with the supervisor or even the director—then there's trouble! His tongue is sharp like a razor! He's got an answer for everything, and the bosses end up covered with embarrassment. He's as wise as Solomon—that's what! Ask him about anything—he's an expert: not only in witty remarks, but in telling it like it is. In a word—a man who can take care of business. He examines, questions, noses about in everything—only then is he ready to say what's at the heart of the matter; and his answer cuts to the point. And where hasn't he been, what people hasn't he mingled with! He's even made the acquaintance of young noblemen: from them he learned to read, write, and all kinds of knowledge. It happens that you read a book, you ask: "What's this book say, Stepan?"— And, he says, "It's like this!" And as he spells it out, your ears are swallowing everything: it's so clear, everything's spread before your eyes. And we loved and respected him for this" (156).[50]

Stepan is heroic, a reassuring defender of the common worker and passionate fighter of injustice: described in this way, Varzar probably intended to prime the reader to accept "Stepan's" analysis and conclusions. The information is conveyed at second hand, as the narrator (named Andrei, we learn) relates to his audience what he learned from Stepan. Andrei, it seems, serves as the representative of the working-class reader. His reactions anticipate those of the audience, as they are presented with new and at times hard to believe information about the economy and a new way of looking at Russian society. As with other illegal pamphlets, this one not only presents information but serves as an example of how to instruct others. Stepan's character is not beside the point—he is not cowed by the bosses, not passive, timid, or discouraged. Andrei's conversations with Stepan are reproduced in dialogue form. The key conversation takes place in a tavern, where our protagonists are drinking tea. The dialogue is conducted in the presumed colloquial speech of the peasant, liberally sprinkled with folk sayings. Stepan directs sarcastic barbs at the exploiters: the nobles, merchants, *kulaks*, even the tsar, and at times cannot restrain himself from cursing them, which initially makes Andrei very uncomfortable. Similarly, the audience for *The Clever Trick* may also have found this "forbidden" language shocking. Whatever workers may have thought or said among themselves, the use of such language in a printed work must have been a novelty and underlined the illegality of the revolutionary worldview to which the audience was being introduced.

---

[50] Page references for *Khitraia mekhanika* are from the version reprinted in Bazanov, *Agitatsionnaia literatura*.

As his contribution to revolutionary literature for the *narod*, Varzar chose to focus on finances, or as the subtitle puts it, "A true account of where money comes from and where it goes." It was important for workers to understand their financial situation and the implications of the burden of taxes—one aspect of the general oppression of the *narod*. As the popularity of this brochure attests, these were the kinds of hard facts that workers appreciated, that helped them understand their impoverished situation. Sitting in the tavern over drinks, Andrei receives his first lesson in finance. "Why don't we have another one to wet our whistles?" he asks. "That wouldn't be a bad idea," Stepan responds, "if only the tsar, nobles, and merchants wouldn't stick in our throat." "What does this have to do with the tsar, or merchants? It's our money." But as Stepan explains, to Andrei's dismay, while five kopecks should get him five glasses, four of them get stolen right out from under his nose by the tsar, the owner, various nobles. Andrei doesn't get it: then they'd all be drunk. But Stepan explains that they don't drink, they just "put your money in their pocket. Understand?" Andrei does not understand—how does it work? (157). Here Stepan begins an explanation of indirect taxes, a concept workers might not be aware of, with alcohol as the main example. All those who sell alcohol must pay for a permit (*patentnyi sbor*), and they pass the cost on to the customers. Similarly with salt—you can't collect and sell salt without paying an excise tax. Tobacco is another example of an indirect tax. Andrei begins to catch on—"It's indirect all right! Pay if you want, don't pay if you don't want.… In the end it's all the same, because you just can't get by without salt, vodka, other things" (158). Stepan goes on to note other taxes people might pay without realizing—stamped paper for official business, customs tax for machines imported by merchants, for example a spinning machine sent from England ("there is such a country"—159). All of this ends up coming out of the peasant's pocket. Andrei objects that even the rich eat salt and drink vodka—don't they pay too? Yes, Stepan answers, of course they pay: "but it all amounts to dry spit" (159) compared to the burden on the *muzhiki* (peasants). These items, he explains, make up a bigger part of peasant's budget, since the nobles comprise only a small percentage of the Russian population. Here we have a digression to comment on the lifestyle of the nobility—the emaciated *muzhik* stumbling home from the tavern is cursed as a drunk—while the nobles and merchants drink much more, but in a more private setting. *The Clever Trick* throughout makes extensive use of statistics to prove its points. When Andrei seems to think that nobles must pay more for alcohol, Stepan explains that the nobility as a group comprise less than 2 million people, while the "simple, black *narod*" number some 70 million, about 40 times more (160).

According to Stepan, indirect taxes are worse than direct, because people pay and don't notice. He brings in the figures—how many millions the state treasury brings in from taxes on vodka, salt—all from the peasant's pocket. Consider in addition the taxes on stamps, mining, roads and railroads, passports, etc. From all of this the government gets 230 million rubles from the peasants alone—and 20 million from the nobility. So families of peasants and *meshchane* (the urban lower-class estate) pay about 13 rubles each (161). The rich are robbing the people in broad daylight—and the poor don't even complain. He shows how any person who understands what's going on can get the details on state income—for example, how much the government gets from the import tax—all the information is published. And the "Godfearing people" (*pravoslavnyi liud*) end up paying for this through taxes on farm tools and other items they use. The nobles and merchants purchasing luxury goods have the nerve to complain that duties are too high. Here Stepan begins to curse: "Oh messieurs the rich, I wish you at the bottom of the sea!" (162). Stepan asks rhetorically, "Do the nobles plow one desiatina, do the merchants weave one piece of cloth?... Our peasant hands made everything." Rising to a peroration, Stepan enumerates: "[W]e built their stone palaces, gold-topped churches, wove their cloth, built their factories, plowed, harvested.... We do everything! We support everyone, feed and clothe everyone. Everyone lives by our labor, our sweat and blood.... Cursed devils!" (162–63).

Andrei is quite agitated by Stepan's words, he thinks he understands the "clever trick." But Stepan dismisses this as mere "everyday robbery." He's not yet through with his analysis. He next turns to direct taxes (so called because "they rob you directly, without any trickery" (164), where he deals with the tax on land and the peasants' inability to pay. To pay the arrears peasants are forced to sell their livestock—which the kulaks buy up "for a song," often in collusion with the authorities. Noting that the "tsar-batiushka" is not guiltless here, Stepan directs Andrei's attention to the Emancipation, who benefited from it, the new taxes, including the redemption payments, that came with it. His references to the tsar are sarcastic, disrespectful: so "the *muzhik* is really getting fat off freedom [*volia*].... Thanks, Little Father!" (164). This is the kind of "freedom" the tsar granted: the peasants' land is overcultivated, there's nothing to sow, they're in debt, some manage to find work elsewhere in exploitative circumstances. The peasant is ruined economically, but the kulaks and contractors profit. Stepan is so indignant he can barely sit still: "Into whose pocket do our bloody pennies slip?" (165). He reveals the existence of the state budget, printed in the newspapers, and proceeds to a breakdown of expenses, starting with those of the tsar, to whom are allocated 25,000 roubles a day—"with that you could feed half a province for a year!" (165). A basic goal of propaganda was to lead peasants to lose their (presumed) faith in the tsar as their benevolent patriarch and ruler. To this end, Varzar has Stepan address the tsar directly and disrespectfully, with the familiar *ty* form: "We believed in you, but no longer. You live in stone palaces, and your heart has become just like stone" (166). The tsar, as Stepan explains to his comrade, is himself a landowner, lord, and factory owner—why do we expect any different from him? We have only ourselves to rely on.

Discussion of the state budget leads to the topic of the state debt: 1700 million rubles. Stepan once again adduces the numbers in an effort to make such a large sum meaningful. A family of four, for example, would owe 84 rubles; just to pay the interest on the debt, each family would owe 5 rubles a year. Or—imagine that this debt is made up of silver rubles, each weighing almost 1 pud, 11 funts: if you loaded them onto railroad cars, it would take 4300 cars, and the train would be 26 versts long (167). He provides further details on government expenses (all paid from the peasant's pocket) and explains interest and the role of investors, Russian and foreign. He pays special attention to "the worst tax of all"—the recruitment of soldiers, and the training of soldiers to kill their own. Don't the people get anything, Andrei wants to know? The budget allocates a mere 760,000 rubles for schools, Stepan responds (compared to 9 million for the tsar, 170 million for the military, etc.). The extensive use of statistics in Varzar's exposition is striking, compared with other works of this genre—but perhaps not surprising in the work of a budding statistician.

This long conversation ends on a rather discouraging note: the rich will always reap the privileges of taxation, while the poor will pay. The narrator says that, since this unforgettable conversation, he's wised up considerably. He now sees that the tsar, boyars, factory owners, kulaks have constructed a mechanism for exploitation of the peasantry—and this mechanism is so clever that if you leave just a thread, the whole system will rebuild itself. When Andrei next meets up with Stepan, he's feeling pretty depressed about the situation: "everything is in our enemies' hands. ... there's nothing to be done, you might as well lie down and die!" (170). Varzar, however, feels the need to do something more than unmask the bias of the economic system: he ends *The Clever Trick* with suggestions for a better kind of society, although this section is much briefer. Stepan attempts to buoy Andrei's spirits with basic messages of the revolutionary movement: "They're just a little handful of people: we spit on them and grind them to powder. But we, *muzhiki*, are many millions...." (170). Things will be different when the people wake up. If they stop paying taxes, if the soldiers are on our side—that will be the end of their strength. Andrei objects that those with power are educated and use their knowledge to further their exploitation of the people. Stepan, however, reveals his contacts with some young nobles who are friends of the people, want to help, told him that some books showed that the "clever trick" was figured out long ago. Unfortunately, books like this are forbidden, but these young members of the educated classes learned a lot from them. Stepan read these books for himself, saw how workers in other countries managed to overcome the *mekhanika*. As further encouragement to the still doubtful Andrei, Stepan recalls Pugachev, who, with workers and Cossacks, almost seized Moscow.

The key, however, is brotherhood and communal living. Stepan explains that everyone will contribute according to his ability and receive what he needs. This socialist solution, however, will not be attained without a struggle. At some point, the *narod* will rise up, the tsar will send an army, and the formerly powerful will receive no mercy. "In the end," Stepan concludes, "we'll purge Mother Russia of all her tormentors. Then we'll set up our peasant brotherhood, freely, where there will be neither mine nor yours, neither profit nor oppression—work will be for common use amid brotherly help. We won't construct a clever trick. …. All that is false [*nepravda*] will be rooted out, and eternal truth will stand" (174).

The Clever Trick is no neutral academic treatise but rather a work of revolutionary propaganda. The concluding section of *The Clever Trick* echoes the language of *The Tale of Four Brothers*[51] and enunciates basic principles constantly reiterated in revolutionary propaganda of the period. The need for brotherhood (*bratstvo*), perhaps the most frequent watchword of socialist propaganda, is stressed. Although not developed at any length, the future society, completely at variance with the existing one, is characterized by socialist collectivism. As in other works of the period, violent revolution is necessary to overturn the existing order and destroy the people's oppressors. A *lavrovist* shading can also be seen in the work's conclusion, with its emphasis on knowledge, assistance from sympathetic members of the educated classes, and the need for workers and like-minded intelligentsia to work together as allies. Interestingly, the conclusion to *The Clever Trick* may have been something of a collective effort, unknown to the author. Varzar later noted that he was told the concluding paragraph was rewritten by Valerian Smirnov of the *Vpered!* press, and other evidence claims even further revisions, possibly by Lavrov himself.[52] These revisions may have aligned the brochure more closely with the thinking of Lavrov and others at the *Vpered!* press. In any case, Lavrov's reaction to *The Clever Trick* was quite positive. He named it as one of the brochures that was most popular with the *narod*. (He found that other titles seemed to be more often read by members of the revolutionary youth.) Lavrov also noted that these agitational works, including *The Clever Trick*, tended to be revised according

---

[51] See the concluding passage of *Gde luchshe? Skazka o chetyrikh brat´iakh i ob ikh prikliucheniiakh*, in Bazanov, *Agitatsionnaia literatura*, 294–95.

[52] Varzar, "Vospominaniia starogo statistika," 7. See Sapir, "*Vpered!*" *1873–1877*, 381–82 n. 91.

to shifts in the thinking of the revolutionary intelligentsia—for example, whether the *narod* or the radical youth would play the most decisive role in the revolution. He makes a point of emphasizing, however, that propaganda literature for the people was one aspect of the movement that remained apart from factional disagreements. While different publishing groups might make some changes, they published and disseminated the same works.[53] The use of the same readings by radical groups of different ideological persuasions was to remain a distinctive characteristic of the workers' revolutionary movement.

While taxes may seem like a dry subject to many, Varzar understood that this kind of knowledge was crucial for workers. Making no attempt to simplify, Varzar uses the same terms any educated person would be familiar with: direct and indirect taxes, customs duty, etc. As with other fields of "revolutionary pedagogy," the goal of this treatment of economics was to lead workers or peasants to see that their society did not have to be "just that way"—it was a human creation, not a fact of nature, and served certain interests. Taxation was thus explained as one vehicle for exploiting the *narod*. *The Clever Trick* also differed from other pamphlets of the 1870s in its use of statistics. Workers, probably encountering this information for the first time, may have been impressed by this appeal to logic. Workers with even a rudimentary education could follow the author's argument and, armed with these facts, workers could support their sense of injustice. Correspondence in *Vpered!* made mention of the impact this brochure was having on workers. According to a correspondent from Petersburg, the booklet was being "read to shreds," especially by skilled workers, and causing quite a stir. Even the cab drivers were reading it: "it was the topic of much discussion among them, and almost all agreed with the truth of what was written." Writing from Moscow, another correspondent was pleased to see that workers in that city were so warmly receptive to propaganda. "They read revolutionary booklets eagerly, especially *The Clever Trick*." Demand was such that at the workers' request, propagandists had to copy out 20 more copies.[54]

The Clever Trick was used for propaganda for decades—the sign of a successful work of radical literature. In addition to the various hectographed and printed editions of the 1880s and 1890s,[55] there were also significantly revised and expanded versions in the 20th century, including by the Socialist Revolutionary Party. Varzar was probably referring to one of these editions, which he "could hardly recognize," with the inclusion of such later events as the

---

[53] Lavrov, *Narodniki-propagandisty*, 136–37.

[54] *Vpered!*, 15 May 1875, no. 9, col. 269; 1 July 1876, no. 36, col. 404.

[55] See above, pp. 14–15; and Itenberg et al., *Svodnyi katalog*, 1: 54–57 (nos. 266–82), 3: 6–7 (nos. 37–41).

Russo-Japanese War.[56] A new spate of editions appeared in the revolutionary year 1917, published by various organizations.[57] With this pamphlet, Varzar, as a young economist and statistician, made a lasting contribution to the movement.

ଔ ଯ

Of the three widely-known brochures on political economy, the second, *Tsar Hunger*, was the most comprehensive in its treatment of the subject and was the only one to issue directly from a propagandist's experience leading studies in workers' circles, thus offering insight into this central institution of the workers' revolutionary movement. The work's author, Aleksei Bakh, was a native of Poltava province who had been expelled from Kiev University in 1878 for his role in student unrest. After several years in internal exile, he returned to Kiev in 1882, was readmitted to the university, and joined the local People's Will group, in which he soon became a central figure. The Kiev organization of the People's Will Party, as it called itself, was fairly well organized. Bakh headed one of the two subgroups devoted to propaganda among workers and maintained contacts with a circle of students at the theological seminary and with groups of village schoolteachers. The Kiev *narodovol'tsy* supervised a network of at least seven or eight workers' circles, including workers at the local railroad workshops, artisans, and some factory workers.[58] Bakh later wrote that he began his propaganda among Kiev workers according to the outline later presented in *Tsar Hunger*, and covered the same material in his training sessions for young propagandists who visited the workers' circles. Bakh later called these lessons in political economy "completely orthodox from a Marxist point of view."[59]

Forced to go underground to avoid arrest in February 1883, Bakh spent the next two years as a party organizer in Khar'kov, Iaroslavl', Kazan', Kiev, and Rostov-on-Don. In Kazan' Bakh again assisted a circle of radical youth

---

[56] Varzar, "Vospominaniia starogo statistika," 7.

[57] The Hoover archive includes 1917 editions by "Luch" (Petrograd), "Edinenie" (Odessa), and the All-Russian Soviet of Peasant Deputies; see also "Svobodnaia Rossiia" (Petrograd).

[58] Bakh, *Zapiski narodovol'tsa*, 2nd ed., 26–29, 33–34; "A. N. Bakh" [autobiography], in *Entsiklopedicheskii slovar' Russkogo bibliograficheskogo instituta Granat*, 7th ed., supplement to vol. 40, col. 20, and *Deiateli SSSR i revoliutsionnogo dvizheniia Rossii*, 24 (col. 20); L. S. Zalkind, "Vospominaniia narodovol'tsa," *Katorga i ssylka*, no. 3 (24) (1926): 91–93; RGIA f. 1405, op. 83, d. 11101.

[59] Bakh, *Zapiski narodovol'tsa*, 2nd ed., 32.

engaged in propaganda among workers by giving a series of lectures on political economy. Bakh relates that the local activists received the lectures enthusisastically and recognized their value as a guide for both workers and propagandists. They insisted that Bakh write out his lectures and hectographed them under the title *Tsar Hunger*.[60] Bakh later gave similar lectures for propagandists in Rostov.

Bakh's views on the task of the revolutionary were typical of a certain segment of People's Will activists. Although terrorist activity was central to the popularly perceived image of the People's Will (and still is today), Bakh, like some other members, opposed terror, which he considered a mistake. For Bakh, propaganda and organizing activity at all levels of society, including among workers, was of greater significance. This important, though often unacknowledged, strand of People's Will thought became more noticeable in the 1880s, as the party lost its earlier organizational and ideological coherence.[61]

Bakh's emphasis on the Marxist orthodoxy of his famous work was not, or not only, a retroactive attempt in Soviet times to put a politically correct spin on his earlier beliefs. The emphasis on Marx and his interpreters is not really surprising in a radical milieu dominated by the People's Will and other populists. Student populists of the 1870s had considered *Capital* an essential work, although they read it from a particular perspective, as an object lesson on the evils of capitalism, a disastrous stage of economic development that a peasant Russia could and should avoid. In the 1880s, as radical activists increasingly focused their propaganda on urban workers, many members of the People's Will developed a new perspective on the importance of the working class and began reading Marxist literature somewhat differently. The *narodovol'tsy* of the 1880s tended to accept as applicable even to Russia Marxist principles of political economy, particularly those regarding relations between capital and labor, although they resisted the idea that Russia had irrevocably entered the stage of capitalism. They also now viewed the participation of urban workers as crucial for the Russian revolutionary movement—although Russia's class structure was still not felt to mirror that of Western Europe.[62]

---

[60] Ibid., 73–74.

[61] See ibid., 176, 180–83. Bakh's perspective was much more common inside Russia than it was among members and sympathizers of the People's Will in emigration.

[62] See, for example, the views on the key role of workers in the movement of members of the St. Petersburg People's Will Workers' Group of 1882–84 in I. I. Popov, "Revoliutsionnye organizatsii," 54–55; and I. I. Popov, *Minuvshee i perezhitoe*, 92. On the close relationship between *narodovol'tsy* and Social Democrats in St. Petersburg in the mid-1880s, and a blurring of ideological boundaries, see Martynov-Piker, "Vospominaniia revoliutsionera," *Proletarskaia revoliutsiia*, no. 11 (46) (1925): 264; M. A. Braginskii, "Iz vospominanii o voenno-revoliutsionnoi organizatsii (1884–86)," in

Bakh's brochure, with its close reliance on *Das Kapital* and its attention to the situation of urban workers, reflects this critical shift in People's Will thinking.

In Bakh's hands, political economy became a weapon to unmask and excoriate the current economic system, not to uphold it. Throughout, the listener could hear the note of moral indignation as the oppressed conditions of the common people were revealed.[63] In the introduction to *Tsar Hunger*, a work of about 80 pages, Bakh appeals directly to the typical urban worker of his day, one who had begun life in the peasant village. The introduction presents themes that run as an undercurrent throughout the booklet: Tsar Hunger and his absolute control over workers' lives, the question of fate and powerlessness, and the demand for justice. The epigraph, taken from Nekrasov, was sure to have resonance for the radical reader, as Nekrasov's poems of social conscience enjoyed great popularity among the left and liberal intelligentsia. Several were used as revolutionary literature, including "The Railroad," which was reprinted, in a somewhat modified version, in an illegal poetry collection that circulated in the 1870s.[64] The poem shows the price at which progress, symbolized by the railroad, is bought—the age-old exploitation of the Russian people. The poet raises the question of who built the railroad: Was it Nicholas I's minister Count Kleinmikhel, as the general riding in the luxury of the train carriage maintains, or was it the starved and frozen toilers whose bones lay alongside the tracks? Although the poem was not originally directed to workers, it was frequently used for propaganda purposes and was read in workers' circles.

The introduction brings out what Bakh and his comrades saw as the basic contradiction in society, that between the poor and the rich, those who labor "till they sweat blood … and die like flies of … disease" and those who live in idle luxury (11).[65] Indicting the entire system, the author asks, "Where is justice?" (2). Then he tells the story of a typical worker's hard life, addressing

---

Iakimova-Dikovskaia, *Narodovol'tsy 80-kh i 90-kh godov*, 126; Braginskii, *DRDR* 3, vyp. 1, col. 405.

[63] On the key theme of human rights and dignity in the thinking of Russian workers, see Mark D. Steinberg, "Worker-Authors and the Cult of the Person," in *Cultures in Flux: Lower-Class Values, Practices, and Resistance in Late Imperial Russia*, ed. Stephen P. Frank and Steinberg (Princeton, NJ, 1994), 168–84; and Steinberg, *Moral Communities: The Culture of Class Relations in the Russian Printing Industry, 1867–1907* (Berkeley, CA, 1992), chaps. 3 and 4.

[64] See Zakharina, *Golos revoliutsionnoi Rossii*, 34–35, 90–91. This version is reprinted in *Vol'naia russkaia poeziia vtoroi poloviny XIX veka*, ed. S. A. Reiser and A. A. Shilov (Leningrad, 1959), 243–45.

[65] All references to *Tsar-golod* are to the 1895 edition, published by the Gruppa Narodovol'tsev: *Tsar-golod (Gruppa Narodovol'tsev, 1-go maia 1895 g.)*, 79 pp.

himself directly to the worker, using details and language with which the reader or listener could identify: as soon as you are born,

> sorrow and misfortune lie in wait for you.... For example, you're a peasant's son. When you're four years old you already feel the yoke on your neck. You want to run and play; no, they give you a switch and make you pasture the geese.... You turn eight years old... You want to go to school—it's merry there with the kids.... [But] your dad had a poor harvest and there's heaps of taxes and arrears and nothing to pay them with and many mouths to feed. He struggles with [this] like a fish against ice.

His young son must go to work at a match factory opened by the neighboring nobleman, and so on (2).

Bakh's approach in the introduction is personal, not abstract, and he tells his tale of the worker's life in simple, vivid, and colloquial language, the language of the *narod*: the common man, a "poor devil," is forced to "knock about the world"; if he's lucky some factory machine will not "wring his neck"; factory owners frequently "give workers the sack." Folk sayings are inserted for expressiveness: the rich "live high on the hog" ("tem ne zhizn' a maslianitsa!" [sic]); "this isn't the half of it" ("eto vse tsetochki—a vot tebe i iagodki"); "you want to go work in the factory like a sinner wants to lick a hot frying pan" ("tebe na fabriku tak zhe khochet'sia, kak greshniku lizat' goriachuiu skovorodu") (2–3). Bakh also employs a religious tone, which he clearly felt would appeal to these peasant-workers. He uses expressions like "God alone knows" and "if God is merciful"; he refers to "the laws of God and man" and states that man is created in the image of God (1–4).

In ending the introduction, Bakh dwells on the theme of the worker's apparent powerlessness: Buffeted by fate, the worker has as much free will as "some chip of wood flung about by the river's current." Bakh uses language of moral condemnation, as he tries to elicit the workers' anger at their lot and calls their situation "bitter and humiliating" (4). The force that treats people this way is Tsar Hunger, but, as the author repeats throughout the book, only the evil conditions of human society give this tsar his terrible power. The introduction closes with a ray of hope: Knowledge of what is right and wrong about the present society promises to help bring human suffering to an end— this is the booklet's purpose.

Each of the nine subsequent chapters of *Tsar Hunger* focuses on a different aspect of political economy. In simple terms, Bakh provides explanations of the basic concepts central to such texts as John Stuart Mill's *Principles of Political Economy* and the first volume of *Capital*. The latter, in particular, served as

Bakh's inspiration, in both subject matter and point of view. At several points Bakh goes beyond political economy to consider the history of civilization and of the Russian social and political order. His tone is generally straightforward and pedagogical as he leads the reader/listener through a logical progression of concepts, illustrated with numerous examples. The tone of the first few chapters is not as eloquent and personal as that of the introduction, but Bakh inserts many little conversations to illustrate his points and makes liberal use of colloquial language and pithy sayings. This tone and manner fade by the later chapters, where Bakh emphasizes simple, clear explanation, with little attempt to make the presentation "folksy" or to frame his ideas in the (presumed) language of the Russian peasant-worker. The themes presented in the introduction, however, are always in the background.

Bakh begins his exposition in chapter 1 with an examination of the concept of cooperation and the formation of civil society. He asks the question: Why do people band together into communities and form a society? The answer is that people are social animals (5). Bakh describes primitive savages, at a distinct disadvantage against the natural powers of wild animals, who might even eat them: "Nature gave the bull horns, the wolf sharp teeth, the lion strong claws, and the savage—only a sharpened stick" (5–6). The savages finally have the idea of combining forces to defend themselves against wild beasts. Bakh gives two quite different explanations for this development, referring to the "law of self-preservation" (probably a reflection of the influence of Darwin and his popularizers), as well as to "the divine law that commands that every earthly creature be subordinated to man" (6). Bakh is obviously attempting to do more than explain the fundamentals of economics—he wants to answer the question of society's arrangement. Introducing the vivid image of the "pitiful naked savage" living in his hut and his struggle for survival against the wild beasts was also calculated to pique the curiosity of readers who had surely never before contemplated the isolated existence of primitive people. A propagandist could elaborate on the picture presented in Bakh's brochure and encourage his listeners to think about the virtues of cooperation.

The first chapter also discusses the concepts of division of labor, exchange, and commodities. A community or commune cannot exist in isolation any more than a wild savage can. Because climate and other conditions vary, the exchange of goods between communes becomes necessary. Bakh explains this development by reproducing the thinking of commune members: "Our swamp isn't a good place to grow grain" (8). The processes of division of labor and exchange go on within communes as well: "One man has terrible strength, can pull trees up by the roots—he'd make a great worker in the field"—but he can't stitch a pair of boots; another is so puny he cannot lift a scythe—but he can sew boots. Division of labor is the obvious solution; each does what he does best. A folk saying is interjected: "If you go after two hares, you won't catch even one" (9). Bakh's model is exchange between workers in a self-sufficient village—an idealized image of a peasant Russia of communes without exploiters or overlords.

Each of the next three chapters centers on a single basic concept, accompanied by an extended example related in colloquial style. The labor theory of value is emphasized heavily throughout Bakh's exposition of political economy, beginning with its initial presentation in chapter 2, "The Value of Commodities." Bakh illustrates the theory with a conversation between a shoemaker and a weaver who want to exchange goods. The two artisans become exasperated as they try to find the correct proportions for a fair exchange of their products. Finally, since the shoemaker needs the linen for a pair of trousers, and the weaver is "going around barefoot," an agreement is reached: Goods are valued, the chapter teaches, according to the amount of labor necessary for their production. Bakh's use of conversation adds interest to what might otherwise be a dry and abstract explanation. Reading aloud, the propagandist could take on the roles of the arguing artisans or elaborate on the text; the audience would have a vivid mental picture to go along with the chapter's lesson. Here and throughout the book, the last paragraph of the chapter sums up the major points. Chapter 3, on money, describes the dilemma of a shoemaker who needs to feed his hungry family, but the baker needs not shoes, but cloth. With the aid of rubles, a satisfactory exchange is finally worked out. The discussion that follows describes the function of money, initially in the form of gold and silver, later as paper currency, and demystifies it. Money shows the value of goods, but is also a commodity like any other. Here, too, Bakh emphasizes the labor theory of value, the labor necessary to produce a silver ruble. The shoemaker reappears in chapter 4, as a regiment of soldiers with boot soles "as thin as paper" (21) briefly flood a local market and then just as quickly move on. Here the shoemaker comes to understand supply and demand and competition.

In chapter 5, "The Working Hands," Bakh asks how the producer became separated from the product of his or her labor and was left with nothing to sell but labor power. "A long road of violence and bloodshed, hunger and suffering," he writes, led to the present situation (26). In a lengthy historical digression, the author then proceeds to tell the "sorrowful tale of humanity," tracing the development of human society from a primeval conflict between agriculturalists and forest dwellers through warfare to the formation of the state. In storybook fashion, Bakh first conjures up the picture of a peaceful agricultural commune, then recreates the debate among the people of a nearby forest commune, as they decide to use their superior physical power to plunder the rich agricultural commune. The "bold spirit" who led the forest people to victory gains authority over the others: If anyone disobeys him, his men (*druzhina*) "will learn them some sense." "In this way," the author notes, "most social power arises" (28). The leader ultimately becomes a prince and settles down to regular collection of tribute, living off the fat of the land. He eventually forgets the origins of his power—"from war and violence"—and "orders everyone to believe that his power is from God" (29).

Moving closer to home ("A thousand years ago there were many such princes in Rus'"), Bakh next discusses the growth of the Russian state and explains the rise of the Muscovite tsar and the institution of serfdom. Bakh emphasizes the unjust nature of the Emancipation of 1861. Under serfdom, land was the property of the peasant commune, although the landowner owned the peasant souls. With the Emancipation settlement the peasants were given their freedom, but the landowners took the land, "which the peasants had worked from time immemorial." The peasant's situation remained the same: "Gavrilo didn't die: a sore spot did him in!" (Ne umer Gavrilo, a boliachka ego zadavila!; 40. The peasant with an insufficient allotment had to rent land from the landowner, be hired as a landless agricultural laborer, or be forced to take a job in a factory, ever driven by the specter of Tsar Hunger. Urban artisans fare no better. With the rise of capitalism, the individual artisan is unable to compete with the larger-scale productive systems of manufacture and the factory and has nothing to sell but labor power. Bakh's presentation of the historical evolution of social and economic forms in chapter 5 shows his audience that conditions are not forever fixed and immutable. People had made history and can change it. Bakh traces the origin of political power to violence and warfare and undermines the traditional idea of the sacred authority of the tsar.

Chapter 6 elaborates on the theme of the constant conflict between capital and labor and focuses on surplus value, a concept that the author explains following Marx. Bakh takes a detailed look at the expenses of a hypothetical manufacturer of cotton chintz (setting up the factory, ordering raw cotton, and so forth) and demonstrates that the worker earns only enough for the subsistence of one family, while surplus labor provides a profit for the employer. This discussion is expanded in chapter 7 on workers' wages, which explains why the cost of living can make a worker even worse off with higher pay. Bakh compares the needs and lifestyle of the Russian worker with those of workers in Western Europe. Here the propagandist has the opportunity to compare the situation of the Russian worker to that of workers elsewhere. Implicit in the text is a profile of the typical Russian worker of the day—a recent arrival from the peasant village not yet acculturated to the modern urban industrial environment. The English worker, for example, needs "meat and coffee every day and drinks a lot of beer." The Russian worker, because of the cold and the poor food, needs a warming glass of vodka. The more educated and cultured English and German workers have greater intellectual requirements than the Russian worker, and their wages must cover the cost of books and newspapers and perhaps an occasional visit to the theater (52). Other factors affecting wages are the degree of skill and training required of the worker and the market value of wages as determined by the "iron law of wages," which also correlates with fluctuations in the working-class population. When wages fall below the amount necessary for subsistence, "Tsar Hunger and his assistant death come into their own" (55). (Bakh attributes this "iron law," popularized by the British economists of the early 19th century, to the German socialist Ferdinand Lassalle.)

Chapter 8 describes the capitalist economy, beginning with explanations of the terms *capital* and *capitalist*. Bakh shows how the effects of capitalism could already be seen in Russia. Widespread peasant landlessness fostered capitalism in agriculture, turning peasants into hired hands for landowners. This process of dispossession is due, according to Bakh, not so much to economic forces, but to the *"naked force of the government, which always sides with the landowners and together with them robs the peasants … and sucks them dry!"* (60–61; italics in the original). Capitalism's effects on the worker-artisan date from the introduction of the manufacturing system, which allows the manufacturer to take full advantage of division of labor. Bakh borrows a famous example from Adam Smith (by way of Marx) to illustrate division of labor, describing the manufacture of a needle, a process involving 72 different workers: "One draws out the wire, one makes the eye, one sharpens the end, etc." (62). The resulting increase in labor productivity, however, comes at the expense of the worker who becomes adapted to this minute task and unable to do any other work: "The crippled artisan is chained to the [particular form of] manufacture that crippled him, like a convict chained to his wheelbarrow" (62–63). As industry develops, the use of machines and unskilled labor gives factory owners even more power over workers. Briefly surveying the larger picture, Bakh describes capitalism as a system in constant motion, with competition among capitalists leading to overproduction, periodic crises, and unemployment. Capitalism's tendency toward large-scale production is "a stick with two ends, both of which beat the worker": machines make the worker superfluous, and factory closings do the same (73).

The last chapter of *Tsar Hunger* describes a contrasting economic system, the socialist economy. Attempting to counteract what many propagandists viewed as the traditional passivity of the common people, the chapter begins with the declaration that problems with human causes can be remedied. Bakh makes a distinction between natural causes of hardship—for example, old age—and the suffering caused by the economic organization of society. Capitalism is not a "law of human nature," an immutable and eternal system, as its supporters claim (76–77):

> The true defenders of the working estate, the socialists, reasonably explain that nature [*priroda*] does not create some people for constant idleness, others for constant work; one belly for all the fine foods, another for bread with chaff; nature does not create capitalists and workers. It creates only people, and for this reason, in life people should be equal. And if in life we see the opposite, nature doesn't have anything to do with it. Not nature, but people created capitalism; for this reason, people can and must change it.

Socialists propose an economic system without hired labor, in which the producer will be restored to the means of production. Unlike other populists, Bakh seems to view capitalism as a progressive force, even a precondition for socialism: rather than turning the clock back to earlier times, which would be impossible in any case, socialism will build on the advances achieved by humanity at such a great cost—cooperation, division of labor, machines— and use them for the benefit of workers. The essence of socialism is that the means of production and surplus value will belong to workers: there will be no capitalists and no profit (79).

Tsar Hunger was still unfinished when Bakh was forced by the threat of arrest to leave Kazan' in February 1883.[66] For the next two decades, the pamphlet continued to circulate in underground circles in the 1883 version. It was particularly well suited for use in circle studies. Bakh's systematic presentation of basic concepts of political economy had already proven successful in his own study sessions with workers and young propagandists. The booklet's nine chapters could be used as readings for successive meetings of a circle. This approach, in fact, was taken by People's Will propagandist (and future Bolshevik) M. S. Aleksandrov (Ol'minskii), a St. Petersburg University student, in one of the workers' circles he led in the mid-1880s.[67] Other distinctive features of *Tsar Hunger* also undoubtedly contributed to its success as a work of propaganda literature: the detailed examples used to illustrate key ideas, the realistic conversations that liven up what otherwise might be dry material, and the language, which ranges from the extremely colloquial to the simple and straightforward to the emotional and personal. The oral element was always important to propaganda, and *Tsar Hunger* gave the propagandist

---

[66] Bakh, *Zapiski narodovol'tsa*, 2nd ed., 74.

[67] Ol'minskii, "Davnie sviazi," 69–70; Ol'minskii, "Iz vospominanii revoliutsionera," *Rabochii mir*, no. 4–5 (1919): 12–13.

numerous opportunities to elaborate or insert examples—for example, in the discussion of Russian history or the references to workers of other lands.

Bakh stated his views on propaganda as follows:

> I was always of the opinion that the first and only important striving of the revolutionary who was active among workers should be to develop their self-knowledge; to achieve this, it was necessary to explain to them their situation in society as a sociological whole. That workers' self-knowledge would of itself become class [self]knowledge was absolutely inevitable.[68]

For workers, *Tsar Hunger* offered what propagandists presented as "scientific knowledge," new concepts with which to think and talk about the economic system and social relations. It explained the significance of the working day and the elements of exploitation faced by factory workers, while giving them the vocabulary with which to discuss their situation and voice their grievances. Bakh's analysis also provided ammunition to disabuse workers of any hope that their economic situation might be improving (because nominal wages had gone up, for example). The booklet told them that neither the power of money nor the causes of unemployment, hunger, and the squeezing of independent artisans out of the marketplace are magical. *Tsar Hunger* appealed to the workers' sense of injustice, of right and wrong, with references to God and nature. The treatment of Russian history in chapter 5 provided a new context for understanding serfdom, and the treatment of the broader subject of the origins of political power encouraged workers to demystify and challenge authority. Little marks *Tsar Hunger* as a work of specifically People's Will propaganda; in fact it was subsequently used by both Social Democrats and *narodovol'tsy*. The influence of Bakh's reading of Marx's *Capital* is noticeable throughout, and his awareness of workers as a social class (seen especially in chapter 9) is a departure from earlier populist thinking.

Like other propaganda works, *Tsar Hunger* can be seen as furthering the relation between the revolutionary intelligentsia and workers, a means of communication and a way to initiate dialogue. While such works can be examined to determine the ideas that the radicals presented to workers and how they were expressed, what workers took away from these works is much more difficult to determine. While direct evidence on workers' responses to *Tsar Hunger* is scarce, information on its dissemination indirectly confirms its role in the revolutionary movement. Numerous references in sources on the revolutionary movement attest to the work's continuous popularity through

---

[68] Bakh, *Zapiski narodovol'tsa*, 2nd ed., 32–33.

the 1880s and 1890s. The booklet was used in circle studies by both Social Democrats and *narodovol'tsy* and circulated for the most part in manuscript, hectographed, and lithographed form. As an illegal work, *Tsar Hunger* was noted in police records made at the time of arrest. Possession of a copy was almost a sure sign of involvement in propaganda among workers, as it was not part of the standard reading list for members of the radical intelligentsia, to whom more "advanced" works on political economy were accessible. A few examples drawn from memoir and archival sources will help to illustrate the widespread dissemination and use of *Tsar Hunger*.

People's Will activist Nikolai Evstifeev had been involved in attempts to found a workers' union in St. Petersburg in 1887. When he was arrested, 40 unbound copies of *Tsar Hunger* were found in his apartment. A copy of the work was also discovered when the *narodovolets* Ivan Gilgenberg was searched and arrested in 1888. The Moscow People's Will group of 1885–86 lithographed *Tsar Hunger* and included it in their library of propaganda literature for workers. The work remained quite popular in Kazan', its town of origin, where it went through at least one hectograph and one lithograph edition and was used in propaganda by local People's Will members and populists. It was also read by workers in other provincial centers, including Ivanovo-Voznesensk and Khar'kov.[69] Members of early social democratic groups in Russia thought highly of Bakh's work. In 1886 the Party of Russian Social Democrats, the first social democratic group founded inside Russia (headed initially by Dmitrii Blagoev) chose *Tsar Hunger* as one of the few works to be printed on its printing press, in an edition of 200 copies. For conspiratorial reasons, the other Petersburg social democratic group of the mid-1880s, the Association of St. Petersburg Workingmen (organized by Pavel Tochisskii), did not favor the distribution of illegal literature to workers. Yet it made *Tsar Hunger* one of the few exceptions to this rule. The Association's collection of illegal literature included ten or twelve copies of the brochure, hectographed by a member who later wrote of the brochure's popularity among workers.[70]

---

[69] RGIA f. 1405, op. 88, d. 10094, 69ob.; GARF f. 102, 3 d-vo 3, d. 334, 3–4ob.; K. Tereshkovich, "Pamiati trekh druzei," in *Iakutskaia tragediia 22 marta (3 aprelia) 1889 goda: Sbornik vospominanii i materialov*, ed. M. A. Braginskii and Tereshkovich (Moscow, 1925), 134–35. See S. Livshits, "Ocherki istorii Kazanskoi sotsial-demokratii (1888–1916 gg.)," *Puti revoliutsii*, no. 1 (March 1922): 92, 112; Livshits, "Podpol'nye tipografii 60-kh, 70-kh i 80-kh godov," *Katorga i ssylka*, no. 2 (51) (1928): 73; Berezin et al., "Vospominaniia iz zhizni narodnicheskikh kruzhkov," 125. On Ivanovo-Voznesensk in the early 1890s, see S. P. Shesternin, *Perezhitoe: Iz istorii rabochego i revoliutsionnogo dvizhenii 1880–1900 gg.* (Ivanovo, 1940), 99; on Khar'kov in the mid-1880s, see Veden'ev, "V khar'kovskikh revoliutsionnykh kruzhkakh," 103; see also RGIA f. 1405, op. 90, d. 10847, l. 76.

[70] GARF f. 102, 3 d-vo, d. 467, 10ob., 25ob.; d. 91, 13ob. The member was Andrei Breitfus ("Tochiskii," 330).

The circulation of *Tsar Hunger* increased in 1895, when a fairly large edition (400 to 500 copies according to one source, 1500 according to another) was printed by the Petersburg Group of Narodovol'tsy on their underground press in nearby Lakhta. The title recurs in police reports and workers' accounts of the movement of the mid-1890s as one of the most widespread propaganda works in Petersburg. The brochure was circulated by members of the social democratic St. Petersburg Union of Struggle for the Emancipation of the Working Class, who made use of publications issued by the Group of Narodovol'tsy. It was studied in circles of the more politically active workers sponsored by the Union and reached a much larger audience of workers during the organizing effort that accompanied the Petersburg textile strikes of the summer of 1896. During the same period, *Tsar Hunger* was also read and distributed to workers by the Social Democratic Workers' Unions in Moscow and Ivanovo-Voznesensk and was circulating among workers' circles in Kiev as well.[71]

In the early years of the 20th century, revised editions of *Tsar Hunger* met the needs of a new phase in the revolutionary movement. In 1902 the Socialist Revolutionary Party published a revised and expanded version, prepared by Bakh himself, in a 10,000-copy edition. The introduction explained the need for a new edition: "At present, when propaganda activity among urban workers and the peasantry has taken on especially broad dimensions, the need for a popular exposition of political economy [is] felt especially strongly."[72] In line with Socialist Revolutionary devotion to propaganda among peasants as well as workers, this edition of *Tsar Hunger* examined the situation of the peasantry more closely by expanding on capitalism's negative effect on agriculture and the peasantry (chapter 8) and adding material on the crisis of village handicraft industry (chapters 5, 6, 8). Bakh also added references to the role of the state in the capitalist system. The revised chapter 3, on money, provided an appropriate context for fresh comments on the condition of the state treasury and Russia's foreign trade problems; in chapter 6, on surplus value, Bakh explained where the workers' taxes went—to support the govern-

---

[71] See Kudelli, *Narodovol'tsy na pereput'i*, 13; Shapovalov, *Po doroge k marksizmu*, 62; N. E. Smirnov, "Cherty iz zhizni lakhtinskoi tipografii," in Iakimova-Dikovskaia, *Narodovol'tsy 80-kh i 90-kh godov*, 198; GARF f. 102, 7 d-vo, d. 257, l. 198. See also "Doklad po delu o voznikshikh v Peterburge v 1894 i 1895 godakh prestupnykh kruzhkakh lits, imenuiushchikh sebia "Sotsial-demokratami,'" in *Sbornik materialov i statei* (Moscow, 1921), 1: 96–97, 99; and GARF f. 102, 7 d-vo, d. 319, t. 1, l. 266ob.; t. 2, l. 239; GARF f. 124 (MIu), op. 5, d. 2/1896, 237a, 238, 272ob. On distribution in Moscow and Ivanovo-Voznesensk, see Pankratova and Ivanov, *Rabochee dvizhenie v Rossii*, 4, ch. 1, 388, 443, 493.

[72] Partiia Sotsialistov-Revoliutsionerov, *Tsar-golod* (n.p., 1902), 2. See "A. N. Bakh" [autobiography], cols. 21, 24.

ment and the army and to aid landowners and manufacturers, leaving the workers with little benefit.[73] Finally, Bakh took the opportunity to give a fuller description of the socialist economy in the last chapter, which had been left unfinished in the original version. He made his case for the feasibility and rationality of socialism and demonstrated the increased productivity of labor, the improved working conditions, and the new opportunities for spiritual and social progress that would result from "the fall of the kingdom of Tsar Hunger": "Freed from the grip of involuntary labor, man will remember that 'man does not live by bread alone'.... Only then will the flame of the thirst of knowledge burn in all people, only then ... will the human mind ... penetrate all the secrets of nature." The revised version ends with a call for laboring people to realize their strength, to "rise up like a hero of old, throw off the tsarist, landowner, and merchant scum that sucks its blood, and with proudly raised head enter the new kingdom of labor and freedom!"[74]

Between 1905 and 1907 *Tsar Hunger* appeared in several new legal editions under the title *Ekonomicheskie ocherki*, and sometimes with the author's name. Comparison of the Rostov-on-Don edition published by Donskaia Rech´ in 1906 with the 1902 edition reveals a superficial attempt to disguise the booklet's identity. The telltale epigraph is omitted, and throughout the work reference to Tsar Hunger is reduced simply to hunger. In places, the radicalism of the original is toned down, particularly in criticism of the Russian government and in the discussion of socialism. (Chapter 9 is retitled "Social Economy" rather than "Socialist Economy.")[75]

At the time of the 1917 revolution new editions appeared in Moscow, Petrograd, Odessa, and Smolensk, and a Ukrainian edition was published in New York. Most of these editions follow those of either 1902 or 1906, with the noteworthy exception of the version published by the Socialist Revolutionary press Zemlia i Volia in Moscow in 1917. This version, expanded by some 150 pages, examines the social, in addition to the economic, effects of capitalism, with a section analyzing the teachings of Marx and Engels on capitalist development in light of recent history. According to his biographers, this version was also written by Bakh and represented a third reworking of his ideas.[76]

---

[73] *Tsar-golod* (1902), 57.

[74] Ibid., 106–07.

[75] A. N. Bakh, *Ekonomicheskie ocherki* (Rostov-na-Donu, 1906).

[76] A. N. Bakh, *Ekonomicheskie ocherki* (Moscow, 1917). See L. A. Bakh and A. I. Oparin [his daughter and his protégé], *Aleksei Nikolaevich Bakh: Biograficheskii ocherk* (Moscow, 1957), 105. Other 20th-century editions are listed in the bibliography of Bakh's works in *Aleksei Nikolaevich Bakh*, with an introduction by A. I. Oparin and N. M. Sisakian,

Bakh's life, in the years following the first hectographed edition of *Tsar Hunger*, took some interesting turns. He remained active in the revolutionary underground in the mid-1880s as a respected figure, known by the pseudonym of "Kashchei [Bessmertnyi]" (among others), trying desperately to resurrect some kind of People's Will network, but was forced to leave Russia in 1885, for good as it then seemed, to avoid arrest. Bakh had always felt torn between two divergent paths: that of scientific scholarship and that of the revolutionary movement. The latter had taken precedence in his early years. Now, first in Paris, and then in Geneva, he turned to science, engaging in research in biochemistry on such processes as oxidation and fermentation. He eventually received a doctorate from the University of Lausanne. He returned to Russia in 1917 and within a few years was setting up the biochemical laboratory at Vysshii Sovet Narodnogo Khoziaistva (VSNKh; Supreme Soviet of the National Economy). He went on to become a noted scientific leader, honored as the founder of Soviet biochemistry, and was an organizer of support by scientists for Stalin's program.[77] As he put it in a speech on the occasion of his 80th birthday jubilee, he felt he had found under the Soviet regime a way to reconcile his desire to work toward his two life goals: scientific progress and improvement for people's lives in a socialist society.[78] During World War II he was evacuated with other members of the Academy of Sciences to Central Asia, and he spent two years in Frunze, Khirghiz SSR. He died in 1946 at the age of 89, a recipient of the Stalin Prize, the Order of Lenin, and other honors.[79]

The model Soviet biography presented in most official sources and in his memoirs, however, leaves out or underplays some intriguing information. The fact that Bakh was Jewish by birth is noted in only one encyclopedia, and does not appear in others;[80] he makes no mention of this in his memoirs, which

---

and bibliography compiled by O. A. Gubyrina, Materialy k biobibliografii uchenykh SSSR, Seriia biokhimii, vyp. 1 (Moscow–Leningrad, 1946).

[77] See Michael David-Fox, *Revolution of the Mind: Higher Learning among the Bolsheviks, 1918–1929* (Ithaca, NY, 1997), 246 ; and Bakh and Oparin, *Aleksei Nikolaevich Bakh*, 128–30.

[78] Bakh and Oparin, *Aleksei Nikolaevich Bakh*, 165–66.

[79] For biographical information on Bakh, see, in edition to his memoirs noted above, entries in *Bol'shaia Sovetskaia Entsiklopediia* (Moscow, 1927), 5: cols. 91–92; *BSE*, 3rd ed. (Moscow, 1970), 3: 51; "Bakh, Aleksei Nikolaevich," *DRDR* 3, vyp. 1, cols. 220–23. See also B. Koz'min, "K istorii 'Molodoi Rossii': Zapiska A. N. Bakha 1886 g.," *Katorga i ssylka*, no. 6 (67) (1930): 51–60; Bakh and Oparin, *Aleksei Nikolaevich Bakh*.

[80] *DRDR* 3, vyp. 1, col. 220, "Bakh, Abram Litmanovich (posle kreshcheniia Aleksei Nikolaevich), evrei iz meshchan...."

begin in 1878 with his university years,[81] although he was born in Poltava province, in the Jewish Pale of Settlement. (I surmise that his conversion may have been on the occasion of his marriage.) After fleeing Russia in the mid-1880s, he did not break all contacts with the revolutionary movement. In the early 1900s he was peripherally involved in the setting up of the Socialist Revolutionary Party, which he apparently joined in 1905. He was something of a link between SR organizations in Russia and the émigré leadership in Europe, and the fact that he was chosen by the SR Party to head the commission to investigate the extent of the damage caused by the double agent Azef speaks to the high regard in which he was held.[82] When he returned to Russia during the Revolution he was still an SR: the question of when he left that party remains murky in the sources. Given his background, especially his role as an SR (and at least one article written in 1918 that was highly critical of Lenin),[83] his survival as a loyal and respected scientific leader is a somewhat curious one, in light of the fate suffered by so many of his old revolutionary colleagues in the 1930s.

A third brochure played a key role in introducing workers to the principles of political economy. While attending an evening school for workers in Petersburg in the late 1880s, Vasilii Shelgunov was given *Capital* to read by a radical worker. When it proved too difficult, the same worker gave him *Who Lives By What?* (*Kto chem zhivet?*) instead. Shelgunov later wrote: "This booklet, in a simple and comprehensible manner, explained what capitalists are, how they exploit workers, and who lives by what." Shelgunov later found this pamphlet very useful in his own propaganda among less-educated workers, who often believed that capitalists did workers a favor by giving them wages, a means to survive. This pamphlet was effective in showing these workers the true state of affairs—that workers gave the capitalists a means to live.[84] *Kto chem zhivet?*,

---

[81] A. N. Bakh, *Zapiski narodovol'tsa* (Moscow–Leningrad, 1929), 3.

[82] The Bakhmeteff Archive at Columbia University contains half a dozen letters from Bakh to Mark Natanson, Leonid Shishko, and other veteran populists (1908–09). See also Nurit Schleifman, *Undercover Agents in the Russian Revolutionary Movement: The SR Party, 1902–14* (New York, 1988), 101. Bakh's autobiography in the supplement to vol. 40 of the *Entsiklopedicheskii slovar' Russkogo bibliograficheskogo instituta Granat* (cols. 19–25), written in 1926, seems to downplay his SR past but does refer to his links with the SR Party in the early 1900s and through 1918. At some unspecified time, he writes that he "definitively broke his connection with the organization of that party, although I considered it inappropriate to declare this publicly" (*Deiateli SSSR i revoliutsionnogo dvizheniia Rossii*, 24–27, here 27).

[83] A. N. Bakh, "Revoliutsiia i sotsializm," in *God russkoi revoliutsii (1917–1918 gg.)* (Moscow, 1918), 6–16.

[84] Shelgunov, "Rabochie na puti k marksizmu," 100.

composed by the Polish socialist Szymon Diksztajn in 1881, was translated and published by the small circle of Russian exiles in Switzerland known as the Emancipation of Labor Group. (Although comprised of only a handful of members, the group, which included Georgii Plekhanov, Pavel Aksel'rod, and Vera Zasulich, occupied a key place in Soviet historiography of the revolutionary movement as the first Russian Marxist group.) The appearance of this work represents the broadening of the revolutionary movement and its ties with the nascent Polish revolutionary and labor movements. As more groups in Russia began to identify themselves as "social democrats," Marxists on the Western model and inspired by the success of the German Social Democratic Party, *Who Lives By What?* was widely read and became arguably the most popular of the three famous pamphlets on political economy.

The origins of the Polish socialist movement came from two groups: Polish students from the Congress Kingdom and Ukrainian provinces who had organized at Russian universities, then returned home to the tsarist Poland when arrests and trials of revolutionaries began in Russia; as well as from circles of radical students in Warsaw in the late 1870s who wanted to create a party with the goal of worker propaganda. Ideological influences on Polish socialism in its early stages included anarchism and Russian populism, as well as Lassalle and Marx and Engels. Contacts with the Russian revolutionary movement, especially the People's Will, and the impact of strikes and labor unrest in the Congress Kingdom contributed to the outlook of Polish radicals. The development of the movement was further complicated by the existence, almost from the movement's inception, of factions with opposing outlooks: Polish nationalist vs. international socialism.[85]

Szymon Diksztajn, born in 1858 into the family of an impoverished Jewish merchant in Warsaw, was an exceptionally gifted student and graduated from Warsaw University in 1878. Together with Ludwik Warynski (the acknowledged leader) and others, he became one of the organizers of the movement which culminated with the founding of the "Proletariat" (1882–84), an organization identifying with Western Marxism and, as its name proclaimed, hoping to provide leadership for a workers' movement as well. Forced to leave Poland, Diksztajn took up residence in Geneva, where he developed close ties with

---

[85] For a comprehensive analysis of this topic, see Naimark, *History of the "Proletariat."* On the early history of the socialist movement in Poland, see also I. S. Iazhborovskaia and N. I. Bukharin, *U istokov pol'skogo sotsialisticheskogo dvizheniia* (Moscow, 1976); Lucjan Blit, *The Origins of Polish Socialism: The History and Ideas of the First Polish Socialist Party 1878–1886* (Cambridge, 1971); A. M. Orekhov, *Stanovlenie pol'skogo sotsialisticheskogo dvizheniia: Struktura, programmnye kontseptsii, deiateli (1874–1893)* (Moscow, 1979); T. G. Snytko, *Russkoe narodnichestvo i pol'skoe obshchestvennoe dvizhenie 1865–1881 gg.* (Moscow, 1969); *Ocherki po istorii sotsialisticheskogo dvizheniia v russkoi Pol'she* (Lwów, 1904).

members of the Russian Black Repartition group: Plekhanov, Aksel′rod, Zasulich, and Deich. Under the pseudonym "Jan Młot," Diksztajn wrote for
the movement's journals, and was especially noted for his translations and
popularizations of foreign works. He published a translated version of Varzar's
Clever Trick, reworked to fit the Polish context, for use in workers' circles.[86] The
first version of *Who Lives By What?*, in which key concepts of Marx's *Capital* were
presented in popular form, was published in the journal *Rownosc (Equality)* as
On Surplus Value. It soon appeared in a separate edition, supplemented by a
history of the First International, a summary of the program of the German
Social Democrats, and remarks on the importance of the Paris Commune for
the international workers' movement.[87] In the version first translated into
Russian by the Emancipation of Labor Group in 1885, *Kto chem zhivet?* enjoyed
decades of popularity in the Russian workers' movement.[88] Unfortunately, the
life of the author himself was cut short by suicide in 1884 at age 27. Russian
radicals mourned his death. An obituary that appeared in the People's Will
émigré journal *Vestnik "Narodnoi Voli"* (*Herald of the "People's Will"*) called him
"one of the most talented representatives of Polish socialism" and praised his
"outstanding literary talent."[89]

    In the early 1880s, the small group of emigrant *chernoperedel′tsy* (Black
Repartitionists) in Geneva shed their identification with Russian revolutionary
populism and, calling themselves the Emancipation of Labor Group, began
to see themselves as European-style Marxists.[90] They dedicated themselves

---

[86] Diksztajn's work was given the bland title *An Interesting Story* (*Interesnaia istoriia*)
(Iazhborovskaia and Bukharin, *U istokov pol′skogo sotsialisticheskogo dvizheniia*, 142).

[87] Orekhov, *Stanovlenie pol′skogo sotsialisticheskogo dvizheniia*, 110.

[88] Iazhborovskaia and Bukharin note that Lenin uses Diksztajn's work as an example
of useful (though old) popular literature. See the reference to V. I. Lenin, *Polnoe sobranie
sochinenii*, 5th ed. (Moscow, 1964), 46: 270, 274, in Iazhborovskaia and Bukharin, *U
istokov pol′skogo sotsialisticheskogo dvizheniia*, 256.

[89] L.T., "Shimon Dikshtein: Nekrolog," *Vestnik "Narodnoi Voli,"* no. 3 (1884): 188 (2nd
pagination). For biographical information on Diksztajn, see above works, and *BSE*,
1st ed. (Moscow, 1935), 22, col. 408; *BSE*, 3rd ed. (Moscow, 1970), 8: 263; *DRDR* 3, vyp.
2, cols. 1164–66. Several archival documents on Diksztajn are published as Appendix
14 in I. Volkovicher, *Nachalo sotsialisticheskogo rabochego dvizheniia v byvshei russkoi
Pol′she: Podgotovitel′nyi period partii "Proletariat." Opyt istoricheskogo issledovaniia*, chap.
1 (Moscow–Leningrad, 1925), 112–16. See also Lev Deich, "Pionery sotsialisticheskogo
dvizheniia v Tsarstve Polskom," *Vestnik Evropy*, bk. 4–6 (1917): 577–79.

[90] On the occasion of the 100th anniversary of the Group's founding, a number of
works on their publishing and other activities appeared. See V. Ia. Laverychev et al.,
eds., *Gruppa "Osvobozhdenie truda" i obshchestvenno-politicheskaia bor′ba v Rossii* (Moscow, 1984); I. N. Kurbatova, *Nachalo rasprostraneniia marksizma v Rossii: Literaturno-
izdatel′skaia deiatel′nost′ gruppy "Osvobozhdenie truda"* (Moscow, 1983); Deborah L.

to disseminating the argument that Marxism was the appropriate ideology for the Russian movement and published theoretical and polemical works directed toward the revolutionary intelligentsia, as well as a series of popular pamphlets, including translations, intended for propaganda among workers. The Russian version of *Who Lives By What?*, issued in the Group's Workers' Library series, was prefaced by a lengthy foreword by Plekhanov, in which he addressed Russian workers and presented a context for appreciation of this Polish work. Plekhanov used his preface as a vehicle for expanding the economic focus of the brochure by making connections with more overtly revolutionary ideas. Plekhanov begins by asking why Russian workers should be interested in this work written in Polish by Polish "rabble rousers" (*buntovshchiki*)? Plekhanov takes this opportunity to address the topic of national prejudices: Russian workers should not have the same attitude toward Polish "rebels" as the tsar, the police, and government officials. "What does the Russian working people gain from the oppression of Poland and the Poles?" (iv),[91] Plekhanov underlines, "No people can be free until it stops oppressing other peoples." An uprising (*bunt*) is not a crime, but rather a "sacred cause, when a class or a whole people rises up against violence for the sake of their happiness, their freedom, and their independence" (v). Plekhanov next brings up another concept: the booklet's author was a *socialist*, and a definition is provided: "he wanted to free working people from the oppression of kulaks, factory owners, and landowners." And he wrote this booklet to explain to workers where their social order comes from, why the mass of the population exhausts themselves with heavy labor only in order to enrich these "entrepreneurs." He emphasizes that the movement is international: the basic causes of suffering, the way to conquer them are the same for workers of all the "civilized" countries; that is why workers of different countries must unite for this great goal, "forgetting their dislike of people with different languages and customs, a viewpoint only found among wild and uneducated people" (vi). Russian workers must thus throw off their prejudices and answer the call "Proletarians of all countries, unite!" (vi; a footnote defines the foreign word *proletarian*"). The introduction concludes with a description of the author Diksztajn and his life: his birth into a poor Warsaw family, his intellectual gifts—"before him lay the peaceful and secure life of a scholar. Instead he put aside his study of zoology and gave himself to the workers' cause. He wrote for the movement, but also to make a living, "just like any proletarian" (viii). With his suicide (which Plekhanov seems to attribute to depression) the

---

Pearl, "Marxism's Russian Centennial: Soviet Scholars and the Emancipation of Labor Group," *The Russian Review* 49, 2 (April 1990): 189–98.

[91] All quotes from S. Dikshtein, *Kto chem zhivet?* (Geneva, 1885).

Polish movement lost an important member. In reading this brochure, the editor hopes that Russian workers also will have good memories of the author, who lived "for the happiness of the working class" (x). A note of tenderness underlies this description of Diksztajn: in fact, Plekhanov had known him well and "had a 'special fondness'" for him.[92]

Diksztajn begins his booklet by holding up to criticism the ideology that justified the capitalist system of rich and poor, the myth of the "self-made man," as widely disseminated in the popular book *Self-Help* (1859) by the Englishman Samuel Smiles. Smiles' work is full of examples of men who "pulled themselves up by their bootstraps," going from poverty to plenty, thanks to their own effort and cleverness. Why is this book such a best seller, asks Diksztajn? It expresses the myth that camouflages the reality of starving workers, reassuring the rich that workers don't have it so bad. If some of them die, they're the lazy, helpless ones: "'Whoever wants to work, can, and let every worker think only of himself. Every man can live and even get rich by his own labor'" (2). The rich, writes Diksztajn, would rather workers not think of how to change things. "Are these gentlemen telling the truth?" This book will closely examine the argument: is self-help the solution to improving workers' lives? (3).

Diksztajn thus frames his analysis with one of the dominant myths of capitalist political economy and illustrates one of the key functions of revolutionary propaganda: to attempt to dispel the false consciousness which had workers blindly accepting the explanations provided by the rich and powerful by providing the knowledge necessary for a true picture of how the economy functions. The 54-page booklet is divided into two sections. The first section opens with a statement of received opinion: "'Every man lives by his own labor'" and then asks: "Is that really so?" (3). This rhetorical style provides the rhythm of the book, raising questions that might occur to the worker-reader, then leading him through an analysis of statements and concepts to the author's intended understanding. "At first glance this statement seems true. Just look at all that is written and pronounced in newspapers, journals, and books, and even from the church pulpit! And doesn't it seem that the shoemaker really lives by his labor at shoemaking, the tailor at tailoring.... You may be surprised when I tell you that not a single person lives by his own labor, not the tsar and his ministers, not factory owners and merchants, and not the whole working people" (3). The author explains that due to increasing specialization, at the present time it is more correct to say that workers "support themselves" by their labor. In the past people were more self-sufficient. "Now the Warsaw shoemaker has begun to make shoes for the

---

[92] Quoted in Naimark, *History of the "Proletariat,"* 95.

Russian artisan" and so on. "From the time that production for profit and sale was introduced—no one any longer worked for himself but for others; no one lives by his own labor, but by that of other people" (6–7).

"But even that's not the whole truth." The pamphlet goes on to explain the labor theory of value: goods are valued according to the amount of labor that goes into them. (The analysis is occasionally interrupted by little objections from the supposed reader: "But that's just the same as the book *Self-Help*." "Wait a bit, don't rush with the reproaches, but listen to me.") If a worker can't set himself up in business, he must become a hired, unfree worker at a factory, obeying the factory owner. ("But factory work isn't slavery." [Oh, no?] "We know what kind of freedom that is!") And the factory owner has two powerful assistants: the government and its army; and hunger (7–12).

The imaginary reader is getting frustrated: "Free or not, what's the difference, you say?" And the narrator responds with words of encouragement: "Don't rush, we'll get it all sorted out" (12). He goes on to explain that the factory worker must sell himself: labor power has a value too. And why does the factory owner buy labor power? To make a profit. The narrator lays out in detail the example of a hypothetical cotton factory, explaining the concept of surplus value and how the factory owner gets this from workers. He follows up with an even more detailed and realistic example, taken from real life, of an English cotton factory. "Now you see how the master gets his income. From his own labor? Obviously not" (27). The lie of the author of *Self-Help* and his ilk is now exposed. Diksztajn similarly explains how merchants, landowners, and bureaucrats obtain their income, and notes that the government sends police and troops to protect the interests of the factory owner. To distract workers from labor problems, even wars are fought. Now, the section concludes, the question posed in the booklet's title can be answered. He divides the population into three categories: 1) those people, such as peasants with land, who still work for themselves; 2) workers and peasants who need to sell themselves; and 3) those who have the tools and make others work: factory owners, merchants, and others (33–34).

The second section addresses the question of what to do about the above state of affairs, where "a small handful of men live in luxury from the labor of the *narod*" (35). Rather than a detailed analysis as in the first section, Diksztajn leads the reader through an argument on the basis of morality and economic utility. The present order must be completely reconfigured, and the tools of labor must be taken from the powerful and given to the whole working people to use. "Taken! By force!! And, please tell us, how do we take them? Is it possible? Is it conceivable? Is it moral?" (36). The author proceeds to address the questions in this catechism. First, is it possible for every worker to have his own means of production (*orudiia truda*)? In the past this was possible; today, with world population growth and interdependence, it is not. Today's solution, rather, is for factories and land to belong to all the workers as common property. A footnote spells out that *obshchaia sobstvennost'* means *gosudarstvennaia* (40). Is this solution possible? Here the situation seems encouraging. "There have always been poor and rich, always and everywhere there have been a mass of opressed people and a handful of oppressors" (41). But now a process of growing impoverishment is going on: artisans put out of business by machines, workers made obsolete by machines: but, "as the saying goes, There's no bad without some good" (45). Small factory owners are ruined by competition—and the owners don't know how to work together, whereas factory workers are used to standing up for each other as brothers, against a common enemy. Workers become aware of their numbers, they have a plan to work for the common good. And finally, would it be right (*spravedlivo*) to seize the land and factories from the owners? Again, a pithy folk saying provides the answer: "Ne nos dlia tabakerka, a tabakerka dlia nosa" (The nose isn't made for the snuffbox, but the snuffbox for the nose). In other words, the purpose of people is not to make material goods, but rather the goods exist to satisfy people's needs. Some say that property is sacred: the author answers, "They robbed us for thousands of years and drank our sweat and blood. Now we're going to take what is *ours*" (47–48). The final question: how to take the factories and land? Here the author begs the question: that's up to the workers, it's their affair, and they must join together to carry it out. Diksztajn concludes with two reminders: the necessity of common ownership of the means of production, and the false teachings of people like the author of *Self-Help*.

Who Lives By What? is less colloquial and folksy compared to the two other brochures, especially *The Clever Trick*. It focuses more directly on the issues of labor and profit and presents more direct explanations of such key concepts of Marx's *Capital* as surplus value. Again, the same villains are named: the factory owner and merchant, the government and police; the landowner is barely mentioned, however, and the priest does not appear. Several factors seem to account for the booklet's extraordinary popularity, factors shared by the other two: it provided "useful knowledge," making clear the extent and causes of injustice. Workers had known they were oppressed: now they had an "objective" explanation. As soon as it became available in the mid-1880s, *Who Lives By What?* was picked up as part of the propaganda repertory. Although Pavel Tochisskii, the organizer of the Association of St. Petersburg Workingmen, was reluctant to give workers illegal literature, he made another rare exception in the case of Diksztajn's work. According to a colleague, *Who Lives By What?* was his favorite work of illegal literature for use with workers.[93]

---

[93] Breitfus, "Tochisskii," 338–39.

The sources reveal numerous references to use of the brochure in the 1890s, where it occupied a key place in the circle curriculum.[94]

Workers' circles were not the only venue in which Diksztajn's booklet figured. Some of the more politicized circle workers engaged in political agitation in the workplace. One activist apparently read *Who Lives By What?* aloud in the "workers' club," or lavatory, at the Baltic shipbuilding plant in Petersburg.[95] By the early 1890s, some Petersburg workers began to chafe under the tutelage of the intelligentsia (not to mention that the students always left town during summer vacation). The solution: to create their own "workers' intelligentsia." To this end, Andrei Fisher and his friend Ivan Keizer arranged private tutoring. With one tutor they studied the "Communist Manifesto" and read *Who Lives By What?* Fisher continued on his own with another tutor. With this student he studied the first nine chapters of *Capital*, no easy task: "[N]orm of exploitation, the working day, wages, surplus value, etc., etc. These were things you really had to mull over, because we were encountering them for the first time, they were completely new ideas. Many of them only became completely clear later."[96] Undoubtedly, Fisher's reading of *Who Lives By What?* aided in the comprehension of Marx's work. Throughout the 1890s in St. Petersburg and in the provinces, *Who Lives By What?* continued to circulate. As with *Tsar Hunger*, new editions were printed in Russia and abroad even beyond the 1917 revolution.[97]

ೞ ೞ

These three brochures lent a tone to the study and organizing efforts of radical workers. Presenting sober and practical information on the economy, offering the incontrovertible truth of hard facts, these hand-sized works emboldened workers with understanding of how the exploitative economy worked and what needed to be changed. While each brochure came out of the revolutionary movement at a particular moment in time and differed in its

---

[94] See, for example, Golubev, "Stranichka," 108; GARF f. 102, 3 d-vo, d. 558, l. 8; RGIA f. 1405, op. 93, d. 10547, l. 310ob.

[95] Norinskii, "Moi vospominaniia," 10.

[96] G. M. Fisher, "Podpol'e, ssylka, emigratsiia: Vospominaniia bol'shevika," in Ol'khovskii, *Avangard*, 45–46.

[97] The Hoover Institution Library holds the following editions: London, 1893 (by the Russian Free Press Fund); Geneva, 1901 (by the League of Russian Social Democrats Abroad); Geneva, 1905 (by Iskra); Petrograd, 1917 (Knigoizd. Luch); Tiflis, 1917 (by the SRs in the Caucasus); Moscow, 1918 (by the Central Executive Committee of the Moscow Soviets); and Petrograd, 1919 (by the Petrograd Soviet of Workers and Red Army Deputies.

manner of presentation, the key concepts overlapped. Revolutionary groups made use of all three brochures: whether originating in the populist period, or from People's Will circle work, or the social democracy of the 1880s—I have seen no evidence to show that the presumed "ideological" slant of these works was even brought up for discussion. Political economy in the workers' circles by the 1880s took on a Marxist or social democratic perspective, but even People's Will activist Bakh rightly refers to his exposition in *Tsar Hunger* as Marxist. While these works may not have been completely interchangeable, some groups, such as the Moscow People's Will organization of 1884–86, made use of all three. Stressing the influence of Marxism on People's Will activists of the time, one member later recalled:

> The group had an excellent library for propaganda among workers, consisting of both legal and illegal publications. We had, by the way, not a few popular expositions of the teaching of Marx, including our own lithographed publications.... [T]he group published a translation of the popular exposition of Marx by the French Marxist Gabriel Deville. We also had translations of several brochures by Wilhelm Liebknecht.... It is not surprising that the group's activity in general, and the publishing activity in particular, was penetrated by a certain Marxist tendency, or as it is now expressed, leaning [*uklon*].[98]

In later years, workers continued to remember the illegal works they first encountered. A member of the first circle of female textile workers in Odessa recalls their clandestine celebration of 1 May in 1895, and that they received the brochures *Who Lives By What?* and *The Clever Trick*.[99] During the mid-1890s, the social democratic group that became known as the St. Petersburg Union of Struggle for the Emancipation of the Working Class was quite active in propaganda in circles, at workers' Sunday Schools, and at various factories. During the industry-wide textile strikes in the capital in 1896 and 1897, radicalized workers made contact with the hitherto unpoliticized textile workers, and these works were encountered by a new audience. *Tsar Hunger* was read to striking workers, and the titles recur in official documents on the movement, together with those of newer works on political economy.[100]

---

[98] Tereshkovich, "Pamiati trekh druzei," 134–35.

[99] I. Dargol'ts (Lipovetskaia), "Beglye zametki o sostoianii odesskoi organizatsii k momentu 1-go partiinogo s"ezda: Po lichnym vospominaniiam," in *K dvadtsatipiatiletiiu pervogo s"ezda partii (1889–1923)* (Moscow–Petrograd, 1923), 119.

[100] See *Rabochee dvizhenii v Rossii*, 4, ch. 1, 1895–97, p. 284. Among the new illegal works on political economy that enjoyed popularity in the 1890s were *The Working*

The importance of political economy as a topic in revolutionary propaganda grew with the emphasis on Russia's urban workers in the revolutionary movement, a perspective consciously adopted by People's Will activists of the early 1880s and later reinforced by Social Democrats and Socialist Revolutionaries. Most often focusing on aspects of the relation between capital and labor, these brochures presented political economy directly to the worker as worker, rather than simply a member of the *narod* or lower classes and addressed questions raised by the worker's day-to-day experiences: low wages, exploitation by the employer, unemployment. The goal of these works was to analyze the worker's desperate situation and, more broadly, the injustice of the existing political and economic order and then to offer an alternative—a socialist organization of society. The remarkable popularity of these pamphlets through the decades attests to their effectiveness in giving workers a sense that they were gaining both knowledge of the economic system that ruled their lives and, with this mastery, the possibility of changing it. In this way, the political economy brochures captured (and it appears transmitted) one of the central messages that the Russian revolutionary movement strove to convey to urban workers.

This literature of political economy has faded from view: the titles may be familiar to specialists, but the form of presentation, the ideas that workers found in these works—these questions, while critical to understanding the mindset of the radical Russian worker, have remained largely unexamined. The names of such outstanding worker *narodovol'tsy* as Vasilii Pankratov and Petr Antonov have been forgotten as well, even by those who study the revolutionary movement, and yet they deserve the recognition given to such workers as Stepan Khalturin in the 1870s and Ivan Babushkin, Vasilii Shelgunov, and Semen Kanatchikov in the 1890s. In addition to providing an analysis of the genre of political economy for workers, it has been my goal in this chapter to contribute as well to uncovering hitherto neglected aspects of the history of the Russian revolutionary movement: the continuity and metamorphosis of the movement after 1 March 1881; the central role of the People's Will, in altered form; the importance of worker-*narodovol'tsy*; and the centrality of propaganda among workers to the revolutionary movement.

Day (*Rabochii den'*) and *What Every Worker Should Know and Remember* (*Chto nuzhno znat' i pomnit' kazhdomu rabochemu*). On propaganda activity and literature before and during the St. Petersburg strikes, see GARF f. 102, 7 d-vo, d. 319, tt. 1–5; and GARF f. 102, 3 d-vo, d. 580, t. 1; also "Doklad po delu o voznikshikh v Peterburge v 1894 i 1895 godakh prestupnykh kruzhkakh lits, imenuiushchikh sebia 'sotsial-demokratami,'" in *Sbornik materialov i statei*, 1: 93–178.

Chapter 4

The Revolutionary Songbook: Poetry and Song

> Flow far our song! Whirl all around!
> Over the world our banner waves...[1]

During the meetings, strikes, and demonstrations of the year 1905, the revolutionary song for the first time "flowed far and whirled all around," in the triumphal words of the powerful anthem "The Red Banner" ("Krasnoe znamia"). An example of how workers in large numbers were introduced to revolutionary songs is recounted in an interesting anecdote from the memoirs of Aleksandr Shapovalov, a Bolshevik organizer in Khar′kov in the fall of 1905. At least 60,000 people, according to Shapovalov, took part in a mass funeral procession for the victims of street fighting following promulgation of the October Manifesto. It was during this event that

> workers for the first time, in the mass, learned to sing revolutionary anthems [gimny]. It turned out that not only workers, but even *intelligenty* sympathizers of the revolution, with rare exceptions, didn't know the revolutionary songs. So I, along with the other organizers of the funeral, had to run alongside the separate large detachments into which [the procession] had been divided, write the words of the revolutionary anthems on the backs of the comrades, then sing the tune, and, when the forward section of the detachment had assimilated and already begun to sing a given revolutionary song, run further. In this way, the crowd learned first "You Fell Victim in the Fateful Struggle," and then other revolutionary "hymns."[2]

By 1905 a repertoire of revolutionary songs already existed, one which had taken shape over the course of previous decades of the movement. A list of the most popular songs of that revolutionary year illustrates their varied

---

[1] "Krasnoe znamia," in *Pesni russkikh poetov: V dvukh tomakh* (hereafter *PRP*), ed. Iu. A. Andreev (Leningrad, 1988), 2: 421.

[2] A. S. Shapovalov, *V podpol′e: Na puti k marksizmu* (Moscow–Leningrad, 1927), 208.

origins and the chronological layering of the repertoire of songs. The most popular song during that revolutionary year was the song known as "The Workers' Marseillaise," composed in the 1870s by Petr Lavrov, leading theorist of Russian revolutionary populism. Other popular songs included "Let's Keep Step Boldly, Comrades!" ("Smelo, tovarishchi, v nogu!"), composed by a Petersburg Social Democrat of the 1890s; the two moving "funeral hymns"— "You Fell Victim" ("Vy zhertvoiu pali") and "Oppressed by Heavy Captivity" ("Zamuchen tiazheloi nevolei")—which first appeared in the 1870s; and two Polish revolutionary songs, "Varshavianka" and "The Red Banner," first sung by Polish revolutionaries in the early 1880s and translated into Russian in the late 1890s. These songs and others had roots deep in the past of the revolutionary underground before springing up in a public role in the first years of the 20th century. At this point, street demonstrations and May First celebrations became increasingly common, though still risky occurrences in cities and provincial towns of the Russian Empire, culminating in the revolutionary events of 1905.

This chapter will focus on the genre of poetry and song in the workers' revolutionary movement. I begin by noting several points and problems unique to the study of this genre. There follow five sections tracing the chronological evolution of this genre from the 1870s through 1905. As a strategy of approach to this diverse topic, I have chosen five poetry/song collections as successive guideposts through this period. In addition to analyzing the evolution of this genre and pointing out major themes and poetic tropes, I examine the context in which these works were composed, printed, and read. Which works of verse proved to be most popular among worker participants in the revolutionary movement? Did groups of different ideological persuasions sing different songs or identify with different works of poetry? The concluding section of the chapter links the key concept of "socialism" to revolutionary poetry and song and more broadly to propaganda literature and the workers' movement. In this final section I suggest some answers to a question that is central to any consideration of workers and their involvement in the Russian revolutionary movement, which was most importantly a socialist one: what did socialism mean to these radical workers? Among the varied aspects of the movement, it was perhaps through song that the idealism embodied in the goal of socialism was most clearly manifest.

Poetry and song were embedded in the workers' revolutionary movement, from its earliest days, when workers might declaim poems by Nekrasov at a social gathering, to the crowds of marchers singing the "Workers' Marseillaise" in 1905 and 1917. Perhaps even more than with other genres of propaganda literature, the "revolutionary songbook" was continuously revised, with some songs and poems persisting for decades in the underground, others dropping from memory, new works composed. In varied historical contexts, revolutionary songs have symbolic resonance, recalling the extraordinary events to which they are forever connected: the "Marseillaise" and the French Revolution, "Viva la Quince Brigada" and the Spanish Civil War, the "Internationale" and the world communist movement come to mind. The memoirs of radical worker Petr Moiseenko (as we have seen in earlier chapters) are studded with references to propaganda literature of various kinds, including poetry and song. Recalling a lifetime of revolutionary activism, Moiseenko not only refers to the presence of specific songs and poems in the workers' movement but quotes from them to explain and represent his own feelings in the past, and in retrospect. He refers to the "striking effect" of certain songs sung by workers at the New Cotton Spinning Factory in Petersburg in the 1870s: "We were all inspired by revolutionary song. Even if we were tired, we forgot everything." (Upon invitation, they would even sing these songs in taverns, although this was done "on a completely illegal basis.")[3]

CҐ ЬƆ

The task of understanding the significance of poetry and song in the revolutionary movement confronts the researcher with several new issues, in comparison with the study of other genres of propaganda literature. As an oral genre, songs (and to some extent poetry as well) are elusive—they convey the ideals and emotions that helped bind radical workers to the movement and each other, but, unlike printed brochures, may leave little trace. The importance of the intangible song is only increased when we keep in mind that workers did not have to be literate to memorize it and grasp its meaning. When it came to song, workers with varying degrees of education, ability, and radicalization were on an equal footing. Some of the particular aspects of the study of revolutionary song should be kept in mind. First, the distinction between poetry and song is often blurred. Many revolutionary songs began as poems; songs were sometimes declaimed, their verses printed in radical leaflets, or reflected in May First speeches. In some cases we may not know if a manuscript verse seized as evidence was also a song. Second, the distinction between the adjectives "workers'" and "revolutionary" when applied to songs/poems is also often blurred or artificial. Compared to other genres of revolutionary propaganda literature—revolutionary *skazki*, pamphlets on political economy, legal works of fiction—radical students or other members of the intelligentsia and workers more often sang the same songs, were inspired by the same poems. Of course, there were often differences:

---

[3] Moiseenko, *Vospominaniia starogo revoliutsionera*, 20.

workers and *intelligenty* might sing somewhat different versions (and songs in particular appear in a number of variations and reworkings); also important are differences in reception. The poetry of Nekrasov, for example, was part of the standard corpus of readings for radically inclined youth, and his poems were also very popular with workers. It appears, however, that these poems may have been more often *sung* by workers, often in slightly different variations. Songs about Stenka Razin, to give another example, were sung by both workers and *intelligenty*, but seem to have been more popular with workers, particularly in the 1870s through early 1890s.

A third point has to do with the difficulties of research in this area. Questions of the origins, composers, and tunes for a number of songs have been debated by scholars for decades (and will be touched on here only in passing). As noted, the oral nature of songs (and the ephemeral quality of verse, often preserved only by accident in manuscript form) means that they often left little physical trace. This could be a positive virtue in the revolutionary context: passed on orally, or in an easily destroyed manuscript form from one worker to another, they were less likely than longer printed works to serve the police as evidence of revolutionary activity. On the other hand, from the point of view of today's researcher, evidence of songs is less clear from the sources, including archival documents from the tsarist secret police, Ministry of Justice, and other official sources, as well as memoirs written by participants in the movement. Reference is frequently made to "revolutionary songs," without mention of specifics. One very important source of evidence, however, is the archival *fond* of "material evidence" (Ministry of Justice)[4] linked to the various revolutionary groups arrested and tried by the government. These files contain illegal literature or lists of works of illegal literature seized on the person of arrested individuals or in their apartments. A number of songs/poems are known only from manuscript versions that have survived in this way.

A final but crucial consideration has to do with the unique characteristics of song as a genre—music as well as words. Songs are usually sung in a group; by definition this is a collective, performative act. Words set to music, songs have an emotional impact, evoking memory, emotion, and solidarity. Those researching the connection between music and cognition have noted some of the physiological effects of song. Daniel Levitin describes the neurochemical effects of singing and the way that synchronous music making creates social bonds.[5] The reciprocal connection between feeling and

---

[4] RGIA f. 1410.

[5] Daniel J. Levitin, *The World in Six Songs: How the Musical Brain Created Human Nature* (New York, 2008), 180. See also Levitin, *This Is Your Brain on Music: The Science of a Human Obsession* (New York, 2006); and Oliver Sacks, *Musicophilia: Tales of Music and the Brain*, rev. ed. (New York, 2008).

song lends itself to further study in the field of "emotionology" or "emotions history." The findings presented in this chapter point to revolutionary song as both a way to encapsulate the feelings engendered by participation in the movement and a means to aid in the creation of feelings of unity, solidarity, and brotherhood—goals constantly promoted by revolutionary propaganda of various genres.[6] As a propaganda tool, songs emphasize revolutionary spirit and aspirations, they are often utopian, maximalist—unlike more pragmatic and straightforward political platforms, or expositions of political economy. More than simply a form of propaganda, however, songs (in the Russian and other contexts) helped to create and symbolize the revolutionary movement itself. Laura Mason, who has studied the "song culture" of the French Revolution, goes so far as to argue that "song culture did more than simply express a politics that had prior existence; singing helped to create the political life of the nation."[7] Songs can help create and represent the political life of a subculture or subgroup of a nation as well. Mason closely links singing during the French Revolution to the sans-culottes and calls songs "the poor person's means of expression *par excellence*."[8] Similarly, Levitin claims that "music has historically been one of the strongest forces binding together the disenfranchised, the alienated."[9] Study of songs thus serves as a means of entry into the subculture of radical workers, their emotional ties to the movement, and their conception of a "social imaginary," the future socialist society. For many workers, the revolutionary movement *was* socialism. By the early 20th century a distinctive new manifestation was added to the movement: the public political demonstration, funeral procession, or revolutionary meeting. In this new setting, the combination of words, music, rhythm, and movement were linked with banners, slogans, red flags in novel forms of commemoration. With song, the revolutionary movement took on new qualities.

CB EO

Collections of revolutionary poetry and song, both printed and in manuscript, became an important genre of propaganda literature beginning in the 1870s, as radicals began to make contact with peasants and workers. The history of revolutionary song begins several decades earlier, however, with the appear-

---

[6] On perspectives and possibilities in the field of emotions history, see Matt and Stearns, *Doing Emotions History*; and Steinberg and Sobol, *Interpreting Emotions*.

[7] Laura Mason, *Singing the French Revolution: Popular Culture and Politics, 1787–1799* (Ithaca, NY, 1996), 60.

[8] Ibid., 128.

[9] Levitin, *World in Six Songs*, 61.

ance of subversive poetry. Some of these works, often reworked or modified and turned into songs, remained popular for decades and turn up in later songbooks. The Decembrists counted a number of poets in their circles and among their associates. The most outstanding of these was the well-known poet Kondratii Ryleev, executed for his role in the failed uprising of December 1825. Together with Aleksandr Bestuzhev-Marlinskii he composed a series of "agitational songs,"[10] including "Our Tsar Is a Russian German" ("Tsar' nash—nemets russkii"), consisting of a series of rhyming couplets making fun of the tsar, the government, and such key officials as Count Arakcheev.[11] Some of the lesser known works of Aleksandr Pushkin found their way into the "revolutionary songbook" as well. These included "The Prisoner" ("Uznik")— "I sit behind bars in the damp darkness"—and "The Dagger" ("Kinzhal"), a poem of revenge. Prison and exile already had a thematic history in Russian folksong. Mikhail Lermontov also wrote a poem entitled "The Prisoner."[12] The Petrashevtsy, a group of Petersburg radicals of the 1840s, had their poetic voice as well in Aleksei Pleshcheev; like Dostoevskii, Pleshcheev also went through the terror of a mock execution after the arrest and conviction of the Petrashevtsy. The words of his powerful verse, beginning "Forward! Without fear or doubt" ("Vpered! Bez strakha i somnen'ia"), were apparently recited by the *petrashevtsy* awaiting their execution.[13] Petr Moiseenko later wrote in his memoirs that this same poem came into his head at the time of the Morozov strike in 1885.[14]

Alexander Herzen and Nikolai Ogarev were outstanding figures of Russian radicalism of the Emancipation era. Their two periodicals, *Polar Star* (*Poliarnaia Zvezda*) and *The Bell* (*Kolokol*), published from exile in Western Europe, were noteworthy for including correspondence from Russia. In this way, they succeeded in reflecting views on Russia's internal situation back

---

[10] Editor's note, in *PRP*, 1: 299.

[11] For a selection of poems by Ryleev and A. A. Bestuzhev, see *PRP*, 1: 299–309; and S. A. Reiser and Iu. A. Andreev, eds., *Vol'naia russkaia poeziia XVIII–XIX vekov: V dvukh tomakh* (hereafter *VRP*) (Leningrad, 1988), 1: 252–84. On the literary significance of the Decembrists, see "Decembrism," in Terras, *Handbook of Russian Literature*, 94–96.

[12] For a selection of poems by Pushkin and Lermontov that were broadly popular and often given special significance in the movement, see *PRP*, 1: 244–58, 437–54; and *VRP*, 1: 216–41 and 401–07.

[13] See on this D. Zhitomirskii, "Pesni revoliutsionnoi bor'by: Ocherk tretii—Pesni na stikhi A. N. Pleshcheeva," *Muzykal'naia zhizn'*, no. 15 (1958): 8. For two of the best-known poems of Pleshcheev, both sung to the same tune, see "Vpered! bez strakha i somnen'ia" and "Po chuvstvam brat'ia my s toboi," in *VRP*, 1: 471–72.

[14] Moiseenko, *Vospominaniia starogo revoliutsionera*, 100.

to Russians in educated society, and even penetrated the court and the royal family. Issues of these journals included poetry as well, some of it written by co-editor Ogarev, an accomplished poet. (Fittingly, he was arrested in 1834 in the case of "persons singing libelous verses.")[15] Ogarev may have been the first to publish songbooks filled with tendentious verse, including the collections entitled *Soldiers' Songs* (1862) and *Free Russian Songs* (1863). Some of Ogarev's poems, later set to music, remained popular throughout the 19th century, including "The Prisoner" ("Arestant"), often known by its first verse, "Dark is the night. Seize the minutes"—the prisoner goes on to dream of an impossible escape.[16]

Soviet-era musicologists have pointed to other early influences on revolutionary song, including "banquet" (*zastol'nye*) songs sung at gatherings of young officers and other upper-class youth, and student songs.[17] The student, revolutionary, and workers' movements frequently overlapped and merged into one another. Songs were sung at student demonstrations, and these radical manifestations often influenced workers as well. One important demonstration was carried out by students at Kazan University, in the form of a requiem mass for the peasants of the village of Bezdna who protested the Emancipation settlement and were killed by government troops in April 1861. The students sang the song "Long Have the Landlords Been Suffocating Us" ("Dolgo nas pomeshchiki dushili"), which later appeared in Ogarev's 1863 collection *Free Russian Songs*.[18] Evidence from later decades shows workers responding to student demonstrations and adopting some of the songs sung by students. Worker K. Mironov, for example, in his memoirs of 1906, describes workers' sympathetic response to demonstrations of St. Petersburg students in 1899, and a similar reaction was observed among Khar'kov workers in the same year.[19]

CB   BO

---

[15] *PRP*, 1: 545.

[16] On Ogarev, see also "Ogaryov, Nikolai Platonovich" in Terras, *Handbook of Russian Literature*, 314–15; and Venturi, *Roots of Revolution*, 74–76.

[17] See V. E. Gusev, introduction to *PRP*, 1: 31–32; M. Druskin, *Russkaia revoliutsionnaia pesnia* (Moscow, 1954), 55–56, 148 n. 11, 149 n. 14.

[18] Druskin, *Russkaia revoliutsionnaia pesnia*, 35–36. Druskin thinks it possible that this song was composed by Kazan University students (148 n. 11). See also *PRP*, 2: 482 n. 694.

[19] Mironov, *Iz vospominanii rabochego* (Moscow, 1906), 25; *Rabochee dvizhenie v Khar'kove* (Geneva, 1900), 8–9.

I will now turn to an examination of five distinct moments in the revolutionary movement of the late 19th and early 20th centuries and the poetic works that were created or preserved at the time: 1) the early revolutionary populism of the Chaikovskii circle and the movement "to the people"; 2) the "heroic" period of Zemlia i Volia and Narodnaia Volia; 3) the little-known period in the mid-1880s, when *narodovol'tsy* tried to keep the revolutionary movement alive; 4) the early 1890s, which saw the growth of a revolutionary workers' movement in St. Petersburg, guided to some extent by social democratic teachings; and finally, 5) the early 20th century, when the revolutionary movement emerged into the street in processions and demonstrations. Each of these five "moments" will be represented below by a collection of poetry or song. As will be seen, poems from earlier years were often reproduced in successive collections. The changing titles in the contents of these collections represent in telling fashion shifts in emphasis and values as the movement continued to evolve. (Note that all of these works printed, copied, and sung were illegal.)

ᘓ ᘔ

The first of our five collections appears in the memoirs of Petr Moiseenko. Moiseenko dates his "revolutionary awakening" from the early 1870s, when, as a young weaver, he first read some illegal brochures. Among the four he mentions was a *Revolutionary Songbook* (*Revoliutsionnyi pesennik*). The combined effect of these brochures was profound: "In fact from that time began my awakening from the old, religious teaching."[20] Moiseenko was probably referring to the *Collection of New Songs and Verses* (*Sbornik novykh pesen i stikhov*), one of the first collections of verse intended for propaganda activity, published by the Chaikovskii circle on their Geneva press in 1873, on the eve of the movement to go "to the people."[21] According to B. S. Itenberg, noted scholar of the populist movement of the 1870s, the *Collection* was the most widely used source of revolutionary poetry used by propagandists among the peasantry during this period.[22]

---

[20] Moiseenko, *Vospominaniia starogo revoliutsionera*, 15.

[21] For publication information, see Itenberg et al., *Svodnyi katalog*, 2: 79 (no. 1659). The sources sometimes make it difficult to distinguish the *Collection* from the *Songbook* also published by the *chaikovtsy* in Geneva in 1873, apparently at a somewhat earlier date. See ibid., 2: 28 (no: 1316). See, for example, Lavrov's brief mention of a "Revoliutsionnyi pesennik" in a list of publications of the Geneva press (*Narodniki-propagandisty*, 38). It appears that of the two collections, the *Collection* was the most widely used. On the identification of the collection mentioned by Moiseenko, see the editor's note in *Vospominaniia starogo revoliutsionera* (240 n. 1).

[22] Itenberg, *Dvizhenie revoliutsionnogo narodnichestva*, 262.

The *chaikovtsy* (as we have seen earlier), a St. Petersburg–based group of *intelligenty*, mostly students and former students, were among the first to establish sustained contact with members of the *narod*. This unusual group of young people left its imprint on the values and goals of the movement which came to be known as populism (*narodnichestvo*). Many were involved in the successive phases of the rapidly evolving revolutionary movement of the 1870s, including membership in the People's Will. The group was noteworthy for the inclusion of women as well as men, and the close personal bonds and the high moral standards required for admission to the group are emphasized in the rich collection of memoir accounts. *Underground Russia* (*Podpol'naia Rossiia*), a colorful and exciting depiction of the revolutionary movement and its young adherents by Sergei Stepniak-Kravchinskii, perhaps did more than any other work to embody the movement in its diverse and sympathetically portrayed members and to begin the creation of its myth and image. (First published in Italian in 1882, this enormously influential work was translated into many languages.) The movement of radical youth of 1873–74 was not, according to Kravchinskii, a political movement, but "rather resembled a religious movement.... People not only sought to attain a distinct practical object, but also to satisfy an inward sentiment of duty, an aspiration towards their own moral perfection." Within the Chaikovskii circle relations were characterized by "reciprocal affection and esteem"; they were, Kravchinskii writes, a fraternal exemplar of Rousseau's ideal.[23] Among the members profiled were Dmitrii Klements, Sof'ia Perovskaia, and Prince Petr Kropotkin. With respect and admiration, Kropotkin, later to become a noted anarchist thinker, describes the *chaikovtsy* in a similar fashion in his memoirs, *Memoirs of a Revolutionist*:

> The two years that I worked with the Circle of Tchaykovsky ... left a deep impression upon all my subsequent life and thought.... I was in a family of men and women so closely united by their common object, and so broadly and delicately humane in their mutual relations, that I cannot now recall a a single moment of even temporary friction marring the life of our circle.[24]

---

[23] Stepniak [Kravchinskii], *Underground Russia*, 23, 119.

[24] Kropotkin, *Memoirs of a Revolutionist*, 317. The life of the Chaikovskii circle is richly illuminated in memoirs of its members. See, among others, Charushin, *O dalekom proshlom*; S. S. Sinegub, *Zapiski chaikovtsa* (Moscow, 1929); Shishko, *Sergei Mikhailovich Kravchinskii*; A. Kornilova-Moroz, *Perovskaia i kruzhok chaikovtsev* (Moscow, 1929).

The idealism and utopianism expressed by the *chaikovtsy* in their personal relations seems to have been inseparable from their identity as revolutionaries and socialists.

The *chaikovtsy* emphasized the importance of literature in propaganda, with publishing activity an important part of their endeavor. They began their "cause of the book" (*knizhnoe delo*) with the distribution of works they considered essential to a political education—including Marx, Lassalle, Bervi-Flerovskii—among students in the capital. At the same time, some members became involved in propaganda among local factory workers, offering lessons in workers' *kruzhki*, an activity seen by some as preparation for propaganda among the peasantry. The *Collection of New Songs and Verses* was one of a series of illegal works destined for the *narod*, including *The Tale of Four Brothers* and *Tale of a Kopeck*. The collection was comprised of 15 poems, among them works by Nikolai Nekrasov, as well as verses by several of the *chaikovtsy*.[25] The genesis of this work is unclear: the sources provide no information on which members were involved and how the contents were chosen. The attribution of the new works and the identity of the primary editor of the collection have been disputed in the scholarship and are subject to contradictory statements in memoir accounts, but it appears that two of the key members responsible for the collection were Dmitrii Klements, a sometime student at St. Petersburg University, and Sergei Sinegub, a student at the Technological Institute. Both were circle propagandists in working-class districts of Petersburg.[26]

The propaganda experiences of Klements and Sinegub and their familiarity with workers open to radical ideas may have guided their selection of works to include in the *Collection*. The poems published in the *Collection* fall

---

[25] For publication information, see Itenberg et al., *Svodnyi katalog*, 2: 79 (no. 1659): first published in an edition of 10,000 copies. The poems are reprinted in *VRP*, 2: 175–86; and *VRP* (1959), 236–58.

[26] On Klements, see Venturi, *Roots of Revolution*, 474–76, 792; *DRDR* 2, vyp. 4, cols. 575–76. Kropotkin describes Klements, with whom he was close, in his memoirs, under the name Dmitri Kelnitz (*Memoirs of a Revolutionist*, 303); Stepniak-Kravchinskii includes a profile of "Clemens" in *Underground Russia*, calling him "perhaps the best of our popular propagandists" and endowed with "one of the most powerful intellects to be found among our party" (59, 67.) On Klements, see also I. S. Vakhrushev and L. P. Roshchevskaia, "D. A. Klements—revoliutsionnyi publitsist i prosvetitel'," in *Ocherki istorii revoliutsionnogo dvizheniia v Rossii v 60–80-kh godakh XIX veka*, ed. E. I. Kiriukhina (Kirov, 1979); and E. Dubenskaia, "Dmitrii Aleksandrovich Klements," *Katorga i ssylka*, no. 5 (66) (1930): 170–76. Sinegub left a fascinating record of his experiences in the movement of the early 1870s, "Vospominaniia chaikovtsa." See also *DRDR* 2, vyp. 4, cols. 500–01. On the conflicting Klements/Sinegub attribution, see, among other sources Itenberg et al., *Svodnyi katalog*, 2: 79 (no. 1659); *VRP*, 2: 584–89; *PRP*, 2: 207–09; Bazanov, *Agitatsionnaia literatura*, notes, 492–98.

into three categories: older works here reprinted, works by the poet Nekrasov, and a series of new, specially composed poems. Five poems were taken from earlier collections. Published shortly after the Emancipation, they represent a response to the false and illusory nature of this "freedom": "There once lived a Russian tsar" ("Zhil na svete russkii tsar'"), by Nikolai Ogarev, to be sung to a popular tune, complains that the tsar promised freedom but did not mean it: nobody could understand the Manifesto, and it seems that everything is just as before: "How can there be freedom without land?"[27] The poem "For Long the Landowners Smothered Us" ("Dolgo nas pomeshchiki dushili"), published in *Kolokol* in 1861, dates from the same period. The poet complains, we've tolerated mistreatment for too long, let ourselves be fleeced like sheep. The tsar sits in Piter writing a decree—and not for us, it's incomprehensible. The poet concludes with a reference to the year '25—then Pestel' and Ryleev "rose against the evil doers ... and laid down their heads for brotherhood. Perhaps we'll find another ... Pugachev?" Moiseenko notes in his memoirs that, as a song, "For Long the Landowners Smothered Us" was used in propaganda at factories in the 1870s.[28] The theme of revolt recurs in a short song by Ogarev, "From Our Mother Volga" ("Iz-za matushki za Volgi"), part of a longer work: "From the icy White Sea to the Black Sea of the steppe, ... let's stand up for our land ... our freedom."[29] The famous song "Glory, glory to our Russian Tsar" from Glinka's opera "A Life for the Tsar" was borrowed for the song "Glory to freedom and our honest labor" ("Slav'sia svoboda i chestnyi nash trud!"): even if they lock us up and torture us, even then we'll sing of freedom.[30] The last of the older songs, defiantly titled "Disobedient Song" ("Oslushnaia pesnia") was to be sung to the tune of the "Marseillaise": the hour of rebellion has come, and all Russia should rise as one. Enough of Germans, soldiers, suffering. We don't need a tsar any longer. Come together for freedom. To arms! The chorus is a free translation from the French.[31] The recurrent themes of these older songs introduce basic tropes in revolutionary propaganda: the false emancipation, resistance, revolution, the land, and freedom.

Among the 15 verses collected in the *Collection* were three poems by Nikolai Nekrasov, the poet most beloved by Russian radicals. Nekrasov

---

[27] Nikolai Ogarev, "Zhil na svete russkii tsar'" (1862), reprinted in *VRP*, 2: 95–97, see also 565 n. 48.

[28] Moiseenko, *Vospominaniia starogo revoliutsionera*, 20. The text of the poem appears in *VRP*, 2: 65–66; see also 559–60 n. 35. The author is tentatively identified as V. S. Kurochkin, though some reworking by Ogarev is possible. See *PRP*, 2: 482–83 n. 694.

[29] This poem is reprinted in *VRP* (1959), 159; see also note on 735.

[30] *VRP* (1959), 163–64; and note on 736.

[31] *VRP* (1959), 162–63; and note on 736.

(1821–78) was a publisher and editor, as well as poet; as editor of the "thick" journals *Sovremennik* (The Contemporary, 1846–66) and *Otechestvennye zapiski* (Fatherland Notes, 1867–78) he played an important role in disseminating the essays and literary works that put the "burning issues of the day" before Russia's intelligentsia. Early in his career as a poet Nekrasov was encouraged by the influential critic Vissarion Belinskii to take a realistic approach to Russian society and its ills. Later labeled a "civic" poet, Nekrasov called on his "muse of vengeance and sorrow." He wrote about and for the *narod*, especially on the oppressive nature of serfdom and the persistent effects of serfdom on peasant society post-Emancipation. Although his sympathy for the peasants is obvious, he did not sugarcoat his portrayal of their difficult lives. The strikingly original nature of his poetic works, in both narrative and lyrical genres, has been noted. One scholar has remarked on "his ability to compose poetry in the spirit and style of Russian folklore" and notes his "skill in recreating the rhythm and style of Russian folksong."[32] Most notable in this regard is the long poem *Who Is Happy in Russia?* (*Komu na Rusi zhit' khorosho?*). Excerpts were published during his lifetime, but the poem was still unfinished at the time of his death.

It may be difficult now to fully appreciate the pervasiveness of Nekrasov's influence on the worldview of Russian radicals of the 1870s (and later). His poems captured the spirit of the radical populist groups of the time and were beloved by both radical intelligentsia and workers. In a sense they provided a common framework of ideas and values spanning the two main social pillars of the revolutionary movement. Because Nekrasov's works were legally published (although often with corrections by the censor), they were more readily obtainable, and were often among the first works read or heard that expressed a sympathy for the *narod* and implored the listener to act. A listing of the readings that were a first step in the radicalization of young members of the intelligentsia, often encountered during the gymnasium years, is a virtually universal trope in the memoirs of members of the revolutionary movement. The influential readings of this period included the triumvirate of Chernyshevskii, Dobroliubov, and Pisarev—and also Nekrasov's poems. In a sense Nekrasov provided the introduction to populism, to its deeply felt resolve to engage in the bettering of the life of the people. Nikolai Charushin later recalled:

> Our favorite poet of that time was undoubtedly Nekrasov, whose works we read and reread; we learned many by heart. His populist leaning,

---

[32] "Nekrasov, Nikolai Alekseevich," in Terras, *Handbook of Russian Literature*, 296. On civic poetry, see also Evelyn Bristol, *A History of Russian Poetry* (New York, 1991), chap. 10; on Nekrasov, see 155.

his passionate love for the unfortunate people, and the civic character of the themes of his poetry, so close already to our own mood, attracted us and made us sincerely attached to the very person of the poet, in whom we refused to see a single dark spot.[33]

Fellow *chaikovets* Petr Kropotkin, in his later work on Russian literature, addresses the question of whether Nekrasov can be considered a great poet. A strictly literary evaluation is difficult to disentangle from the powerful moral impact of his work. Kropotkin writes,

Nekrasoff was a pessimist, but his pessimism had an original character. Although his poetry contains so many depressing pictures representing the misery of the Russian masses, nevertheless the fundamental impression which it leaves upon the reader is an elevating feeling. The poet does not bow his head before the sad reality; he enters into a struggle with it, and he is sure of victory.[34]

Memoirs of radical workers also make note of the presence of Nekrasov's poems in the working-class milieu.[35]

Nekrasov's poems were staples of radical student and workers' circles. Nekrasov straddled the line between legal and illegal: having spent decades as publisher and editor, as well as composing for legal outlets, he knew well how to play the censorship game. Nekrasov's poems appeared in various versions. There were, first of all, censorship considerations: illegal versions were often published with pointed revisions.[36] Some poems and sections of poems became songs, and, as happens with popular works transmitted orally, variations crept in.[37] That Nekrasov's poetry was so well loved and touched such deep chords of feeling is attested to by the fact that it was elevated to the national canon. By the early 20th century Nekrasov was generally praised and

---

[33] Charushin, *O dalekom proshlom*, 43. As an illustration of the way in which Nekrasov's poems provided a frame of reference, note that later in his memoirs, when Charushin describes a trip on the Nikolaevskii Railroad, he adds, "of which Nekrasov sang"—obviously a reference to the poem "Zheleznaia doroga" (96).

[34] Peter Kropotkin, *Russian Literature: Ideals and Realities* (1905; repr., Montreal, 1991), 191. On Nekrasov, see 187–94.

[35] Pankratov, *Vospominaniia*, 7; Moiseenko, *Vospominaniia starogo revoliutsionera*, 71.

[36] See A. M. Garkavi, "Proizvedeniia Nekrasova v revoliutsionnoi agitatsii 1870-kh godov," chap. 4 in his *N. A. Nekrasov i revoliutsionnoe narodnichestvo* (Moscow, 1962).

[37] V. E. Gusev discusses the broader phenomenon of poems becoming songs in his introductory article to *PRP* (1: 5–54).

his works included in primary school primers and read at literary evenings for villagers.[38] Kropotkin noted Nekrasov's universal popularity and added, "[I]t is difficult to imagine, without having seen it, the delight with which Russian children in the poorest village schools are now reading Nekrassof and learning full pages from his verses by heart."[39]

The power and appeal of Nekrasov's poetry can be seen in the three works included in *Collection of New Songs and Verses*. Each of the poems appeared in a reworked form, with obvious efforts made to simplify and popularize the language and to sharpen the content in a revolutionary direction. The poem entitled "Night After the Holiday" ("Noch' posle prazdnika") is a shortened and somewhat revised section of "The Drunken Night" ("P'ianaia noch'"), which appears in part 1 of "Who Is Happy in Russia?" "The Drunken Night" presents a naturalistic scene of peasants at the close of a holiday—the whole crowd is drunk and vulgar; babies are crying, wives and mothers are trying to get their men out of the bars, frightened horses are running around riderless. At the crossroads a nobleman is chatting with the peasants, asking them to repeat a song so he can write it down. He comments on the peasants' disgraceful drunken behavior. One of the peasants responds that no one notices when peasants are working hard, only the rare occasions when they get drunk. The gulf separating nobles—even those who are drawn to the peasants—from the *narod* is striking. As the peasant makes clear, he doesn't like being the object of study and censure: he'll "work till he's dead / drink til he's half-dead."[40] In this verse Nekrasov takes pains to show the peasants "warts and all"—but he also emphasizes their pride, especially in their dealings with the uncomprehending noble.

The other two poems, "A Conversation on the Railroad" ("Razgovor na zheleznoi dorogi" [original version entitled "Zheleznaia doroga"]) and "At the Main Entrance" ("U paradnogo kryl'tsa" [original version entitled "Razmyshleniia y paradnogo pod˝ezda"]), in particular were especially popular in the revolutionary movement. As literary scholar and Nekrasov specialist A. M. Garkavi has pointed out, a comparison of the poet's published versions with those appearing in the *Collection* shows distinct differences.[41] The former

---

[38] See Brooks, *When Russia Learned to Read*, 53, 350.

[39] Kropotkin, *Russian Literature*, 194.

[40] Compare the version in the *Collection* (*VRP* [1959], 236–40) and see note on 753 and the complete version reprinted in N. A. Nekrasov, *Stikhotvoreniia. Komu na Rusi zhit' khorosho?* (Moscow, 1969), 80–91. The changes in the "illegal" version mostly excise the sections that connect this story with the longer poem.

[41] Compare "Zheleznaia doroga" and "Razgovor na zheleznoi dorogoi" in *VRP* (1959), 243–45.

poem relates a conversation between a little boy and his father, a general. Vania asks, who built the railroad? His father answers—engineers. The narrator takes the father to task for not telling his son the truth, and asks the general's permission to enlighten his young son. The fellow passenger explains: Tsar Hunger drove impoverished peasants to build the railroad. The sad song of their ghosts can still be heard, telling their story of suffering and asking if they will be remembered. Responding to this pitiful picture, the general asks if the stranger can't show the youngster the happy side of the peasants' life. The narrator obliges with an ironic look at payday. The businessman comes to inspect the work's progress; it turns out that fines have eaten up the wages—but the entrepreneur will cancel the additional arrears—and treat the workers to a cask of wine. Compared to the version originally published in *Sovremennik* in 1865, the *Collection* version is shorter, and the author's moral is made more pointedly. The editors of the *Collection* also added a foreword, reviewing in prose the main point of the poem, with further explanation for the peasant or worker to whom this collection is addressed.[42] Similarly, "At the Front Entrance" is a shortened and simplified reworking of Nekrasov's original poem. In this work, the poet is observing ragged peasants turned away from the entrance of a grand house, seemingly that of an important government official with the power to grant or deny requests. His anger and despair lead him to wonder at the overwhelming unhappiness of the Russian land: is there any remote corner where the Russian peasant does not groan—in the fields, on the roads, in the prisons? At the formal entrance of the judge's palace in every provincial town? "We call this groan a song—like those the Volga boatmen sing." This portion of the poem, 21 lines in length, became a well-known song, "Just Name for Me One Single Place" ("Nazovi mne takuiu obitel'").[43]

The seven new poems included in the collection were, experts have established, composed by either Dmitrii Klements or Sergei Sinegub, both actively involved in the Chaikovskii group's main project of propaganda among

---

[42] Garkavi, *N. A. Nekrasov*, 52–53. Copies of the *Collection* are quite rare; *Svodnyi katalog* lists only three in major Russian repositories.

[43] Compare Nekrasov's version, "Razmyshleniia u paradnogo pod"ezda," in *Stikhhotvoreniia* (1969), 35–38, and the *Sbornik* version reprinted in *VRP* (1959), 104–07; for publishing history of *Sbornik*, see note on 583. See also Garkavi, *N. A. Nekrasov*, 52–56. On "Nazovi mne takuiu obitel'," see *PRP*, 2: 123. N. V. Os'makov analyzes the reworking of Nekrasov's poems by the editors of the *Sbornik* in his *Poeziia revoliutsionnogo narodnichestva*, 50–53. For a suggestive interpretation of the significance of the "parade entrance" in Russian culture, see Stites, *Passion and Perception*, 47–57.

workers, in the Nevskii Gate region and elsewhere.[44] Sinegub was inspired to
write "Thoughts of a Weaver" ("Duma tkacha") following a visit to a night-
marish textile factory: the thundering noise of the looms, the dust, and the
nauseating smells gave him a headache after only two hours.[45] The poem is
written from the weaver's perspective, describing the painful working conditions and the toll they take: the hellish factory setting, the aching legs of
workers unable to sit down. Worries fill the worker's mind: that a thread will
break, that a foreman will levy a fine. But without work, his family will starve:
"O Lord, ... how long will I live this sorrowful life...?" (A later version of this
poem, known as "Weaver's Song" ("Pesnia tkacha"), was popular among St.
Petersburg workers in the 1890s.) [46]

With the explicit intention of appealing to the common folk, such poems
as "Dear Freedom" ("Svobodushka"), "My Fate" ("Dolia"), and "The Barge"
("Barka") were self-consciously modeled after well-known folksongs, and the
tunes to which they were to be sung were indicated. In this way, poems could
be easily remembered, and everyone already knew the tunes.[47] "Dear Freedom," for example, was to be sung to the tune of "Splinter, little splinter"
("Luchina-luchinushka"), a popular love song.[48] It opens with a folk motif: a
swan is flying over the Russian land in search of a place to nest. But the land
is groaning and falsehood rules. The peasants are not free, the authorities
"suck our blood," the tsar has forgotten them. The song of suffering is heard

---

[44] The attribution of these poems, whether by Klements or Sinegub, was a subject of
debate among Soviet scholars. The evidence leads me to conclude that while Klements
was the author of "Thoughts of a Weaver," and "The Barge" was probably the product
of "collective authorship," the remaining poems composed by the *chaikovtsy* for the
Collection were probably authored by Sinegub. See Gusev's note on D. A. Klements in
PRP, 2: 207, and S. A. Reiser's notes, in *VRP* (1959), 755–60. Both Gusev and Reiser lean
toward Klements as the major author. Bazanov and O. B. Alekseeva support Sinegub's
authorship (*Agitatsionnaia literatura*, notes on 492–94). Interestingly, the 1988 edition of
VRP attributes authorship of most of the poems to Sinegub (2: 583–89 nn. 94–99).

[45] Sinegub, "Vospominaniia chaikovtsa," 52. The poem "Thoughts of a Weaver" is
reprinted in *VRP*, 241–42.

[46] This later version, which begins with the line "The din of machines, unbearable
stuffiness" (Grokhot mashin, dukhota nesterpimaia), based closely on Sinegub's
poem, was also very popular. It was printed, for example, by a worker at the People's
Will Lakhta press in the mid-1890s: GARF f. 102, 7 d-vo, d. 257, l. 363ob. "Grokhot
mashin" is reprinted in *VRP* (1959), 754.

[47] M. Druskin notes that the use of well-known tunes for revolutionary songs was a
tried and true technique. See *Russkaia revoliutsionnaia pesnia*, 146 n. 2. See also Gusev,
introduction to *PRP*, 17.

[48] For the text of "Luchina-luchinushka," see *Russkie pesni XIX veka*, comp. I. N.
Rozanov (Moscow, 1944), 65–66.

throughout the land, "along the Volga, ... in dirty taverns, ... on the road to Siberia...." The poet calls on "dear freedom" to "fly to us," opening the road for a free life. The song "Dear Freedom" picks up some of the same themes we have seen in the revolutionary *skazki*, but here presented in a more poetic fashion, and can be sung. We see the emphasis on freedom (the term *voliushka* is used as well). It is also a song about a song—a song of suffering, and the swan is the symbol of freedom. As in other works of propaganda, there is an enumeration of oppressors, of places. The song doesn't say how freedom will come. It simply voices longing. A. M. Garkavi notes the obvious influence of Nekrasov's "Thoughts on the Main Entrance."[49] The singer of "My Fate" (to the tune of "My land, my dear land"—"Storona l' moia storonka") bemoans the cruel fate that brought him to Siberia—not for drunkenness or robbery, but for standing up for the *mir* (the peasant commune). Sent by the *mir* to petition the tsar for relief from unbearable levies, he was arrested before he even got to St. Petersburg. The song "The Barge" mocks the tsar—the drunken pilot who has run the barge aground. The song is closely modeled on traditional songs of the Volga boatmen, and the chorus is that of the popular "Little Cudgel" ("Dubinushka"—which has several revolutionary variants as well): "From the nobles' stupidity / The peasant barge can't get on an even keel... / In order to get moving / We'll have to toss the nobles into the water!" According to Leonid Shishko, another member of the *chaikovtsy*, "The Barge" was especially popular.[50] "Thoughts of a Smith" ("Duma kuznetsa") by Klements resembles "Thoughts of a Weaver." A smith muses on his 30 years of work with his hammer. Now he's losing strength, but can not afford to put it down. But enough of suffering, he resolves: it's time to do battle and turn the old order upside down. The poem sometimes entitled "A Request" ("Pros'ba")—also known as "The Tsar's Conversation with the People" ("Razgovor tsaria s narodom")— takes the form of a dialog between peasants and the tsar. The peasants beg the tsar for help with their hard lives—little land, officials stealing everything, the hardship caused by recruitment levies. The tsar, however, is hardhearted and unfeeling: "You'll get nothing out of me!" The last of these poems, "When I Was a Russian Tsar" ("Kogda ia byl tsarem rossiiskim," to the tune of the popular song "When I Was an Arcadian Prince" ["Kogda ia byl arkadskim printsom"]), presents another picture of a careless, thoughtless tsar who deceives and ruins the *narod*: he goes hunting for a bear, has had too much to

---

[49] Garkavi, *N. A. Nekrasov*, 41.

[50] See the texts of all three poems in Bazanov, *Agitatsionnaia literatura*: "Svobodushka," 458–60; "Dolia," 461; "Barka," 465–66.

drink, and shoots a peasant! And as for the reforms, the tsar goes on, "what one hand gives, I immediately take back with the other."[51]

The songs included in *Collection of New Songs and Verses* became the first wave of revolutionary songs that were truly widespread and popular among workers. Evidence from memoirs, archival sources, and trial records show that these were songs that workers learned and sang. The sources also to some extent indicate the relative popularity of individual songs. Aleksandra Kornilova, who, together with her two sisters was a core member of the Chaikovskii circle, made a point of noting that some of the verses composed by Klements and Sinegub were "well-known to workers [even] before their publication abroad and thus serve as evidence that the propaganda of the *chaikovtsy* was not limited to literacy and science, but was distinguished by its fully revolutionary character."[52] The *chaikovtsy* were gratified by the success of these songs among the Petersburg workers with whom they came in contact. Leonid Shishko notes "The Barge" and "The Peasants' Request" ("Pros'ba krest'ian") as among the most popular songs from the *Collection*.[53] When several of Sergei Sinegub's worker students were arrested, police found manuscript copies of various illegal works, including the songs "The Barge" ("Barka"), "The Tsar's Conversation with the People," both in Sinegub's hand, as well as the song "Freedom, Dear Freedom" ("Svoboda-svobodushka")."[54] Police records reveal the rapid dissemination of the *Collection*. In the mid-1870s copies were found with arrested workers and propagandists in Moscow, Ivanovo-Voznesensk, and Odessa.[55] The mere possession of the poems of Nekrasov, according to the young worker Pankratov, was grounds for punitive measures.[56] The role of song among radical workers comes through in some memoir accounts of this period. One propagandist from the Chaikovskii circle gave workers copies of a songbook in a Petersburg bar—this made the workers want to sing, and they

---

[51] These three poems are reprinted in Bazanov, *Agitatsionnaia literatura*: "Duma kuznetsa," 463–65; "Pros'ba" (here labeled ["Razgovor tsaria s narodom"]), 461–63; "Kogda ia byl tsarem rossiiskim," 469–70. For further discussion of the *Collection*, as well as the other songbook published by the *chaikovtsy*, *Songbook*, see Os'makov, *Poeziia revoliutsionnogo narodnichestva*, 83–88.

[52] Kornilova-Moroz, *Perovskaia i kruzhok chaikovtsev*, 53–54.

[53] Shishko, *Sergei Mikhailovich Kravchinskii*, 27.

[54] Sinegub, *Zapiski chaikovtsa*, 130. According to V. V. Kallash, the poems "The Barge," "People and Tsar" ("Narod i Tsar'"), and "Thoughts of a Weaver" were found in one worker's pocket (*Protsess 193-kh*, 16).

[55] See Mitskevich, "Moskovskie revoliutsionnye kruzhki," 58–59; Pankratova and Ivanov, *Rabochee dvizhenie v Rossii*, 2, ch. 1, 424–25; ch. 2, 20, 24, 32–33, 49, 113, 146.

[56] Pankratov, *Vospominaniia*, 7, 25.

headed out to the street singing "Long Have the Landlords Been Suffocating Us." Not surprisingly, Petr Moiseenko, who viewed his revolutionary career through the prism of song, quotes Nekrasov from "A Sumptuous Feast" ("Pir na ves mir"): "A good song raises the spirits." Moiseenko made great use of songs in his propaganda at the New Cotton Spinning Factory in Petersburg in the mid-1870s: "We used everything we could, even got up a choir with a tambourine and dancing." Among the favored songs were "Long Have the Landlords Been Suffocating Us" and "Dear Freedom": "The effect was striking. We were all inspired by revolutionary song. In spite of being tired, we forgot everything."[57]

By 1873 young radicals, including members of the Chaikovskii group, were eager to take their message of revolution to the countryside and engage the mass of the *narod*. The colorful story of the "pilgrimage" to the countryside of young radicals from the educated classes, who dressed as common people so their presence in the countryside would not stand out, has been told by historians of the Russian revolutionary movement, as well as participants.[58] Traveling deep into the provinces, sometimes taking work as *artel* members or barge haulers, radicals spoke to groups of peasants and distributed illegal pamphlets. Itenberg judges the *Collection* to be the most widespread illegal publication used in propaganda among the peasantry during the period of the movement "to the people."[59] Itenberg notes that with their outspoken attacks against serfdom, exploitation, and the whole tsarist system, these songs easily appealed to peasants as well as workers (and were, most likely, their intended audience). Within months, hundreds of the youthful propagandists had been arrested. For one thing, their presence could not be concealed from the authorities: it was almost impossible for a young member of the nobility to pass as a peasant. Assessments of the effectiveness of this propaganda effort vary. While the received view holds that peasants could not relate to the revolutionary message, Itenberg's comprehensive study of the movement shows a certain degree of success.[60] The arrested propagandists were defendants in two big trials—the "trial of the 193" and the "trial of the 50"—that were the main political events of 1877–78. In addition to peasant propaganda, those on

---

[57] M. P. Ovchinnikov, "Iz moikh narodovol'cheskikh vospominanii," *Sibir'skaia letopis'*, no. 6–8 (September–October 1916): 272; Moiseenko, *Vospominaniia starogo revoliutsionera*, 20, 55.

[58] See especially Itenberg, *Dvizhenie revoliutsionnogo narodnichestva*; and Venturi, "The Chaikovskists and the Movement 'To Go to the People,'" chap. 18 in *Roots of Revolution*.

[59] Itenberg, *Dvizhenie revoliutsionnogo narodnichestva*, 262–63.

[60] Ibid., 266–345.

trial, particularly in the "trial of the 50," included a number of youth who had been involved in propaganda among workers, especially in Moscow.

Records from the two umbrella trials give a detailed picture of the nature of revolutionary propaganda in the mid-1870s. The *Collection*, as well as *Songbook*, the other popular songbook published by the *chaikovtsy*, are mentioned frequently, in testimony on the use of the booklet and the singing of songs, and in enumeration of illegal literature seized during arrests.[61] Witnesses frequently note occasions on which revolutionary songs, those printed in the *Collection*, were sung. "The Barge" seems to have been particularly popular. Sinegub taught this song to workers, and another propagandist set up a village carpentry workshop where he taught local peasants "The Barge," "Freedom," and other revolutionary songs, and even organized social events (*narodnye gulianiia*) which featured the singing of revolutionary songs. In another instance, peasants were witnessed singing "Freedom, Dear Freedom" right on the street. Under questioning, one of those involved maintained that he "didn't consider them [songs] revolutionary." Peasants and workers often gave disingenuous answers when confronted with the illegal literature in their possession. One worker, for example, claimed that he "burned it [illegal pamphlet] as soon as he realized it was bad." Other songs that proved popular included "My Fate" ("Volia-voliushka"), "When I Was a Russian Tsar," and "Little Cudgel."[62]

Activists felt that a combination of oral and written (read aloud) propaganda would be most effective. They would speak to peasants, read to them, and teach them songs. In one instance, a propagandist in Ivanovo-Voznesensk gave workers legal but tendentious works to read, then held discussions about the books and explained their contents.[63] As described in trial materials, the ideas propounded by the propagandists were fairly blunt. According to the testimony of witnesses, members of the *chaikovtsy* told workers that "to free

---

[61] For materials from these trials, see Kallash, *Protsess 193-kh*, and Kallash, *Protsess 50-ti*. While both songbooks are mentioned repeatedly, *Collection* dominates references in the Trial of the 50. For references to the Collection in *Protsess 193-kh*, see pages 35, 41, 49, among many others. One load of contraband seized included 533 copies of the *Collection* (63).

[62] Kallash, *Protsess 50-ti*, 7. Among the many references to "The Barge" and other songs, see Kallash, *Protsess 193-kh*, 17, 115–16, 120–21. One propagandist also met with local gymnasium students in Penza. Meetings regularly concluded with the singing of revolutionary songs (*Protsess 193-kh*, 133). Songs were an oral genre, and as such they were often referred to by slightly different titles. For example, "Svobodushka" (Dear Freedom), "Svoboda-svobodushka" (Freedom, Dear Freedom), and "Svoboda" (Freedom) all undoubtedly referred to the song printed in the *Collection* as "Svobodushka."

[63] See Kallash, *Protsess 193-kh*, 55, 69, 73, 93, 110; and Kallash, *Protsess 50-ti*, 12.

themselves from government oppression, it was necessary to destroy the government by means of an uprising, after which the land would be at the disposition of the peasantry and the factories in the hands of the workers."[64] Another propagandist told peasants that "in order to have a better life, it was necessary to destroy the government and the bureaucrats, after which everyone would be equal."[65] The goal of "leveling" society was one repeated by various propagandists, according to witnesses: these radicals wanted "to equalize the poor and the rich, to organize a *bunt* and slaughter, so as to destroy the government, the *chinovniki*, and the nobles."[66] One propagandist gave out books and explained that "in Russia there would soon be an uprising, the government would be destroyed, and the *narod* would govern itself."[67]

Although the "movement to go to the people" is almost exclusively associated with propaganda among the peasantry, documents from the trials show that even in the countryside, propagandists continued to associate with workers. They often set up carpentry workshops or metal shops as a basis for propagandizing workers. (Of course, in many cases it is impossible to draw a clear line between "peasants" and "workers.") In the summer of 1874 propaganda was carried out among members of an *artel* of carpenters working on a zemstvo hospital in Samara. These workers also provided addresses of nearby peasants, and propaganda spread in this fashion.[68] Elsewhere, a propagandist set up a joiners' workshop, where he taught village workers revolutionary songs; several propagandists joined a coopers' workshop, and in another case radicals opened a metal shop to operate on socialist principles.[69]

The songs published in the illegal *Collection* by the Chaikovskii circle continued to be sung by workers up to the turn of the century. A variant of Sinegub's "Thoughts of a Weaver" was sung at the turn of the century. One worker, recalled the abysmal conditions at his factory in Ivanovo-Voznesensk, which brought to mind the "Weaver's Song" ("Pesn' tkacha") published by the local committee of social democrats: "the pages on which it [the song] was hectographed were read to pieces. And one could hear this carefully learned song

---

[64] Kallash, *Protsess 193-kh*, 21.

[65] Ibid., 32.

[66] Kallash, *Protsess 50-ti*, 3; see also Kallash, *Protsess 193-kh*, 159, 161.

[67] Kallash, *Protsess 193-kh*, 161.

[68] Ibid., 106, 166–68.

[69] See ibid., 113, 115, 98–99. The two volumes published by Kallash contain much more interesting information on propaganda activity of the period.

among the youth somewhere in the woods or far from the eyes of the police."[70] Nekrasov's verse, especially "At the Main Entrance" and "The Railroad," both included in the *Collection*, remained widely popular among workers. Workers in one Moscow circle of the mid-1890s learned these and other poems by heart "and recited them everywhere at parties."[71] Similarly, a Petersburg worker of the same period later recalled that "Nekrasov made the greatest impression on us. His verse achieved through suffering, his muse of sorrow and anger went straight to our heart."[72]

∞   ∞

The second chronological grouping of revolutionary verse I will consider are works that appeared in revolutionary journals in the period following the "movement to the people." From the mid-1870s to the mid-1880s, a series of "underground" revolutionary journals served as a common reference point for the groups that made up the Russian revolutionary movement. The first of these was Petr Lavrov's *Vpered!*, published in Zurich and London, followed by the official organs of the parties of populism's "heroic period"— *Zemlia i Volia* (Land and Freedom) and *Narodnaia Volia* (The People's Will). Single issues of these journals circulated for years and turned up repeatedly in police searches. They served as vehicles for the dissemination of a number of poems (some of which were later set to music) which remained popular in the movement, including among workers, for decades. Taken as a whole, these poems reflect the rapid evolution of the revolutionary movement in the second half of the 1870s: the movement now had a history. Poems might commemorate events or enshrine martyrs: those who, in the words of the revolutionaries, suffered for their heroic service in the people's cause, victims of unjust trials, inhumane punishment, imprisonment, execution. It is worth noting that the half decade of the late 1870s/early 1880s was a key period for the composition and publication of revolutionary verse that remained popular into the early 20th century.

As Franco Venturi and others have shown, the figure of Petr Lavrov was at the theoretical heart of the revolutionary populism that developed in

---

[70] M. Kiselev, *Iz revoliutsionnogo proshlogo: Zapiski starogo bol'shevika* (Moscow, 1934), 20–21. This later version of Sinegub's verse is reprinted in *VRP* (1959 ed.), 754.

[71] Mironov, *Iz vospominanii rabochego*, 10.

[72] Shapovalov, *Po doroge k marksizmu*, 45. See also Zelnik, *A Radical Worker*: "[W]e often remained awake well past midnight reading aloud the simple, angry verses of Nekrasov, henceforward our favorite, most beloved poet" (75). See also Fomin, "Vospominaniia o podpol'noi rabote," 204; and Egorov, "[Iz vospominanii o rabochikh kruzhkakh]," 241.

Russia in the 1870s. He began his career as a mathematics instructor at the Mikhailovskii Military Academy in Petersburg in the late 1840s. Described by Philip Pomper as a "courtly, gentle, comically myopic teacher of mathematics,[73] the writings and contacts of this unlikely radical led to his arrest in 1866 following Karakozov's attempt on the life of the tsar. While in exile he wrote his influential *Historical Letters*, a book which made a strong impact on radical youth, with the call for the "critically thinking individuals" from among the educated minority to repay their "debt to the *narod*" and to prepare themselves for revolution by educating themselves and carrying out propaganda among the *narod*. Having escaped Siberia in 1870, Lavrov spent the rest of his life in Western Europe. There, encouraged in his own idea of publishing a journal by requests from young radicals in Russia, he published a journal and a biweekly, both with the title *Vpered!* (Four volumes of the review *Vpered!* were published under Lavrov's editorship in 1873–76; the biweekly was published in 1875–76.) Setting up presses first in Zurich, then in London, Lavrov took up the mantle of Herzen and Ogarev's *Kolokol*. Copies were smuggled into Russia and provided material for debate, as well as bolstering the nascent revolutionary movement. Many of the poems published in *Vpered!* were written by Lavrov himself.[74]

The revolutionary movement evolved rapidly, soon leaving Lavrov behind. Following the spontaneous and disorganized movement "to the people" and the ensuing arrests, radicals sought greater strength through structure, and by 1878 a nationwide umbrella organization, termed a "party," was formed: Land and Freedom (Zemlia i Volia). Notes Venturi, "The very name … implies a programme."[75] A centralized organization, Land and Freedom united far-flung circles and groups throughout the empire and made use of division of labor as well, with different groups focusing on literary activities, propaganda among different segments of the population (students, workers), and those

---

[73] Pomper, *Peter Lavrov*, xviii.

[74] On Lavrov and *Vpered!*, see Pomper, *Peter Lavrov*; Itenberg, *P. L. Lavrov*; Itenberg, *Dvizhenie revoliutsionnogo narodnichestva*, 77–92, 194–218; Venturi, "Bakunin and Lavrov," chap. 17 in *Roots of Revolution*; Sapir, "*Vpered!*" *1873–1877*; and Sapir, ed., *Lavrov—gody emigratsii: Arkhivnye materialy v dvukh tomakh* (Dordrecht, Netherlands, 1974). These works convey a detailed picture of the varying views and factions confronting Lavrov and of the workings of the press operation and its contacts with groups in Russia. Lavrov withdrew as editor of *Vpered!* in 1876. Although never a member of a revolutionary party, he drew closer to the People's Will in later years and served on the editorial board of that party's emigré journal, *Vestnik Narodnoi voli* (Herald of the People's Will), which appeared in five issues (1883–86). For a reprint of the review *Vpered!*, see *Vpered! Neperiodicheskoe obozrenie*; for the biweekly *Vpered!*, see *Vpered! Dvukhnedel'noe obozrenie* (The Hague, 1969).

[75] Venturi, *Roots of Revolution*, 558. On Land and Freedom, see Deborah Hardy, *Land and Freedom: The Origins of Russian Terrorism, 1876–1879* (Westport, CT, 1987).

charged with "disorganization" activities, or reprisals against spies. From this point, the growing tension between the government and the revolutionaries, tellingly viewed by the public as a "duel," became a central feature of Russian life, manifest in a series of assassinations and attempted assassinations, armed resistance to arrest, and arrests, imprisonment, and executions. In 1879, however, the basic ideological disagreement dividing the members—whether the party should continue to focus on its former goal of propaganda among the peasantry, or whether revolutionaries needed to do battle with the tsarist state directly, hoping either to provoke a popular revolution or to wrest the essential freedoms without which revolutionary propaganda and organization could not take place—could no longer be papered over. The resulting schism resulted in the creation of two new parties, Black Repartition (Chernyi Peredel—voicing the peasants' presumed desire for a new and equitable land distribution) and the People's Will (Narodnaia Volia). The People's Will quickly attracted more members and was destined for a much greater historical role. The official party journal published by the People's Will, in addition to the preceding journal *Zemlia i Volia*, occasionally included among the editorials, ideological debates, and news of workers' movement in the West and revolutionary activity in Russia, published poetry as well.[76] Throughout the rest of the century illegal journals and newspapers were published by revolutionary groups. The ability to set up an underground press, or even to produce literature by hectograph, in itself attested to the strength of a group and was a point of pride. Such revolutionary periodicals comprised an essential element of the movement as well as literature that served the purpose of propaganda.

Publication in these party periodicals was a major factor in the widespread dissemination of revolutionary poetry throughout the Russian Empire. The most famous revolutionary song through 1917 was the "New Song" ("Novaia pesnia"), usually known as the "Workers' Marseillaise," composed by Lavrov and published in *Vpered!* in 1875. From the mid-1880s this song was sung by

---

[76] For information on the party presses and publications of Land and Freedom, the People's Will, and Black Repartition, see Venturi, *Roots of Revolution*, 620–21, 629–30, 640, 664–65, 684–85. See reprints of *Zemlia i Volia* and *Listok Zemli i Voli* in *Revoliutsionnaia zhurnalistika semidesiatykh godov: Vtoroe prilozhenie k sbornikam "Gosudarstvennye prestupleniia v Rossii,"* ed. B. Bazilevskii [V. Bogucharskii], Slavica-reprint 52; Russkaia istoricheskaia biblioteka 7 (Düsseldorf, 1970). A reprint of the 1905 edition of *Literatura sotsial'no-revoliutsionnoi partii "Narodnoi Voli"* (published by the Socialist Revolutionary Party) was published in Leipzig, 1977. It includes all issues of *Narodnaia Volia*, *Listok Narodnoi Voli*, *Rabochaia Gazeta* (nos. 1 and 2), and other documents. On the publication of *Rabochaia Gazeta*, the People's Will's newspaper for workers, see Venturi, *Roots of Revolution*, 704–06. For more information on *Rabochaia Gazeta* and *Zerno* (The Seed), the newspaper for workers put out by the rival Black Repartition, see Pearl, "Educating Workers for Revolution," 273–79.

radicals of all ideological persuasions and burst forth into the public domain in the political demonstrations of the early 1900s and the revolutions of 1905 and 1917. (In 1917 the Provisional Goverment made it the national anthem.) The tune is a modified version of the famous French "Marseillaise"; the lyrics, however, differ, reflecting the struggle for social revolution, rather than war against foreign powers. Infused with determination and hope, the song calls on the "starving working people" to rise up against the rich, who feast at the expense of the people, and against the tsar-vampire, who drinks the people's blood and sucks their veins dry. The chorus calls: "Arise working people, rise against your enemies, starving brother! Let the cry of the people's vengeance ring out! Forward!" The last stanza pictures the new dawn, under the sun of truth and brotherhood, when all people will join together in the "free kingdom of holy labor."[77] (A number of variations of the "workers' Marseillaise" were composed, including the "peasant Marseillaise" and a "Jewish workers' Marseillaise.")[78]

The funeral march titled "Final Farewell" ("Poslednee prosti") by Grigorii Machtet, a participant in the revolutionary movement, was also published in *Vpered!* (1876). The song, commonly known by its first line, "Tormented by terrible captivity" ("Zamuchennyi tiazhkoi nevolei"), was dedicated to Pavel Chernyshev, a student slated for trial with "the 193." Incarcerated for the crime of carrying out propaganda among peasants, Chernyshev contracted tuberculosis in prison and was released days before his death. (Chernyshev's funeral on 30 March 1876, was deliberately turned into a political demonstration with about 1000 mourners, mostly students.) In the song, the hero's brothers in struggle bid him farewell: "In battle for the people's cause / You lay down your impetuous bones." They too are ready to make the supreme sacrifice: "Our road is one with yours." But they are sure that "soon from our bones / Will arise a stern avenger / And he will be stronger than us!"[79] Similar sentiments are expressed in another funeral march, probably also composed in the mid-

---

[77] "Novaia pesnia" was first published in the biweekly *Vpered!*, no. 12 (1875). See the reprint in *VRP* (1959 ed.), 262–63. The song is recorded on the compact disc *Pesni rossiiskogo proletariata*" (Melodiia, 1998).

[78] See a reference to the latter in N. A. Bukhbinder, *Istoriia evreiskogo rabochego dvizheniia v Rossii: Po neizdannym arkhivnym materialam* (Leningrad, 1925), 155.

[79] "Poslednee prosti" reprinted in *VRP*, 2: 197–98. See also 593–94 n. 109. On P. F. Chernyshev, see *DRDR* 2, vyp. 4, cols. 1949–51. A lengthy correspondence on Chernyshev's funeral was published in *Vpered!*: "Pokhorony Pavla Chernysheva," *Vpered!*, no. 34 (1 June [20 May] 1876): cols. 320–25. For details on the interesting career of Machtet, see *DRDR* 2, vyp. 3, cols. 896–99. On the song and the funeral demonstration, see T. G. Polianskaia, "K istorii izvestnoi revoliutsionnoi pesni (K 100-letiiu pesni 'Zamuchen tiazheloi nevolei')," *Sovetskoe zdravookhranenie*, no. 6 (1976): 69–71.

1870s, but not published at that time. Usually referred to simply as "Funeral March" ("Pokhoronnyi marsh") or by the opening words, "You fell victim..." ("Vy zhertvoiu pali"), the funeral hymn bids farewell to brothers who have fallen in the struggle for the people's freedom. Their suffering is acknowledged, and the song concludes with a prophecy of a future time when the struggle will be taken up by the awakened people: "You fell victim in a fatal battle / With selfless love for the people.... / At times you languished in damp prisons... / And you went, with shackles clanking." The days of tyranny are numbered: "a fateful hand has long since drawn / The fateful letters are on the wall.... / The time will come—and the people will awaken, / Great, powerful, and free."[80] These two songs remained the most popular funeral songs through the early 20th century, sung at demonstrations, funerals, and on the journey to Siberia. From the 1870s, when the movement was small, to the mass revolutionary and workers' movement of the early 20th century, these songs retained their place of honor as a means of paying last respects to fallen revolutionaries of all parties.

Other poems also honored individual revolutionaries and their sacrifices. "To the Judges" ("K sudiam"), published in the review *Vpered!* in 1877, was dedicated to Lidiia Figner, one of the defendants in the "trial of the 50," by Aleksandr Borovikovskii, one of a notable group of liberal-minded jurists who served as defense attorneys for revolutionaries on trial in the mid to late 1870s. Written in the voice of its female defendant, the poem was most commonly known by its first line: "My Grievous Sin, My Evil Intention," as the narrator ironically admits to her "crime" of going to the *narod* and asks, why bother with this hypocritical trial? Yes, she is guilty of love for her native land. But as she is seriously ill, her punishment will be brief.[81] "After the Execution of

---

[80] "Vy zhertvoiu pali," reprinted in *VRP* (1959), 562–63. Authorship of this song is disputed and many variants exist. See ibid., 825–27n. See also the variant "My zhertvoiu pali," in *VPR*, 2: 440–42 and 643–44 n. 208. For an excellent detailed analysis of this song, see E. Kann-Novikova, *Vy zhertvoiu pali v bor´be rokovoi: Rasskazy o pesniakh* (Moscow, 1968). Kann-Novikova delves into the complicated history of the text, which she links to the executions of revolutionaries in the late 1870s and 1880s. She concludes that while the identity of the song's author is still "unknown," it may well be the fruit of collaborative work. Kann-Novikova's work also includes an interesting discussion of the poetic images common to so many verses of the period.

[81] Published in *Vpered!* 5 (1877); reprinted in *VRP* (1959), 275–76 and 768–69n. Lidiia Figner was a sister of noted revolutionary Vera Figner. See biographical note on Borovikovskii in V. G. Bazanov, B. L. Bessonov, and A. M. Bikhter, eds., *Poety-demokraty 1870–1880-kh godov* (Leningrad, 1968), 486. See mention of his activity in V. N. Ginev and S. S. Volk, eds., *Revoliutsionery 1870-kh godov: Vospominaniia uchastnikov narodnicheskogo dvizheniia v Peterburge* (Leningrad, 1986), 208, 209, 211, 219; and N. A. Troitskii, *Tsarizm pod sudom progressivnoi obshchestvennosti 1866–1895 gg.* (Moscow, 1979), 186, 194. The

4 November" ("Posle kazni 4 noiabria") was composed by Nikolai Morozov, a prominent member of the People's Will. The title refers to the execution of Aleksandr Kviatkovskii and Andrei Presniakov, two members of the party's Executive Committee, and was published in the journal *Narodnaia Volia* in December 1880, one month after the event. The opening lines convey the heartwrenching spectacle: "And again executioners! Keep silent my scream-ing heart!... / Again corpses swing in the noose." The author cries out over their deaths: we'll fight the tsar and his gang: "Death for death! Blood for blood! Revenge for execution!" Some day the light will dawn, "even if over our grave," and our descendants in a free land will "remember us with a good word."[82]

Vpered! regularly published correspondence and articles on the workers' and socialist movements in Western Europe, and similar news was frequently featured in the other journals as well. The history of the workers' movement in the West was a major topic discussed in workers' circles throughout the 19th century. One of the most widely disseminated poems of this period, published in *Vpered!*, took as its subject the revolution of 1848—specifically, the mood of Parisian workers on the eve of the June Days, when the workers fought street battles at the barricades in a doomed attempt to hang on to their revolution in the face of General Cavaignac's army and the fears of the increasingly conservative government of the Second Republic. "In Memory of the June Days of 1848" ("V pamiat' iiun'skikh dnei 1848 goda") opens with the

---

judicial reform of 1864 introduced aspects of a modern Western-style legal system, including defense attorneys. For a fuller discussion of the role of lawyers and the legal system in cases involving revolutionaries, see Troitskii, "Politicheskie protsessy i russkaia advokatura," chap. 4 in *Tsarizm pod sudom.*

[82] The poem is reprinted in *VRP* (1959), 468, with author unknown. According to the 1988 edition of *VRP* (Leningrad, 1988), Morozov has been established as the author. See 632 n. 254. A. K. Presniakov, and A. A. Kviatkovskii, at one time a student at the Technological Institute, were fully involved in the revolutionary activities of the 1870s. They were both members of the "Disorganization Group" of Land and Freedom, formed in 1877 to counter spies in the movement; later both joined the Executive Committee of the People's Will and participated in terrorist activities. Upon arrest, Presniakov put up armed resistance. See Volk, *Narodnaia Volia 1879–1882*, 307, 407; and Venturi, *Roots of Revolution*, 641, 698. See also Hardy, *Land and Freedom*, 56–58, 85–86. On Nikolai Morozov's revolutionary activities, see Venturi, *Roots of Revolution*, 505, 640–41, 649, 653; Volk, *Narodnaia Volia 1879–1882*, 85–92, 95–97, 232–34, 251–56. 440–44; Bazanov, Bessonov, and Bikhter, *Poety-demokraty*, 184–86; and Morozov's memoirs: N. A. Morozov, *Povesti moei zhizni: Memuary*, 2 vols. (Moscow, 1961). Morozov was a fairly prolific writer of revolutionary verse. See especially his poems published in the illegal collection *Iz-za reshetki: Sbornik stikhotvorenii russkikh zakliuchennykh po politicheskim prichinam v period 1873–1877 gg., osuzhdennykh i ozhidaiushchikh "suda"* (Geneva, 1877); reprinted in *VRP* (1959), 338–48.

starving family of an unemployed worker. The father comforts his children: tomorrow our suffering will come to an end; "the Republic has promised us bread or a bullet." A determined crowd gathers on the street with song and banner, building a barricade and awaiting the next day's battle with grim determination. They face the stark alternatives: "either bread or a bullet."[83] News from abroad provided workers with information on the lives and movements of their fellow workers in Western countries. A poem such as "In Memory of the June Days of 1848" could also build sympathy, showing the suffering and determination of the Parisian workers, so similar to their own.

γ ў

The People's Will persisted as the major trend in the 1880s, one of the most understudied periods in the history of the revolutionary movement. Groups of radical *intelligenty* and in some cases workers calling themselves *narodovol'tsy* continued to exist in urban centers and provincial towns throughout the empire. Revolutionary activity took the predominant form of contacts and circle organization among workers, building on foundations laid during the 1870s.[84] One attempt to resurrect the formerly centralized leadership core of the People's Will was undertaken by a group of professional revolutionaries (including Natan Bogoraz, Boris Orzhikh, and others) operating in Rostov-on-Don, Novocherkassk, and other southern towns in 1885–86. They set up a sizeable underground press in Taganrog, on which they printed the last issue of *Narodnaia Volia* (no. 11–12) and other material. Significantly, publication of an extensive collection of revolutionary verse, to be called *Echoes of the Revolution* (*Otgoloski revoliutsii*), was a top priority, and it serves as the third guidepost in this chapter's analysis. (An edition of 1000 copies of the 150-page collection

---

[83] The poem is dated 27 June 1875, Paris. It is reprinted in *VRP* (1959), 264. Authorship has been disputed: the 1959 edition of *VRP* attributes the poem to poet and journalist N. S. Kurochkin; see note on 765. The 1988 edition of *VRP* attributes the poem to D. A. Klements; see 592 n. 105. Klements is also named as the author in Sapir, *"Vpered!" 1873–77*, 163.

[84] On the Russian revolutionary movement in the 1880s, see Naimark, *Terrorists and Social Democrats*; and Offord, *The Russian Revolutionary Movement*. On worker-*narodovol'tsy*, see Pearl, "From Worker to Revolutionary." In 1928–31 the All-Union Society of Political Prisoners and Exiles (Vsesoiuznoe obshchestvo politicheskikh katorzhan i ssyl'no-poselentsev), in which many former members of the People's Will were active, published three invaluable collections of memoirs of this period. See Iakimova-Dikovskaia, *Narodovol'tsy posle 1-go marta 1881 goda*; Iakimova-Dikovskaia et al., *Narodovol'tsy 80-kh i 90-kh godov*; and Iakimova-Dikovskaia et al., eds., *Narodovol'tsy: Sbornik III, sostavlen uchastnikami narodovol'cheskogo dvizheniia* (Moscow, 1931).

was printed.)[85] This collection never circulated, however, as the police raided the premises of the press on the eve of publication (January 1886): the pages were printed, but not yet bound. Nevertheless, this work is of interest for the light it sheds on the body of revolutionary poetry circulating in the mid-1880s. As the editors note in the preface to the volume, the collection

> represents an extraction from the voluminous material we have at hand. In it are included not only original new works from the editors' portfolio, but also many poems printed in various revolutionary publications or passed from hand to hand for the past ten years.[86]

Several poems from the period of the celebrated trials and exploits of the late 1870s/early 1880s had become well-known and were frequently recopied and circulated in manuscript form. Three of these were reprinted in *Echoes of the Revolution*: "To the Judges" ("Moi tiazhkii grekh, moi umysel zlodeiskii!") and "After the Execution of 4 November," both noted above, and the longer work "By the Coffin" ("U groba") by Aleksandr Ol'khin, first published in the journal *Zemlia i Volia* in 1878. Ol'khin, the author of several poems popular in the revolutionary movement, was a defense lawyer in a number of trials of radicals, including the trial of the *nechaevtsy*, those arrested in the Kazan Square demonstration (St. Petersburg, 1876), and the trials of "the 50" and "the 193." While never a member of a revolutionary party, Ol'khin's assistance to radicals and his well-known anti-government views ultimately led to his brief imprisonment and years of surveillance and exile.[87] "By the Coffin" is dedicated to "the one who struck down Mezentsev," a reference to the daredevil radical Sergei Kravchinskii, who in August 1878 fatally stabbed the head of the Third Section, General Mezentsev, in broad daylight and

---

[85] Boris Orzhikh later wrote a detailed essay on his travels around Russia attempting to forge links between scattered radical groups: Orzhikh, "V riadakh 'Narodnoi voli,'" in Iakimova-Dikovskaia et al., *Narodovol'tsy*, 75–176. On the Taganrog press and the collection of revolutionary verse, see ibid., 126, 130–31, 154, 167. On Orzhikh and the Taganrog press, see also A. Shekhter-Minor, "Iuzhno-russkaia narodovol'cheskaia organizatsiia," in Iakimova-Dikovskaia, *Narodovol'tsy posle 1-go marta*, 131, 133. Additional information on the group connected with the press is found in the police file: GARF f. 102, DP, 7 d-vo, d. 42, ch. 3. See also Ministry of Justice files: RGIA f. 1405, op. 87, d. 10138; f. 1410, op. 1, dd. 523, 524. For bibliographical information on the collection, see Itenberg et al., *Svodnyi katalog*, 2: 20 (no. 1272); and *VRP* (1959), 821–22.

[86] RGIA f. 1410, op. 1, d. 524, l. 11.

[87] See biographical information on Ol'khin in *DRDR* 2, vyp. 3, cols. 1087–90. See also Bazanov et al., *Poety-demokraty 1870–1880-kh godov*, 502–03; *VRP* (1959), 803–04; Troitskii, *Tsarizm pod sudom*, 203, 207; Ginev and Volk, *Revoliutsionery 1870-kh godov*, 208, 209; and Os'makov, *Poeziia revoliutsionnogo narodnichestva*, 66.

then managed a successful escape.[88] This lengthy poem (39 verses) pictures the disconsolate tsar at Mezentsev's coffin, wondering who had dared to execute his favorite. Suddenly at midnight the lamp goes out and the tsar is confronted with a multitude of wraithlike apparitions, the spectres of those whose suffering he had caused. The phantoms carry out a grim funeral mass for the deceased, forcing the tsar to confront the death and devastation he has caused: "Surrounded by a galaxy of palace luminaries,... Didn't you hear the wailing of your native land / Over the tune of the court musicians?" Following verses detailing devastation and suffering, the speaker issues a threat: "[A]n immense storm cloud hangs over your throne.... And your hour will strike!... Every groan, every sigh, the falling tears / Will turn into a firebreathing serpent / And your heart, hardened long ago, / Will be pierced by millions of teeth!'"[89] As in other examples of revolutionary verse, "By the Coffin" describes an unfeeling autocrat and the suffering of the people; it sounds themes of vengeance and coming vindication. According to one scholar, "U groba" "in the course of several decades played the role of the populist Marseillaise ... and was recited at literally all revolutionary *vecherinki* right up until the revolution of 1917."[90] Another important song found among the papers seized at the Taganrog press was a manuscript version of the famous funeral hymn "You Fell Victim," noted above.[91]

A group of Moscow *narodovol'tsy* made a similarly unsuccessful attempt to publish a collection of revolutionary poetry in 1886. Here too the printed sheets, for an intended edition of 1000, were seized by the police. Natan Bogoraz, one of the most active *narodovol'tsy* of the mid-1880s and a composer of revolutionary verse as well, had eluded arrest at the time of the discovery of

---

[88] See Venturi, *Roots of Revolution*, 610–11.

[89] The poem is reprinted in *VRP* (1959), 440–45. See also note on 803–04, where "By the Coffin" is called "one of the most popular verses in Russian revolutionary poetry of the 1870–1880s."

[90] D. Kuzmin, *Narodovol'cheskaia zhurnalistika* (Moscow, 1930), 218, quoted in M. Druskin, "Revoliutsionnaia pesnia narodovol'tsev," *Sovetskaia muzyka*, no. 3 (1934): 49 n. 5. Worker Petr Moiseenko notes in his memoirs that "By the Coffin" made a strong impact on workers in the late 1870s, shortly after Mezentsev's assassination (*Vospominaniia starogo revoliutsionera*, 33).

[91] This poem/song appeared in many variants, sometimes as "You Fell Victim" ("Vy zhertvoiu pali"). For the version found at the Taganrog press, see *VRP* (1959), 562–63. This version is felt by some scholars to be "contaminated" by verses from another poem. More frequently, the version reprinted in *PRP*, 2: 346 was sung. For a detailed historical and musicological analysis of this hymn, see Kann-Novikova, *Vy zhertvoiu pali*. She notes the striking similarity between these two most popular of funeral hymns and calls "Oppressed by Heavy Captivity" the "direct ancestor" of "You Fell Victim" (60). She also notes the manuscript found at the Taganrog press (48ff.).

the Taganrog press. He then made his way to Moscow and linked up with the local group of *narodovol´tsy*, for the most part students.[92] It is thus no accident that the Moscow group planned to include some of the poems from *Echoes of the Revolution*, which were undoubtedly brought to them by Bogoraz, in their *Verses and Songs* (*Stikhi i pesni*).[93] One of the poems included in this collection, beginning "Brothers, forward!" ("Brat´ia, vpered!"), was popular among radical students and others from the 1860s, appearing in handwritten form in a number of variants. In the verses of this song revolutionaries encourage each other: they will defend their native land and fight for the *narod*: "Even if we must perish / in prisons and damp mines, / Our cause will find an answer / In the living generations / in the generations that follow."[94] This song, sometimes called the "People's Will [*narodovol´cheskii*] hymn"—retained its popularity into the period of the 1917 revolution.[95] (As for Bogoraz, later known as Vladimir Bogoraz-Tan, while in Siberian exile he began a distinguished career as an

---

[92] See *DRDR* 3, vyp. 1, col. 352. Bogoraz turned up in Moscow, where he had contacts with the People's Will circle around Mikhail Gots, in the fall of 1886. He was arrested there in December. On Bogoraz as a poet and activist, see E. Bushkanets, "Neizvestnye pamiatniki revoliutsionnoi poezii 1880-kh godov," *Russkaia literatura*, no. 1 (1962): 233–35. On the Moscow People's Will group, see the memoir account of M. R. Gots, "Moskovskaia tsentral´naia gruppa partii 'Narodnaia Volia,' 1883–1885 gg.: Otryvok iz neizdannoi avtobiografii," in Iakimova-Dikovskaia et al., *Narodovol´tsy posle 1-go marta*, 96–108; and Tereshkovich, "Neskol´ko slov," 109–28. On *Verses and Songs* and Bogoraz's trip to Moscow, see Tereshkovich, "Neskol´ko slov," 113–14.

[93] On this verse collection, see *VRP* (1959), 828–30. The collection was subtitled *Collection of Verse by Various Authors. With a Supplement of Verses from the Unpublished Collection "Echoes of the Revolution"* (*Sbornik stikhotvorenii raznykh avtorov. S prilozheniem stikhotvorenii iz nenapechatannogo sbornika "Otgoloski revoliutsii"*). The volume's cover announced the forthcoming publication of *Tsar Hunger, The Clever Trick*, and *Who Lives By What?*", the three major pamphlets on political economy used in propaganda among workers and a sure sign of the group's involvement in this activity. This intention is also noted by Tereshkovich ("Neskol´ko slov," 113). See also Itenberg et al., *Svodnyi katalog*, 2: 103 (no. 1804): although part of the edition was seized by the police, part was salvaged and distributed.

[94] This version is reprinted in *VRP* (1959), 578. The history of this song and its versions has been the subject of controversy among Soviet scholars of revolutionary song. See *VRP* (1959), 829n; *VRP* (1988), 647n. One frequently heard version, attributed to M. L. Mikhailov, begins "Bravely, friends! Don't lose courage..." (reprinted in VRP [1959], 655; see *PRP*, 2: 43–44 and note 469 on 444. The poem is often attributed to M. L. Mikhailov and dated to 1861. This is disputed, however, by E. G. Bushkanets in "Ob oshibochnoi atributsii stikhotvoreniia 'Smelo, druz´ia, ne teriaite...," *Russkaia literatura*, no. 2 (1968): 111–14. See also M. Druskin, "Revoliutsionnaia pesnia narodovol´tsev," *Sovetskaia muzyka*, no. 3 (1934): 56–57. For analysis of the melody of "Smelo, druz´ia," see Druskin, *Russkaia revoliutsionnaia pesnia*, 60–61, 156–57 n. 28.

[95] *VRP* (1959), 829n.

ethnographer of the indigenous peoples of Siberia; after the 1917 revolution he continued his work as ethnographer, professor, and member of the Academy of Sciences.)[96]

These two overlapping collections, *Echoes of the Revolution* and *Verses and Songs*, attest to the communications network linking far-flung revolutionary groups. The links between the southern *narodovol'tsy* and their comrades in Moscow are further illustrated in archival files of the 1880s, which reveal a web of connections between *narodovol'tsy* groups in various urban centers; the files usually present evidence of propaganda among workers as well. To ask who was the intended audience for these songbooks is perhaps to oversimplify the distinction between songs and verse intended for propaganda among workers and those directed at the intelligentsia. In the genre of poetry and song, in particular, no clear lines can be drawn, and any songs available to local *narodovol'tsy* were apt to be passed on to workers as well. Propaganda materials seized at the arrest of a revolutionary group, for example, frequently included works directed at workers, as well as songs and the particular works circulating among radical-minded students at the time.[97] When the Taganrog press was discovered, police seized not just the pages of *Echoes of Revolution*, but 85 copies of *Tale of Four Brothers*—as we have seen, one of the popular works of propaganda used among workers.[98]

In addition to the widespread circulation of poetry among *intelligenty* involved in propaganda among workers, by the 1880s we find that radical workers had developed their own attachment to revolutionary verse and had made it their own. In the first half of the 1880s a rather autonomous group of worker *narodovol'tsy* in Rostov-on-Don functioned as propagandists as well as providing leadership in the local labor movement. (They had initially been radicalized in circles led by members of the local People's Will organization, mostly students.) In 1883 these Rostov worker *narodovol'tsy* even managed to put

---

[96] On Bogoraz, see *DRDR* 3, vyp. 1, cols. 351–55 and note 92 above.

[97] To give several examples: among literature seized at the arrest of an Odessa People's Will circle of primarily gymnasium students (active in 1884) were copies of the verse "You Fell Victim" (in one copy, "We Fell Victim"). The group's main figure was also reading propaganda literature to workers (GARF f. 112, op. 1, d. 619, ll. 299 ob., 331–331ob.). A similar People's Will circle of secondary school students in Kishinev was arrested with copies of *Tale of Four Brothers* and *On Truth and Falsehood*, both used for propaganda among workers, as well as a copy of the funeral hymn "Oppressed by Heavy Captivity" (GARF f. 102, 7 d-vo, d. 573, ll. 18–20, 29ob.). At the arrest of Kiev *narodovol'tsy* involved in propaganda among workers, a copy of "By the Coffin" was seized, among other works of literature (RGIA f. 1405, op. 83, d. 11101, l. 147).

[98] GARF f. 102, 7 d-vo, d. 42, ch. 3, l. 8ob. On literature seized at the press, see ibid., ll. 8ob.–9ob.

out a hectographed journal, *Rabochii* (The Worker), written entirely by workers and addressed to a worker audience. Poetry features in several instances in *Rabochii*'s single issue. As was often the case in revolutionary writings, a verse from Nekrasov's *Who Lives Well in Russia?* appears as the epigraph to an article explaining the dire effects of the development of capitalism: "Homeless, without kith or kin—this is the lot / Of more than a few of the *narod* in Rus'." An untitled poem beginning "The new tsar promised us..." is also included. It expresses the people's resolve to obtain the land that is theirs, as well as the factories. They will show the tyrants that one does not live by might alone, but rather "honest people from the *narod*" will be in charge of the new society.[99] In a third poetic reference, the final article, "How the Workers are Living," a lengthy survey of working conditions concluding with a call to revolution, closes with the chorus from Lavrov's "Workers' Marseillaise": "Arise, stand up, working people."[100] In Khar'kov, a major center of People's Will activity in the 1880s, a similar group of radical workers managed to keep a network of circles going, engaged in organizing work among broader strata of the working class, and escaped arrest for nearly a decade, until 1889.[101] The bonds of personal friendship uniting these activists are revealed in a poem written by one of the workers on the eve of his departure for Siberian exile. In "My Dear Brothers and Comrades," the poet bids farewell to individually named activists, wives, and associates.[102]

Cʒ ʕʊ

The archaelogy of the "revolutionary songbook" reveals successive layers, with each new phase of the revolutionary movement contributing certain poems and songs that remained popular in later periods. The songbook's contents shifted and overlapped. Some older poems remained popular, then dropped out of use; newer works were added. As we see in the analysis of

---

[99] "'Rabochii'—rostovskii zhurnal," 85–86. I have not been able to find an attribution for this poem.

[100] On this group, see ibid., with extensive commentary by Nevskii and Volk, 75–100. See also Peshekerov, "Propaganda narodovol'tsev," 116–28. On V. Pankratov's experiences as a propagandist in Rostov, see Pankratov, *Vospominaniia*, 64–81; Pankratov, "Iz deiatel'nosti sredi rabochikh," 249–51.

[101] On this Khar'kov group, see Veden'ev, "V Khar'kovskikh revoliutsionnykh kruzhkakh," 98–111; and Denisenko, "Khar'kovskaia gruppa," 128–42.

[102] The poem is reprinted in V. I. Nevskii, "Khar'kovskoe delo Iuvenaliia Mel'nikova i drugikh," in *Ot "Zemli i Voli" k gruppe "Osvobozhdenie Truda,"* ed. Nevskii (Moscow, 1930), 28–82. For additional discussion of the Rostov and Khar'kov organizations of worker-revolutionaries, see Pearl, "From Worker to Revolutionary," 19–24.

these song collections, the poetic works of very different chapters in the history of the revolutionary movement could mingle and form one repertoire, transcending organizational and ideological differences of the various revolutionary groups. Poetry originating in and appreciated by such diverse groups as the peasant-oriented *narodniki* of the 1870s; *narodovol'tsy* waging their struggle against the government in the late 1870s and early 1880s; and isolated circles of radicals and workers in provincial towns in the 1880s: these same works apparently retained their appeal among participants in the social democratic workers' movement of the 1890s. In 1892, the police uncovered a network of workers' circles in St. Petersburg. This city-wide social democratic organization has been discussed above in chapter 1. It brought together a number of activist workers, mostly from the Baltic plant, the Franco-Russian Company, and other metalworking plants, who distributed underground literature and organized workers' *kruzhki*. As we have seen, circle studies were led by *intelligenty*: for example, a science student at St. Petersburg University who gave lectures on political economy and sociology, as well as providing revolutionary publications.[103] By the early 1890s these radical workers were exercising a major role in political activity under the umbrella of the Workers' Union, which brought together representatives of working-class districts and leading student radicals. The worker activists managed, despite police surveillance, to hold a clandestine meeting with speeches to celebrate 1 May. (The first such commemoration occurred in 1891 in St. Petersburg.) The tsarist regime saw these radical workers as a definite threat. Petr Durnovo, head of the Department of Police, noted in a report of 1892 that workers had recently become the focus of revolutionary propaganda: "and at the present time in St. Petersburg there are a fair number of workers who have completely assimilated revolutionary teachings."[104]

This organization of St. Petersburg workers appears to be the source for an intriguing archival discovery: a manuscript collection of poems in a police file labeled "Collection of verses which are being passed around among workers."[105] This collection will serve as the fourth guidepost as we trace the evolution of the corpus of revolutionary verse in this chapter. Among the dozen

---

[103] GARF f. 102, 3 d-vo, d. 558, ll. 7–8.

[104] GARF f. 102, 3 d-vo, d. 888, ll. 189–189ob. For more information on the Petersburg "Workers' Union," also known as the "Brusnev Organization," see Kazakevich, *Sotsialdemokraticheskie organizatsii Peterburga*; Polevoi, *Zarozhdenie marksizma v Rossii*; and Orekhov, *Pervye marksisty*. See also the numerous memoir accounts of participants, including those published in *Ot gruppy Blagoeva k "Soiuzu Bor'by"* and Korol'chuk, *V nachale puti.*

[105] The document has the title "Echo from the Volga" ("Otklik s Volgi") (GARF f. 102, 3 d-vo, d. 558, ll. 44–68).

works included are some of the poems mentioned above: "Dear Freedom," from the *Collection of New Songs and Verses* (1873); "In Memory of the June Days, 1848" by Dmitrii Klements and the funeral march "Oppressed by Heavy Captivity," both published in *Vpered!*, and four very popular poems printed in the above-mentioned 1886 collections: "By the Coffin," "After the Execution of 4 November," "To the Judges," and "Brothers, forward! Don't lose... "[106] Overall, the collection has a definite "People's Will"—or maybe we should just say "revolutionary"—flavor: not surprising, as that was the revolutionary tradition to that point. The significance of the circulation of this particular group of poems among presumably social democratic St. Petersburg workers (and we know that most of the propagandists considered themselves social democrats, a claim supported by the types of other literature used or seized at searches—many standard SD works, especially writings of Plekhanov and the Emancipation of Labor Group) calls into question the nature of the political identity of these radical workers and the significance of ideological distinctions at the grassroots level. Most accounts of the revolutionary movement in this period emphasize competition between populists and Marxists. Memoirs of revolutionary St. Petersburg workers refer to debates between People's Will and social democratic *intelligenty* in the mid-1890s, and some workers were clearly aware of a distinction. But at the same time, these workers had assimilated a sense of a revolutionary movement and revolutionary tradition that went back to the earliest contacts between workers and members of the intelligentsia. The songs seem to be serving their intended purpose, creating

---

[106] The complete listing of poems in the collection is as follows: 1) "Virgin Soil" ("Nov'") by N. A. Sablin, first published in *Na rodine*, no. 1 (1882), reprinted in *Otgoloski revoliutsii* (hereafter *OR*); 2) "By the Coffin" ("U groba") by Ol'khin, reprinted in *OR*; 3) "Dear Freedom" ("Svobodushka"); 4) "Thus the soul is torn to pieces" ("Tak i rvetsia dusha") by A. V. Kol'tsov, first published in *Otechestvennye zapiski*, no. 12 (1840); 5) "Quiet in the prison" ("Tikhko v t'iurme") by an unknown author, from *Stikhi i pesni* (Moscow, 1886); 6) "Brothers, forward! Don't lose... " ("Brat'ia vpered! Ne teriaite...") from *Stikhi i pesni*; 7) "In Memory of the June Days, 1848" ("V pamiat' iiunskikh dnei 1848 g.") by N. S. Kurochkin, *Vpered!*, no. 3 (1875), reprinted in *OR*; 8) "Great Fedor, He's a Fool" ("Velika Fedora, da—dura") and "Noblewoman, her lordship, the little mother of little Fedor" ("Barynia sudarynia, matushka fedorushka"), first published in *Vestnik Narodnoi Voli* 2 (1884); 9) "After the Execution of 4 November" ("Posle kazni 4-go noiabria 1880 g.") by an unknown author, first published in *Narodnaia Volia*, no. 4 (1909)—reprinted in *OR*; 10) "My Grievous Sin, My Evil Intention" ("Moi tiazhkii grekh, moi umysel zlodeiskii..."—"K sudiam") by Borovikovskii, reprinted in *OR*; 11) "On the death of V. Osinskii" ("The trumpet rang out...") ("Na smert' V. Osinskogo" ("Pogremela truba...")—this is the poem "Execution" ("Kazn'"), author unknown, manuscript seized with arrest of the *OR* press; 12) "Oppressed by Heavy Captivity" ("Zamuchen tiazheloi nevolei"—"Poslednee prosti") by G. A. Machtet, published in *Vpered!*, no. 33 (1876): col. 284.

an emotional connection between workers and the revolutionary movement. The collection also reveals the overlapping layers of the movement's cultural history.

I have found no other references to this collection, and its intriguing, somewhat idiosyncratic selection of poems, including both the well known and the quite obscure, raises the question—who put together this collection? Individual poems from the collection, however, were being read and circulated among workers. We have already come across, in chapter 1, one of these poems. Among the illegal literature found when two 21-year-old factory workers were arrested in November 1891 was a handwritten copy of "To the Judges" ("K sudiam"—here titled "Rech' podsudimoi" ["Words of the Accused"]), written, as we have seen, at the time of the "trial of the 50" in 1877, in the voice of one of the noble-born female defendants, and published in *Vpered!* and *Echoes of the Revolution*, as well as being included in the 1892 collection. Archival files also give some information on the use of this poem. One of the two workers, Nikolai Bogdanov (the poem was written in his hand), once recited the poem to two female workers at his factory (the card [*kartochnaia*] factory of the Imperial Foundling Home), apparently, according to one of the women, to show that "women used to be more energetic, than at present." She liked the poem so much that she in turn copied it down (and indeed, the copy was found in her apartment).[107] The "Workers' Union" frequently held parties with dancing, drinking, and guitar music as a cover both for socializing and making contacts among the population of active workers, and as a way to draw new recruits into the movement. The singing of revolutionary songs was central to the social and emotional life of this group of workers. One participant recalled that everyone gathered round and sang "with joy and anger, knowing that the song was like a bridge leading right to the road to the police station or the thrice-cursed 'rodina' [one's village], or even to Siberia."[108] The press belonging to a People's Will-identifying group (Gruppa Narodovol'tsev) provided a good part of the revolutionary literature available in St. Petersburg during the first half of the 1890s. While the press did not officially print any poems, one of the workers testified that he "personally printed 'The Weaver's Song' ['Pesnia tkacha'] on our press (as I recall, five copies)."[109] Individual poems and songs did not "belong" to different groups but were part of a common culture of revolution.

---

[107] RGIA f. 1405, op. 92, d. 10979, l. 39. For Bogdanov and his activities, see chapter 1 of this book.

[108] Quoted in Kazakevich, *Sotsial-demokraticheskie organizatsii*, 161.

[109] This may have been Sinegub's "Duma tkacha" of the 1870s. GARF f. 102, 7 d-vo, d. 257, l. 363ob.

 C3   80

In the early 20th century the revolutionary song reached its final stage of development. No longer restricted to clandestine meetings, revolutionary song became part of public life and was heard openly in the street, as in the 1905 demonstration described by Shapovalov at the beginning of this chapter. The workers' revolutionary movement underwent a rapid evolution in the period 1900–05, and this was reflected in a new importance given to song in this era. In Saratov, for example, the first May Day demonstration took place in 1902, accompanied by singing of the "Workers' Marseillaise." Those arrested continued to sing the "Marseillaise," as well as "Bravely, Comrades, Let's March" in a "harmonious and inspiring" fashion. The authorities actually tried to drown out the singing with drums—but the beat somehow matched the "Marseillaise," "so the singing was even more effective and rang out with redoubled force."[110] Strikes, street demonstrations, and the public celebration of May Day all highlighted a new and, from the perspective of the government, more threatening image of workers in Russian society. The revolutionary movement had continued to evolve as well, with the formation of the Social Democratic and Socialist Revolutionary Parties. *Intelligenty* and workers associated with these parties were often (but not always) in leadership roles in these new manifestations of the movement. Among the most important of these strikes and demonstrations were, in 1901: street demonstrations in major cities; the May First demonstration in Khar'kov; and the strike at the St. Petersburg Obukhov plant, which culminated in armed battle between workers and the police (often referred to as the "Obukhov defense"). Revolutionary songs also accompanied demonstrations in Ekaterinoslav in 1901 and 1902, as well as, in 1902, May Day demonstrations in Nizhnii Novgorod and Sormovo and a strike of railroad workers in Rostov-on-Don. In 1903 strikes broke out throughout the southern part of the empire; 1903 also witnessed many attempts to celebrate May Day.[111] By the revolutionary year 1905 striking

---

[110] Partiia Sotsialistov-Revoliutsionerov, *Demonstranty pered sudom: Delo o saratovskoi demonstratsii s prilozheniem izvlechenii iz obvinititel'nykh aktov o nizhegorodskoi i sormovskoi demonstratsiiakh* (1902), 5, 6, 10.

[111] Major secondary studies of the labor movement of this period include Surh, *1905 in St. Petersburg*; Reichman, *Railwaymen and Revolution*; Wynn, *Workers, Strikes, and Pogroms*; Theodore H. Friedgut, *Iuzovka and Revolution, 2: Politics and Revolution in Russia's Donbass, 1869–1924* (Princeton, NJ, 1994); Weinberg, *The Revolution of 1905 in Odessa*; Wade and Seregny, *Politics and Society in Provincial Russia*; Engelstein, *Moscow, 1905*; Jeremiah Schneiderman, *Sergei Zubatov and Revolutionary Marxism: The Struggle for the Working Class in Tsarist Russia* (Ithaca, NY, 1976). See also M. Rozanov, *Obukhovtsy* (Leningrad, 1938); and I. Bortnikov, *Iul'skie dni 1903 goda na iuge Rossii*

and demonstrating workers and radicals had become part of the lexicon of political activity. The public nature of these demonstrations and meetings brought the existence and issues of the movement, along with revolutionary songs, to increasing numbers of workers and bystanders.[112] Workers often participated in student demonstrations, also characteristic of these years, and learned from them. According to a social democratic report on local activity, the student "disorders" which took place in Khar'kov in 1899 made a big impression on workers: "The student demonstrations, which excited the whole town and aroused general sympathy among the Khar'kov population, found an especially lively response in the working-class milieu."[113] Although SDs and SRs vied for leadership of the workers' movement, in the area of song unity prevailed. Adherents of both of Russia's mutually antagonistic socialist parties taught and sang the same songs.[114]

As we saw in Shapovalov's description of workers learning "The Red Banner" "on the run," in the midst of a street demonstration, workers in the early 20th century learned revolutionary songs through various means. More than was the case with other genres of propaganda, the revolutionary song was learned by heart, and by many workers simultaneously. O. Alekseeva notes: "this [revolutionary] poetry helped introduce socialist consciousness into the proletarian movement," and in the years leading up to 1905 their sound was everywhere.[115] These songs captured the movement in their phrases and ideas

---

(Odessa, 1953). In these works, however, little attention is paid to the physiognomy of street demonstrations, and revolutionary song is mentioned briefly, if at all.

[112] A. Iu. Drugovskaia finds that the songs sung at demonstrations "exerted enormous influence on all strata of the urban population." Drugovskaia, "Propaganda mestnymi organizatsiiami RSDRP revoliutsionnoi pesni," *Voprosy istorii KPSS*, no. 8 (1988): 118.

[113] "Rabochee dvizhenie v Khar'kove," 8. Memoir and other evidence show that workers were aware of and sympathetic to student demonstrations. In many cases, demonstrators consisted of both students and workers. See, for example, the memoirs of Mironov, *Iz vospominanii rabochego*, 25; V. Zalezhskii, *Na putiakh k revoliutsii: 1896–1906 gg.* (Moscow–Leningrad, 1925), 36; E. P. Onufriev, *Za nevskoi zastavoi: Vospominaniia starogo bol'shevika* (Moscow, 1968), 34; N. Drokhanov, "Na zare," in Rubach, *Istoriia ekaterinoslavskoi sotsial-demokraticheskoi organizatsii*, 260–61; and Shesternin, *Perezhitoe*, 32. On the participation of workers in student demonstrations of the early 20th century, see A. V. Ushakov, *Revoliutsionnoe dvizhenie demokraticheskoi intelligentsii v Rossii 1895–1904* (Moscow, 1976), 141–68.

[114] See, for example, RGIA f. 1405, op. 530, d. 79, 1903 g., ll. 78–83ob. (Prosecutor's report on SR activity in Kiev, 1903). Found at search: hectographed words to "Workers' Marseillaise," other songs.

[115] O. Alekseeva, "Pesni russkikh rabochikh," *Russkaia literatura*, no. 4 (1964): 131–32. Alekseeva's treatment of revolutionary song is one of the least tendentious and a good introduction to Soviet-era historiography on the subject.

and wove a network linking workers in cities and industrial areas throughout the empire. Songs spread in both written and oral form. G. N. Kotov, a worker, recalled that before he ever read illegal literature, he learned a couple of revolutionary songs from some politicized workers.[116] Songs were printed in the growing number of revolutionary periodicals and were also published as leaflets. Verses and quotations from songs were frequently inserted in articles and used as epigraphs and concluding exhortations.[117] Local revolutionary groups devoted a major effort to organizing demonstrations for May Day, often publishing special 1 May proclamations; a number of these included songs. A typical 1 May proclamation was issued by the Ekaterinoslav SDs in 1903. The one-page broadside concluded with the chorus from the "Workers' Marseillaise," followed by slogans.[118] Songbooks were also popular and were

---

[116] G. N. Kotov, *V bor'be za revoliutsii: Vospominaniia rabochego-bol'shevika* (Moscow–Leningrad, 1930), 23. M. Essen recalls leading circle studies with a group of railroad workers in Saratov in the late 1890s. He sometimes recited revolutionary poems and songs, and the workers would copy them down: "It sometimes happened that I'd go to the circle, and the day's topic would be 'The Decline of Petty Bourgeois Handicrafts'— and the workers would sharpen their pencils and request that I dictate the 'Marseillaise' or the 'Internationale.'" M. Essen, "Pesni revoliutsionnogo podpol'ia," *Sovetskaia muzyka*, no. 12 (1955): 7. For analysis of how songs were disseminated, see A. M. Novikova, "Rol' i znachenie revoliutsionnoi literaturnoi pesni v rabochem fol'klore," in *Ustnaia poeziia rabochikh Rossii*, ed. V. G. Bazanov (Moscow–Leningrad, 1965), 72. See also N. V. Os'makov, *Russkaia proletarskaia poeziia, 1890–1917* (Moscow, 1968), 75–76, 87–89.

[117] See the following examples of songs in periodicals: "Varshavianka" was published in full in *Iuzhnii Rabochii*, no. 4 (1901). ("By far the outstanding achievement of the talented Southern [SD] *praktiki* was the regional underground paper, *Iuzhnii Rabochii* [*Southern Worker*], founded early in 1900" [Wildman, *Making of a Workers' Revolution*, 222]. See 222–25 for a more detailed discussion.) Issue no. 5 (no date) of the same paper includes a song, "Song of the Spring" ("Pesnia vesny"), as well as an article on the history of 1 May, ending with a poetic verse. "Krasnoe Znamia" was published in *Rabochee Slovo*, no. 3 (1902) by the Odessa SDs, and a different poem with the same title was published in *Nashe Delo*, no. 5 (1902) in Nikolaev (both RGIA f. 1410, op. 2, d. 138).

[118] "Pervoe Maia: Ko vsem rabochim i rabotnitsam g. Ekaterinoslav," in Rubach, *Istoriia ekaterinoslavskoi sotsial-demokraticheskoi organizatsii*, 373. The SD organization in Ivanovo-Voznesensk put out a leaflet, *Pervoe maia*, in 1907 devoted to an explanation of the holiday and the symbolism of the red banner; lines from "Krasnoe Znamia" were included (*Pervoe maia v tsarskoi Rossii 1890–1916 gg.: Sbornik dokumentov* [Moscow, 1939], 175).

Radical groups occasionally made use of caricatures in their efforts to familiarize workers with the ideas of the movement. A picture entitled *Marseillaise* was listed among works of illegal literature circulating in Ekaterinoslav in 1900 ("Literaturno-izdatel'skaia deiatel'nost' 1899–1900 g.," in Rubach, *Istoriia ekaterinoslavskoi sotsial-demokraticheskoi organizatsii*, 203). In a report on the workers' movement in Khar'kov,

printed and hectographed in increasing numbers from the early 20th century through the 1917 revolution and the Civil War.[119]

One of the earliest songbooks, *Songs of Revolution* (*Pesni revoliutsii*), was published in 1902 by the "Iskra" press maintained by the émigré faction of social democrats associated with Lenin in Geneva.[120] This is the fifth and final song collection highlighted in this chapter. The collection consisted of only four songs, with notes: but as any perusal of the sources will show, they were the songs sung repeatedly during strikes and at meetings and demonstrations. These songs were: the "Workers' Marseillaise," "Warsaw Song" ("Varshavianka"), "The Red Banner" ("Krasnoe Znamia"), and "Step Bravely, Comrades" ("Smelo, tovarishchi, v nogu"). The first of these by the early 20th century had a long history in the movement; the other three were relatively recent. (Although intended for oral, collective song, the songbook itself could serve as propaganda literature.) F. N. Samoilov, a worker who began life in a poor peasant village, was a teenager when he joined his father in a textile factory in Ivanovo-Voznesensk. He later recalled that the first illegal brochure

---

a Social Democrat activist noted with dismay that the 1 May leaflet published in 1899 was poorly understood by "the lower strata of the working masses." On the other hand, workers very much liked the May Day pictures issued by *Rabochee Delo*; leaflets with drawings published by the St. Petersburg SDs were similarly successful (*Rabochee dvizhenie v Khar'kove*, 7). *Iskra* occasionally published political caricatures as supplements: several are reproduced in TSK KPSS, Vysshaia partiinaia shkola, Kafedra zhurnalistiki, *Bol'shevistskaia pechat': Sbornik materialov*, 1: *1895–1903 gg.* (Moscow, 1959), 305–10. See also Zelnik, *A Radical Worker*, 287.

[119] Among the early songbooks were *Pesni bor'by: Sbornik revoliutsionnykh stikhotvorenii i pesen* (Geneva, 1902); *Pesni bor'by: Sbornik stikhotvorenii* (Rostov-na-Donu, 1906); *Sbornik revoliutsionnykh pesen i stikhotvorenii* (Nizhnii Novgorod, January 1904 [GARF f. 1741, op. 2, d. 1516]); *Revoliutsionnye pesni* (Kostroma, February 1905 [GARF f. 1741, op. 2, d. 1441]).

[120] On this songbook, see S. D. Dreiden, *Muzyka—revoliutsiia*, 2nd ed. (Moscow, 1970), 12–16. According to Dreiden, few copies of the songbook are extant; Dreiden edited a reprint in 1968 (published by Sovetskii kompozitor) (Dreiden, *Muzyka*, 567 n. 7). A small group of Russian Social Democrats formed a party (RSDRP) in 1898. While key figures attempted to provide leadership from emigration, social democracy continued to gain adherents among workers and organizers in Russia. As is well known, at the second Party Congress in 1903, the Social Democrats split into the Bolshevik and Menshevik factions. Meanwhile, former populists and *narodovol'tsy*, with an updated agenda, had also by the early 20th century united in the Socialist Revolutionary Party. On the formation of the RSDRP, see Leopold H. Haimson, *The Russian Marxists and the Origins of Bolshevism*. Cambridge, MA, 1955; on the Socialist Revolutionary Party, see Maureen Perrie, *The Agrarian Policy of the Russian Socialist-Revolutionary Party from Its Origins through the Revolution of 1905–1907* (Cambridge, 1976).

he read was *Pesni revoliutsii,* which he "quickly learned by heart."[121] Together with the funeral marches "You Fell Victim" and "Oppressed by Heavy Captivity," both of which also dated, as we have seen, from an earlier period, this group of six songs remained the most popular, through the revolution of 1917 and beyond.

Songs of this type were usually referred to as revolutionary *gimny* or hymns (a terminology which, with its religious overtones, seems at first somewhat awkward). M. Druskin provides the following definition of this musical genre:

> songs which join together the consciousness, will and feelings of the masses in *action.* These works are filled with a *heroic-uplifting,* resonant tone. They are marked by a *high level of generalization* in text and music, to which is foreign any storytelling [narrative] or lyric, subjective character. This abstractness is joined with maximum *accessibility and concreteness* of political appeals directed to the broad strata of the *narod.*[122]

Lavrov's "New Song," popularly known as the "Workers' Marseillaise," was well known from the 1870s but received a new lease on life at the turn of the century and was without a doubt the most popular revolutionary "hymn."[123] Druskin traces shifts in melody from that of its model, the French "Marseillaise" and concludes that a new variant was created at this time.[124] As we have

---

[121] Samoilov, *Po sledam minuvshego,* 43. Samoilov dates this to 1902–03, so this is likely the songbook in question.

[122] Druskin, *Russkaia revoliutsionnaia pesnia,* 85–86. See Druskin's further analysis of this genre throughout chap. 4, "Pesni massovogo rabochego dvizheniia."

[123] Soviet-era musicologists, who have made the most detailed study of these songs, are in agreement on the overwhelming popularity of the "Workers' Marseillaise" at the marches and demonstrations of the early 20th century. See E. Gippius and P. Shiriaeva, "Rabochaia Marsel'eza," in *Biografii pesen* (Moscow, 1965), 53–73; and A. M. Novikova, "Revoliutsionnye pesni XIX veka v epokhu massovogo rabochego dvizheniia," *Uchenye zapiski Moskovskogo oblastnogo pedagogicheskogo instituta* 40, 2 (1956): 183–84.

[124] Druskin, *Russkaia revoliutsionnaia pesnia,* 95. Gippius and Shiriaeva note that the song was first sung in 1876 at Chernyshev's funeral demonstration, but that the earliest version of the tune has not survived. Various early versions were close to that of the French Marseillaise, and it was not until 1905, they claim, that the song acquired its current melody ("Rabochaia Marsel'eza," 68–69).

Although many sources, including secondary works, refer simply to the singing of "The Marseillaise," the song in question was *always,* according to Boris Sapir, the "Workers' Marseillaise" (personal communication to the author, August 1979).

seen, the song is a call to battle, pitting the "ranks of suffering brotherhood" against the "golden idols," the palaces of the rich, and the "tsar-vampire." The hunger, suffering, and exploitation of the *narod* are contrasted with the bonds of brotherhood and struggle that unite people "from the Dniepr to the White Sea, / from the Volga to the far-off Caucasus." With this final struggle, we will redeem the world, merge all peoples into one, and create a "free kingdom of holy labor." The chorus summons: "Get up, arise, working people! / Rise against your enemies, starving brother! / And let the cry of the people's vengeance ring out! / Forward!" Among events surrounding the 1898 *maevka* (1 May celebration) in St. Petersburg, Kolpino worker I. V. Mikhailov recalls the singing of the "Marseillaise" during a small spontaneous demonstration. The "Workers' Marseillaise" also resounded during the first street demonstration in Ekaterinoslav in December 1901. Saratov radicals of the same era loved to sing this song at their small social gatherings, and it figured in the first Saratov May Day demonstration in 1901 as well.[125] According to one account, someone began to sing the "Internationale," but few people knew the words. On the other hand, almost everyone knew the "Marseillaise" and sang out loudly, followed by two other songs of the era, the "Warsaw Song" ("Varshavianka") and "All Together, Comrades, Step in Time!" ("Druzhno, tovarishchi, v nogu," a variant of "Step Bravely, Comrades"). "In fact song was one of the most powerful and, in addition, the most accessible means of revolutionary agitation and propaganda."[126]

One of the first new songs to enter the revolutionary repertoire was "Boldly, Comrades, Step in Time!" ("Smelo, tovarishchi, v nogu!); the song was also known by its original title, "Druzhno, tovarishchi, v nogu!" ("All Together, Comrades, Step in Time!").[127] The author, Leonid Petrovich Radin, was a promising young chemist, a graduate of St. Petersburg University and a favorite pupil of the chemist Dmitrii Mendeleev. He abandoned his scientific pursuits, however, in favor of the revolutionary movement. He was active in the Moscow social democratic organization, the Rabochii Soiuz (Workers Union) in the mid-1890s. Charged with setting up an underground press, he "invented" a mimeograph (after carefully studying an American machine on display in a Moscow shop). Arrested in 1896, he composed a number of verses

---

[125] I. K. Mikhailov, *Chetvert´ veka podpol'shchika* (Moscow, 1957), 24–26; Wynn, *Workers, Strikes, and Pogroms*, 129. Kanatchikov describes "Auntie Marseillaise," who received her nickname from her vigorous piano renditions of this song (Zelnik, *A Radical Worker*, 191).

[126] G. G. Sushkin, *Maevki proshlogo* (Moscow, 1926), 7–9.

[127] See the text of "Smelo, tovarishchi!" reprinted in *PRP*, 2: 286–87 and 474–75 n. 657.

in prison, few of which survived. Radin died of tuberculosis in 1900, at the age of 40.[128]

"Boldly, Comrades" was, for many workers, the most popular revolutionary song. Its march rhythm was well suited to street demonstrations; it was sometimes called the "Fighting March" ("Boevoi marsh") or "Workers' March." In tone and message, it bears comparison to the *narodovol'cheskii* hymn" "Brothers, forward!" ("Brat'ia, vpered!"), also sometimes with the words "Boldly, friends, do not fear" (Smelo, druz'ia, ne teriaite) mentioned above. Significantly, the later song is voiced in the first person, its most famous lines: "We all came from the *narod*, / Children of the laboring family." Rather than dwelling on hardships and suffering, the song is a call to battle, expressing the confidence of workers: "Can our fighters be afraid / Of the spectral forces of tsars? / Everything that supports their thrones / Is the work of the laborers' hands." Victory, rather than vengeance, is the guiding goal: "And we'll raise over the earth / The red banner of labor!" (The earlier song, by contrast, dwells on the hardships the revolutionaries are willing to go through to help the "poor, oppressed people." The small band of fighters "in this unequal battle" will die—but the people will remember them.) Learning the songs "Boldly, Comrades" and the "Marseillaise" served as the introduction to revolutionary ideas for one Urals factory worker in 1902–03; he then advanced to reading propaganda literature.[129] "Boldly, Comrades" was the favorite song of workers at the Sormovo industrial plant near Nizhnii Novgorod; meetings regularly concluded with the singing of "our favorite" "All Together [sic], Comrades, Step in Time!"[130]

The other two songs in the 1902 *Iskra* songbook, the "Warsaw Song" and "The Red Banner," came to the Russian revolutionary movement from its Polish counterpart. Social democrats arrested as members of the St. Petersburg

---

[128] On Radin and "Smelo, tovarishchi, v nogu!" see also A. L. Dymshits, ed., *Revoliutsionnaia poeziia (1890–1917)*, 2nd ed. (Leningrad, 1954), 548; Gippius and Shiriaeva, "Smelo, tovarishchi, v nogu," in *Biografii pesen*, 74–89; Druskin, *Russkaia revoliutsionnaia pesnia*, 102–03; Os'makov, *Russkaia proletarskaia poeziia*, 69–71; A. I. Nutrikhin, "Gimny proletarskoi revoliutsii," *Vestnik Leningradskogo universiteta* 2, 8 (1958): 112–13; Iu. Dmitriev, "Smelo, tovarishchi, v nogu!" *Znanie—sila*, no. 4 (1961): 16–18. Dmitriev notes that the song was heard in 1917, during the Civil War, and during World War II as well (16). See also Vladimir Bonch-Bruevich, "Pervyi russkii mimeograf: Pamiati Leonida Petrovicha Radina," *Proletarskaia revoliutsiia*, no. 1 (1921): 167–80.

[129] Kotov, *V bor'be za revoliutsii*, 23–24.

[130] See recollections of Sormovo workers in V. T. Illarionov, ed., *Materialy po istorii revoliutsionnogo dvizheniia* (Nizhnii Novgorod, 1920), 1: 98, 102. The song was first published in the local underground newspaper, *Nizhegorodskaia rabochaia gazeta*, November 1901. See I. S. Eventov, ed., *Poeziia v bol'shevistskikh izdaniiakh 1901–1917* (Leningrad, 1967), 416–17 n. 2.

Union of Struggle and the Moscow Workers' Union first heard these songs in the Moscow transit prison in 1897, while awaiting exile to Siberia. "Warsaw Song" was composed by Vatslav Sventsitskii (1848–1901), a member of the Polish socialist organization "Proletariat," and published in the underground journal *Proletariat* in 1883.[131] One of the Russian prisoners inspired by the song was Gleb Maksimilianovich Krzhizhanovskii, who both translated and modified the song.[132] (Krzhizhanovskii was a close associate of Lenin in the St. Petersburg Union of Struggle and in Siberian exile. After the 1917 revolution he played a prominent role in developing electrical power in the Soviet Union.) "Warsaw Song" begins in a minor key: "Hostile whirlwinds circle around us, / Dark forces maliciously pursue us," then shows its true colors: it is a song of battle, raising the banner of struggle for the worker's cause. A song of vengeance ("death to … all the parasites of the working masses, … to all tsar-plutocrats"), but also of victory, the melody switches to the major mode as the famous chorus rings out: "To the bloody struggle, /Holy and true / March, march forward, /Working people!"[133] Musicologist D. Zhitomirskii describes the tune of "Warsaw Song" as "at the same time severe, energetic, and full of heartfelt passion." M. Druskin compares the Russian version of "Warsaw Song" with its Polish predecessor, emphasizing the way in which Krzhizhanovskii reworked the original, and finds that the "the heroic form is strengthened in the Russian melody."[134] The other song learned from Polish revolutionaries, "The Red Banner" ("Krasnoe Znamia"), became equally famous. This song's origins are much more complicated, beginning as a French song written to commemorate the anniversary of the Paris Commune, and reworked by the Polish socialist Boleslav Czerwieński (1851–88) in the early 1880s. The authorship of the Russian version, composed around 1900 and first published in that year, has been a subject of dispute among Soviet-era musicologists. It can most likely be attributed to Vladimir Akimov-

---

[131] The roots of the Polish song have been traced to the "March of the Zouaves" ("Marsh zhuavov") popularized by the insurgents of the failed Warsaw uprising of 1863. E. V. Gippius, quoted by D. Zhitomirskii in "Pesni na stikhi G. M. Krzhizhanovskogo," in *Biografii pesen*, 93.

[132] See G. Krzhizhanovskii, "Pesni bor'by," *Sovetskaia muzyka*, no. 12 (1955): 3–4. On the Petersburg "Union of Struggle" (Soiuz Bor'by), see Wildman, *Making of a Workers' Revolution*, 64-78, 97–100. For another account of the song's inception, see P. N. Lepeshinskii, *Na povorote* (Moscow, 1955), 68. See also Lepeshinskii, "Starye pesni revoliutsii," *Ogonek*, no. 32 (228), 7 August 1927 [pages unnumbered].

[133] See the text of "Varshavianka," reprinted in *PRP* (3rd ed.), 2: 288–89 and 475 n. 658.

[134] See Zhitomirskii, "Pesni na stikhi," 91; Druskin, *Russkaia revoliutsionnaia pesnia*, 96–101; Nutrikhin, "Gimny," 114–15.

Makhnovets, a Russian social democrat in emigration.[135] Like "Warsaw Song," "The Red Banner" opens on a foreboding note—"The boundless world is flooded with tears, / Our whole life is nothing but heavy labor"—but the first two lines are immediately followed by "But the inevitable day will come / Of the implacable stern judgment." The workers' song and their banner symbolize the bright future. The old order will fall, powerless before the workers' unity: "We don't need the old slave ways! ... Labor will be the ruler of the earth!" Once again, the song derives much of its emotional pull from its chorus, so closely matched with the melody: "Flow far, our song! ... Our banner waves over the world ... It shines and brightly glows, / Just like our blood, it shines like fire, / Because the worker's blood is on it!"[136]

The two revolutionary funeral hymns, "You Fell Victim" and "Oppressed by Heavy Captivity," both composed in the populist period, continued to grow in popularity. S. P. Shesternin, describing his group of radicalized gymnasium students in the years around 1880, recalls the special place held by the first of these: when news reached them of the execution of revolutionaries, they would sing "You Fell Victim."[137] By the early 20th century the two funeral hymns were taken up by workers as well; together with the four songs that comprised the *Iskra* songbook, these were undoubtedly the songs most often sung in marches and demonstrations of the workers' movement. Taken as a whole, the words and phrases of these six songs comprise a revolutionary vocabulary, one quite distinct from that of the various prose forms of propaganda literature. They speak in the voice of warriors, sometimes martyrs, who comprise a revolutionary brotherhood. For the sake of the hungry, exploited people they are ready to engage in battle/struggle, often termed "bloody," with the "tsar-

---

[135] E. Gippius and P. Shiriaeva present a detailed analysis of "The Red Banner" in *"Krasnoe Znamia": Iz istorii pesni trekh russkikh revoliutsii* (Moscow, 1969). The authors discuss the thorny question of the song's attribution, concluding that the main reason Akimov-Makhnovets could not be named as the author in the Stalinist period was due to "vulgar sociology"—a Menshevik could not have written this key revolutionary song (128–29). See also the version in E. Gippius and P. Shiriaeva, "Krasnoe Znamia," in *Biografii pesen*, 101–16. The song was first published in the workers' newspaper *Rabochaia mysl'*, no. 8 (February 1900). On the reworking and reception of the Polish songs "Warsaw Song," "The Red Banner," and "Rage, tyrants..." ("Besnuites', tirany..."), see Os'makov, *Russkaia proletarskaia poeziia*, 63–65.

[136] For the text, see *PRP*, 2: 421–22 and 498–99 n. 797. .

[137] Shesternin, *Perezhitoe*, 14. See Druskin, "Revoliutsionnaia pesnia 1905 g.," 14–15. Druskin notes that "Oppressed by Heavy Captivity" was "V. I. Lenin's favorite song." See also P. G. Shiriaeva, "Revoliutsionnaia pesnia v rabochei pechati 1905–1907 godov," in *Revoliutsiia 1905 goda i russkaia literatura*, ed. V. A. Desnitskii and K. D. Muratova (Moscow–Leningrad, 1950), 397–99; Novikova, "Revoliutsionnye pesni XIX veka," 157, 171, 190–95; *VRP* (1959), note on 766–67.

vampire" and other enemies. The goal is not just vengeance, but a society of freedom and brotherhood under the banner of labor. As the last verse of the "Marseillaise" puts it, "The sun of truth and brotherhood will rise ... Falsehood, evil will vanish forever." The "red banner" symbolizes these goals, won at the cost of the blood of revolutionary workers; the song's chorus is their battle cry.

The red banner literally waved in the streets over crowds of workers and other demonstrators in the course of strikes, May First celebrations, and other manifestations of the workers and revolutionary movements in the period 1900–05. The new songs and "hymns" of the early 20th century were closely linked with this new urban political manifestation, the demonstration—the newest form taken by the revolutionary movement. Revolutionary politics and goals, spelled out in slogans and the words of songs, were now visible to all who thronged the street; the boundary between demonstrators and bystanders was porous. Demonstrations were noisy and fraught with danger: marchers were frequently attacked by police; thus the revolutionary struggle was dramatized. Richard Stites compares the demonstration to a parade or a religious procession and writes that "the visual austerity was more than compensated for by the emotional texture and quasi-religious aura."[138] Michelle Perrot's analysis of the cultural significance of strikes in France also seems applicable: "A strike is a festival because it is a gathering and, therefore, also a communion." It "produce[s] the ... feeling that 'We are many.'"[139] Musicologists have pointed to the function of music in binding people together. "The binding is accomplished by rhythm," according to Oliver Sacks, "not only heard but internalized, identically, in all who are present. Rhythm turns listeners into participants."[140]

Evidence on the songs as an integral part of early 20th-century demonstrations is plentiful. Most frequently, articles in underground publications and accounts by participants refer simply to the "singing of revolutionary songs." In many cases, however, specific songs are mentioned by name, as illustrated by the following examples. Along with students and other members of the intelligentsia, workers also participated in the demonstration organized to

---

[138] Richard Stites, "The Role of Ritual and Symbols," in Acton, Cherniaev, and Rosenberg, *Critical Companion to the Russian Revolution*, 565–71; reprinted in Stites, *Passion and Perception*, 187.

[139] Michelle Perrot, *Workers on Strike: France, 1871–1890*, trans. Chris Turner (New Haven, 1987), 149.

[140] Sacks, *Musicophilia*, 266. Daniel Levitin similarly emphasizes the bonds created by "synchronous, coordinated song and movement," and speculates that "the strong emotional, even neurochemical pleasure that resulted from synchronized movement may well have had a prehistoric antecedent" (Levitin, *World in Six Songs*, 50, 56.)

accompany the writer Maksim Gor'kii on the first stage of his journey into exile (November 1901, Nizhnii Novgorod). The account published in *Iskra* names seven songs, including the "Workers' Marseillaise," the *"narodovol'cheskii gimn"* "Bravely, friends! Don't lose courage...," and "You Fell Victim." This lengthy correspondence also provides a detailed illustration of the demonstration as a means of linking the radicalized participants with bystanders and providing opportunities of explaining the revolutionary cause.[141] The first workers to participate in political demonstrations in Ekaterinoslav were artisans, rather than industrial workers, Charters Wynn has found. A description of one of the earliest demonstrations, organized by social democrats in 1901, points out several characteristic attributes. It involved "a few hundred demonstrators, many wearing red jackets and red ties," who marched to the town center "singing the 'Marseillaise," waving a red banner, and shouting 'Long live political freedom!' and 'Down with the autocracy!'"[142] Local revolutionary groups made special efforts to mount May Day celebrations, issuing proclamations beforehand to familiarize workers with the significance of the day and planning for street demonstrations. A Kiev factory worker recalls singing the "Marseillaise," "The Red Banner," "Dubinushka," and other songs during a large May Day meeting in 1900: "That day will never be erased from my memory. And the same deep impression, it was clear, was also made on the rest of the comrades, many of whom had tears in their eyes and were deeply moved." Similarly, the celebration of May Day in 1903, marked by the singing of "Varshavianka," had a great effect on the morale of Jewish workers in Gomel' (although, according to one account, police hostility toward the Jewish population of Gomel' increased following the demonstration). The May Day proclamation distributed by the Social Democrats in Ekaterinoslav in 1903 quoted the chorus of "Varshavianka": "To the bloody battle, sacred and true, / March, march forward, working people!"[143]

Cities and towns throughout Russia witnessed successive waves of strikes and demonstrations during the 1905 revolution, inaugurated by the procession of Petersburg workers to the Winter Palace on Bloody Sunday. The

---

[141] Correspondence from Nizhnii Novgorod, December 1901, reprinted in *Bol'shevistskaia pechat'*, 1: 213–16.

[142] Wynn, *Workers, Strikes, and Pogroms*, 129.

[143] Aleksandr Voronin, "Kruzhok na zavode Gretera-Krivanek," in *K dvadtstatipiatiletiiu pervogo s"ezda partii (1898–1923)* (Moscow–Petrograd, 1923), 92–93; N. A. Bukhbinder, "Evreiskoe rabochee dvizhenie v Gomele (1890–1905 gg.): Po neizdannym arkhivnym materialam," *Krasnaia letopis'*, no. 2–3 (1922): 67–68; Rubach, *Istoriia ekaterinoslavskoi sotsial-demokraticheskoi organizatsii*, proclamation reprinted, 372–73. For other examples of May First celebrations, see *Pervoe maia v tsarskoi Rossii 1890–1916 gg.: Sbornik dokumentov* (Moscow, 1939).

street demonstration, with its crowds of people; songs, banners, and slogans; and the danger posed by police and cossacks became emblematic of the events of that year. One memorable scene in Boris Pasternak's *Doctor Zhivago* depicts a demonstration in Petersburg following promulgation of the October Manifesto:

> Down the street people came pouring in a torrent—faces, faces, faces, quilted winter coats and sheepskin hats, male and female students, old men, children, railwaymen in uniform, workers from the trolley depot and the telephone exchange in knee boots and leather jackets, girls and schoolboys. For some time they sang the "Marseillaise," the "Varshavianka," and "Victims You Fell."[144]

This demonstration was dispersed violently by cossacks on horseback. The sources contain numerous other descriptions of demonstrations during 1905 and the central role played by songs. Railroad workers in the small town of Verkhneudinsk participated in a strike and demonstration, the town's first, in October 1905. Crowds of workers, employees, and soldiers took part, and a military group played the "Marseillaise"—although not very well. "Songbooks appeared, given out to those who wanted to sing.… At first uncertainly, unsure, the song then grew, broadened, attracted others." The procession grew as people marched to the city center singing "You Fell Victim." A participant struggles to recapture the impact of this first demonstration: "Rapture took hold of everyone, from the worker, to the intelligent, to the soldier; the singing of revolutionary songs—the 'Marseillaise,' 'Boldly, Comrades, Keep Step,' 'Hostile Whirlwinds' (the 'Varshavianka')—all of this for the first time, never before seen—fired up the whole demonstration as with a passionate breath."[145] Many other examples of the role of song in 1905 could be given.[146] A. M. Novikova claims that by the turn of the 20th-century revolutionary songs had become part of workers' daily life; this was especially true during 1905. She quotes correspondence from Kostroma that appeared in the SD

---

[144] Boris Pasternak, *Doctor Zhivago*, trans. Max Hayward and Manya Harari (New York, 1958), 35. This dramatic scene also figures in the 1965 film version of *Doctor Zhivago*, directed by David Lean.

[145] G. A. Vasil'ev, *Iz revoliutsionnogo proshlogo: Vospominaniia* (Ulan-Ude, 1954), 17–18.

[146] See, for example, Moiseenko, *Vospominaniia starogo revoliutsionera*, 193 (Iuzovka); Shapovalov, *V podpol'e*, 207–08 (Khar'kov); Onufriev, *Za Nevskoi zastavoi*, 65–68 (St. Petersburg); *Pervoe Maia v tsarskoi Rossii*; Wynn, *Workers, Strikes, and Pogroms*, 188, 196 (Ekaterinoslav). See the analysis of the "demonstratsionnoe dvizhenie" in Iu. I. Kir'ianov's *Perekhod k massovoi politicheskoi bor'be: Rabochii klass nakanune pervoi rossiiskoi revoliutsii* (Moscow, 1987).

journal *Proletarii* in 1905: "Even children adopted revolutionary songs. In the evening after a strike the workers' neighborhood resounded from all sides the sounds of the 'Marseillaise' and 'Varshavianka,' carried in all directions on the evening air. The police just gave up."[147]

03 80

Revolutionary song expressed the struggles, the solidarity, and the goals of the workers' revolutionary movement, and the movement's core concept was that of socialism. What did socialism mean to radical workers? How was the goal of a future socialist society expressed in propaganda literature of various genres, and in revolutionary song in particular? In this section I will suggest some ways to approach this elusive topic, which takes us to the heart of the workers' revolutionary movement.

As the strikes, meetings, and demonstrations of 1905 made clear, revolutions are not normal times. Ordinary people become involved; In Russia, new numbers of workers became politicized. Teodor Shanin notes:

> For its participants, a revolution is a moment of truth.... Within the process of revolution, images and realities confront and shape each other in a massive and fundamental process of learning. The major break of continuity rips the veils of the taken-for-granted, common sense and party rhetoric, offering an objective, hard and un-negotiable political lesson, the most dramatic of them all.[148]

The revolutionary song embodied this new revolutionary awareness: "Every participant in revolutionary activity knows from his own experience that a good mass song is a powerful weapon.... It creates solidarity and inspires action."[149] The message of revolutionary songs was reinforced by the slogans printed on red banners: "Down with the Autocracy!", "Long live the 8-hour working day!", "Long live political freedom!", "Long live May 1!" During 1905 and after, the slogan "Long live socialism!" appeared with increasing frequency on banners and was included in the slogans with which May Day and other revolutionary *listovki* concluded. Underground newspapers and leaflets frequently devoted articles to socialism, especially in connection

---

[147] Novikova, "Revoliutsionnye pesni XIX veka," 157.

[148] Teodor Shanin, *The Roots of Otherness: Russia's Turn of Century, 2: Russia 1905–07: Revolution as a Moment of Truth* (New Haven, 1986), 184.

[149] Aaron Copeland, quoted in David King Dunaway and Molly Beer, *Singing Out: An Oral History of America's Folk Revivals* (Oxford, 2010), 32.

with the celebration of May 1. The head of the Kazan' provincial gendarme department reported that about 200 local workers celebrated 1 May 1905 with a gathering at which several workers gave speeches. One was on the topic, "On Socialism."[150] What did this key concept mean to radical workers and the workers' revolutionary movement?

From its inception, the Russian revolutionary movement was a socialist movement. This basic goal united the two frequently discordant strands of the movement, Populism and Marxism. Revolutionary propaganda, in study circles and other venues, had several major emphases: among others, it explained the exploitative nature of the capitalist economic system, criticized the autocracy, raised revolutionary demands, and sketched a picture of the future socialist society. For some movement participants, the revolutionary subculture itself seems to have represented an alternative society. The revolutionary subculture certainly had its negative and iconoclastic elements, and recent studies of the revolutionary culture of 1917 have indeed emphasized these elements. Donald Raleigh argues that attacking the autocracy was the primary aim of revolutionary culture: "[T]he ideological origin of the Russian Revolution was less a matter of imagining a brave new world—although it was that, too—than it was of delegitimizing the autocratic system."[151]

---

[150] "Iz doneseniia nachal'nika Kazanskogo Gubernskogo Zhandarmskogo Upravleniia v Departament Politsii 4 maia 1905 g. No. 2155," in *Pervoe Maia v tsarskoi Rossii*, 142–43. See the description of Nikolai Bauman's funeral in Moscow in October 1905 in Engelstein, *Moscow, 1905*, 141. *Pervoe Maia* includes many Social Democratic proclamations of the early 20th century, with growing use of the slogan "Long Live Socialism!" See, for example: proclamation of the Southern Revolutionary Group of SDs in Odessa, 1 May 1902 (79–80); proclamation of the Kremenchug Committee of RSDRP, 16 April 1902 (83); RSDRP proclamation to Petersburg workers, 1 May 1903 (97–98); proclamation of the Moscow committee of RSDRP, April 1905 (138–39), and others. See, in M. A. Zaborov, ed., *Pervoe maia v dokumentakh i svidetel'stvakh sovremennikov, 1886–1918* (Moscow, 1989): leaflet of Petersburg committee RSDRP calling for strike 1 and 2 May 1905, 151–54; Moscow district of Petersburg, RSDRP leaflet for 1 May 1909, 190–91. According to correspondence published in *Iskra* radicals put a lot of effort into organizing a *maevka* in 1903. A series of proclamations was issued in April, including one "on socialism"; "political freedom," "what is a demonstration," and "a chronicle of the struggle with the autocracy" were among the other topics covered (107–08). See also the 1905 Kostroma May Day speech, reported in "Korrespondentsii iz Kostromy v gazetu 'Vpered,' mai 1905 g.," in *Pervoe maia v tsarskoi Rossii*, 143–44; and Semen Kanatchikov's description of a Saratov *maevka* in 1902 (Zelnik, *A Radical Worker*, 313).

See the analysis of topics covered in Socialist Revolutionary proclamations and propaganda activity in Rice, *Russian Workers*, 38–46.

[151] Donald Raleigh, *Experiencing Russia's Civil War: Politics, Society, and Revolutionary Culture in Saratov, 1917–1922* (Princeton, NJ, 2002), 23. Orlando Figes and Boris Kolonitskii, in *Interpreting the Russian Revolution: The Language and Symbols of 1917* (New Haven, 1999), similarly emphasize the central place in revolutionary culture of "de-

Consideration of a future, alternative society, however, was also part of the movement's appeal for workers. Mark Steinberg stresses the two-sided nature of the "language of revolution" of 1917: demands for freedom and justice, as well as class identification and hostility.[152] In attempting to answer the question of "what workers thought," in particular their understanding of socialism and their vision of the future socialist society, the concept of the "social imaginary" as presented by Bronislaw Baczko is useful. Baczko associates modern political myths with the dream of a perfectly transparent society and emphasizes that such representations of social reality do not simply reflect but also affect collective mentality. In referring to visions of the future, the idea of utopia, he writes: "The great political and social question of modernity [is] how to imagine and think about society as self-constituted, having full mastery of itself and resting on no order external to itself."[153] The concepts of socialism and utopia (and, in the Russian case, revolution) were closely linked. Revolutionary culture of necessity had its aspect of utopia, of the imaginary. As Ronald Suny has put it, "utopia can ... be understood to be an ideal, a goal toward which people aspire.... In a sense, every political movement seeking change contains within it a utopia, a place where if all were possible people would like to end up."[154] Richard Stites, in *Revolutionary Dreams*, his impressive study of the varying alternatives envisioned by Russians under the name *revolution*, similarly writes that

> utopianism ... is the key to the emotional force of the Russian Revolution—as it is to any successful revolution.... Both social reverie and social design were alternatives to a system that seemed unable to deliver the two things essential to human happiness: a victory over

---

sacralization of the monarchy," iconoclasm, and "anti-burzhui" hostility, along with more positive symbolic aspects.

[152] Mark D. Steinberg, "Introduction: The Language of Popular Revolution," in *Voices of Revolution, 1917*, ed. Steinberg (New Haven, 2001).

[153] Baczko, *Les imaginaires sociaux*, 7. This protean concept of the "social imaginary" has been given different meanings by other authors. See, for example, its use by Sarah Maza in her study *The Myth of the French Bourgeoisie: An Essay on the Social Imaginary, 1750–1850* (Cambridge, MA, 2003), in which she argues that while "the bourgeoisie" was basically an imaginary entity, the construct tells us something important about French society.

[154] Ronald Grigor Suny, *The Soviet Experiment: Russia, the USSR, and the Successor States* (Oxford, 1998), xiv.

nature to insure material abundance and a victory over egoism and exploitation to insure social justice.[155]

What did radical workers mean when they talked of socialism or called themselves socialists? How did they envision the future, post-revolution society? Two kinds of sources shed light on the "social imaginary" of radical workers: works of propaganda literature, including poetry and song, and memoirs written by participants in the revolutionary workers' movement.

As we have seen, a variety of genres of propaganda literature circulated in the subculture of radical workers: revolutionary *skazki*, pamphlets on political economy, poetry and song, newspapers, and others. Most of these works were composed or selected by *intelligenty* involved in propaganda activity, and one can not automatically assume that the views expressed were those of workers. Rather, they represent the views that these students and other radicals hoped to convey. On the other hand, we do have information as to the use and popularity of many works and thus can indirectly gauge their effectiveness. We also have some evidence that the ideas expressed were not adopted automatically or uncritically—they were adapted and used by workers in ways that made sense to them. (In some cases, we do have examples of literature and speeches composed by workers in this period.) The topics of socialism and the future socialist society are treated in many formats: in programs and speeches, through the genres of the *skazka* and pamphlets on political economy analyzed above, as well as in revolutionary poetry and song. A sampling of these varied formats follows.

From the 1870s, the various parties and groups in contact with peasants and workers issued programs and programmatic statements. The demands expressed present the future socialist society in its most basic outlines. Indeed, key demands remain unchanged from the 1870s through the 1917 revolution. The oft-reprinted "Program of the Executive Committee" of the People's Will Party (1879) called for self-government, "the possession of the land by

---

[155] Richard Stites, *Revolutionary Dreams: Utopian Vision and Experimental Life in the Russian Revolution* (Oxford, 1989), 4. Stephen Kotkin also emphasizes "socialism" as a key category for understanding the Russian Revolution and its meaning for the Soviet period: "By now ... it should be obvious that, from beginning to end, the Russian Revolution was fought over socialism." Stephen Kotkin, "1991 and the Russian Revolution: Sources, Conceptual Categories, Analytical Frameworks," *Journal of Modern History* 70, 2 (June 1998): 387.

For discussion of the concept of "utopia," see Karl Mannheim, *Ideology and Utopia: An Introduction to the Sociology of Knowledge* (New York, 1936); Jay Winter, *Dreams of Peace and Freedom: Utopian Moments in the Twentieth Century* (New Haven, 2006), 2–4; Susan Buck-Morss, *Dreamworld and Catastrophe: The Passing of Mass Utopia in East and West* (Cambridge, MA, 2000).

the *narod*," and the "transfer of all factories into the hands of the workers." The "Program of the Worker-Members of the 'People's Will' Party" (1880), perhaps the propaganda work with the most widespread circulation among radical workers at the time, explicitly calls for life to be established "according to socialist theory": in addition to a government elected by the people, other points state that "all the land [is to be] transferred into the hands of the working people and is considered the people's property," and "factories are considered the people's property."[156] The international socialist holiday of 1 May was first celebrated in Russia in 1891 by 70 or 80 Petersburg workers, members of the underground revolutionary (mostly social democratic) network. The clandestine meeting featured several speeches, which, all sources insist, were written by workers. One of these activists set forth in his speech a program to be followed, with the ultimate goal of attaining a socialist society. Aspects of the "transitional phase" would include "nationalization of land" and the establishment of a bank making loans to workers for the purpose of setting up factories.[157] The paired demands for land to be given to the peasants and factories to the workers continue to sound through the revolutionary year 1917. This seems to have been a basic understanding of socialism, voiced by that time not only by the politicized, but in the voices of ordinary lower-class citizens.[158]

Propaganda literature also contained more extended discussions of socialism. The main article in one issue of *Zerno*, the special "newspaper" for workers issued by the Black Repartition Party in 1880–81, was devoted to an extended definition of the concept of socialism, with emphasis on its communal elements, democratic self-government, protection of individual rights, and the core principle "The land, the factories, and capital will belong to all the working people."[159] Another description of the socialist economy, in contrast to the capitalist one, is presented in the last chapter of *Tsar Hunger*. After analyzing capitalism at length, the author, Aleksei Bakh, declares that capitalism is not "a law of human nature.... In life people should be equal." Capitalism was created by people, who must now change it. Socialists, the booklet continues, propose an economic system without hired labor, in which

---

[156] See programs reprinted in Valk et al., *Revoliutsionnoe narodnichestvo*, 2: 172, 184, 188–89.

[157] Reprinted in A. M. Orekhov, *Sotsial-demokraticheskoe dvizhenie v Rossii i pol'skie revoliutsionery* (Moscow, 1973), 174.

[158] See resolutions published in Steinberg, *Voices of Revolution, 1917*, for example, 95, 131, 140, 298.

[159] *Zerno*, no. 3 (June 1881), reprinted in *Istoriko-revoliutsionnyi sbornik*, ed. V. I. Nevskii (Moscow–Leningrad, 1924), 2: 360.

the means of production will be restored to the producer. The essence of socialism is that the means of production and surplus value will belong to workers: "There will be no capitalists and no profit."[160] The brochure *What Should Every Worker Know and Remember?* (published by Social Democrats, 1897) also concluded with a description of the future socialist society. Years later the worker Semen Kanatchikov remembered the electrifying effect of this vision, and noted in his memoirs:

> Clearly written, in a popular but passionate style, this book produced a total transformation in my ideas. A complete revelation for me was the elegant exposition of its views of the socialist society of the future. Factories, workshops, the land, the forests, the mines—everything would become the common property of the toilers!

For workers, the future goal of socialism was bound up with a sense of struggle for what was seen as a specifically *workers'* cause. This perspective is seen, for example, in the worker-composed 1891 May First speeches, which stress (as did circle propaganda) the struggle and achivements of workers in the West. As Kanatchikov continues, in the passage quoted above: "The organized struggle of the working class against the capitalists, the landowners, and the tsar—that was the meaning of life and work for every conscious worker."[161]

But the vision of socialism held out in works of propaganda literature went beyond the oft-repeated programmatic basics to a more utopian level: to the longed-for society of equality, justice, truth, material well-being, and brotherhood. In *Revolutionary Dreams*, Richard Stites stresses the close link between utopianism and revolution and underlines (following the Soviet scholar V. F. Zakharina) the distinction between party programs and visions of the utopian future: "It is clear from reading the programs that they deal in a different order of perception from utopias.... They ... tend to be tabular, static, flat, dry and singularly unemotional.... Utopian social daydreaming is something else. It is visionary in the extreme."[162]

Some of the revolutionary *skazki* of the 1870s, as we have seen, depict a utopian vision of socialism. In *Tale of a Kopeck* the picture of a better society appears in a dream: there will be no landowners, work will be cooperative, and brotherly love will reign. *Tale of Four Brothers* closes by invoking "that happy

---

[160] *Tsar-golod* (Gruppa Narodovol'tsev, 1895), 76–79.

[161] Zelnik, *A Radical Worker*, 34.

[162] Stites, *Revolutionary Dreams*, 13.

time, when there will be on earth no evil, injustice, oppression, or violence.[163] The tale *On Truth and Falsehood* promises with assurance that "all falsehood will perish with the old world," along with poverty, slavery, and violence. In the new world, "all will be equal, like brothers, all will love one another like brothers, because the kingdom of truth and love is approaching ... which Jesus Christ first preached to the people and for which he was tormented by the enemies of the people."[164] In his 1 May speech, Nikolai Bogdanov voiced this utopian vision, anticipating a society where "there will be neither poor nor rich, and all will enjoy happiness and contentment to the same degree."[165] That the teachings of socialism are those of Jesus is a recurring subtheme. Petr Antonov, a worker-*narodovolets* of the 1880s, later wrote that when he began to carry out revolutionary propaganda he started with the Gospels, "which in my opinion comprised socialist teaching, if you left out the elements of mystification."[166]

The socialism of the radical Russian worker had multiple aspects: the need to fundamentally change the existing social order, the pragmatic goal of land to the peasants and factories to the workers, and the above ideal of a utopian future. Revolutionary songs tended to be particularly utopian and maximalist. The first four verses of the "Workers' Marseillaise," the most popular revolutionary song into 1917, call for war against the hated tsarist order and enumerate the wrongdoings of the oppressors. But the last verse turns to the socialist future and shows what makes the struggle worthwhile: "The sun of truth and brotherhood will rise.... the age of freedom will begin, falsehood and evil will be extinguished forever, and the people will join together in the free kingdom of holy labor."[167] Other well-known songs referred to the "kingdom of freedom" ("Let's Keep Step Boldly, Comrades!") and summoned comrades to rise "for our holy workers' cause, for happiness, freedom, and truth" ("Foreward!").[168]

There is some evidence that radical workers put even more emphasis on the utopian ideals of the revolutionary movement than did revolutionaries

---

[163] *Gde luchshe? Skazka of chetyrekh brat'iakh i ob ikh prikliucheniiakh*, in Bazanov, *Agitatsionnaia literatura*, 294.

[164] *O pravde i krivde*, in Bazanov, *Agitatsionnaia literatura*, 117.

[165] Bogdanov's speech in Orekhov, *Sotsial-demokraticheskoe dvizhenie*, 170.

[166] "Avtobiografiia P. L. Antonova," 85. See also Bergman, "The Image of Jesus," 220–48; and Steinberg, *Proletarian Imagination*, chaps. 6 and 7.

[167] Bazanov, *Agitatsionnaia literatura*, 476.

[168] Dymshits, *Revoliutsionnaia poeziia*, 61–69. See also "The Red Banner": "We'll show the earth a new way, / Labor will be the ruler of the earth!" (ibid., 66).

from the intelligentsia. While the latter may have favored more concretely expressed goals—the transfer of land to the peasantry, the calling of a constituent assembly—one radical worker writes in his memoirs that the revolutionary movement of the period (late 1870s/early 1880s) was "a struggle for human ideas, happiness, light, freedom, brotherhood, and equality—not in words alone, but in deed." In the workers' May Day speeches of 1891 similar ideas are expressed. One worker voices hopes for a society where there will be "neither poor nor rich, and all will enjoy happiness and contentment to the same degree." Another speech calls on workers to fight "for truth, equality, brotherhood, freedom."[169]

In many literary works, songs, and speeches, the goal of socialism is tied to the need for struggle and (often violent) revolution. Workers read in the tale *On Truth and Falsehood* that "the people's uprising is a high and holy cause," and the *Tale of Four Brothers* ends with a call for a bloody uprising. The chorus of the "Workers' Marseillaise" commmands: "Stand up, arise, working people! Rise up against your enemies, starving brother! And the people's call for vengeance will ring out: Forward!"[170] The story of the Roman slave revolt led by Spartacus similarly stuck a responsive chord with Russian workers (as we will see in the next chapter). Russian workers too saw themselves engaged in a struggle for freedom and equality, one of the fundamental principles of socialism.

Memoirs provide another point of entry into the worldview of radical workers, although here at first glance the meaning attached to the conception of socialism appears rather opaque. The assumption is that the reader understands the meaning. For example, workers might refer simply to the "social idea" or to propaganda of the "collective idea." One worker notes that he "quickly assimilated the ideas of the socialists"; another refers to propaganda of "socialist ideas." For workers, socialism was closely linked to the working-class struggle and to revolution. As one "conscious" worker recalled, the first *intelligent* to conduct regular studies for his circle "acquainted the workers in general outlines with socialism as the future ideal—and how to achieve this better future: only by the efforts of the whole working class, which must organize for the struggle."[171]

When the question is rephrased as "What is a socialist?" memoirs provide more explicit answers. One of the few women active in the Petersburg network of the early 1890s asks, "Were we socialists at that time?" and answers,

---

[169] Pankratov, *Vospominaniia*, 9; workers' speeches reprinted in Orekhov, *Sotsial-demokraticheskoe dvizhenie*, 170, 172.

[170] Bazanov, *Agitatsionnaia literatura*, 122, 475.

[171] *V nachale puti*, 141, 144, 193, 227.

"The revolutionary 'virus' sat deep within each of us, and if we perhaps hadn't fully assimilated the theory and practice of class struggle, we understood quite well who the enemies of the working class were." Another worker explains that by being in a circle, a worker was considered "socialist." Memoirs sometimes use the expression *"rabochaia molodezh'"* (worker youth) to refer to radical workers; for some this was a synonym for "socialist." Other related terms were *intelligentnye rabochie* (intelligentsia-like workers) or even "students." Judging from the memoirs, some workers quickly came to see themselves as "socialists"; for others it seems that the term "revolutionary" was more comprehensible. Sometimes further distinctions were made. According to one worker, the 1891 May First speeches were "of a fully defined social democratic tendency."[172] The brochure *What Should Every Worker Know and Remember?* differentiated between "socialists" and "social democrats": the latter were "those who believe that workers can only achieve this [socialism] by their own efforts."[173]

For many politicized workers, socialism meant both the movement and the future society. From the 1890s, in particular, many came to see socialism as related to them, "the cause of the 'liberation of the working class,'" rather than to society as a whole.[174] (This probably shows the influence of social democratic propaganda, with its emphasis on the leading role of the proletariat.) The orientation of some activists could be termed "workerist," as well as socialist; they believed, as one wrote in a manuscript of the early 1890s: "The movement to improve the workers' situation rests first of all on [workers] themselves."[175] Some workers called for the creation of a *worker* intelligentsia to replace the tutelary role of *intelligenty* from the upper classes. Another worker, referring to the period around 1890 in Petersburg, on the question of "political tendency" recalls, "we did not yet call our circles social democratic, but were simply a circle, of a distinct revolutionary bent—and that one a firm, workerist bent."[176]

Reflecting on the birth of their political identity, some workers noted that the factory was their teacher: "It would be incorrect to say that we were studying Marxism at that time—because our main teacher of Marxism was the factory where we worked, where we, knowing nothing of Marx, never having

[172] Korol'chuk, *V nachale puti*, 259, 234, 233; Rubach, *Istoriia Ekaterinoslavskoi sotsial-demokraticheskoi organizatsii*, 15, 22.

[173] *Chto nuzhno znat' i pomnit' kazhdomu rabochemu* (Geneva, 1897), 36.

[174] Karelina, "Vospominaniia o podpol'nykh rabochikh kruzhkakh," 278.

[175] N. Bogdanov: RGIA f. 1405, op. 92, d. 10979, 1891, l. 8; reprinted in Orekhov, *Pervye marksisty*, 176.

[176] Egorov, "[Iz vospominanii o rabochikh kruzhkakh]," 239.

heard of him, were already becoming Marxists." When workers heard about the "autocratic yoke" or the oppression of the factory owners, they already felt its weight directly.[177] Occurrences in one's factory, a labor dispute, a political event—all had a radicalizing effect, were ingredients in what workers thought of as socialism. An event like the Khodynka catastrophe at Nicholas II's coronation had a profound effect on Semen Kanatchikov, at that time a young Petersburg worker with a growing interest in the revolutionary movement:

> [A]t that time, when my understanding of political questions was still very weak, I could already sense that these three events—Khodynka, the Petersburg weavers' strike, and the shift to the ten-hour day—were closely connected to one another and somehow stood in a state of causal interdependency.[178]

The experience of exploitation—the arbitrary power of the factory administration, beatings by the police—made workers more aware of the way their society functioned. Hatred of the police, in particular, was widespread, according to the memoirs. The topic of "workers in the West," a key focus in workers' study circles, also made an impression on Russian workers, confirming the movement's identity as a *workers'* revolutionary movement.

The "culture of revolution" itself, the subculture of radical workers, provided a taste of an alternative society and likely also informed their vision of socialism. As described in a number of memoirs—for example those of Vera Karelina on the Petersburg network of the early 1890s, or the circle of Khar'kov worker activists in the late 1880s—the comradeship, focus, and common experiences and goals that drew these workers together were fulfilling in their own right. We might see this as a form of "living the revolution."

ଓଃ ଃ

This chapter has surveyed the genre of revolutionary poetry and song over a significant span of the history of the revolutionary movement, from the 1870s through the revolution of 1905. While the titles of some of the most well-known poems/songs are familiar to those who study the revolutionary movement, the actual words, and the themes, contents, and lived experiences of these works, are virtually unknown. Faced with the special difficulties attendant on a study of this genre—the vast number of individual songs and poems, the many variants, their often ephemeral nature (songs were often

---

[177] V. A. Shelgunov in *V nachale puti*, 340–41.

[178] Zelnik, *A Radical Worker*, 45.

transmitted orally, with no written or printed copy required)—I have chosen to approach this subject through examination of five "collections" of poetry/ song, using them as guideposts through this period. These five "moments" are: 1) populist poetry of the early 1870s, published in the *Collection of New Songs and Verses*; 2) poetry of *narodniki* and *narodovol'tsy* published in revolutionary periodicals from the mid-1870s through the early 1880s; 3) two song collections by *narodovol'tsy* of the mid-1880s, *Echoes of the Revolution* and *Verses and Songs*; 4) a manuscript collection of songs circulating among St. Petersburg workers in 1892; and 5) songs of the early 20th century, especially those in the *Iskra* songbook of 1902, *Songs of the Revolution*. By comparing these different collections, the longevity of certain works, and the shifting emphasis of certain themes, become clear. We begin to see the parameters permitting a definition of the revolutionary song. One striking conclusion from this study (as was true of other genres) is that revolutionary songs were common to the whole movement; they were not particular to ostensibly separate rival political ideologies or groups. Again, we see the key role of the People's Will and later *narodovol'tsy* in composing, publishing, and disseminating works of this genre. I have also attempted to convey a sense of the emotional valence of poetry and song, their role in creating bonds of solidarity among workers who participated in the movement, and a way for workers to express and demonstrate their hopes for a socialist future.

The works of poetry and song that went to make up the "revolutionary songbook" of 1870–1905 were added not in separate chapters, but in overlapping waves. As with some of the prose works of propaganda literature, such as *Tsar Hunger*, some songs remained in the popular revolutionary repertoire throughout this period, and even through the revolution of 1917: the "Workers' Marseillaise" is one such example. While shifting, old themes were not completely replaced by new ones. Many verses and songs of the 1870s focused on the exploitation of the *narod*, on victims of the tsarist system, and revolutionary martyrs, and called for revenge, yet the popular song "Dear Freedom" (1873), included in the *Collection of New Songs and Verses*, while lamenting the hardships the Russian people must endure, holds out the dream of a better future, when freedom will come to the land. The two famous funeral marches, "Oppressed by Heavy Captivity" (1876) and "You Fell Victim" (late 1870s/early 1880s), took on new resonance in the early 20th century, no longer sung or circulated within small circles but, in the context of urban street demonstrations, showing the strength of the workers' movement. Songs and the collective experience of marching together were central to the meaning and impact of demonstrations and marches. The emotional connection provided by song is illustrated in the powerful verse of "Boldly, Comrades, March in Step" (1897): "We all came from the people, / Children of the laboring family. / "Brotherly union and freedom"— / That's our fighting slogan." The poems that appeared in underground publications of the early 20th century also manifested a more optimistic outlook. The "Song on 1 May " by an unknown author, gives meaning to the "bright and free holiday": "labor has given us brave strength.... We only need to stand together in harmony: / Our enemies will be worth nothing."[179]

Of all the genres of revolutionary literature, song embodied the emotions and feelings of the movement, linked on the 1 May holiday with visual collective representation and the promise of socialism. A May First pamphlet of 1901 summons to celebration, the form to be taken depending on the number of worker participants:

> Where you are many, go to the noisy streets of the city, to the populated squares and let the banner bearer raise before you the red banner— the symbol of the struggle for socialism instead of the old order, the symbol of the coming victory.[180]

In 1905 strikes, meetings, and demonstrations were the order of the day. In addition to calling for the end to autocracy, workers expressed their desire for the ultimate goal of socialism. In the revolutionary spirit characteristic of the October general strike, a meeting of the Assembly of Railroad Workers Deputies in Ekaterinoslav passed a resolution which answers the question of what at least one group of workers envisioned when they spoke of socialism. The resolution called for "the establishment of the 'kingdom of socialism,' under which 'all land, factories, and establishments of art and science will belong to the people. In the kingdom of socialism there will be neither rich nor poor, oppressed nor oppressors; all will labor equally and everyone will have everything necessary for the satisfaction of their physical and spiritual needs.'"[181] In his study of radical workers in Germany, Eric Weitz concludes that socialism was linked to the workers' sense of injustice, that in fact, "socialism meant justice." As a short definition, this would seem to hold for Russian workers as well.[182]

---

[179] "Krivaia dolia" (no publ. info. but probably early 20th century), RGIA f. 1410, op. 2, d. 162, 60–61.

[180] "Pervoe maia 1901 goda. Izd. Soiuza russkikh sotsialdemokratov" (Geneva, 1901), 2.

[181] Quoted in Wynn, *Workers, Strikes, and Pogroms*, 196.

[182] Eric Weitz, *Creating German Communism, 1890–1990: From Popular Protests to Socialist State* (Princeton, NJ, 1997), 51. See pp. 39–55.

Revolutionary poetry and song linked movement activists with workers and the many other people in the street who may have had little previous contact with the movement. Poetry and song were integral to the revolutionary movement and had great staying power: songs composed in the 1870s were still heard in 1917. In this respect the genre is similar to that of political economy, with certain key works were still current during the 1917 revolution. With the next chapter, we turn from poetry to prose and a fourth distinctive genre of literature, the foreign novel in Russian translation.

Chapter 5

The Revolutionary Novel: Foreign Literature in Translation

> "Is it possible that the gods established
> inequality among people? Aren't we born with
> the same needs, the same weakness? ... and
> if crude force was the basis for establishing
> the first inequality, usurpation, slavery, then
> why shouldn't we also use force to reestablish
> equality, justice, freedom!"
> —Spartacus[1]

> "Is there any story we tell in which justice is not
> at issue?"[2]

Looking back on the revolutionary activity of his student days as a member of the People's Will organization in Moscow in the mid-1880s, Mikhail Gots recalled the group's "workers' library," a collection of legal literature—books, pamphlets, and journal articles—considered appropriate for reading to workers. He notes that several of these works were extremely successful with their worker-readers, but mentions by name only one: the novel *Spartacus* by the Italian author Raffaello Giovagnoli, which had recently appeared in a Russian translation. The novel was so popular, in fact, that the group had to purchase several copies. As Gots remembered, the fictional Spartacus even became something of a local hero: "the leader of the insurgent Roman slaves became, by all accounts, one of the most popular heroes of our [workers'] districts."[3] What was it about this novel of a slave revolt in ancient Rome—

---

[1] Rafael Dzhiovanioli [Raffaello Giovagnoli], *Spartak: Istoricheskii roman* (n.p., [1881]), 273–74.

[2] Melvyn A. Hill, "The Fictions of Mankind and the Stories of Men," in *Hannah Arendt: The Recovery of the Public World*, ed. Hill (New York, 1979), 290.

[3] Gots, "Moskovskaia tsentral'naia gruppa," 104. Gots became a prominent figure in the Socialist Revolutionary Party of the early 20th century. For biographical information, see "Gots, Mikhail (Movsha) Rafailovich," in *DRDR* 3, vyp. 2, cols. 938–42.

and moreover a novel by no means notable from the standpoint of "great" literature—that captured the imagination of members of a new group on the Russian social landscape in the late 19th century, Russian urban workers? Obviously the theme of revolt against oppression linked this book with the goals of revolutionary propaganda, but would there not have been easier and more concise ways to convey this idea than in a novel of close to 500 pages? In fact, a number of other foreign novels of the late 19th century, legally published in Russian translation, proved highly successful as propaganda literature among workers in contact with the revolutionary movement. This body of works included Zola's *Germinal* and Edward Bellamy's *Looking Backward*, as well as select European works dealing with movements of national liberation, revolution, and workers' movements.

The titles of some of these novels, most of them fairly obscure, are familiar to scholars of the Russian revolutionary and workers' movements of this period. With a couple of notable exceptions, however, scholars have ignored the significance of these works as a genre of literature used for propaganda.[4] This chapter will focus on the three most widely used works of this genre: *Story of a Peasant* (*Istoriia krest'ianina*) by Erckmann-Chatrian, *Emma* by Johann Baptist von Schweitzer, and *Spartacus* (*Spartak*) by Rafaello Giovagnoli. To broaden the analysis, six other works, also very popular among workers, will be considered as well. Analysis of these novels also raises the question of how imaginative literature, particularly the historical novel, was received and appropriated by workers. In becoming part of the revolutionary canon, these works contributed to the creation of a culture of revolution that developed among radical workers in late 19th-century Russia. Historical novels fit well with the curriculum of workers' circles, which typically included relevant historical topics, such as past revolutions and revolts and the history of workers' movements. As the revolutionary workers' movement persisted over the decades, it too gained a history, and a martyrology. The historical perspective presented in revolutionary propaganda, together with the experience of participation

---

[4] N. S. Travushkin is the pioneer in examining this topic, with a series of articles published in the Soviet Union in the late 1960s–70s. See, for example, his "Zarubezhnaia belletristika." His pathbreaking doctoral dissertation was apparently not published as a separate work (Travushkin, "Zarubezhnaia khudozhestvennaia literatura"). V. F. Zakharina, a scholar of the populist literature of the 1870s, has published an article on *Istoriia odnogo frantsuzskogo krest'ianina*, to be discussed below. See V. F. Zakharina, "Roman Erkmana-Shatriana 'Istoriia krest'ianina' i ego peredelka v revoliutsionnoi narodnicheskoi propagande," *Russkaia literatura*, no. 2 (1964): 117–25. Neither scholar, however, attempts a comprehensive analysis of the corpus of propaganda literature over the span of the revolutionary movement, nor do they go into depth on the role of these works in the workers' revolutionary subculture.

in the movement, may have created or deepened an awareness among these workers of their role as actors in history.

As we have seen, from the beginnings of an organized movement in contact with the *narod*, members of Russian revolutionary groups recognized the need for a special literature of propaganda, including both specially composed works of illegal literature and legally published works suitable for this purpose. While a member of the Chaikovskii circle in the 1870s, the future anarchist Petr Kropotkin produced an early formulation of the goals of propaganda literature: he saw a need for "books which would make it possible for people who do not easily know how to raise certain questions to nevertheless deal with these issues." He also called for "books which arouse a spirit of independence, an awareness in the *narod* of their strength …, which support … a consciousness of common interests and common enemies."[5] Each of the genres of literature used for propaganda—including revolutionary *skazki*, expositions of political economy, and poetry and song—presented different types of ideas and varied in appeal and response. *Belletristika*, as works of fiction were known (from the French *belles-lettres*), was an important category in lists of recommended reading for propaganda and self-education circles.[6] Workers often recollected these literary works with enthusiasm. As I. I. Egorov, a worker at the Baltic shipbuilding plant in St. Petersburg in the 1880s, later wrote: "We were carried away by *belletristika* of a revolutionary [tendency]."[7] By definition, these works had passed the censor and been published legally, although in some cases offending passages had been cut, and in others books were "removed from circulation" after publication. As we will see, legal works had a special function, as their possession or dissemination carried no official penalty (although certain "tendentious" works did draw suspicion). For this reason, propagandists often gave these works first to workers just beginning their contact with the movement. A. K. Petrov, a worker involved in organizing work in the industrial town of Sormovo in the mid-1890s, noted the difficulty in introducing these uneducated workers to revolutionary ideas, given the need for conspiratorial measures so as not to alert the authorities. He and other activist workers found that legal literature played a "great role" in this endeavor: "this kind of [legal] literature broadened the worker's worldview;

---

[5] P. A. Kropotkin, "Dolzhny li my zaniat'sia rassmotreniem ideala budushchego stroia?" (November 1873), reprinted in Valk et al., *Revoliutsionnoe narodnichestvo*, 1: 105.

[6] *Belletristika* was the first section in the "Odessa" and "Cheliabinsk" catalogs, guides to legal literature from a revolutionary viewpoint much perused by circles of radical youth; they were published in the early 1880s. These catalogs are discussed below.

[7] Egorov, ["Iz vospominanii o rabochikh kruzhkakh"], 237. Other workers noted in their memoirs titles of works they remembered or which were popular. See, for example, Norinskii, *Pod nadzorom politsii*, 23.

he read it with eagerness, even fascination"—leading to a gradual transition, in successful cases, to the reading of illegal literature.[8] (Legal literature also complicates the task of the historian: such works were not included in the lists of illegal literature seized during arrests, which are perhaps the best indicator of the use of specific works of propaganda literature. Memoirs then become the most important source on the use of these novels, although they are frequently referred to simply by the blanket term *belletristika*—without any mention of specific titles.)

∞ ∞

As with the other genres of propaganda literature we have examined, several key works of foreign literature in translation used for purposes of propaganda among workers in the period 1870–1905 stand out in the frequency with which they are referred to in memoirs of participants in the movement. The major part of this chapter will focus on the three most widely used works of this genre, as noted above: *Istoriia krest´ianina* by Erckmann-Chatrian, *Emma* by Schweitzer, and *Spartak* by Giovagnoli. The analysis of these three works will be followed by briefer consideration of six other well-known works of foreign literature in translation, in order to give a fuller picture of the parameters of this genre, which drew on works from a variety of national literatures. These works (five novels and a play) are: *Germinal* by Émile Zola, *The Weavers* by the playwright Gerhardt Hauptmann, *Looking Backward* by Edward Bellamy, *Quatrevingt-treize* by Victor Hugo, *At Dawn (Na rassvete)* by T. T. Jez, and *The Gadfly* by Ethel Lilian Voinich.

The first of the three major works, *The Story of a Peasant (Istoriia krest´ianina)*, was the translation of a work by the popular French writing team, Émile Erckmann and Alexandre Chatrian.[9] This prolific duo authored a series of novels, most dealing with the period of the French Revolution and Napoleon. *Histoire*

---

[8] A. K. Petrov, *Rabochii bol´shevik v podpol´e* (Moscow, 1969), 43. The distinction between legal and illegal literature is almost always mentioned in memoirs. See comments by intelligentsia propagandists: Liadov, "Kak zarodilas´ Moskovskaia rabochaia organizatsiia," 66; S. I. Mitskevich, *Revoliutsionnaia Moskva, 1888–1905* (Moscow, 1940). Mitskevich lists translated works read by leading workers in Moscow in the 1890s, adding, "We distributed these translated works ourselves and also recommended that they be obtained for workers' libraries" (170–71).

[9] On Erckmann, Chatrian, and their intertwined history as authors, see Jean-Pierre Rioux, *Erckmann et Chatrian ou le trait d'union* (Paris, 1989); René Dumesnil, *Le Réalisme* (Paris, 1936), 197–202; and "Erckmann-Chatrian," in *La Grande Encyclopédie* (Paris, 1982), 16: 167–68.

d'un paysan, published in four volumes in 1868–70,[10] was one of the novels that comprised the series Romans nationaux (National Novels). The authors' native Lorraine is the setting for *The Story of a Peasant*, told in the first person by the peasant Michel Bastien, looking back from the vantage point of old age on his youth during the years of revolution.[11] The novel opens with a letter from Bastien to his "friends," the readers. He admits that many books have been written about the revolution, some lauding the role of the "great man," others the actions of the bourgeoisie (whether seen as positive or negative). Bastien proclaims, however: "I am a man of the people, and I write for the people.... So this is the story of your grandparents, I write for all of you, bourgeois, workers, soldiers, and peasants" (pt. 1, 2–3). He promises to relate only those events in which he himself participated; other events, however, are recounted by people returning from Paris, for example, or by letter. The book focuses on the French Revolution as experienced in the provinces and by peasants, as opposed to the traditionally privileged role of the Parisian sans-culottes. This perspective serves to highlight the socially divisive nature of the revolution, fought out on the battlefield against both internal and external enemies.

The novel is informed by the authors' political viewpoint, which is democratic, populist, and republican. Michel begins by describing life under the Old Regime, characterized by social inequality and a disproportionate burden on the poor. Broad national divisions are mirrored within the village, as is the case, for example, with the church: the hierarchy sides with the royalists and wins the support of many ignorant villagers, particularly women (including the narrator's mother), while the parish clergy side with the people. Christophe, the parish priest, deems the revolutionary constitution in accord with the Gospels and claims that the Rights of Man were predicted by Jesus (pt. 2, 42). Vignettes of daily life, involving Michel's family members and neighbors, are used to teach lessons on politics and society. Various political positions are personified by the novel's characters. Particularly important is the role of Chauvel, the *colporteur* (peddler) who becomes the book's most admirable political figure and uncompromising supporter of the Revolution. Chauvel is, moreover, a Calvinist, an anomaly in the village; he is old enough to remember the bitter persecution of Calvinists in earlier times. The pamphlets he carries in his pack help to spread the ideas of, for example, the Abbé Sieyès on the Third Estate before 1789. Chauvel serves as a deputy to the Estates General and the National Assembly and later opens a public reading room in the village.

---

[10] Erckmann-Chatrian, *Histoire d'un paysan 1789–1815*, pts. 1–4 (Paris, 1870).

[11] Bastien lives throughout his life in a small village near the town of Phalsbourg. Erckmann was born in Phalsbourg, and both men spent a large part of their lives in that town.

Bastien speaks with the voice of the people, translating abstract concepts—Nation, Republic, Terror—into common speech. Against the backdrop of historic events—the calling of the Estates General, war against the Habsburg armies—Michel grows up, courts Chauvel's daughter Marguerite, and marries. Called up as part of the *levée en masse*, Michel is involved in fighting the royalist peasants of the Vendée as well as the Germans, and the authors are not sparing in their descriptions of bloody battles and the horrors of war. Truly the revolution was a civil war, not just in the Vendée, but among Michel's associates, including journeyman Valentin at the forge, who continued to support the king, and in Michel's own family, with his brother fighting in the royalist army. The cultural aspects of the revolution are portrayed as well. The Parisian sans-culottes, more animated and excitable than the peasants, seem to Michel to be forever singing "Ça ira" (It'll Be Fine) and dancing the Carmagnole. Even on campaign, the sans-culottes (as Michel refers to the Parisians) come up with inventive dishes from dogs and rats and "never lose their gaity or good humor" (pt. 3, 51). Chauvel had hoped that the revolution would produce a truly grand song. Upon hearing the "Marseillaise" for the first time, Michel recognizes: "here is the song Chauvel had hoped for to replace the Carmagnole" (pt. 2, 103).

The narrator also provides a running critique of political figures and trends, explaining his opposition to the bourgeois Girondists, expressing disapproval of Robespierre's rigid policies, and castigating Napoleon's destruction of the revolution with his autocratic rule. Chauvel laments that the revolution was only half made: "the peasants got their share; they have the land without fees and privileges; the other half remains to be made: the workers also must obtain their share" (pt. 4, 28). Michel hopes these lessons will be taken to heart and provide his listeners with guidelines for the future. Erckmann and Chatrian show that revolution is difficult, often ugly and bloody. People do not easily give up the old ways. Most important, however, the novel shows the role of ordinary people in political events and emphasizes that revolution is not made by heroes, but by the mass of ordinary people. For all these reasons, the book seems a natural choice for use in political education.

The works of Erckmann-Chatrian (as they signed themselves) were extremely popular with French readers, although they failed to attain a lasting place in the literary canon. They were popular in Russia as well, where a handful were translated in the mid-1860s. Even before *Histoire d'un paysan* appeared in Russian translation, it was the subject of a lengthy review by the critic Dmitrii Pisarev which was published in *Otechestvennye zapiski* (Notes of the Fatherland), one of the "thick" journals read devotedly by the intelligentsia, in 1868. Referring to the entire corpus of novels by Erckmann-Chatrian, Pisarev noted that the authors pursued the same goal in all: "They attempted to view great historical events from below, through the eyes of the ordinarily voiceless and submissive masses."[12] Turning to the question of reader reception, Pisarev asserted that

> [t]hese novels develop in their readers the capacity to respect the *narod*, to rely on it, to consider its interests, to regard current events from the point of view of these interests, to call evil that which lulls popular consciousness to sleep, and good that which arouses it.

While ostensibly reviewing a novel on the French Revolution, Pisarev seems to be using the coded, "Aesopian" language that readers of serious articles were trained to look for. In what sounds in hindsight like a broad hint to future propagandists, Pisarev refers several times to the effect these novels have on the "simple worker" (*prostoi rabotnik*):

> When these novels fall into the hands of the simple worker, they inspire him with legitimate and reasonable self-respect; from them he sees that there is not the slightest necessity for him to be the passive instrument of another's whim and a submissive servant of another's interests; he sees that the members of that mass to which he himself belongs, and moreover people of the most ordinary qualities, are capable not only of thinking for themselves, and discussing social issues in sensible fashion, but of influencing the direction of the life of the people.

Pisarev then proceeds to a sociological and political analysis of *Histoire d'un paysan*, constructed around three characters, each of which has a different influence on the young Michel: the local smith and innkeeper, representing to Pisarev the new bourgeoisie; the local curé; and Chauvel, the "hero" and "fanatic of the common good," the peddler who distributes radical literature and hews to an uncompromising revolutionary line. In this way, Pisarev reads the novel as a way to grasp the "influences which prepared the French people for its political awakening."[13]

---

[12] D. I. Pisarev, "Frantsuzskii krest'ianin v 1789 godu: *Histoire d'un paysan 1789*, par Erckmann-Chatrian," reprinted in D. I. Pisarev, *Polnoe sobranie sochinenii v shesti tomakh* (St. Petersburg, 1894), 519.

[13] Ibid., 524. Dmitrii Ivanovich Pisarev, an uncompromising radical and materialist, was arrested in 1862 and imprisoned, where he continued to write. Pisarev's article on *Histoire d'un paysan* was published shortly before his death in 1868. For biographical information on Pisarev, see "Pisarev, Dmitry Ivanovich," in Terras, *Handbook of Russian Literature*, 339–40. See also the discussion of Pisarev's review in N. P. Emel'ianov, *"Otechestvennye zapiski" N. A. Nekrasova (1868–1877)* (Leningrad, 1977), 58–61; for

Thus the Russian reading public was fully primed and the proper reading of the novel had already been suggested before a Russian translation appeared. Following a condensed translation in the journal *Delo* (The Cause), the full text of this lengthy novel was then published separately in 1870 and 1872 in two parts, in an excellent translation by Marko Vovchok (pseudonym of Mariia Aleksandrovna Vilinskaia, a well-known writer and translator).[14] Her rendition is complete, accurate, and faithfully captures the tone of the original. Inevitably, however, her choice of terms gives *Story of a Peasant* something of a Russian flavor: *muzhik* for "peasant," *barshchina* for "corvée." The local moneylender becomes a *kulak*; Père Chauvel becomes *Diadia Shovelev*. (Names are russified as well.) This translation also includes many of the original illustrations—carefully executed engravings that complement the text.

Erckmann-Chatrian's novel had thus achieved a certain degree of notoriety when members of the Chaikovskii circle, the leading group of radicals in St. Petersburg in the early 1870s, were struck by the propaganda possibilities inherent in the novel. As we have seen, the group had begun to make contact with local workers and meet with them in small circles, and a literary committee (including Kropotkin, Kravchinskii, Klements, and Tikhomirov) was charged with composing (illegal) works suitable for propaganda among the *narod*. The length of the novel did pose a problem, solved by what was termed a "reworking" (*peredelka*) that significantly condensed the original. This brochure, still rather lengthy at 225 small-format pages, was published on the Chaikovskii circle's printing press in Geneva in 1873, under the modified title *The Story of a French Peasant* (*Istoriia odnogo frantsuzskogo krest'ianina*). The question of the authorship of the *peredelka* remains unresolved; one or more members of the literary committee were likely involved.[15]

---

critical reception of this and other French novels, see P. R. Zaborov, "Russkaia kritika kontsa 60-kh–nachala 70-kh godov XIX veka i frantsuzskii demokraticheskii roman," in *Problemy realizma russkoi literatury XIX veka*, ed. B. I. Bursov and I. Z. Serman (Moscow–Leningrad, 1961), 368–78; for a broader treatment of the French Revolution in Russian intellectual life, see B. S. Itenberg, *Rossiia i Velikaia frantsuzskaia revoliutsiia* (Moscow, 1988).

[14] Erkman-Shatrian [Erckmann-Shatrian], *Istoriia krest'ianina 1789–1792*, trans. Marko Vovchok, pts. 1 and 2 (St. Petersburg, 1870); *Istoriia krest'ianina 1793–1815*, trans. Marko Vovchok, pts. 3 and 4 (St. Petersburg, 1872). For further information on Vilinskaia/ Vovchok (1834–1907), see "Vovchok, Marko" in Terras, *Handbook of Russian Literature*, 513–14; and A. F. Martynov, "Obshchestvennaia deiatel'nost' Marko Vovchok," *Voprosy literatury*, no. 6 (1962): 184–86. Her friendship with Alexander Herzen can be glimpsed in Herzen's correspondence: "Pis'ma Gertsena k Marko-Vovchoku," *Byloe*, no. 10 (22 October 1907): 63–75.

[15] *Istoriia odnogo frantsuzskogo krest'ianina* (Chaikovskii group press, Geneva, 1873). See entry in Itenberg et al., *Svodnyi katalog*, 1: 119 (no. 658). On the publication history

This version of Erckmann-Chatrian's novel appears with the subtitle "This book was written by a French peasant as a mark of brotherly love to the Russian peasants"—and differs from the Marko Vovchok translation in significant respects. Rather than addressing the younger generation of French peasants, Mikhail (as he is now called) now addresses his Russian counterparts, and there are frequent asides analyzing Russian conditions and exhorting Russian peasants to learn from the French example and hopefully avoid some of their errors. Authors of the illegal work highlight Robespierre as the best revolutionary leader, as opposed to support for Danton in the original, and the village notables are portrayed more negatively: they do not really have the people's interests at heart. In this version Shovelev is opposed to war, and Napoleon is termed a simple robber (*razboinik*) (206). Socialism is preached directly: "Brothers, it's time to wise up and get rid of all nobles, merchants, and owners.... Without them, everything will be easier ... you will work only for yourself, ... and you will have THE KINGDOM OF WORKING PEOPLE" (123). Typical propaganda points of 1870s populism are made clearly: the land should not be divided, but rather held in common; the selling off of church lands has led to inequality (104–05, 121, 110). Compared to the translation, the *peredelka* is characterized by additional aspects of russification: the Bastille is compared to the Peter-Paul Fortress in St. Petersburg; dates are often indicated in relation to traditional holy days—"near Pokrov Day," "near the end of the Petrov fast"—and folk sayings are sprinkled throughout: "Whoever stirs up the porridge is going to have to deal with the mess"; "Here's a fine how do you do!"[16] The original work devoted hundreds of pages to Michel's military experiences, at war against both foreign armies and local uprisings as in the Vendee. Most of this is excised in the abbreviated version, but in general plot and characters follow the original quite closely. Although Zakharina calls the propaganda version "a completely new work, for which Erckmann-Chatrian's novel served only as an outline,"[17] this seems to be something of an overstatement. While the authors use more conversational language and more pointed political polemic, the central themes carry over well from the original to the reworked version, and the warnings issued by Erckmann and

---

and authorship of the illegal work, see Zakharina, "Roman Erkmana-Shatriana." Zakharina feels the evidence points to the writer Zasodimskii as the author, or at least a contributor to a collectively authored version (119–21). N. Iakushin, however, disputes Zasodimskii's authorship and concludes that the question requires further research. N. Iakushin, "Byl li P. V. Zasodimskii avtorom peredelki romana Erkmana-Shatriana 'Istoriia krest'ianina'?" *Russkaia literatura*, no. 1 (1965): 191–93.

[16] Sayings: "Kto zavaril etu kashu, tot ee i raskhlebyvai" (112); "Vot tebe, babushka, i budet Iur'ev den'" (154); and many others.

[17] Zakharina, "Roman Erkmana-Shatriana," 119.

Chatrian remain the same: the need to complete the revolution, to make sure that city workers achieve their goals too, to protect revolutionary leaders like Robespierre, and, most important, to fight against popular indifference (215).

The Story of a French Peasant was one of the most popular works used for propaganda among both peasants and workers throughout the 1870s. The title was mentioned numerous times in testimony relating to the two important mass trials of revolutionary propagandists in this period, the "Trial of the 193" and the "Trial of the 50" (1877–78).[18] An indication of how urban workers responded to this work is provided in Kropotkin's memoirs. He mentions reading to a group of St. Petersburg workers the history of the French Revolution as recounted in "the reworking of the excellent 'Story of a Peasant' by Erckmann-Chatrian. Everyone was enraptured with 'M. Shovelev,' who traveled around the villages and distributed prohibited books. Everyone burned with the desire to follow his example."[19] Other members of the Chaikovskii group mention use of this work in propaganda as well. O. V. Aptekman participated in the movement "to the people" and worked as a *fel'dsher* (medical assistant) in a village in Penza province. He found a ready audience for his readings of *Story of a French Peasant* and other works. He had learned from experience to review the works beforehand and make modifications. While peasants reacted negatively to attacks on the tsar or religion (although, according to Aptekman, there was little of this in the brochures), he was struck by "how keenly the *narod* related to truth, how they were sickened by injustice."[20] Solomon Chudnovskii, a member of the Odessa branch of the *chaikovtsy*, notes that although he did little direct propaganda among workers, he visited workers' taverns a few times, bringing with him *Story of a French Peasant* and other illegal brochures. He explained the contents briefly and encouraged the workers to purchase the works for a nominal sum.[21] By the mid-1870s radical workers in St. Petersburg were maintaining

---

[18] See Kallash, *Protsess 193-kh*; and Kallash, *Protsess 50-ti*. On the trials, see Venturi, *Roots of Revolution*, 533–35, 586–91, and elsewhere; I. S. Dzhabadari, "Protsess 50-ti (Vserossiiskaia Sotsial'no-Revoliutsionnaia Organizatsiia) 1874–77 gg.," *Byloe*, no. 8 (20) (August 1907): 1–26, and no. 10 (22) (October 1907): 168–97; A. Iakimova, "'Bol'shoi protsess,' ili 'protsess 193-kh': O revoliutsionnoi propagande v imperii (1877 18/X–1878 23/1)," *Katorga i ssylka*, no. 8 (37) (1927): 7–31.

[19] Kropotkin, *Zapiski revoliutsionera*, 200.

[20] O. V. Aptekman, *Iz istorii revoliutsnionnogo narodnichestva: "Zemlia i Volia" 70-kh godov. Po lichnym vospominaniiam* (Rostov-na-Donu, [1907]), 70.

[21] S. L. Chudnovskii, *Iz davnikh let* (Moscow, 1934), 84. Chudnovskii's memoirs give an interesting picture of developments in the South in this period, including the student movement (Chudnovskii attended New Russia University in Odessa), the anti-Jewish pogrom in 1871 which he witnessed, and the activity of contrabandists, for which

their own library, which held many works of *belletristika*, including *Story of a French Peasant*.[22]

The first work of subversive literature encountered by a worker was often *Story of a French Peasant* or another legal work of fiction; similarly workers who formed their own self-education circles often made use of this and other works.[23] Although the illegal version of Erckmann-Chatrian's novel predominated during the early period of mass propaganda by populists, it appears that in subsequent years—the 1880s and 1890s—the legal translation of the novel was more widely used. (Note that it is often difficult to distinguish between the two versions in the sources: reference is frequently made to *Istoriia odnogo krest´ianina* [sic].)[24] To give one later example, the novel was frequently given to workers attending one of the Sunday/evening schools for workers in St. Petersburg in the 1890s. (Staffed by a contingent of female teachers with connections to local radicals, such schools sometimes served as a recruiting ground for the underground workers' circles.) One copy of the novel was found to be peppered with questionable marginal notes: for example, "opposite the place where the execution of Louis XVI was mentioned, someone had written: 'That's how we should take care of our own [king].'"[25]

Chudnovskii was finally arrested in 1874. He was tried as one of the "193" and spent years in prison and exile. See also a reference to the work in the memoirs of L. E. Shishko, *Obshchestvennoe dvizhenie v shestidesiatykh i pervoi polovine semidesiatykh godov* (Moscow, 1920), 84.

[22] From correspondence published in *Vpered!*, no. 3 (15) (February 1875), col. 76. Two Petersburg workers arrived in Zurich and presented an important first-hand account of the movement's doings.

[23] See, for example, Volynkin, "Iz vospominanii rabochego," in Mitskevich, *Na zare rabochego dvizheniia v Moskve*, 210 (on use of *Istoriia odnogo frantsuzskogo krest´ianina* in a self-education circle of young workers, Moscow, c. 1894); and Shapovalov, *Po doroge k marksizmu*, 75 (the work is also included in a listing of legal literature used when beginning propaganda).

[24] For example, Kanatchikov refers to reading "Erkmann-Chatrian's *The Peasant*" while in prison (Zelnik, *A Radical Worker in Tsarist Russia*, 250.) To illustrate the difficulty that sometimes occurs in identifying works: Moiseenko mentions that he borrowed "the History of the French revolution" from a student (1875)—this could be a reference to Erckmann-Chatrian (P. A. Moiseenko, "[Revoliutsionnoe dvizhenie 1875–1879 godov sredi rabochikh Peterburga]," in *V nachale puti*, 168).

[25] N. K. Krupskaia, *Iz dalekikh vremen: Politprosvetrabota sredi peterburgskikh rabochikh 90-e gody* (Moscow–Leningrad, 1930), 15, quoted in L. K. Fedorov, "Nelegal'nye biblioteki s nachala 70-kh godov do vtoroi poloviny 90-kh godov proshlogo stoletiia," in *Iz istorii nelegal'nykh bibliotek revoliutsionnykh organizatsii v tsarskoi Rossii: Sbornik materialov*, ed. E. D. Stasova (Moscow, 1956), 56–57. A new translation of Erckmann-Chatrian's work appeared in 1906: Erkman-Shatrian, *Istoriia odnogo krest´ianina*:

CR RO

Another foreign novel popular with the Russian radical reading public from the early 1870s was the work entitled *Emma* by Johann Baptist von Schweitzer (sometimes Jean Baptista von Schweitzer), translated from the German. This tale of revolution was a perennial on reading lists circulated by radical youth and was frequently chosen for distribution to workers and discussion in workers' circles. We have noted that the memoirs of radical worker Petr Moiseenko are distinctive for their numerous references to works of propaganda literature, with comments on how they affected him and their value in his radical organizing activity. Referring to the readings which animated his circle of Petersburg worker activists in the mid-1870s, he notes that "Shveitser's novel *Emma* (1848 revolution) produced a strong effect on all of us. We were chomping at the bit to spring into action [*my vse rvalis' k boiu*]." Elsewhere Moiseenko recalls gathering a large group of workers together to hear *Emma* read aloud: "Everyone was delighted with the deeds of the revolutionaries; the mood was uplifted."[26] Many other workers and intelligentsia propagandists also recalled the importance of *Emma* in their arsenal of radical novels. S. I. Mitskevich (a medical student, then doctor active in Moscow social democratic circles in the mid-1890s), for example, placed the novel on the list of translated literature most often given out to leading workers and recommended for inclusion in libraries for workers.[27]

Moiseenko's recollection was correct in general, but somewhat mistaken in the particulars: *Emma* did not in fact depict the Revolution of 1848, but rather an 1848-like revolution occurring in a nameless German state some time later. The author, Schweitzer, was a prominent follower of Lassalle and organizer of the German socialist labor movement. His novel *Lucinda, or Capital and Labor*

V chetyrekh chastiakh, translated from the German [sic] by A. Annenskaia and T. Bogdanovich (St. Petersburg, 1906).

[26] Moiseenko, *Vospominaniia starogo rabochego*, 18; and Moiseenko, "[Revoliutsionnoe dvizhenie 1875–1879 godov]," in Korol'chuk, *V nachale puti*, 168.

[27] Mitskevich, *Revoliutsionnaia Moskva*, 170–71 (Moscow, mid-1890s). Workers who recalled reading *Emma* included Karelin, "[Vospominaniia o rabochikh kruzhkakh]," 244; A. K. Petrov, *Rabochii bol'shevik*, 43; Pankratov, "Iz deiatel'nosti sredi rabochikh," 252; Samoilov, *Po sledam minuvshego*, 45 (Ivanovo-Voznesensk, early 20th century). Correspondence on a workers' library in St. Petersburg that included *Emma* among the belletristic works appeared in Lavrov's biweekly *Vpered!* (no. 3 [15/3 February 1875], col. 76, reprinted in *Vpered! Dvukhnedel'noe obozrenie*, 1: *1875* (The Hague: Mouton, 1969). Following the arrest of a workers' group in Kharkov in 1888, Kharkov university student and propagandist Vladimir Perazich testified that he read to a couple of workers selections from various works, including *Emma*, and then "conversed with them on the material read" (RGIA f. 1405, op. 80, d. 10847, l. 90ob.).

(*Lucinde, oder Kapital und Arbeit*), was published in Frankfurt in 1864.[28] As the title implies, the novel portrays the recurrent mid–19th-century conflict between proletariat and bourgeoisie that erupted in repeated revolutions.[29] These two groups are embodied in various characters, including workers like the brave organizer Emil Blankendorf and members of the bourgeoisie,

---

[28] Ferdinand Lassalle (1825–64), a brilliant, erratic, and flamboyant figure, is now best known for his complex and competitive relationship with Marx and Engels (a circumstance which has perhaps distorted his historical significance). Lassalle, an early leader of the German workers' movement, founded the General German Workers' Association in 1863. Although his theoretical writings were not especially innovative, several of his speeches and letters, during his brief period as movement organizer, met with an enthusiastic response from workers. Among his key goals for workers were universal suffrage and state-supported workers' enterprises to overcome the negative consequences of the "iron law of wages." An opponent of the German bourgeois liberal movement, he felt that the state could be used in the workers' favor and even went so far as to present his ideas to Bismarck, the Prussian minister.

On Lassalle's life and ideas, see Hans Mommsen, "Lassalle, Ferdinand," in *Marxism, Communism, and Western Society: A Comparative Encyclopedia*, ed. C. D. Kernig (New York, 1972–73), 5: 107–27; G. D. H. Cole, *Socialist Thought: Marxism and Anarchism, 1850–1890* (London, 1957), 2: 71–87; Vernon L. Lidtke, *The Outlawed Party: Social Democracy in Germany (1878–1890)* (Princeton, NJ, 1966), 18–27; "Lassall'," in *Entsikopedicheskii slovar' Brokgauza i Efrona* (St. Petersburg, 1896), 17: 363–66; David Footman, *Ferdinand Lassalle: Romantic Revolutionary* (New Haven, 1947); Edward Bernstein, *Ferdinand Lassalle as a Social Reformer*, trans. Eleanor Marx Aveling (London, 1893); Fritz Mehring, *Karl Marx: The Story of His Life* (Ann Arbor, MI; 1962), 176, 251; George Lichtheim, *The Origins of Socialism* (New York, 1969), 172, 173; Lichtheim, *Marxism: An Historical and Critical Study*, 2nd ed. (New York, 1963), 92 ff.

Johann Baptist von Schweitzer (1833–75), a close associate of Lassalle, edited the journal *Social Democrat* and headed the General German Workers' Association (ADAV) from 1867 to 1871. In 1867 he was elected to the North German Confederation Parliament, one of the first Socialists to win a parliamentary election in Germany. Schweitzer was also involved in literary activity, producing a series of didactic plays, as well as the novel *Lucinde, oder Kapital und Arbeit* (Frankfurt am-Main, 1864). On Schweitzer, see Cole, *Socialist Thought*, 2: 238–39; Mommsen, "Lassalle," 119–23; Footman, *Ferdinand Lassalle*, 181–82; and Lidtke, *Outlawed Party*, 21, 29. See reference to Schweitzer's literary activity in Lidtke, *The Alternative Culture: Socialist Labor in Imperial Germany* (New York, 1985), 138–39. For consideration of Lassalle and Lassalleanism in the context of European socialism, see Albert S. Lindemann, *A History of European Socialism* (New Haven, 1983), 102–05, 135, 155. Geoff Eley makes only a brief mention of Lassalle in *Forging Democracy: The History of the Left in Europe, 1850–2000* (Oxford, 2002), 45.

[29] The Russian version of Schweitzer's novel was published in two volumes: the first half as *Emma: Roman Shveitsera, perevod s nemetskogo* (St. Petersburg, 1871); the second half under the title *Liutsinda: Roman Shveitsera (avtora romana "Emma")* (St. Petersburg, 1872). On the publication and censorship history of the Russian translation, see Travushkin, "Zarubezhnaia belletristika," 85–89.

including factory owners, bankers, a professor, and others who are caricatured and treated with irony. A third group is also portrayed—the aristocratic rulers of the state.

The novel develops on three levels: a melodramatic, ultimately tragic tale of inter-class love; a political novel of revolution; and an exposition of current theories of political economy, the theme expressed in the German subtitle: Capital and Labor. *Emma* opens on a dramatic, one could say operatic note: the title character, a working-class girl, is visiting her father's grave, then gets lost walking home through the woods. A drunken soldier appears and tries to rape her, but in the nick of time handsome young Count Theodor von Lindenval´ (son of the prime minister) rides up on his horse and saves her. The two are forced to take shelter from a storm in a grotto—as lightning flashes, they fall in love. Emma and the young Count have several meetings, but the Count finds it difficult to break from his aristocratic, high society world. The romance is marked by the count's mistakes and by various convoluted plot turns. Theodor becomes converted to the workers' cause, and he and Emma finally find each other again on the barricades.

Entwined with this love story is a political novel which depicts in fictional form the social structure and conflicts of mid–19th-century Western Europe: the parties and classes, and the causes that lead to the outbreak of revolution. After extensive description of the untenable situation of the workers, the reader witnesses plans for organization and revolution by both workers and the capitalist class, the latter, through their "Society of Progress and Freedom," attempting to co-opt the workers' movement for their own ends. Two of the leaders of the growing workers' movement are Emil´ Blankendorf, Emma's brother, and his friend Dr. Nollo, who begins to lead a study circle for workers at the apartment of the Blankendorf family. In the words of Emile, referring to the vast inequality in society, it is time "to resolve the great question of labor and capital."[30] As opposed to the realistic and sympathetic treatment of the working class, the representatives of the bourgeois liberals, including factory owners, bankers, and a professor, are depicted in caricature fashion. The liberals, for example the banker Isaak Levi German Itsinger, have luxurious homes, handsome carriages, attractive mistresses. (Jewish names are prominent in this group, but there is also a sympathetic portrayal of a Jewish factory owner who helps the workers. Whatever significance this is supposed to have in the novel is not explained.) Schweitzer consistently uses the ironic device of showing the ridiculous goings-on at meetings of the liberal group, followed by the inflated, heroic treatment of these same events in the liberal organ *Popular Representative*. In this way, the novel shows how the press

---

[30] Shveitser [Schweitzer], *Emma*, 36.

is manipulated. After revolution breaks out in an unnamed neighboring state, pamphlets appear, and workers start discussing the "social question" and the "workers' question." Some workers are initially naive and taken in by the liberals. The revolutionary uprising is portrayed in cinematic detail—from the construction of barricades to the strategy of street fighting against government troops. The workers and the bourgeoisie are ostensibly allies—but when the fighting is over the capitalists are in control (as the old count, a victim of the revolutionary mob, had earlier predicted). The new provisional government dominated by the liberals decides to set up national workshops, à la France in 1848, with the purpose of discrediting the socialists. It turns out (through plot developments too complicated to explain briefly) that Emma subsequently takes the place of another woman from the lower classes, Lucinda, the mistress of a wealthy entrepreneur. As the account continues in the second half of the novel (published as *Lucinda* in Russian translation), the workers become more knowledgeable and better organized. In the workers' study circle Dr. Nollo patiently explains that the crucial social relationship and conflict of the day is that between Capital and Labor. A second revolutionary uprising takes place. Although they fight with desperation, the workers are once more defeated. The cross-class love story ends tragically, as do the workers' attempts at revolution. In the final act, the state—the old aristocratic order headed by the king and his generals—disbands the liberals' provisional government.

The novel's third strand is comprised of the exposition of political economy, through Emile's speeches, Dr. Nollo's talks at the workers' gatherings, and in excerpts from Nollo's diary. Various political positions and theories are presented. The old count mounts a defense of conservative monarchist principles for the good of society. The bourgeoisie wants power for itself, he explains; but the decisive force rests with the masses—they just don't know it yet.[31] Emile asks the novel's key question: why do workers work so hard, but have nothing to show for it?[32] Nollo expounds at length on the ideas of mid-century economists and socialists, including Lassalle, Proudhon, and Louis Blanc. The "Iron Law of Wages" is repeatedly invoked (as it was by Lassalle). Nollo teaches that the capitalists operate according to this 'law," so detrimental to workers, but refuse to acknowledge it—it is their "secret" knowledge. Lassalle's central ideas come through clearly, both in the expository passages and in the action of the novel: the demand for universal suffrage, the goal of organizing producers' associations with government support.[33] The workers' movement is also a socialist one, as Nollo writes in

---

[31] Ibid., 51–59.

[32] *Emma*, 63.

[33] *Emma*, 280–81.

his diary: "the cause of the workers' estate is the cause of all humanity ... the workers' cause is the cause of equality."[34] Schweitzer's main rhetorical attacks are directed against the liberal bourgeoisie—the common enemy of workers and monarchists. Old Count Lindenval' is portrayed more sympathetically than the liberal characters, who barely rise above the level of caricature. In addition to economic and socialist ideas, Schweitzer quotes at length from a history of workers' associations in France, describing the events in Lyons in the 1830s and Paris in June 1848. The closing of the national workshops and the mass executions that followed in June are described in detail. The author of *Emma/Lucinda* wants to make the point that these events are not fantastic, but actually occurred in the not too distant past.[35]

The centrality of Lassalle's ideas to the novel *Emma* serves to highlight the importance of Lassalle to the revolutionary movement of this period. The works of Lassalle were considered essential reading for young members of the intelligentsia in the 1870s and 1880s, and propagandists shared Lassalle's ideas in workers' circles as well. A two-volume Russian edition of Lassalle's writings was completed in 1870. While the censor initially approved the first volume, the second volume was banned and the publisher prosecuted. In 1872 the Ministry of Internal Affairs ordered that the first volume be confiscated and destroyed as well.[36] Nonetheless, copies of volume 1 continued to circulate. Debagorii-Mokrievich lists in his memoirs the works read by members of radical circles in Kiev in the early 1870s, including volume 1 of Lassalle. He notes the peculiarly populist way in which Lassalle was read and adapted to the Russian context:

> [F]rom Lassalle we drew arguments in support of our populist views, even though Lassalle, speaking of workers in his book, indicated only the factory proletariat and not at all the peasants, who elsewhere he directly called a reactionary element.... We especially took to heart Lassalle's reasoning that the worker ... served the cause of the interests of all humanity.[37]

---

[34] *Liutsinda*, 31.

[35] *Liutsinda*, 384–94: ch. 28, "Fiction or History?"

[36] See L. M. Dobrovol'skii, *Zapreshchennaia kniga v Rossii: Arkhivno-bibliograficheskie razyskaniia* (Moscow, 1962), 72–73; L. I. Polianskaia, "Arkhivnyi fond glavnogo upravleniia po delam pechati," *Literaturnoe nasledstvo*, no. 22–24 (1935): 616.

[37] P. L. Lavrov, *Narodniki-propagandisty 1873–78 godov* (St. Petersburg, 1907), 50–51. See also references to the reading of Lassalle by the radical intelligentsia in B. S. Itenberg, *Dvizhenie revoliutsionnogo narodnichestva: Narodnicheskie kruzhki i "khozhdenie v narod"*

Several of Lassalle's speeches and shorter works composed for the audience of the German workers' movement were translated and published as illegal pamphlets for use in propaganda among Russian workers. They continued to be influential into the early 20th century. The most popular of these were Lassalle's *Workers' Program* (*Programma rabotnikov*) and *On the Essence of Constitution* (*O sushchnosti konstitutsii*).[38] Some of the radical Petersburg workers involved in the Workers' Union of the early 1890s carried on propaganda among female workers at the Foundling Home. When one of these workers, Natasha, was arrested, police found a notebook in which Genrikh Fisher, one of the more knowledgeable workers, "had copied the 'iron law of wages' from Schweitzer's *Emma*."[39] Describing his work with a circle of Petersburg factory workers in the late 1890s, one of the social democratic *intelligenty* active in propaganda lists among literature read by his workers the speeches of Lassalle, as well as the novel *Emma*.[40]

As a literary work, *Emma* suffers by comparison with *Story of a Peasant*. The novel is overly long, repetitious, and sentimental, and the plot lacks believability. Yet its popularity was such that a new edition was published in 1906. What were the novel's virtues from a radical perspective? First, it provided a literary depiction of an archetypal 1848-style revolution, analyzed the political groups involved, and cautioned workers not to be taken in by the bourgeoisie, who know they cannot succeed without working-class support. Second, there is the appeal of the melodramatic love story, capturing the readers' interest in how things will turn out that drew many new readers from the people to "boulevard" literature and newspaper "feuilletons" in the same period. Schweitzer also takes the opportunity to include lengthy passages from contemporary works of political economy, including those by J. B. Say, Proudhon, and Lassalle.

Schweitzer's novel had a somewhat complicated publishing history in Russia. The first half appeared in Russian translation under the title *Emma* in 1871. The second half appeared in 1872 under the title *Lucinda* (*Liutsinda*). (No translator is indicated on either, and I have found no information on this

---

v 70-kh godakh XIX v. (Moscow, 1965), 99, 140. On Lassalle's ideas in Russian radical thinking, see Venturi, *Roots of Revolution*, 323, 414.

[38] F. Lassalle, "Programma rabotnikov" (Geneva, 1902); Lassalle, "O sushchnosti konstitutsii" (Geneva, 1897). For a complete listing of illegal works by Lassalle in Russian, see *Svodnyi katalog*, 1: 160–62; 3: 16–17.

[39] G. M. Fisher, "Podpol'e, ssylka, emigratsiia," in *Proletarskii prolog: Vospominaniia uchastnikov revoliutsionnogo dvizheniia v Peterburge v 1893–1904 godakh*, comp. E. R. Ol'khovskii, ed. L. M. Spirin (Leningrad, 1983), 130, 389 n. 7.

[40] K.Ia., "Pervye shagi," *Byloe*, no. 9 (21) (1907): 143.

point.) This time the St. Petersburg censorship committee took notice and pro-hibited the work as subversive. The Ministry of Internal Affairs expressed its position as follows:

> The author of this novel, Schweitzer, well known in German literature as a representative of democratic interests, in this work, entitled *Lucinda*, sets himself the task of introducing socialist ideas into the reading public in the form of a novel.... The struggle of the workers' estate against both the government and those estates privileged in terms of material and political relations is presented as a completely rightful struggle, in which in the end, after many failures, the victors will be the people of labor, that is, the workers. Moreover, the novel repeatedly and manifestly condemns the social and economic order, preaches hatred toward the upper and possessing classes; approves of revolution.[41]

The harmful influence of *Emma* was also soon noted: although not coming under a blanket prohibition, the book was removed from public libraries and reading rooms.[42] Thus, although copies were not easy to obtain, small num-bers of both *Emma* and *Lucinda* circulated.[43]

A brief review on the occasion of *Emma*'s reissue in 1906 sheds some light on the nature of the book's appeal. The reviewer notes that "most members of the Russian intelligentsia remember this book from their youth, if not the contents, then at least the title." Like Chernyshevskii's *What Is to Be Done?*, such "secretly read books" shaped the young readers' lives and social con-sciousness. The reviewer notes: "We're in the habit of speaking about the low literary quality [*nekhudozhestvennost'*] of these novels, which we all read. But this is unfair." The best of these works, he contends, have what might be termed a kind of social aesthetic (*estetika obshchestvennosti*). The reviewer allows that Schweitzer's novel might lack even this—there's too much preaching of outdated Lassallean ideas:

> But it is possible that *Emma* will nonetheless find a wide circle of readers, because it deals with the clash of workers with both capitalists and governing powers, with workers' unions, with revolution in the

---

[41] Quoted in Dobrovol'skii, *Zapreshchennaia kniga*, 102–03; see also Itenberg, *Svodnyi katalog*, 2: 184 (no. 2366 [*Liutsinda*]).

[42] B. S. Itenberg et al., eds., *Svodnyi katalog russkoi nelegal'noi i zapreshchennoi pechati XIX veka: Knigi i periodicheskie izdaniia* (Moscow, 1971), ch. 9, 1169, no. 193 (*Emma*).

[43] See publication information in note 29, above.

streets. The tone and views [of the book] have aged. But the struggle has not.[44]

Both *Story of a Peasant* and *Emma* found their way into illegal bibliographies of recommended reading. The importance of works of fiction in the corpus of radical literature is reflected in the prominent place given to *belletristika* in these guides. The two most widely disseminated, the so-called "Odessa" and "Cheliabinsk" catalogs, both date from the early 1880s and were compiled by radical *intelligenty* affiliated with provincial revolutionary circles and were disseminated widely throughout the empire. Although they appeared to be legal publications, their subversive slant was quickly recognized, and the catalogs were put on the censors' prohibited list.[45] These lengthy catalogs were comprised for the most part of legal works, arranged under such rubrics as History, Natural Science, and Political Economy, with further subdivisions. The "Cheliabinsk catalog" in particular focused on articles from the "thick" journals of the intelligentsia. In both catalogs, the first rubric was *Belletristika*, including both Russian and foreign works, among them the above two novels. These politicized reading lists enjoyed great popularity among radical university and gymnasium student circles. They provided a kind of revolutionary countereducation, opposed to the one officially prescribed for secondary and higher educational institutions.[46] Consulted by student propagandists, they also served as guides to readings in workers'

---

[44] Vergezhskii, review of *Emma*, *Byloe*, no. 5 (May 1906): 296–97.

[45] The "Odessa catalog" appeared in two editions. The first came out in 1882. References here are to the second edition: *Katalog sistematicheskogo chteniia*, 2nd ed. (Odessa, 1883). The "Cheliabinsk catalog" is *Sistematicheskii ukazatel´ luchshikh knig i zhurnal´nykh statei (1856–1883 g.)* (Cheliabinsk, 1883). See Dobrovol´skii, *Zapreshchennaia kniga*, no. 130 (*Katalog sistematicheskogo chteniia*) and no. 131 (*Sistematicheskii ukazatel´ luchshikh knig i zhurnal´nykh statei*), 148–49; Itenberg, *Svodnyi katalog*, 1: 126–27 (nos. 710–15, *Katalog sistematicheskogo chteniia*, 1st and 2nd eds.); and Itenberg, *Svodnyi katalog*, 2: 85 (no. 1693, *Sistematicheskii ukazatel´ luchshikh knig i zhurnal´nykh statei* [Cheliabinsk, 1883]).

On these two catalogs, see: N. V. Zdobnov, "Konfiskovannye bibliograficheskie izdaniia 80-kh godov," *Katorga i ssylka*, no. 4 (113) (1934): 106–22; N. V. Zdobnov, "Iz istorii rekomendatel´noi bibliografii 80-kh godov: Odesskii i cheliabinskii ukazateli," *Sovetskaia bibliografiia*, no. 1 (19) (1941): 152–74; N. V. Zdobnov, *Istoriia russkoi bibliografii do nachala XX veka*, 3rd ed. (Moscow, 1955), 485–500; S. A. Reiser, "Podpol´naia rekomendatel´naia bibliografiia 70–80-kh godov XIX veka," *Sovetskaia bibliografiia*, no. 1 (59) (1960): 54–69; M. V. Mashkova, "Nikolai Vasil´evich Zdobnov: K 90-ketiiu so dnia rozhdeniia," *Sovetskaia bibliografiia*, no. 2 (1978): 64–72.

[46] A hectographed copy of the 1882 edition of the Odessa catalog was found among the papers of arrested members of the People's Will circle in the town of Kamenets in 1883 (RGIA f. 1410, op. 1, d. 420, 1883g., ll. 9–34ob.).

circles as well, one sign of the overlap between these two segments of the revolutionary movement. As noted in the foreword to the Odessa catalog, "In the first section are placed the easiest works of belletristic literature, which, together with critical and historical literature, have important developmental significance for the reader who is young, inexperienced, or unused to serious reading."[47] Many other reading lists circulated in manuscript, printed, or hectographed form. Vera Karelina recalled that, due to the great demand for suitable reading material on the part of Petersburg workers in the early 1890s, a special "catalog of books" was compiled for the workers. One section of the catalog was devoted to *belletristika*.[48] The foreword to a 1902 catalog stated that its purpose was to improve on its Odessa and Cheliabinsk predecessors. The former, the author A. V. Panov felt, were too much addressed to the "aristocracy of the intelligentsia," rather than the uneducated. He hoped to include more "booklets accessible to the working masses and at the same time to broaden their worldview until it approached that of educated people."[49] *The Story of a Peasant* is deemed appropriate for acquainting the popular reader with the lives of peasants in other lands. Along with *Emma*, it is also included in section 2, readings for the intelligentsia, under the heading of *Belletristika*, comprising works "which describe the struggle for the ideal."[50]

C3   80

The third foreign novel to rank at the top of the underground popularity list was *Spartacus*, by the Italian author Rafaello Giovagnoli. Giovagnoli, a participant in the Risorgimento, campaigned alongside the revolutionary nationalist Garibaldi.[51] He subsequently wrote a series of historical novels set in ancient Rome, the most popular of which, *Spartacus*, commemorated

---

[47] "Katalog sistematicheskogo chteniia," p. III.

[48] Karelina, "Vospominaniia o podpol'nykh rabochikh kruzhkakh," 287.

[49] A. V. Panov, *Domashnie biblioteki: Opyt sostavleniia predmetnogo ukazatelia knig dlia domashnego chteniia* (Nizhnii Novgorod, 1902), 4.

[50] Ibid., 14, 39, 43. It appears that Panov's bibliography was legally published, which may explain the rather "Aesopian" language framing the selections. On Panov's bibliographical work, see V. M. Mashkova, "Aleksandr Vasil'evich Panov: Iz istorii russkoi rekomendatel'noi bibliografii nachala XX veka," *Trudy gosudarstvennoi Publichnoi biblioteki im. M. E. Saltykova-Shchedrina* 10 (13) (1962): 141–52. For another early 20th-century radical bibliography, see St. Strumilin, *Chto chitat' sotsialdemokratu?* (n.p., n.d.).

[51] On Garibaldi's revolutionary and colorful life, see Denis Mack Smith, *Garibaldi: A Great Life in Brief* (New York, 1956). For a recent and revisionist treatment of Garibaldi, see Lucy Riall, *Garibaldi: Invention of a Hero* (New Haven, 2007). Tim Parks counters Riall's portrayal in an essay which captures Garibaldi's achievements and appeal: Tim

the famous slave revolt of 73–71 BC.[52] The novel was published in 1874 and was extremely popular with Italian readers. Garibaldi himself praised it highly, and his letter to Giovagnoli was added as a preface to the novel. Giovagnoli in fact explicitly compares Spartacus to the equally charismatic leader Garibaldi.[53] The Russian translation, penned by noted radical Sergei Stepniak-Kravchinskii, was published first in the journal *Delo* in 1880–81 and then separately in 1881. (We have already noted the earliest stages of Stepniak-Kravchinskii's revolutionary career as a member of the Chaikovskii circle and a propagandist among Petersburg workers. His subsequent adventures included participation in the uprisings of the Balkan Slavs as a volunteer; arrest together with a group of Italian anarchists in connection with a failed uprising in Benevento in 1877; and the assassination of the head of the Russian Secret Police (Third Section) in 1878—after which he made a successful escape.)[54]

The novel *Spartacus* combines elements of history and melodrama, successfully melded in a seamless exposition. It can be read as a tale of love and jealousy—and also as a chronicle of honor, brotherhood, and the struggle for

---

Parks, "The Insurgent: Garibaldi and His Enemies," *The New Yorker*, 9 and 16 July 2007, 92–97.

[52] On slave revolts against Rome, Spartacus, and the revolt he led, see Brent D. Shaw, ed., *Spartacus and the Slave Wars: A Brief History with Documents* (Boston, 2001); Barry Strauss, *The Spartacus War* (New York, 2009); and M. J. Trow, *Spartacus: The Myth and the Man* (Stroud, UK, 2006).

[53] In a footnote Giovagnoli writes of Spartacus: "The striking simplicity and modesty of this truly great man was recognized even by his enemies" and supports this statement with a quotation from Plutarch. He continues, "Of all the fighters for freedom who have raised themselves from complete obscurity to immeasurable heights, only one resembles in this Spartacus—Giuseppe Garibaldi" (Dzhiovanioli, *Spartak: Istoricheskii roman*, translated from the Italian [n.p., n.d.]).

[54] On Stepniak-Kravchinskii's Italian connections, see Taratuta, *S. M. Stepniak-Kravchinskii*, 136–45, 225–44, and elsewhere, and E. A. Taratuta, "S. M. Stepniak-Kravchinskii v Italii," in *Rossiia i Italiia: Iz istorii russko-ital'ianskikh kul'turnykh i obshchestvennykh otnoshenii* (Moscow, 1968), 227–58. Taratuta's monograph is aptly subtitled: in addition to his devotion to revolution, Kravchinskii was heavily involved in literary activity—his own books, articles, and correspondence for journals, as well as translations—primarily as a means of financial support for himself and his wife. See also Z. M. Potapova, *Russko-ital'ianskie literaturnye sviazi: Vtoraia polovina XIX veka* (Moscow, 1973), 174–86. Garibaldi was a heroic figure for this Russian radical. After Garibaldi's death in 1882, Kravchinskii wrote an essay on his life and role in the Italian national movement. See S. Stepniak-Kravchinskii, *Sochineniia: V dvukh tomakh* (Moscow, 1958), 2: 355–98. According to one reference, Kravchinskii translated *Spartak* with some assistance from Ol'ga Liubatovich, a fellow Russian revolutionary in exile in Switzerland. See O. Liubatovich, *Dalekoe i nedavnee*, ed. V. Nevskii and P. Anatol'ev (Moscow, 1930), 52.

freedom. It recounts the history of the slave/gladiator uprising led by Spartacus, and Giovagnoli emphasizes the historical truth of his account with reference to contemporary sources, including Livy, Pliny, Plutarch, and Cicero, sometimes quoting these sources directly. The novel opens with a detailed description of gladiator games in Rome, in which the reader meets the hero Spartacus, a Thracian slave and gladiator. The games depicted, organized by Sulla, are horrible and bloody. A complex plot unfolds, which interweaves fictional characters and such noted historical figures as Sulla, Catiline, and Julius Caesar. Spartacus, for example, has a clandestine meeting with Caesar, the latter at this time a young patrician with a promising political future. Neither convinces the other of his position—Rome as the ruler of the world vs. a peaceful future for all peoples—but each admires and respects the other. Giovagnoli traces the story of the slave revolt to its ultimately tragic end. Spartacus was a brilliant military leader and strategist. The revolt began among gladiators at the prominent training school in Capua, but grew with an influx of slaves to a size of 80,000 over a three-year period. Giovagnoli shows how Spartacus was able to organize and inspire the downtrodden people. The main theme is that of the struggle of freedom against slavery. No one is born with the right to rule over others, Spartacus repeatedly maintains; he holds out a vision of a society without slavery. The gladiator fights symbolize the profoundly flawed nature of the Roman system: the slave gladiators train in schools together, then must fight each other to the death. Although for a period of time successful in battle against the Roman legions, Spartacus's forces are eventually weakened by betrayal and discord: while Spartacus wants to take his troops outside Italy to join with subject peoples, his rivals want to march on Rome directly, a move which Spartacus holds will lead to certain defeat. In the end, the rebel forces are defeated, the body of Spartacus has been spirited away, and 6000 prisoners are hanged [sic] by the Romans along the road from Capua to Rome.

In addition to the story of preparation for the revolt and then the lengthy series of battles, there is also a romantic narrative. Spartacus falls in love with the patrician Valeria, the wife, then widow of the former dictator Sulla, and they have a child. Although Valeria begs Spartacus to leave his gladiators and enjoy a life of luxury with her, his sense of honor and commitment to the cause make this impossible. In a major plot complication, the beautiful Greek slave Evtibida, now a noted courtesan, is also in love with Spartacus. Blinded by jealousy and seeking only revenge, she takes every opportunity to betray Spartacus's plans to the enemy. Many other characters are also introduced, including Spartacus's sister Mirtsa as well as Artorix, Oknoman, and other gladiator leaders. Giovagnoli emphasizes the different national origins of gladiators and slaves and notes Spartacus's strategies for holding his disparate forces together. The bulky novel—nearly 500 pages in the first Russian translation—is filled with details about Roman life and history: holidays such as the lupercalia and the saturnalia are explained, and dress, food, and forms of gladiator combat are described. Oaths and religious beliefs of different nationalities—Germanic, Gallic, Thracian—are interspersed; the scene ranges from the homes of the patricians to the dark and somewhat menacing "Buried Venus" tavern (so-named for its proximity to the graves of slaves, criminals, and the poor), a dive bar over which "one-eyed" Lutatia presides, to the gladiators' camp on Mt. Vesuvius.

Evidence shows that the experience of reading *Spartacus* lingered in the memories of radical workers. Konstantin Norinskii, a worker active at the Baltic Shipbuilding Plant in Petersburg in the early 1890s, includes in his memoirs a detailed list of works, headed by *Spartacus*, that were the most successful among circle workers. A. K. Petrov, a worker-organizer in Nizhnii Novgorod in the 1890s noted that *Spartak* and other works were purchased from used book sellers: "These books began to circulate briskly from hand to hand among our workers."[55] Ekaterinoslav activists in the late 1890s could draw on a fairly well-stocked library of legal literature. Copies of *Spartacus* were among the most well-worn volumes: since they "only had one, or at most two copies of each title, most of them, even with the most careful handling by the readers, soon took on a ragged, worn-out look."[56] Workers continued to read *Spartacus* into the early 20th century. Ekaterinoslav workers took pride in their library of legal works, which had eight to ten copies of the most popular works, including Giovagnoli's novel. The novel was also popular among workers in the technical class at the Petersburg Obukhov plant during the same period.[57]

Anna Boldyreva, a textile worker involved in Petersburg workers' circles in the early 1890s, recalls passionate discussions of the books they read and listened to, among them *Spartak*: "'Heroic' literature seized hold of us, we were raised on it, it formed our characters."[58] Clearly, this book would interest radical workers, with its attractive hero, Spartacus, and the many other

---

[55] Norinskii, *Pod nadzoram politsii*, 23; Petrov, *Rabochii bol'shevik*, 31. See also Shapovalov, *Po doroge k marksizmu*, 75; K. Ia. [V. N. Katin-Iartsev], "Pervye shagi," *Byloe*, no. 9 (21) (1907): 143; "Polozhenie tverskikh rabochikh: Pis'mo iz Rossii" (Prilozhenie k no. 4 "Rabochego Dela") (Geneva, 1899), 5.

[56] I. Lalaiants, *U istokov bol'shevizma. Zarozhdenie RSDRP* (Moscow, 1934), 36–37.

[57] Drokhanov, "Na zare," 255; U. A. Shuster, *Peterburgskie rabochie v 1905–1907 gg.* (Leningrad, 1976), 56.

[58] Anna Boldyreva, "Minuvshie gody: Vospominaniia rabotnitsy," *Tekstil'shchik*, no. 1–2 (42–43) (1923): 119.

characters with which to identify. The novel could encourage by example, showing how others had united to revolt against oppression for equality and freedom. It revealed important details of conspiratorial organization: passwords and handshakes. Although this revolt failed, it showed what people had managed to achieve even in ancient times and raised the banner of equality, so central to socialism, in contrast to the grave inequalities of life in Rome. The figure of Spartacus retained symbolic significance into Soviet times. As the victorious Bolsheviks attempted to create a new Soviet culture after the October Revolution, Spartacus was an iconic figure in revolutionary festivals and plans for new monumental heroes to replace the old.[59] Spartacus continued to live on as the name of the most popular Moscow soccer team, Spartak. As one fan put it, recalling life in a communal apartment in the 1930s: "Today I understand most clearly that Spartak was the home team ... of ordinary people.... Why? The name had meaning for us. Then all the kids and even the grown-ups knew the name of the leader of the slave revolt in ancient Rome...."[60]

The Story of a Peasant, Emma, and *Spartacus* were arguably the most popular foreign works used in propaganda among workers.[61] The body of translated works of fiction continued to evolve, however, and by the 1890s newer works began to circulate as well. To more accurately capture the scope of this genre, a handful of other frequently encountered titles will be noted here. Among the most popular were *Germinal* by the French author Emile Zola, *The Weavers* by the German playwright Gerhardt Hauptmann, and *Looking Backward* by the

---

[59] See Stites, *Revolutionary Dreams*, 89–95, 111; James von Geldern, *Bolshevik Festivals, 1917–1920* (Berkeley, CA, 1993), 112, 159–60.

[60] Quoted in Robert Edelman, "A Small Way of Saying 'No': Moscow Working Men, Spartak Soccer, and the Communist Party, 1900–1945," *American Historical Review* 107, 5 (December 2002): 1454. On the naming of the team, see also Edelman, *Spartak Moscow: A History of the People's Team in the Workers' State* (Ithaca, NY, 2009), p. 73. In analyzing the iconic significance of the historical figure "Spartacus," N. S. Travushkin writes, "Spartacus became part of the cohort of *eternal images*, close in their universal content to the worlds of Prometheus, Hercules, Anteus, Icarus, etc. The image of Spartacus embodied the conception ... of the hero-liberator, of the tragedy of inequality, the proud struggle with the enslavers, promising in time victory to the oppressed" ("Zarubezhnaia khudozhestvennaia literatura," 164). On Lenin's high evaluation of Spartacus, see Travushkin, "Revoliutsionno-propagandistskaia zarubezhnaia belletristika v Rossii," in *Materialy nauchnoi konferentsii Astrakhanskogo pedagogicheskogo instituta im. S. M. Kirova* (Volgograd, 1972), 61–62.

[61] Frequently all three were listed in catalogs of suggested reading. The People's Will "Program of Propaganda Among Workers" (1881) placed these three works at the head of a listing of works of Russian and foreign fiction. See "Programma propagandy sredi rabochikh," in *Revoliutsionnoe narodnichestvo*, 2: 358.

American author Edward Bellamy.[62] Zola's great work *Germinal* (1885) depicts a miners' strike in northern France, set in the 1860s under the Second Empire. In preparation for writing the novel, Zola researched the mining industry and the history of earlier strikes, and visited a mining town during an ongoing strike in 1884. Following his stated principles of naturalism, *Germinal* and his other works were characterized by stark, often violent realism. Zola describes the hard lives of the miners and depicts both individuals and social classes: miners, the mine owner and his family, priests, the shopkeeper, the tavern keeper, and others. The socialist movement appears too, in the person of a representative of the International and of a Russian anarchist. The novel takes as its theme the critical struggle of capital and labor (as did *Emma*). The strike ends in death and destruction, but the appearance of the new leaves and shoots of April promises a true spring (whence the title of *Germinal* from the calendar of the French Revolution): "New men were starting into life, ... slowly germinating in the furrows, ... and soon this germination would tear the earth apart."[63] Zola's works were very popular in Russia, *Germinal* in particular, which was most frequently referred to by the title *The Coalminers* (*Uglekopy*). A number of Russian workers mention reading *Germinal*, which was deemed "very successful" by Konstantin Norinskii and, according to another worker, was among those works which "definitively strengthened our class consciousness."[64]

Gerhart Hauptmann's play *The Weavers* encountered censorship problems in Germany,[65] as well as Russia. Like Zola a proponent of literary naturalism, Hauptmann took as the subject of his 1892 drama the weavers' uprising in Silesia in 1844. As critics noted, the play lacked a hero—what it presented instead was a "collective hero,"[66] the working people. The play's five acts, while not developing a straightforward plot, are linked by repeated and overlapping

---

[62] See the entries for *Uglekopy* and *Cherez sto let* in K. I. Dikson, A. V. Mez'er, and D. P. Braginskij, *Bibliograficheskie ukazateli perevodnoi belletristiki*, with an introduction by J. S. G. Simmons (London, 1971), 31, 52. See the entries for all three works in Panov, *Domashnie biblioteki*.

[63] Emile Zola, *Germinal*, trans. Roger Pearson (London, 2004), 532.

[64] Norinskii, *Pod nadzorom politsii*, 23; G. M. Petrovskii, "S 1898 goda po 1905 god: Vospominaniia," in Rubach, *Istoriia ekaterinoslavskoi sotsial-demokraticheskoi organizatsii*, 52.

[65] Warren R. Maurer, *Understanding Gerhart Hauptmann* (Columbia, SC, 1992), 48. The play was also banned in Newark, New Jersey in 1893 (ibid., 50).

[66] Evgenii Degen, "Gergard Gauptmann," *Novoe Slovo*, no. 3 (December 1895): 51.

themes and the singing of the threatening song, "Bloody Justice."[67] The action builds to a crescendo of revolt. Hauptmann's play was also distinguished by the use of Silesian dialect and the unique portrayal of each of the characters. Readers and viewers are moved to sympathy for these handloom weavers and their families, a departure from the more removed and dispassionate naturalism of Zola. *The Weavers*, so well-suited for revolutionary propaganda, was rejected by the Russian censorship. Its first appearance in Russian translation was as an illegal work. Two nearly simultaneous translations were published in 1895: one in hectographed form by the social democratic Moscow "Workers' Union" (Rabochii Soiuz) in a translation by Anna Elizarova (Lenin's sister); and the other printed on the press of the St. Petersburg "Group of Narodovol'tsy" in a translation by Praskov'ia Kudelli, a teacher in a Sunday school for workers.[68] Both versions circulated among workers in the mid- to late 1890s. S. I. Mitskevich, a leader of the Moscow Workers' Union, noted that "the drama [in Elizarova's translation] was very successful among the workers."[69] *The Weavers* (*Tkachi*) was the first illegal work read by Semen Kanatchikov as a young worker recently arrived in Moscow:

> The book made a rather strong impression on me. I soon learned the "song of the weavers" by heart and would recite it to the other apprentices of my age group in the workshop. The words kept echoing again and again in my ears.... The book had a very disturbing effect on me, stirring up my animosity toward the rich and my pity for the oppressed and awakening many new, previously unknown emotions....[70]

---

[67] Also known as "Dreissiger's Song," Dreissiger being the name of the employer. For the lyrics, see *The Weavers*, in Gerhart Hauptmann, *Three Plays: The Weavers, Hannele, The Beaver Coat*, trans. Horst Frenz (New York, 1977), 34–35. For brief treatments of Hauptmann and his works, see Warren R. Maurer, *Gerhart Hauptmann* (Boston, 1982); and Maurer, *Understanding Gerhart Hauptmann*.

[68] For a detailed comparison of the German and Russian versions of the play, see Zelnik, "Weber into Tkachi," 216–41.

[69] Mitskevich, *Revoliutsionnaia Moskva*, 146. See also the reference by a worker member of the Union who was close to the Ul'ianov family: V. Maslennikov, "Stranichki proshlogo," in Mitskevich, *Na zare rabochego dvizheniia v Moskve*, 120.

[70] Zelnik, *A Radical Worker*, 33–34. For other references to the circulation of *Tkachi*, see Mironov, *Iz vospominanii rabochego*, 10; and Shesternin, *Perezhitoe*, 96 (Ivanovo-Voznesensk). On the printing of *Tkachi* on the press of the Group of Narodovol'tsy, see Shapovalov, *Po doroge k marksizmu*, 62. The group apparently also had made a translation of *Germinal*, which they planned to print in an edition of 3800 copies. See GARF f. 102, 7 d-vo, d. 257, ll. 31ob., 176ob., 346. On the Group of Narodovol'tsy and their press, see Kudelli, *Narodovol'tsy na pereput'i*.

Looking Backward (1888), a utopian novel by the American writer and political thinker Edward Bellamy, also enjoyed significant popularity among Russian workers. In the United States the novel was at the center of the National movement founded by Bellamy (a movement which did much to inspire the socialist movement in the U.S.).[71] Within a few years the novel appeared in Russian translation under the title *A Hundred Years Later* (*Cherez sto let*).[72] The novel's protagonist and narrator, Julian West, is a wealthy young man living in late 19th-century Boston, with its rampant capitalism, poverty, class divisions, and suffering. Through a twist of circumstances, he falls asleep only to awaken in the year 2000. Bellamy depicts a society of cooperation and order, with an economic and political system that have solved the problems of the former world, resulting in a society of equality for men and women, rational political and economic organization, and freedom from want, ignorance, and injustice. The novel includes a love story as well: as it happens, Julian falls in love with the descendant of his fiancée of 1888.[73] In fact, the society depicted could easily be called socialist, though the movement it gave birth to in the 1890s and early 20th century was known as Nationalism. The novel was read enthusiastically by radical workers in the United States and had a similar effect on Russian workers at the turn of the century. Mitskevich read the translation as soon as it came out:

> In this utopian novel the action takes place in North America, in which in the year 2000 a socialist society has been established, one that is vividly depicted in the novel. We thought that things would surely be that way; and that America, as a leading industrial country, would quite likely be the first to establish a socialist order, and that would in turn influence the less developed countries. This novel had an invigorating effect on us.[74] The novel was also found to be useful for propaganda in Ivanovo-Voznesensk and was read by circle workers in St. Petersburg and elsewhere.[75]

---

[71] See the interesting treatment of Bellamy's influence on American socialism in Franklin Rosemont, "Bellamy's Radicalism Reclaimed," in *Looking Backward, 1988–1888: Essays on Edward Bellamy*, ed. Daphne Patai (Amherst, MA, 1988), 147–209.

[72] See entry no. 4821 in the Dikson-Mez'er-Braginskii bibliography of foreign literature in translation (*Bibliograficheskie ukazateli*, 62). Translations appeared in 1891 and 1893.

[73] The novel is reprinted in Edward Bellamy, *Looking Backward* (New York, 1996).

[74] Mitskevich, *Revoliutsionnaia Moskva*, 76.

[75] "Rabochee dvizhenie v Ivanovo-Voznesenske za poslednie 15 let," 21; Shesternin, *Perezhitoe*, 96; Boldyreva, "Minuvshie gody," 259.

A number of other works continued to expand the genre of foreign literature in translation used for propaganda. The works of Victor Hugo enjoyed great popularity, particularly the novel *Ninety-Three* (*Quatrevingt-treize*), translated in 1893 under the title *93 god*. A work of historical fiction, *Ninety-Three* tells the story of the French Revolution at its most terrible in 1793, bringing out the contrast between Paris and the provinces, supporters of the revolution and those of the king. Hugo shows the human element of both sides and the complexity of political and moral decisions.[76] The novel was read in workers' circles and distributed as legal literature with hopes of attracting workers to the movement.[77] Other works circulating among radical workers included *At Dawn* (*Na rassvete*) by the Polish author T. T. Jez (Ezh), a tale of the Bulgarian uprising against the Ottoman Empire; and *The Gadfly* (*Ovod*) by Ethel Lilian Voinich, a novel which took as its setting the Italian liberation struggle during the 1830s and 40s. Worker-organizer Shapovalov noted that his circle of radicalized workers (Ivanovo-Voznesensk, 1901) were inspired by, for example, *At Dawn*, and attempted to emulate the "heroism of [these] revolutionaries of previous eras."[78] Voinich's *Gadfly* (1897; Russian translation 1898) appears to have been quite popular among Ekaterinoslav workers at the turn of the century, listed as one of the workers' favorites. According to one

---

For further discussion of Bellamy and *Looking Backward*, see the essays in Patai, *Looking Backward 1988–1888;* and Sylvia Bowman, *Edward Bellamy* (Boston, 1986). For a detailed analysis of the impact of *Looking Backward* and other utopian novels in the milieu of radical workers, see Travushkin, "Zarubezhnyi utopicheskii roman," 93–114. See also Scott McLemee, "Back to the Future," *New York Times Book Review*, 24 December 2000, 23.

[76] For information on early Russian translations of Hugo's works, see Dikson-Mez'er-Braginskii, *Bibliograficheskie ukazateli*, 24–25. An English translation has been reprinted: Victor Hugo, *Ninety-Three* (New York, 1988). For a thought-provoking analysis of Hugo's work, see Priscilla Parkhurst Ferguson, "*Quatrevingt-treize*: Turning the Terror to Account," in *Unfinished Revolutions: Legacies of Upheaval in Modern French Culture*, ed. Robert T. Denommé and Roland H. Simon (University Park, PA, 1998), 65–80.

[77] See Shapovalov, *Po doroge k marksizmu*, 75; Mironov, *Iz vospominanii rabochego*, 10; Petrov, "Moi vospominaniia," 188. References simply to works by Hugo quite likely indicate this work as well, for example, Volynkin in Mitskevich, *Na zare rabochego dvizheniia v Moskve*, 210.

[78] *At Dawn* first appeared in a Russian translation in 1889. See Dikson-Mez'er-Braginskii, *Bibliograficheskie ukazateli*, 98. Teodor Tomasz Jez was the pen name of Zygmunt Milkowski (1824–1915); he authored a number of historical novels. For biographical information, see "Milkovskii (Sigizmund Miłkowski)," in *Entsiklopedicheskii slovar' Brokgauz-Efron* (St. Petersburg, 1896), 19: 296–97; and Shapovalov, *V podpol'e*, 52. Semen Kanatchikov also recalled reading this work (Zelnik, *A Radical Worker*, 115).

worker, their library included multiple copies of *Ovod* which were always in circulation.[79]

cs   so

How did these novels gain a place in the canon of revolutionary literature, what function did they serve, and what did they mean to workers? Initially, these works were chosen and introduced into the movement by propagandists from the intelligentsia (in this period, frequently students). These were usually not obscure works, but well known to the educated public. Often they had appeared in serial form in the widely read "thick" journals. Thus the corpus of "tendentious" novels popular with radical workers shaded over into works read by young members of the radical intelligentsia as well. Only rarely were these novels rewritten for the reader from the *narod*—the *"peredelka"* of *Story of a Peasant* may be a unique case in this regard. The books were discussed in workers' circles, or more frequently read aloud in circles or perhaps retold by the propagandist with suitable explanation. The subjects and themes of these novels fit quite well into the circle curriculum, which retained its basic outlines from the 1870s into the early 20th century: slave and peasant revolts, revolutions, class struggle, movements of national liberation, and workers' movements in Western Europe.[80] In this way, works of imaginative literature, for the most part legally published, broadened the workers' perspective on history and brought to life topics of circle discussion that might otherwise have remained abstract.[81]

It bears emphasis that workers' circles associated with presumably competing ideological trends in the revolutionary movement—People's Will/Black

---

[79] See Dikson-Mez'er-Braginskii, *Bibliograficheskie ukazateli*, ch. 2, 9; and Drokhanov, "Na zare," 255. On Ethel Voinich (1864–1960) and *Ovod*, see E. Taratuta, *Etel' Lilian Voinich: Sud'ba pisatelia i sud'ba knigi* (Moscow, 1964).

[80] Among the topics listed in various programs for workers' circles were "the workers' situation in Western Europe, ... the development of capitalism ... and the various methods used by Western European workers in their struggle with their situation"; "the history of the workers' movement in the West"; and the "history of social movements in Europe."

Testimony of Anton Boreisha, quoted in I. I. Mindlina, "Deiatel'nost' revoliutsionnykh narodnikov sredi rabochikh Peterburga i Moskvy (1879–1882 gg.)," in *Uchenye zapiski 1-go Moskovskogo pedagogicheskogo instituta inostrannykh iazykov*, no. 34 (1965): 201, 204; "Ustav Moskovskoi rabochei gruppy partii 'Narodnoi Voli,'" reprinted in *Revoliutsionnoe narodnichestvo*, 2: 215; Program of Brusnev group, reprinted in Pankratova and Ivanov, *Rabochee dvizhenie v Rossii*, 3, ch. 2, 131–32.

[81] For fairly complete bibliographies of *belletristika* available to the Russian reading public, see Dikson-Mez'er-Braginskii, *Bibliograficheskie ukazateli*, 25 n. 62.

Repartition, populist/Marxist, Social Democratic/Socialist Revolutionary—used the *same* works of literature. These novels also circulated outside the circle setting, and here their standing as (for the most part) *legal* literature was important. Some propagandists in fact preferred to avoid illegal literature altogether, or to begin with legal works when approaching workers not yet committed to the movement, as there was less liability involved. (As noted, possession or dissemination of illegal literature was a crime that could carry harsh penalties.) As one worker-activist noted:

> We used the latter works [*Spartacus* and other works of legally published fiction] as agitational material: you give a newcomer *Spartacus* to read— if you see that the book has an effect, infects him with enthusiasm for the struggle, then you can give illegal [literature]; if it doesn't work, then you continue to educated with *belletristika*, until the fellow is inspired and doesn't waiver.[82]

But literature originally chosen by *intelligenty* propagandists was ultimately appropriated by the subculture of radical workers. First, there was a selection process: only certain works introduced by propagandists gained popularity among workers. The context and manner of reading in which these two groups engaged in reading differed as well. While members of the intelligentsia probably first read radical works silently, workers often first listened to them, or even heard them retold. Nor should we assume that these works had the same function in the workers' milieu. Once again, the concept of appropriation is helpful in understanding the cultural role of literature. As Roger Chartier emphasizes:

> [T]he diffusion of ideas cannot be held to be a simple imposition. Reception always involves appropriation, which transforms, reformulates, and exceeds what it receives. Opinion is in no way a receptacle, nor is it soft wax to be written upon. The circulation of thoughts or cultural models is always a dynamic and creative process. Texts, to invert the question, do not bear within them a stable and univocal meaning, and their migrations within a given society produce interpretations that are mobile, plural, and even contradictory.[83]

The topic of the variable reception and appropriation of revolutionary literature, crucial for understanding revolutionary culture, has been virtually

---

[82] Mikhailov, *Chetvert' veka podpol'shchika*, 27.

[83] Roger Chartier, *The Cultural Origins of the French Revolution* (Durham, NC, 1991), 19.

ignored to date and calls for attention. For example, Vera Karelina, one of the first women workers active in the movement, recalls that workers in the Petersburg circle network of the early 1890s chose revolutionary *klichki* for purposes of conspiracy: "because we loved reading *Spartak*, we called ourselves by the names of the heroes of that novel: Natasha was called Lucretia, I— Valeria, and Kolia Lialia—Spartacus."[84] Was it strange that this working-class woman chose the name of a patrician woman? Clearly, the novel's meaning to workers transcended some kind of mechanistic sociological correspondence.

To answer this question we might raise a related one: why make use of *belles lettres*/imaginative literature at all? Why not simply present ideas in a straightforward pamphlet? Of course, as we have seen, using legal literature in propaganda was safer, and Vera Karelina noted that *belletristika* was "easily read and assimilated in the circles."[85] But could it be that imaginative literature has a particular effect, even in the case of works of "lesser" quality? It seems that these fictional works are not merely more palatable vehicles for embedded social/political/economic ideas (although they are often treated as such). Engrossing plots, attractive and inspirational heroes, and characters with which readers can identify are not simply incidental, but rather are crucial to their effect.

An answer to this question is suggested by Nikolai Rubakin, the turn-of-the-century Russian scholar of the popular reader. He stressed the impor-tance of historical novels (a category which includes many of the kinds of works discussed above) not only in teaching history, but in fostering critical understanding of society and wakening the desire to work for the common good. Even bad historical novels, he maintained, had this effect. Noting the popularity of historical novels among readers from the *narod*, as well as the divergent reception of such works by upper- and lower-class readers, he proposed an explanation for their effect: for the reader from the people, the reader with little education, such a novel is a "kind of discovery: it opens up [new] horizons, ... removes historical figures from a pedestal to the level of ordinary mortals."[86] The historical novel serves as a bridge between images and ideas. It leads to an understanding of history, culture, and social relations, and shows how ordinary people are affected by historical events. As the reader brings his/her own life experiences to the reading of the novel, s/he begins to see how ideas are embodied in society, including their own. Among the examples Rubakin gives of such novels are *Spartacus* and the works of

---

[84] Karelina, "Na zare rabochego dvizheniia v S.-Peterburge," 19.

[85] Karelina, "Leonid Borisovich," 90.

[86] N. A. Rubakin, "Istoricheskii roman i prepodavanie istorii," introduction to Mez′ier, *Ukazatel′ istoricheskikh romanov*, 7.

Erckmann-Chatrian. Similarly Georg Lukács, in his study of the historical novel, argues that "the historical novel in its origin, development, rise and decline follows inevitably upon the great social transformations of modern times...." Following the French Revolution history became "a *mass* experience ... on a European scale," with "concrete possibilities for men to comprehend their own existence as something historically conditioned, for them to see in history something which deeply affects their daily lives and immediately concerns them."[87]

Works of foreign literature, including many of the historical novels noted above, remained popular among Russian workers into the 20th century. A survey of workers taking technical classes at the St. Petersburg Obukhov plant in 1902 noted among their favorite works *Spartak*, *Germinal*, and works by Victor Hugo.[88] The workers who read and were inspired by these novels can be seen as acquiring a sense of themselves as actors in history, as in this way entering the public sphere. Hannah Arendt called history "the storybook of mankind," produced by the web of relationships linking individual lives. Using this metaphor, we might see these workers—as they read about the peasant Michel Bastien and the French Revolution, Spartacus and the Roman slave revolt, and Emma and the struggle of German workers to transform their society through revolution—as reading themselves into history and realizing the possibility of action. These novels encouraged identification with these heroes and with the common people as a collective hero:

> The hero the story discloses needs no heroic qualities.... The connotation of courage, which we now feel to be an indispensable quality of the hero, is in fact already present in a willingness to act and speak at all, to insert one's self into the world and begin a story of one's own.[89]

The works that made up the genre of foreign novels in translation contributed to a common vocabulary of revolution. They emphasized values such as solidarity, resistance to oppression, and a striving for justice; presented concepts of citizenship; and explained the political issues of 19th–early 20th-century society. They helped to create a "usable past," highlighting particular historical events and stressing the possibility of action. This sense of themselves

---

[87] Georg Lukács, *The Historical Novel* (Lincoln, NE, 1983), 17, 23, 24. On Erckmann-Chatrian, see 212–14 and elsewhere; on *The Weavers*, see 96, 116. David Lowenthal's discussion of the complex relationship between history and fiction questions any neat separation of the two. See his *The Past Is a Foreign Country* (Cambridge, 1985), 224–31.

[88] Shuster, *Peterburgskie rabochie*, 56.

[89] Hannah Arendt, *The Human Condition*, 2nd ed. (Chicago, 1998), 183–84.

as actors in history seems to have been reflected in the use of the fictional characters in the novels as revolutionary sobriquets, as recalled above by Vera Karelina.[90] By the late 19th century there is evidence that radical workers had a revolutionary history and heritage as well. A worker in the Petersburg suburb of Kolpino recalled that even in the late 1890s traces of the "terrorist" movement of the 1870s and 80s lingered in the person of workers who had participated in the movement at that time. When they'd been drinking they would recite revolutionary verse and tell of Zheliabov, Perovskaia, and others. These tales had a revolutionizing effect on some of the younger workers.[91] Some workers' circles could trace their lineage back through a number of successive "generations," and there often appeared to be one of the "last of the Mohicans of Narodnaia Volia" in the workplace.[92] Development of the concept of history was one of the goals of revolutionary propaganda: seeing one's position in society and realizing that the social order was not ordained by fate but was under human control. This recognition was central to the socialist perspective as well and was integral to the culture common to the workers' revolutionary movement as a whole, the shared culture of radical workers regardless of ostensible ideological differences.

---

[90] Radical workers in Ivanovo-Voznesensk and Rostov-on-Don took *klichki* from *At Daybreak* by T. Ezh. See references in Travushkin, "Zarubezhnaia belletristika," 94–95.

[91] Ia. A. Andreev, "1897–98 v Kolpine," *Proletarskaia revoliutsiia*, no. 2 (14) (1923): 77.

[92] Ol'minskii, "O vospominaniiakh N. D. Bogdanova," 39. One example of a long-lived circle is given in B---------[Bartenev], "Vospominaniia peterburzhtsa o vtoroi polovine 80-kh godov," *Minuvshie gody*, no. 10 (October 1908): 175.

Conclusion

Propaganda literature was at the heart of the subculture of radical workers who participated in the revolutionary workers' movement in late 19th-century Russia. This literature, comprised of various genres, embodied the ideals, the goals, and the world outlook that were held in common by those workers. Although for the most part composed or selected by members of the radical intelligentsia, only those works which were adopted by workers and validated by their repeated use became part of the revolutionary canon. The varied genres are distinguished by their forms and manner of approach to the goal of imparting revolutionary knowledge. We have examined four of these genres. Revolutionary *skazki*, cloaked in the age-old form of the traditional folktale, presented uncensored criticism and scathing indictment of the existing social order, leading the reader/listener to the need for revolution and presenting the language in which to call for it. Expositions of political economy laid bare the framework of the economic system of capitalism and exploitation; with understanding of how the system was created and who benefited from it, workers could contrast the desired socialist economy. Revolutionary poetry and song conveyed with words and music the emotional commitment to the revolutionary struggle, the bonds of solidarity uniting workers with their comrades, and the utopian vision of a socialist future. A selected list of foreign novels in translation drew workers into history, highlighting struggles for freedom, equality, and justice in the recent and distant past.

This literature was embedded in the world of the workers' circle, the key institution of the workers' movement and the main locus of revolutionary activity in the late 19th century. As we have seen, the experience of participation in the *kruzhok*, the ties with small groups of radical-minded workers and with radicals from the intelligentsia, was critical to the creation of the dense web of organization and ideas that made up the Russian revolutionary workers' movement. The revolutionary movement is typically sketched in terms of a series of antagonistic ideological camps—populists vs. Marxists, Socialist Revolutionaries vs. Social Democrats—culminating in the victory of the Bolsheviks in 1917. Highlights of the movement's history in the late 19th century are propaganda among the peasantry in the 1870s and the dramatic terrorist exploits of the People's Will in the late 1870s and early 1880s. I have attempted in this study to view the workers' movement not through the grid of well-worn historiography but through the experiences of workers and the lens provided by the propaganda literature and ideas that comprised the intellectual and moral core of the movement. A major finding that revises the long-accepted story is that of the essential unity of the movement. At the grassroots level of the workers' revolutionary movement, ideological differences were of minor significance. Workers saw the movement as a workers' movement and a revolutionary one; differences between revolutionary theories and parties were of lesser importance. Significantly, throughout the period 1870–1905, propagandists from ostensibly rival groups made use of the same propaganda literature, thrilled to the same songs, and followed the same curriculum in the *kruzhki*. By the early 20th century street demonstrations and May Day celebrations were distinguished by their banners, red flags, and songs: the common symbolic heritage of the revolutionary movement. A second major revision concerns the significance of the People's Will Party, whose history is usually relegated to a few dramatic terrorist acts. In fact, the People's Will was Russia's major revolutionary party in the late 19th century, with social democratic groups becoming prominent only in the 1890s. In the 1880s, in particular, the revolutionary movement was represented for the most part by circles of *narodovol'tsy* scattered throughout the cities, provincial towns, and industrial centers of the Russian empire, with radicals engaged in the quintessential revolutionary activity of the time: propaganda in workers' circles.

Without acknowledging the decades-long history of the Russian workers' movement, workers' revolutionary activism in 1917 seems to come out of nowhere (and is often presented in this way). What happened to the subculture of radical workers during 1917? Was it discarded, or was it changed? An analysis of the workers' movement after 1905 is beyond the scope of this study. Recent research, however, provides some answers to the question of the fate of the culture of the revolutionary movement in 1917 and after. It appears that the symbols, language, and ideals that marked this culture were carried over into the charged atmosphere of revolution, a liminal time when questions of politics and utopian yearnings become everyday topics. During the revolutionary months of 1917, workers and others drew on the "discourse of socialism" that, as S. A. Smith has noted, had been in circulation for decades, "characterized by strident hostility to autocracy and 'arbitrariness' ..., burning hatred of class exploitation, a passionate commitment to equality and social justice, and a utopian vision of a new society."[1] The street procession, with a history going back to the early 20th century, became the primary mode of political expression; the color red was seen on flags and bunting; the "Workers' Marseillaise" and other revolutionary songs were sung. The

---

[1] S. A. Smith, *Revolution and the People in Russia and China: A Comparative History* (Cambridge, 2008), 31.

language of class, Marxism and the heroic role of the proletariat, ideas of revolution and socialism: these were not new for radical workers and the urban lower-class milieu of which they were a part. When the revolution began in February the culture of revolution was ready to hand, the symbols, forms of activity, and the socialist outlook accepted without debate. As Donald J. Raleigh puts it in a telling phrase, "[r]evolution became a tradition in Russia before it was a fact."[2] Orlando Figes and Boris Kolonitskii similarly note that "the symbolic systems of the revolutionary underground ... dominated the political culture of the February Revolution.... No one doubted for a moment that the symbols of the revolutionary movement would become the emblems of the future state."[3] Once again in 1917 the demonstrations and crowds in the streets were among the enduring images of revolution. Familiar songs were heard once again. John Reed, in *Ten Days That Shook the World*, recalls military bands playing the "Marseillaise," along with the "International," and the "Funeral March" (probably "You Fell Victim") was heard as well.[4] Similarly, a newspaper account of May Day festivities in Petrograd in 1917 noted that "the bold sounds of the 'Workers' Marseillaise' rang out, the triumphal motif of the 'Internationale' was carried on the air, and the incendiary words of the 'Red Banner' [were heard]."[5] The potency of revolutionary song, and the emotions released by the words and melodies of the most popular songs, were irresistible at the moment of actual revolution. In song, as in other respects, the culture of the revolutionary movement was transformed and integrated into the newborn culture of the revolution. After the February Revolution even peasant villagers were heard singing the "Marseillaise." In Viatka district, to give one example, local officials and members of the intelligentsia were assigned to prepare villagers for the celebration of May First in 1917 by teaching the old revolutionary songs: the "Marseillaise," "Bravely, Comrades, Keep Together," the "Varshavianka," and the "Funeral March."[6] The general acceptance of this powerful symbolic heritage by workers and other ordinary people, as well as radical minded members of the intelligentsia, undoubtedly

---

[2] Donald J. Raleigh, *Experiencing Russia's Civil War: Politics, Society, and Revolutionary Culture in Saratov, 1917–1922* (Princeton, NJ, 2002), 23.

[3] Orlando Figes and Boris Kolonitskii, *Interpreting the Russian Revolution: The Language and Symbols of 1917* (New Haven, 1999), 187–88.

[4] John Reed, *Ten Days That Shook the World* (New York, 1934/1967), 243, 258, 309.

[5] *Pervoe maia v dokumentakh i svidetel'stvakh sovremennikov 1886–1918* (Moscow, 1989), 214–15.

[6] See Aaron B. Retish, *Russia's Peasants in Revolution and Civil War: Citizenship, Identity, and the Creation of the Soviet State, 1914–1922* (Cambridge, 2008), 69, 78.

contributed to widespread support for the overthrow of the autocracy and the significant degree of popular unity as the revolution began to unfold.

During the politicized eight months between the February and October Revolutions, broader layers of the population, urban and rural, became familiar with these symbols and ideas. The political press, street demonstrations, slogans, and the new language of class, socialism, and "the democracy" became familiar and helped to concretize revolutionary change. Revolutionary funerals and the celebration of May First further provided words and symbols to express the revolution. At the same time, scholars have noted a fragmentation of the once unified revolutionary culture and the focus on symbols as a stage for contestation. Figes and Kolonitskii in *Interpreting the Russian Revolution* focus on the struggle over the revolutionary heritage, seen particularly in the shifting significance of songs: which version of "The Marseillaise" was to be played, or the replacement of the old revolutionary "Workers' Marseillaise" of Lavrov by the "Internationale," which ranged the Revolution unequivocally with the Western Marxist movement.[7]

The utopian goal of a socialist society, a goal which it shared with the rest of the revolutionary movement of which it was a part, was at the heart of Bolshevik ideology. In his treatment of the 1917 revolution and the Civil War Christopher Read brings out the link between revolution and utopia, emphasizing that "[w]ithout recognizing the utopian foundation of the Leninist outlook one cannot understand Bolshevism."[8] After their October victory, the Bolsheviks needed to create a new culture for the new society, and much effort was directed to this task. Holidays such as 1 May, the anniversaries of the February and October Revolutions, and funerals and commemorations of revolutionary martyrs were occasions for showcasing the meaning of the revolution. The class nature of the new society headed by the heroic proletariat; the ideology of socialism, symbolized by the red banner; "You Fell Victim," "Bravely, Comrades, Keep Step," and other revolutionary songs: in these and other respects the new Communist state appeared as the revolutionary movement in power. A major effort was devoted to planning appropriate celebrations where the meaning of the victorious revolution could be presented in song, story, and dramatic tableaux.[9] The new regime replaced

---

[7] Figes and Kolonitskii, *Interpreting the Russian Revolution*, 39–43.

[8] Christopher Read, *From Tsar to Soviets; The Russian People and Their Revolution, 1917–21* (Oxford, 1996), 161–62; Richard Stites, *Revolutionary Dreams: Utopan Vision and Experimental Life in the Russian Revolution* (Oxford, 1989).

[9] For studies of Soviet celebrations, see James von Geldern, *Bolshevik Festivals, 1917–1920* (Berkeley, CA, 1993); Karen Petrone, *Life Has Become More Joyous, Comrades: Celebrations in the Time of Stalin* (Bloomington, IN; 2000); Malte Rolf, *Soviet Mass Festivals, 1917–1991* (Pittsburgh, 2013).

the old with the new, renaming streets and dismantling symbols of the tsarist regime. In April 1918 the Plan for Monumental Propaganda was unveiled, presenting a new list of heroes: among them was Spartacus, who had figured in the curriculum of the underground workers' circle. The Revolution could be taught, the Bolsheviks believed. In Petrograd, for example, the Commissariat of the Enlightenment organized school choruses and taught revolutionary songs in its preparation for the commemoration of the October Revolution.[10]

The culture of a revolutionary movement striving to take power and create a new socialist society and the newly adapted culture of a victorious revolutionary government attempting to retain power amid the difficult circumstances of the Civil War years and after: these of necessity could not be the same. Workers who had been participants in the pre-1917 movement, together with broader groups of workers who joined them, had a perspective developed through the movement over decades: their ethos was collective and egalitarian; they strove for social justice and a revolution that was theirs, that of the working class. This had been the focus of propaganda in *kruzhki* and in revolutionary literature for decades. All of this was captured in the slogan of "Soviet power." As scholars have shown, Russian workers in the 1920s and early 1930s retained a "workerist" and "shop floor" identity.[11] They continued to commemorate past events in the history of the movement and continued to see themselves as the true representatives of 1917. As official Soviet culture "stiffened," to use Richard Stites's expression, the utopian dreams of the Revolution died. This transition could be seen in the realm of public festivals, among other areas: "The transformation of Soviet public holiday celebration from a festival of revolution to a panegyric ritual of power and solidarity was the public emblem of the changing nature of the system and its supporting myths."[12] Diane Koenker and Jeffrey Rossman have shown that into the early 1930s workers were still speaking the language of revolution: they wanted true "soviet power," and some felt that the Bolsheviks had betrayed the revolution. They had the confidence that grew from their certainty that 1917 had indeed been the workers' revolution, the culmination of their movement.[13]

Tracing the workers' revolutionary movement into the Soviet period goes beyond the boundaries of this book. Nonetheless, scholarly research

---

[10] Alexander Rabinowitch, *The Bolsheviks in Power: The First Year of Soviet Rule in Petrograd* (Bloomington, IN; 2007), 367.

[11] See Diane Koenker, *Republic of Labor: Russian Printers and Soviet Socialism, 1918–1930* (Ithaca, NY, 2005).

[12] Stites, *Revolutionary Dreams*, 228.

[13] See Koenker, *Republic of Labor*; Jeffrey J. Rossman, *Worker Resistance under Stalin: Class and Revolution on the Shop Floor* (Cambridge, MA, 2005).

has shown that at least through the early Soviet period the heritage of the workers' revolutionary movement was not lost. Many workers active in the movement of the late 19th and early 20th centuries lived to see the victory of their revolution, with what degree of satisfaction or disappointment remains to be investigated. There can be no doubt, however, that the goals of the workers' revolutionary movement, the hopes and goals that gave strength to the workers' movement in 1917, were those presented in propaganda literature and taken up by workers in the *kruzhki* of the late 19th century. Equality, social justice, solidarity, the vision of a future socialist society—these were the ideals that workers fought for, and this, to workers, was the meaning of the revolution of 1917.

Selected Bibliography

Archives

GARF, Gosudarstvennyi arkhiv Rossiiskoi Federatsii (State Archive of the Russian Federation), Moscow, Russia

RGIA, Rossiiskii gosudarstvennyi istoricheskii arkhiv (Russian State Historical Archive), St. Petersburg, Russia

Books and Articles

Acton, Edward, V. Iu. Cherniaev, and William G. Rosenberg, eds. *Critical Companion to the Russian Revolution, 1914–1921.* Bloomington, IN, 1997.

Aleksandrov, M. S. [Ol'minskii]. "'Gruppa narodovol'tsev' (1891–1894 gg.)." *Byloe*, no. 11 (November 1906): 1–27.

Alekseev, P. A. et al. *Rabochee dvizhenie v Rossii v opisanii samykh rabochikh: Ot 70-kh do 90-kh godov.* Moscow, 1933.

Alekseeva, O. "Pesni russkikh rabochikh." *Russkaia literatura*, no. 4 (1964): 119–34.

Aleksei Nikolaevich Bakh. Introduction by A. I. Oparin and N. M. Sisakian. Bibliography compiled by O. A. Gubyrina. Materialy k biobibliografii uchenykh SSSR; Seriia biokhimii. Vyp. 1. Moscow-Leningrad, 1946.

Andreev, Ia. A. "1897–98 v Kolpine." *Proletarskaia revoliutsiia*, no. 2 (14) (1923): 77–87.

Andreev, Iu. A., ed. *Pesni russkikh poetov.* 2 vols. Leningrad, 1988.

Antonov, P. L. "Avtobiografiia P. L. Antonova." *Golos minuvshego*, no. 2 (1923): 77–96.

Aptekman, O. V. *Iz istorii revoliutsionnogo narodnichestva: "Zemlia i Volia" 70-kh godov. Po lichnym vospominaniiam.* Rostov-na-Donu, [1907].

Aptekman, O. V. *Obshchestvo "Zemlia i Volia" 70-kh gg.: Po lichnym vospomina niiam.* 2nd ed. Petrograd, 1924.

Arendt, Hannah. *The Human Condition.* 2nd ed. Chicago, 1998.

Artamonov, A. *Ot derevni do katorgi: Vospominaniia.* Moscow–Leningrad, 1925.

Babushkin, I. V. *Vospominaniia I. V. Babushkina, 1893–1900 gg.* Moscow, 1955.

Baczko, Bronislaw. *Les imaginaires sociaux: Mémoires et espoirs collectifs.* Paris, 1984.

Bakh, A. N. *Zapiski narodovol'tsa.* Moscow–Leningrad, 1929.

———. *Zapiski narodovol'tsa.* 2nd ed. Leningrad, 1931.

Bakh, L. A., and A. I. Oparin. *Aleksei Nikolaevich Bakh: Biograficheskii ocherk.* Moscow, 1957.

Bakunin, Mikhail. *Statism and Anarchy.* Translated and edited by Marshall S. Shatz. Cambridge, 1990.

B_____, V. [V. V. Bartenev]. "Vospominaniia peterburzhtsa o vtoroi polovine 80-kh godov." *Minuvshie gody,* no. 10 (October 1908): 169–97; no. 11 (November 1908): 168–88.

Bazanov, V. G. *Ot fol'klora k narodnoi knige.* Leningrad, 1973.

———. *Russkie revoliutsionnye demokraty i narodoznanie.* Leningrad, 1974.

Bazanov, V. G., ed. *Agitatsionnaia literatura russkikh revoliutsionnykh narodnikov: Potaennye proizvedeniia 1873–1875 gg.* Leningrad, 1970.

Bazanov, V. G., B. L. Bessonov, and A. M. Bikhter, eds. *Poety-demokraty 1870–1880-kh godov.* Leningrad, 1968.

Bazilevskii, B. [V. Bogucharskii], ed. *Revoliutsionnaia zhurnalistika semidesiatykh godov: Vtoroe prilozhenie k sbornikam "Gosudarstvennye prestupleniia v Rossii."* Slavica-reprint 52; Russkaia istoricheskaia biblioteka 7. Düsseldorf, 1970.

Berezin, M. E. et al. "Vospominaniia iz zhizni narodnicheskikh kruzhkov v Kazani (1875–1892 gg.)." *Katorga i ssylka,* no. 10 (71) (1930): 111–36.

Bergman, Jay. "The Image of Jesus in the Russian Revolutionary Movement: The Case of Russian Marxism." *International Review of Social History* 35, 2 (August 1990): 220–48.

Bernstein, Edward. *Ferdinand Lassalle as a Social Reformer.* Translated by Eleanor Marx Aveling. London, 1893.

Blit, Lucjan. *The Origins of Polish Socialism: The History and Ideas of the First Polish Socialist Party 1878–1886.* Cambridge, 1971.

Bogucharskii, V. Ia. *Aktivnoe narodnichestvo semidesiatykh godov.* Moscow, 1912.

Boldyreva, Anna. "Minuvshie gody: Vospominaniia rabotnitsy." *Tekstil'shchik,* no. 1–2 (42–43) (1923): 109–22.

Bonch-Bruevich, Vladimir. "Pervyi russkii mimeograf: Pamiati Leonida Petrovicha Radina." *Proletarskaia revoliutsiia*, no. 2 (1921): 167–80.

Borodin, N. D. *Idealy i deistvitel'nost': Sorok let zhizni i raboty riadovogo russkogo intelligenta (1879–1919)*. Berlin, 1930.

Bortnikov, I. *Iul'skie dni 1903 goda na iuge Rossii*. Odessa, 1953.

Borziakov, Gr. "Revoliutsionnaia molodezh' v Odesse v 1882–1884 gg." *Katorga i ssylka*, no. 8–9 (1929): 129–58.

Bowman, Sylvia. *Edward Bellamy*. Boston, 1986.

Breitfus, A. "Tochisskii i ego kruzhok." *Krasnaia letopis'*, no. 7 (1923): 324–43.

Bristol, Evelyn. *A History of Russian Poetry*. New York, 1991.

Brooks, Jeffrey. *When Russia Learned to Read: Literacy and Popular Literature, 1861–1917*. Princeton, NJ, 1985.

Brusnev, M. I. "Vozniknovenie pervykh sotsial-demokraticheskikh organizatsii: Vospominaniia." *Proletarskaia revoliutsiia*, no. 2 (14) (1923): 12–33.

Buck-Morss, Susan. *Dreamworld and Catastrophe: The Passing of Mass Utopia in East and West*. Cambridge, MA, 2000.

Budnitskii, O. V. *Istoriia terrorizma v Rossii v dokumentakh, biografiiakh, issledovaniiakh*. 2nd ed. Rostov-na-Donu, 1996.

———. *Terrorizm v rossiiskom osvoboditel'nom dvizhenii: Ideologiia, etika, psikhologiia (vtoraia polovina XIX–nachalo XX v.)*. Moscow, 2000.

———. *Zhenshchiny-terroristki v Rossii*. Rostov-na-Donu, 1996.

Buiko, A. M. *Put' rabochego: Vospominaniia putilovtsa*. Leningrad, 1964.

Bukhbinder, N. A. "Evreiskoe rabochee dvizhenie v Gomele (1890–1905 gg.): Po neizdannym arkhivnym materialam." *Krasnaia letopis'*, no. 2–3 (1922): 38–102.

———. *Istoriia evreiskogo rabochego dvizheniia v Rossii: Po neizdannym arkhivnym materialam*. Leningrad, 1925.

Bulanova, O. K. "'Chernyi Peredel': Vospominaniia." In *Gruppa "Osvobozhdenie Truda": Iz arkhivov G. V. Plekhanova, V. I. Zasulich i L. G. Deicha*, edited by Deich, 1: 112–22. Moscow, 1924.

Bushkanets, E. "Neizvestnye pamiatniki revoliutsionnoi poezii 1880-kh godov." *Russkaia literatura*, no. 1 (1962): 230–35.

Bushkanets, E. "Ob oshibochnoi atributsii stikhotvoreniia 'Smelo, druz'ia, ne teriaite....'" *Russkaia literatura*, no. 2 (1968): 111–14.

Bychkov, A. I. "Delo o revoliutsionnykh kruzhkakh v Kieve v 1879, 1880 i 1881 gg." *Letopis´ revoliutsii*, no. 2 (7) (1924): 39–62; 3 (8) (1924): 161–74.

Calhoun, Craig, ed. *Habermas and the Public Sphere*. Cambridge, MA, 1992.

Chartier, Roger. *The Cultural Origins of the French Revolution*. Durham, NC, 1991.

———. *The Cultural Uses of Print in Early Modern France*. Princeton, NJ, 1987.

———. *On the Edge of the Cliff: History, Language, and Practices*. Baltimore, 1997.

———. "Texts, Printing, Readings." In *The New Cultural History*, edited by Lynn Hunt, 154–75. Berkeley, CA, 1989.

Charushin, N. A. *O dalekom proshlom: Iz vospominanii o revoliutsionnom dvizhenii 70-kh godov XIX veka*. 2nd ed. Moscow, 1973.

Cherniavsky, Michael. *Tsar and People: Studies in Russian Myths*. New York, 1969.

Chudnovskii, S. L. *Iz davnikh let*. Moscow, 1934.

Clarke, John et al. "Subcultures, Cultures and Class: A Theoretical Overview." In *Resistance Through Rituals: Youth Subcultures in Post-War Britain*, edited by Stuart Hall and Tony Jefferson, 9–74. London, 1975.

Clowes, Edith, Samuel D. Kassow, and James L. West, eds. *Between Tsar and People: Educated Society and the Quest for Public Identity in Late Imperial Russia*. Princeton, NJ, 1995.

Cole, G. D. H. *Socialist Thought: Marxism and Anarchism, 1850–1890*. 3 vols. London, 1953–60.

Confino, Alon. "Collective Memory and Cultural History: Problems of Method." *American Historical Review* 102, 5 (December 1997): 1386–1403.

Corney, Frederic C. *Telling October: Memory and the Making of the Bolshevik Revolution*. Ithaca, NY, 2004.

Dargol´ts, I. [Lipovetskaia]. "Beglye zametki o sostoianii odesskoi organizatsii k momentu 1-go partiinogo s˝ezda: Po lichnym vospominaniiam." In *K dvadtsatipiatiletiiu pervogo s˝ezda partii (1898–1903)*, 95–134. Moscow–Petrograd, 1923.

David-Fox, Michael. *Revolution of the Mind: Higher Learning among the Bolsheviks, 1918–1929*. Ithaca, NY, 1997.

"Delo o prestupnoi propagande v srede s.-peterburgskikh rabochikh (1881 god)." *Byloe*, no. 1 (13) (1907): 288–94.

Denisenko, V. "Khar'kovskaia gruppa partii "Narodnoi Voli' 1885–1887 gg." In Iakimova-Dikovskaia et al., *Narodovol'tsy 80-kh i 90-kh godov*, 128–42.

Departament Politsii. *Obzor vazhneishikh doznanii po delam o gosudarstvennykh prestupleniiakh proizvodivshikhsia v Zhandarmskikh Upravleniiakh Imperii*. 17 vols. St. Petersburg, 1881–94.

Diakin, V. S., ed. *Istoriia rabochikh Leningrada*, 1: *1703–fevral' 1917*. Leningrad, 1972.

Dikson, K. I., A. V. Mez'er, and D. P. Braginskii. *Bibliograficheskie ukazateli perevodnoi belletristiki*. With an introduction by J. S. G. Simmons. London, 1971.

Dmitriev, Iu. "Smelo, tovarishchi, v nogu!" *Znanie—sila*, no. 4 (1961): 16–18.

Dobrovol'skii, L. M. *Zapreshchennaia kniga v Rossii: Arkhivno-bibliograficheskie razyskaniia*. Moscow, 1962.

"Doklad po delu o voznikshikh v Peterburge v 1894 i 1895 godakh prestupnykh kruzhkakh lits, imenuiushchikh sebia 'Sotsial-demokratami.'" In *Sbornik materialov i statei*, by RSFSR, Tsentral'noe arkhivnoe upravlenie, 1: 93–178. Moscow, 1921.

Drei, M. I. "Zametki o rabochem dvizhenii v Odesse v 1880–1881 gg." *Katorga i ssylka*, no. 5 (12) (1924): 73–77.

Dreiden, Sim. *Muzyka—revoliutsiia*. 2nd ed. Moscow, 1970.

Drugovskaia, A. Iu. "Propaganda mestnymi organizatsiami RSDRP revoliutsionnoi pesni." *Voprosy istorii KPSS*, no. 8 (1988): 111–21.

Druskin, M. "Revoliutsionnaia pesnia narodovol'tsev." *Sovetskaia muzyka*, no. 3 (1934): 48–62.

———. "Revoliutsionnaia pesnia 1905 g." *Sovetskaia muzyka*, no. 12 (1935): 11–22.

———. *Russkaia revoliutsionnaia pesnia*. Moscow, 1954.

Dubenskaia, E. "Dmitrii Aleksandrovich Klements." *Katorga i ssylka*, 5 (66) (1930): 170–76.

Dunaway, David King, and Molly Beer. *Singing Out: An Oral History of America's Folk Revivals*. Oxford, 2010.

Dymshits, A. L., ed. *Revoliutsionnaia poeziia (1890–1917)*. 2nd ed. Leningrad, 1954.

Dzhabadari, I. S. "Protsess 50-ti (Vserossiiskaia Sotsial'no-Revoliutsionnaia Organizatsiia) 1874–77 gg." *Byloe*, no. 8 (20) (August 1907): 1–26; no. 10 (22) (October 1907): 168–97.

Edelman, Robert. "A Small Way of Saying 'No': Moscow Working Men, Spartak Soccer, and the Communist Party, 1900–1945." *American Historical Review* 107, 5 (December 2002): 1441–74.

——. *Spartak Moscow: A History of the People's Team in the Workers' State.* Ithaca, NY, 2009.

Eklof, Ben. *Russian Peasant Schools: Officialdom, Village Culture, and Popular Pedagogy, 1861–1914.* Berkeley, CA, 1986.

Eley, Geoff. *Forging Democracy: The History of the Left in Europe, 1850–2000.* Oxford, 2002.

Emel'ianov, N. P. *"Otechestvennye zapiski" N. A. Nekrasova (1868–1877).* Leningrad, 1977.

Engelstein, Laura. *Moscow, 1905: Working-Class Organization and Political Conflict.* Stanford, CA, 1982.

Essen, M. "Pesni revoliutsionnogo podpol'ia." *Sovetskaia muzyka*, no. 12 (1955): 7–10.

Eventov, I. S., ed. *Poeziia v bol'shevistskikh izdaniiakh 1901–1917.* Leningrad, 1967.

Evtukhov, Catherine et al. *A History of Russia: Peoples, Legends, Events, Forces.* Boston, 2004.

Ferguson, Priscilla Parkhurst. *"Quatrevingt-treize*: Turning the Terror to Account." In *Unfinished Revolutions: Legaacies of Upheaval in Modern French Culture,* edited by Robert T. Denommé and Roland H. Simon, 65–80. University Park, PA, 1998.

Field, Daniel. *Rebels in the Name of the Tsar.* Boston, 1976.

Figes, Orlando, and Boris Kolonitskii. *Interpreting the Russian Revolution: The Language and Symbols of 1917.* New Haven, 1999.

Figner, V. N. *Zapechatlennyi trud.* 2 vols. Moscow, 1964.

Fisher, A. *V Rossii i v Anglii: Nabliudeniia i vospominaniia peterburgskogo rabochego (1890–1921 gg.).* Moscow, 1922.

Footman, David. *Ferdinand Lassalle: Romantic Revolutionary.* New Haven, 1947.

Forgacs, David, ed. *The Antonio Gramsci Reader: Selected Writings 1916–1935.* New York, 2000.

Frank, Stephen P., and Mark D. Steinberg, eds. *Culture in Flux: Lower-Class Values, Practices, and Resistance in Late Imperial Russia.* Princeton, NJ, 1994.

Frankel, J. "Roots of 'Jewish Socialism' (1881–1892): From 'Populism' to 'Cosmopolitanism'?" In *Imperial Russia, 1700–1917: State, Society, Opposition. Essays in Honor of Marc Raeff,* edited by Ezra Mendelsohn and Marshall S. Shatz, 241–69. DeKalb, IL, 1988.

Freeze, Gregory, ed. *Russia: A History.* 2nd ed. Oxford, 2002.

Freifel'd, L. V. "Iz zhizni narodovol'cheskikh organizatsii kontsa 80-kh godov." In Iakimova-Dikovskaia et al., *Narodovol'tsy 80-kh i 90-kh godov,* 143–56.

———. "Zapozdalaia popravka." *Katorga i ssylka,* no. 4 (113) (1934): 122–28.

Freire, Paulo. *Pedagogy of the Oppressed.* New York, 2000.

Friedgut, Theodore H. *Iuzovka and Revolution, 2: Politics and Revolution in Russia's Donbass, 1869–1924.* Princeton, NJ, 1994.

Garkavi, A. M. *N. A. Nekrasov i revoliutsionnoe narodnichestvo.* Moscow, 1962.

Geifman, Anna. *Thou Shalt Kill: Revolutionary Terrorism in Russia, 1894–1917.* Princeton, NJ, 1993.

Ginev, V. N., and S. S. Volk, eds. *Revoliutsionery 1870-kh godov: Vospominaniia uchastnikov narodnicheskogo dvizheniia v Peterburge.* Leningrad, 1986.

Gippius, E., and P. Shiriaeva. *"Krasnoe Znamia": Iz istorii pesni trekh russkikh revoliutsii.* Moscow, 1969.

———. "Rabochaia Marsel'eza." In Shapovalova, *Biografii pesen,* 53–73.

———. "Smelo, tovarishchi, v nogu." In Shapovalova, *Biografii pesen,* 74–89.

Glickman, Rose. *Russian Factory Women: Workplace and Society, 1880–1914.* Berkeley, CA, 1984.

Golubev, Vas. "Stranichka iz istorii rabochego dvizheniia: Pamiati N. V. Shelgunova." *Byloe,* no. 12 (December 1906): 105–26.

Gots, M. R. "Moskovskaia tsentral'naia gruppa partii 'Narodnaia Volia,' 1883–1885 gg.: Otryvok iz neizdannoi avtobiografii." In Iakimova-Dikovskaia et al., *Narodovol'tsy posle 1-go marta 1881 goda,* 96–108.

Gramsci, Antonio. *Selections from the Prison Notebooks.* Edited by Quenton Hoare and Geoffrey Nowell Smith. New York, 1971.

Gusev, K. V. *Rytsari terrora.* Moscow, 1992.

Habermas, Jurgen. *The Structural Transformation of the Public Sphere: An Inquiry into a Category of Bourgeois Society.* Translated by Thomas Burger with the assistance of Frederick Lawrence. Cambridge, MA, 1989.

Haimson, Leopold H. *The Russian Marxists and the Origins of Bolshevism.* Cambridge, MA, 1955.

Haney, Jack V. *An Introduction to the Russian Folktale.* Armonk, NY, 1999.

Hardy, Deborah. *Land and Freedom: The Origins of Russian Terrorism, 1876–1879.* Westport, CT, 1987.

Hebdige, Dick. *Subculture: The Meaning of Style.* London, 1986.

Hemenway, Elizabeth Jones. "Mother Russia and the Crisis of the Russian National Family: The Puzzle of Gender in Revolutionary Russia." *Nationalities Papers* 25, 1 (1997): 103–21.

———. "Nicholas in Hell: Rewriting the Tsarist Narrative in the Revolutionary *Skazki* of 1917." *Russian Review* 60 (April 2001): 185–204.

Herrlinger, Page. *Working Souls: Russian Orthodoxy and Factory Labor in St. Petersburg, 1881–1914.* Bloomington, IN, 2007.

Hill, Melvyn A. "The Fictions of Mankind and the Stories of Men." In *Hannah Arendt: The Recovery of the Public World,* edited by Hill, 275–300. New York, 1979.

Hobsbawm, Eric. *Workers: Worlds of Labor.* New York, 1984.

Iakimova, A. "'Bol'shoi protsess,' ili 'protsess 193-kh': O revoliutsionnoi propagande v imperii (1877 18/X–1878 23/I)." *Katorga i ssylka,* no. 8 (37) (1927): 7–31.

———. *See also* Iakimova-Dikovskaia, A. V.

Iakimova-Dikovskaia, A. V. et al., eds. *Narodovol'tsy: Sbornik III, sostavlen uchastnikami narodovol'cheskogo dvizheniia.* Moscow, 1931.

———. *Narodovol'tsy posle 1-go marta 1881 goda.* Moscow, 1928

———. *Narodovol'tsy 80-kh i 90-kh godov: Sbornik statei i materialov, sostavlennyi uchastnikami narodovol'cheskogo dvizheniia.* Moscow, 1929.

Iakovenko, E. I. *Petr Abramovich Tellalov.* Moscow, 1930.

Iakovlev, V. Ia., ed. *Literatura sotsial'no-revoliutsionnoi partii "Narodnoi Voli."* 1905. Reprint, Leipzig, 1977.

Iakushin, N. "Byl li P. V. Zasodimskii avtorom peredelki romana Erkmana-Shatriana 'Istoriia krest'ianina'?" *Russkaia literatura,* no. 1 (1965): 191–93.

Iakutskaia tragediia 22 marta (3 aprelia) 1889 goda – Sbornik vospominanii i materialov. Edited by M. A. Braginskii and K. M. Tereshkovich. Moscow, 1925.

Iazhborovskaia, I. S., and N. I. Bukharin. *U istokov pol'skogo sotsialisticheskogo dvizheniia.* Moscow, 1976.

Itenberg, B. S. *Dvizhenie revoliutsionnogo narodnichestva: Narodnicheskie kruzhki i "khozhdenie v narod" v 70-kh godakh XIX v.* Moscow, 1965.

Itenberg, B. S. *Iuzhno-rossiiskii soiuz rabochikh: Vozniknovenie i deiatel'nost'.* Moscow, 1974.

———. *P. L. Lavarov v russkom revoliutsionnom dvizhenii.* Moscow, 1988.

———. "Revoliutsionnye narodniki i voprosy religii: Iz istorii 'khozhdenie v narod.'" *Voprosy istorii religii i ateizma: Sbornik statei,* no. 11 (1963): 293–305.

———. *Rossiia i Velikaia frantsuzskaia revoliutsiia.* Moscow, 1988.

Itenberg, B. S. et al., eds. *Svodnyi katalog russkoi nelegal'noi i zapreshchennoi pechati XIX veka: Knigi i periodicheskie izdaniia.* 2nd ed. Moscow, 1981–82.

Ivanov, L. M., ed. *Istoriia rabochego klassa Rossii 1861–1900 gg.* Moscow, 1972.

———. *Rossiiskii proletariat: Oblik, bor'ba, gegemoniia.* Moscow, 1970.

Ivanov, N. A. et al., eds. *Morozovskaia stachka 1885 g. i rabochie tsentral'nogo promyshlennogo raiona Rossii v kontse XIX–nachale XX v.: Tezisy vystuplenii uchastnikov XV zonal'noi mezhvuzovskoi nauchnoi konferentsii, posviashchennoi 100-letiiu Morozovskoi stachki.* Moscow, 1984.

Ivanov, Sergei. "Iz vospominanii o 1881 gode." *Byloe,* no. 4 (1906): 222–36.

Izd. Soiuza russkikh sotsial-demokratov, *Iz rabochego dvizheniia v Odesse i Nikolaeve.* Geneva, July 1900.

Iz-za reshetki: Sbornik stikhotvorenii russkikh zakliuchennykh po politicheskim prichinam v period 1873–1877 gg., osuzhdennykh i ozhidaiushchikh "suda." Geneva, 1877. Reprinted in *Vol'naia russkaia poeziia vtoroi poloviny XIX veka,* edited by S. A. Reiser and A. A. Shilov, 338–48. Leningrad, 1959.

Kallash, V., ed. *Protsess 50-ti.* Moscow, 1906.

———. *Protsess 193-kh.* Moscow, 1906.

Kann-Novikova, E. *Vy zhertvoiu pali v bor'be rokovoi: Rasskazy o pesniakh.* Moscow, 1968.

Karelina, V. M. "Leonid Borisovich—propagandist i organizator rabochikh kruzhkov." In *Leonid Borisovich Krasin ("Nikitich"): Gody pod'polia. Sbornik vospominanii, statei i dokumentov,* edited by M. N. Liadov and S. M. Pozner, 86–92. Moscow–Leningrad, 1928.

———. "Na zare rabochego dvizheniia v S.-Peterburge." *Krasnaia letopis',* no. 4 (1922): 12–20.

Katalog sistematicheskogo chteniia [Odessa catalog]. 2nd ed. Odessa, 1883.

Katrenko, A. N. *V bor'be za probuzhdenie narodnoi revoliutsii: Iz istorii revoliutsionno-demokraticheskogo dvizheniia na Ukraine v 80-kh–nachale 90-kh godov XIX v.* Kiev, 1988.

Kazakevich, R. A. *Sotsial-demokraticheskie organizatsii Peterburga kontsa 80-kh– nachala 90-kh godov: Kruzhki P. V. Tochisskogo i M. L. Brusneva.* Leningrad, 1960.

Kelly, Aileen. *Mikhail Bakunin: A Study in the Psychology and Politics of Utopianism.* New Haven, 1987.

Kelly, Catriona, and David Shepherd, eds. *Constructing Russian Culture in the Age of Revolution: 1881–1940.* Oxford, 1998.

Kharitonov, V. "Iz vospominanii uchastnika gruppy Blagoeva." *Proletarskaia revoliutsiia,* no. 8 (79) (1928): 152–66.

Kir'ianov, Iu. I. *Perekhod k massovoi politicheskoi bor'be: Rabochii klass nakanune pervoi rossiiskoi revoliutsii.* Moscow, 1987.

Kiselev, M. *Iz revoliutsionnogo proshlogo: Zapiski starogo bol'shevika.* Moscow, 1934.

Kizenko, Nadieszda. *A Prodigal Saint: Father John of Kronstadt and the Russian People.* University Park, PA, 2000.

Klevenskii, M. M. "Khudozhestvennaia literatura 70-kh godov na sluzhbe revoliutsii ('Skazka Kota-Murlyki')." *Literatura i marksizm,* no. 4 (1931): 117–25.

Klibanov, A. I. *History of Religious Sectarianism in Russia (1860s–1917).* Translated by Ethel Dunn. Edited by Stephen Dunn. Oxford, 1982.

Kline, George L. *Religious and Anti-Religious Thought in Russia.* Chicago, 1968.

Koenker, Diane. *Moscow Workers and the 1917 Revolution.* Princeton, NJ, 1981.

———. *Republic of Labor: Russian Printers and Soviet Socialism, 1918–1930.* Ithaca, NY, 2005.

Kornilova-Moroz, A. *Perovskaia i kruzhok chaikovtsev.* Moscow, 1929.

———. *Sof'ia L'vovna Perovskaia: Chlen ispolnitel'nogo komiteta partii "Narodnaia volia."* Moscow, 1930.

Korol'chuk, E. A. *Severnyi Soiuz Russkikh Rabochikh.* Leningrad, 1946.

———. *"Severnyi soiuz russkikh rabochikh" i revoliutsionnoe rabochee dvizhenie 70-kh godov XIX v. v Peterburge.* Edited by K. G. Sharikov. Leningrad, 1971.

———, ed. *V nachale puti: Vospominaniia peterburgskikh rabochikh 1872–1897 gg.* Leningrad, 1975.

Kotkin, Stephen. "1991 and the Russian Revolution: Sources, Conceptual Categories, Analytical Frameworks." *Journal of Modern History* 70, 2 (June 1998): 384–425.

Kotov, G. N. *V bor′be za revoliutsii: Vospominaniia rabochego-bol′shevika*. Moscow–Leningrad, 1930.

Koval′skaia, Ekaterina. *Iuzhno-russkii rabochii soiuz, 1880–1881*. Moscow, 1926.

Koz′min, B. "K istorii 'Molodoi Rossii': Zapiska A. N. Bakha 1886 g." *Katorga i ssylka*, no. 6 (67) (1930): 51–60.

Krol′, M. A. *Stranitsy moei zhizni*. New York, 1944.

Kropotkin, Petr Alekseevich. *Memoirs of a Revolutionist*. 1899; repr., New York, 1968.

———. *Russian Literature: Ideals and Realities*. 1905; repr., Montreal, 1991.

———. *Zapiski revoliutsionera*. Moscow, 1966.

Krzhizhanovskii, G. "Pesni bor′by." *Sovetskaia muzyka*, no. 12 (1955): 3–4.

Kudelli, P. *Narodovol′tsy na pereput′i: Delo lakhtinskoi tipografii*. Leningrad, 1926.

Kuliabko-Koretskii, I. G. *Iz davnikh let: Vospominaniia lavrista*. Moscow, 1931.

Kurbatova, I. N. *Nachalo rasprostraneniia marksizma v Rossii: Literaturno-izdatel′skaia deiatel′nost′ gruppy "Osvobozhdenie truda."* Moscow, 1983.

Kuzmin, D. *Narodovol′cheskaia zhurnalistika*. Moscow, 1930.

Lalaiants, I. *U istokov bol′shevizma: Zarozhdenie RSDRP*. Moscow, 1934.

Larin, A. E. "Pamflet V. Libknekhta 'Pauki i mukhi' v Rossii nakanune i v gody pervoi russkoi revoliutsii." *Voprosy istochnikovedeniia i istoriografii* (Vladivostok) 4 (1975): 21–34.

Laverychev, V. Ia., and A. M. Solov′eva. *Boevoi pochin rossiiskogo proletariata: K 100-letiiu Morozovskoi stachki 1885 g.* Moscow, 1985.

Laverychev, V. Ia. et al., eds. *Gruppa "Osvobozhdenie truda" i obshchestvenno-politicheskaia bor′ba v Rossii*. Moscow, 1984.

Lavrov, P. L. *Narodniki-propagandisty 1873–78 godov*. St. Petersburg, 1907.

Lepeshinskii, P. N. *Na povorote*. Moscow, 1955.

———. "Starye pesni revoliutsii." *Ogonek*, 7 August 1927 [pages unnumbered].

Levitin, Daniel J. *The World in Six Songs: How the Musical Brain Created Human Nature*. New York, 2008.

———. *This Is Your Brain on Music: The Science of a Human Obsession*. New York, 2006.

Liadov, M. "Kak zarodilas′ Moskovskaia rabochaia organizatsiia." In *Na zare rabochego dvizheniia v Moskve: Vospominaniia uchastnikov moskovskogo rabochego soiuza 1893–95 gg. i dokumenty,* edited by S. I. Mitskevich, 42–96. Moscow, 1932.

Liadov, M. L., and S. M. Pozner, eds. *Leonid Borisovich Krasin ("Nikitich"): Gody podpol'ia. Sbornik vospominanii, statei i dokumentov.* Moscow–Leningrad, 1928.

Lichtheim, George. *Marxism: An Historical and Critical Study.* 2nd ed. New York, 1963.

———. *The Origins of Socialism.* New York, 1969.

Lidtke, Vernon L. *The Alternative Culture: Socialist Labor in Imperial Germany.* New York, 1985.

———. *The Outlawed Party: Social Democracy in Germany (1878–1890).* Princeton, NJ, 1966.

Lindemann, Albert S. *A History of European Socialism.* New Haven, 1983.

Lion, S. E. "Ot propagandy k terroru." *Katorga i ssylka,* no. 5 (12) (1924): 9–24.

Liubatovich, O. *Dalekoe i nedavnee.* Edited by V. Nevskii and P. Anatol'ev. Moscow, 1930.

Livshits, S. "Ocherki istorii Kazanskoi sotsial-demokratii (1888–1916 gg.)." *Puti revoliutsii,* no. 1 (March 1922): 85–142.

———. "Podpol'nye tipografii 60-kh, 70-kh i 80-kh godov." *Katorga i ssylka,* no. 41 (1928): 23–33; no. 43 (1928): 60–78; no. 50 (1929): 64–80; no. 51 (1929): 57–74; no. 55 (1929): 44–59.

Loiko, Lidiia. *Ot "Zemli i Voli" k VKP(b): 1877–1928. Vospominaniia.* Moscow–Leningrad, 1929.

Lowenthal, David. *The Past Is a Foreign Country.* Cambridge, 1985.

Lukács, Georg. *The Historical Novel.* Introduction by Fredric Jameson. Lincoln, NE, 1983.

Makarevskii, A. N. "Rabochii-narodovolets P. L. Antonov: Vospominaniia." *Katorga i ssylka,* no. 5 (12) (1924): 272–81.

Mannheim, Karl. *Ideology and Utopia: An Introduction to the Sociology of Knowledge.* New York, 1936.

Martynov, A. F. "Obshchestvennaia deiatel'nost' Marko Vovchok." *Voprosy literatury,* no. 6 (1962): 184–86.

Martynov-Piker. "Vospominaniia revoliutsionera." *Proletarskaia revoliutsiia,* no. 11 (46) (1925): 262-83.

Mashkova, M. V. *A. V. Mez'er (1869–1935): Ocherk zhizni i deiatel'nosti*. Moscow, 1962.

———. "Aleksandr Vasil'evich Panov: Iz istorii russkoi rekomendatel'noi bibliografii nachala XX veka." *Trudy gosudarstvennoi Publichnoi biblioteki im. M. E. Saltykova-Shchedrina* 10 (13) (1962): 141–52.

———. "Nikolai Vasil'evich Zdobnov: K 90-letiiu so dnia rozhdeniia." *Sovetskaia bibliografiia*, no. 2 (1978): 64–72.

Mason, Laura. *Singing the French Revolution: Popular Culture and Politics, 1787–1799*. Ithaca, NY, 1996.

Matt, Susan J., and Peter N. Stearns, eds. *Doing Emotions History*. Urbana, IL, 2014.

Maurer, Warren R. *Gerhart Hauptmann*. Boston, 1982.

———. *Understanding Gerhart Hauptmann*. Columbia, SC, 1992.

Maza, Sarah. *The Myth of the French Bourgeoisie: An Essay on the Social Imaginary, 1750–1850*. Cambridge, MA, 2003.

McReynolds, Louise. *The News Under Russia's Old Regime: The Development of a Mass-Circulation Press*. Princeton, NJ, 1991.

Mehring, Fritz. *Karl Marx: The Story of His Life*. Ann Arbor, MI, 1962.

Mekhontsev, N. I., comp. *Probuzhdenie: K 100 letiiu Morozovskoi stachki*. Moscow, 1984.

Melancon, Michael. "Athens or Babylon? The Birth of the Socialist Revolutionary and Social Democratic Parties in Saratov, 1890–1905." In *Politics and Society in Provincial Russia: Saratov, 1590–1917*, edited by Rex A. Wade and Scott J. Seregny, 73–112. Columbus, OH, 1989.

———. *The Lena Goldfields Massacre and the Crisis of the Late Tsarist State*. College Station, TX, 2006.

———. "The Socialist Revolutionaries from 1902 to 1907: Peasant and Workers' Party." *Russian History* 12, 1 (Spring 1985): 2–47.

———. *"Stormy Petrels": The Socialist Revolutionaries in Russia's Labor Organizations 1905–1914*. The Carl Beck Papers in Russian and East European Studies, no. 703. Pittsburgh, 1988.

Melancon, Michael, and Alice K. Pate. "Bakhtin contra Marx and Lenin: A Polyphonic Approach to Russia's Labor and Revolutionary Movements." *Russian History* 31, 4 (Winter 2004): 387–417.

Melancon, Michael, and Alice K. Pate, eds., *New Labor History: Worker Identity and Experience in Russia, 1840–1918*. Bloomington, IN, 2002.

Mikhailov, I. K. *Chetvert´ veka podpol´shchika.* Moscow, 1957.

Mindlina, I. I. "Deiatel´nost´ revoliutsionnykh narodnikov sredi rabochikh Peterburga i Moskvy (1879–1882 gg.)." *Uchenye zapiski 1-go Moskovskogo pedagogicheskogo instituta innostrannykh iazykov* 34 (1965): 103–208.

Mironov, K. *Iz vospominanii rabochego.* Moscow, 1906.

Mitskevich, S. I. "Moskovskie revoliutsionnye kruzhki vtoroi poloviny 1870-kh godov." *Katorga i ssylka,* no. 4 (11) (1924): 57–78.

———. *Na grani dvukh epokh: Ot narodnichestva k marksizmu.* Moscow, 1937.

———. *Revoliutsionnaia Moskva, 1888–1905.* Moscow, 1940.

Mitskevich, S. I., ed. *Na zare rabochego dvizheniia v Moskve: Vospominaniia uchastnikov moskovskogo rabochego soiuza (1893–95 gg.). Dokumenty.* Moscow, 1922.

Moiseenko, P. A. "Iz vospominanii P. A. Moiseenko." In *Rabochee dvizhenie v Rossii v opisanii samykh rabochikh: Ot 70-kh do 90-kh godov,* by P. A. Alekseev et al., 131–73. Moscow, 1933.

———. *Vospominaniia starogo revoliutsionera.* Moscow, 1966.

Mommsen, Hans. "Lassalle, Ferdinand." In *Marxism, Communism, and Western Society: A Comparative Encyclopedia,* edited by C. D. Kernig, 5: 107–27. New York, 1972–73.

Moon, David. *The Russian Peasantry, 1600–1930: The World the Peasants Made.* London, 1999.

———. *Russian Peasants and Tsarist Legislation on the Eve of Reform: Interaction between Peasants and Officialdom, 1825–1855.* London, 1992.

Morozov, N. A. *Povesti moei zhizni: Memuary.* 2 vols. Moscow, 1961.

Naimark, Norman M. *The History of the "Proletariat": The Emergence of Marxism in the Kingdom of Poland, 1870–1887.* Boulder, CO, 1979.

———. *Terrorists and Social Democrats: The Russian Revolutionary Movement under Alexander III.* Cambridge, MA, 1983.

Nekrasov, N. A. *Stikhotvorenie. Komu na Rusi zhit´ khorosho.* Moscow, 1969.

Nevskii, V. I. "K istorii 'Partii russkikh sotsial-demokratov' (Blagoevskaia gruppa)." *Proletarskaia revoliutsiia,* no. 5 (1922): 297–302.

———. *Ot "Zemli i Voli" k gruppe "Osvobozhdenie Truda."* Moscow, 1930.

———, ed. "Rabochii Sbornik." *Krasnaia letopis´* 4 (1922): 339–70.

Nikolaevskii, B., ed. "Programma pervogo v Rossii s.-d. kruzhka." *Byloe,* no. 13 (July 1918): 38–52.

N___skii, B. [B. Nikolaevskii]. "K istorii 'Partii russkikh sotsial-demokratov' v 1884–86 g." *Katorga i ssylka*, no. 5 (54) (1929): 44–67.

Norinskii, K. M. *Pod nadzorom politsii: Vospominaniia.* Moscow, 1974.

K. M. Norinskii et al. *Ot gruppy Blagoeva k "Soiuzu Bor'by" (1886–1894 gg.): Stat'i i vospominaniia K. M. Norinskogo, V. A. Shelgunova, V. Nevskogo, M. Ol'minskogo. Materialy po delu M. I. Brusneva i Iu. V. Mel'nikova. Rechi rabochikh 1 maia 1891 goda.* Rostov-na-Donu, 1921.

Norton, Barbara T. "The Making of a Female Marxist: D. D. Kuskova's Conversion to Russian Social Democracy." *International Review of Social History* 34, 2 (1989): 227–47.

Novikova, A. M. "Revoliutsionnye pesni XIX veka v epokhu massovogo rabochego dvizheniia." *Uchenye Zapiski moskovskogo oblastnogo pedagogicheskogo instituta* 40, 2 (1956): 153–97.

———. "Rol' i znachenie revoliutsionnoi literaturnoi pesni v rabochem fol'klore." In *Ustnaia poeziia rabochikh Rossii*, edited by V. G. Bazanov, 69–80. Moscow-Leningrad, 1965.

[Novopolin, G.]. "Poslednie usiliia: Iz revoliutsionnogo proshlogo Ekaterinoslavshchiny." *Puti revoliutsii*, no. 2–3 (5–6) (1926): 44–61.

N___in, G. [G. Novopolin]. "Iz zhizni rabochikh narodovol'cheskikh kruzhkov: Pamiati Andreia Karpenko. *Katorga i ssylka*, no. 8–9 (1929): 203–13.

Nutrikhin, A. I. "Gimny proletarskoi revoliutsii." *Vestnik Leningradskogo universiteta* 2, 8 (1958): 112–18.

Ocherki po istorii sotsialisticheskogo dvizheniia v russkoi Pol'she. [Lwów], 1904.

Odinets, D. M. "V kruzhke 'chaikovtsev.'" In *Nikolai Vasil'evich Chaikovskii: Religioznye i obshchestvennye iskaniia*, edited by A. A. Titov, 39–96. Paris, 1929.

Offord, Derek. *The Russian Revolutionary Movement in the 1880s.* Cambridge, 1986.

Ol'khovskii, E. R. "K istorii 'Chernogo Peredela.' (1879–1881 gg.)." In *Obshchestvennoe dvizhenie v poreformennoi Rossii.* Moscow, 1965.

———, comp. *Proletarskii prolog: Vospominaniia uchastnikov revoliutsionnogo dvizheniia v Peterburge v 1893–1904 godakh.* Edited by L. M. Spirin. Leningrad, 1983.

Ol'khovskii, E. R., ed. *Avangard: Vospominaniia i dokumenty piterskikh rabochikh 1890-kh godov.* Leningrad, 1990.

Ol'minskii, M. "Iz vospominanii revoliutsionera." *Rabochii mir*, no. 4–5 (1919): 12–13.

Onufriev, E. P. *Za nevskoi zastavoi: Vospominaniia starogo bol'shevika.* Moscow, 1968.

Orekhov, A. M. *Pervye marksisty v Rossii: Peterburgskii "rabochii soiuz" 1887–1893 gg.* Moscow, 1979.

———. *Sotsial-demokraticheskoe dvizhenie v Rossii i pol'skie revoliutsionery.* Moscow, 1973.

———. *Stanovlenie pol'skogo sotsialisticheskogo dvizheniia: Struktura, programmnye kontseptsii, deiateli (1874–1893).* Moscow, 1979.

Orzhikh, Boris. "V riadakh 'Narodnoi voli.'" In Iakimova-Dikovskaia et al., *Narodovol'tsy,* 75–182.

Os'makov, N. V. *Poeziia revoliutsionnogo narodnichestva.* Moscow, 1961.

Ovsiannikova, S. A. *Gruppa Blagoeva: Iz istorii rasprostraneniia marksizma v Rossii.* Moscow, 1959.

"Pamiati Grinevitskogo." *Byloe* (Rostov-na-Donu), vyp. 1 (1906): 6–13.

Pankratov, V. S. "Iz deiatel'nosti sredi rabochikh v 1880–1884 gg." *Byloe*, no. 3 (1906): 236–57.

———. *Vospominaniia: Kak prikhodilos' rabotat' sredi rabochikh v 1880–1884 gg.* Moscow, 1923.

———. *Zhizn' v Shlissel'burgskoi kreposti 1884–1898.* 1902; Petrograd, 1922.

Pankratova, A. M., and L. M. Ivanov, eds. *Rabochee dvizhenie v Rossii v XIX veke: Sbornik dokumentov i materialov.* 4 vols. Moscow–Leningrad, 1950–63.

Partiia Sotsialistov-Revoliutsionerov. *Demonstranty pered sudom: Delo o saratovskoi demonstratsii s prilozheniem izvlechenii iz obvinititel'nykh aktov o nizhegorodskoi i sormovskoi demonstratsiiakh.* 1902.

Pate, Alice K. "Workers and *Obshchestvennost'*: St. Petersburg, 1906–1914." *Revolutionary Russia* 15, 2 (2002): 53–71.

Pearl, Deborah L. "Educating Workers for Revolution: Populist Propaganda in St. Petersburg, 1879–1882." *Russian History* 15, 2–4 (1988): 255–84. Reprinted in *Articles on Russian and Soviet History 1500–1991*, ed. Alexander Dallin, 3: *Imperial Russian History II 1861–1917*, ed. Gary M. Hamburg, 181–200. New York, 1991.

Pearl, Deborah L. "From Worker to Revolutionary: The Making of Worker *Narodovol'tsy.*" *Russian History* 23, no. 1–4 (1996): 11–26.

Pearl, Deborah L. "Marxism's Russian Centennial: Soviet Scholars and the Emancipation of Labor Group." *The Russian Review* 49, 2 (April 1990): 189–98.

———. "Narodnaia Volia and the Worker." In *Workers and Intelligentsia in Late Imperial Russia: Realities, Representations, Reflections,* edited by Reginald E. Zelnik, 55–75. Berkeley, CA, 1999.

———. "Political Economy for Workers: A. N. Bakh's *Tsar-Golod.*" *Slavic Review* 50, 4 (Winter 1991): 768–78.

———. "Revolutionaries and Workers: A Study of Revolutionary Propaganda among Russian Workers, 1880–1892." Ph.D. diss., University of California, Berkeley, 1984.

———. *Tales of Revolution: Workers and Propaganda* Skazki *in the Late Nineteenth Century.* The Carl Beck Papers in Russian and East European Studies, no. 1303. Pittsburgh, 1998.

———. "Tsar and Religion in Russian Revolutionary Propaganda." *Russian History,* 20, 1–4 (1993): 81–107.

Perrie, Maureen. *The Agrarian Policy of the Russian Socialist-Revolutionary Party from Its Origins through the Revolution of 1905–1907.* Cambridge, 1976.

———. "Folklore as Evidence of Peasant *Mentalité*: Social Attitudes and Values in Russian Popular Culture." *Russian Review* 48, 2 (April 1989): 119–43.

———. "Popular Monarchism: The Myth of the Ruler from Ivan the Terrible to Stalin." In *Reinterpreting Russia,* edited by Geoffrey Hosking and Robert Service, 156–69. London, 1999.

Perrot, Michelle. *Workers on Strike: France, 1871–1890.* Translated by Chris Turner. New Haven, 1987.

Pervoe maia v tsarskoi Rossii 1890–1916 gg.: Sbornik dokumentov. Moscow, 1939.

Peshekerov, P. "Propaganda narodovol'tsev sredi rabochikh v Rostove-na-Donu v 1882–84 gg." In Iakimova-Dikovskaia et al., *Narodovol'tsy posle 1 marta 1881 g.,* 116–28.

———. "Rabochii narodovolets G. G. Rudometov." *Katorga i ssylka,* no. 11 (60) (1929): 164–71.

Petrogradskoe biuro komissii po istorii Oktiabr'skoi revoliutsii i Rossiiskoi Kommunisticheskoi Partii. *Chernyi Peredel: Organ sotsialistov-federalistov, 1880–1881 g.* Moscow–Petrograd, 1923.

Petrone, Karen. *Life Has Become More Joyous, Comrades: Celebrations in the Time of Stalin.* Bloomington, IN, 2000.

Petrov, A. K. *Rabochii bol'shevik v podpol'e.* Moscow, 1969.

Pipes, Richard. *The Degaev Affair: Terror and Treason in Tsarist Russia.* New Haven, 2003.

———. *Social Democracy and the St. Petersburg Labor Movement: 1880–1897.* Cambridge, MA, 1963.

Pirumova, N. M. *Bakunin.* Moscow, 1970.

Pisarev, D. I. "Frantsuzskii krest'ianin v 1789 godu. (*Histoire d'un paysan 1789, par Erckmann-Chatrian*)." Reprinted in D. I. Pisarev, *Polnoe sobranie sochinenii v shesti tomakh,* 6: 519–48. St. Petersburg, 1894.

Plamper, Ian [Jan Plamper], Shamma Shakhadat [Schamma Schahadat], and Mark Eli [Marc Elie], eds. *Rossiiskaia imperiia chuvstv: Podkhody k kul'turnoi istorii emotsii.* Moscow, 2010.

Plekhanov, G. V. *Russkii rabochii v revoliutsionnom dvizhenii: Po lichnym vospominaniiam.* Leningrad, 1940.

"Pokazaniia pervo-martovtsev." *Byloe,* no. 4–5 (1918): 230–304.

Polevoi, Iu. Z. *Stepan Khalturin: K 100-letiiu "Severnogo soiuza russkikh rabochikh."* Moscow, 1979.

———. *Zarozhdenie marksizma v Rossii, 1883–1894 gg.* Moscow, 1959.

Polianskaia, L. I. "Arkhivnyi fond glavnogo upravleniia po delam pechati." *Literaturnoe nasledstvo,* no. 22–24 (1935): 603–34.

Polianskaia, T. G. "K istorii izvestnoi revoliutsionnoi pesni: K 100-letiiu pesni 'Zamuchen tiazheloi nevolei.'" *Sovetskoe zdravookhranenie,* no. 6 (1976): 69–71.

Pomper, Philip. *Lenin's Brother: The Origins of the Russian Revolution.* New York, 2010.

———. *Peter Lavrov and the Russian Revolutionary Movement.* Chicago, 1972.

———. *The Russian Revolutionary Intelligentsia.* New York, 1970.

Popov, I. I. "Fedor Vasil'evich Olesinov." *Katorga i ssylka,* no. 5–6 (114–15) (1934): 227–30.

———. *Minuvshee i perezhitoe: Vospominaniia za 50 let. 1: Detstvo i gody bor'by.* 2nd ed. Leningrad, 1924.

———. "Revoliutsionnye organizatsii v Peterburge v 1882–1885 gg." In Iakimova-Dikovskaia et al., *Narodovol'tsy posle 1-go marta 1881 goda,* 49–80.

Popov, I. I. "Venedikt Arsen'evich Bodaev." *Katorga i ssylka,* no. 9 (106) (1933): 145–49.

Popov, M. R. "Iz moego proshlogo." *Minuvshie gody*, no. 2 (February 1908): 170–204.

Potapova, Z. M. *Russko-ital´ianskie literaturnye sviazi: Vtoraia polovina XIX veka.* Moscow, 1973.

Rabinowitch, Alexander. *The Bolsheviks in Power: The First Year of Soviet Rule in Petrograd.* Bloomington, IN, 2007.

Rabochee dvizhenie v Khar´kove. Izd. Soiuza russkikh sotsial-demokratov. (Geneva, September 1900).

"'Rabochii'—rostovskii zhurnal 1883 goda." With foreword by V. Nevskii and afterword by S. N. Valk. *Literaturnoe nasledstvo*, no. 2 (1932): 75–100.

Raleigh, Donald. *Experiencing Russia's Civil War: Politics, Society, and Revolutionary Culture in Saratov, 1917–1922.* Princeton, NJ, 2002.

Rancière, Jacques. *Nights of Labor: The Workers' Dream in Nineteenth-Century France.* Translated by John Drury. Philadelphia, 1989.

———. *Staging the People: The Proletarian and His Double.* Translated by David Fernbach. London, 2011.

Read, Christopher. *From Tsar to Soviets: The Russian People and Their Revolution, 1917–21.* Oxford, 1996.

Reed, John. *Ten Days That Shook the World.* 1934; New York, 1967.

Reichman, Henry. *Railwaymen and Revolution: Russia, 1905.* Berkeley, CA, 1987.

Reiser, S. A. "Podpol´naia rekomendatel´naia bibliografiia 70–80-kh godov XIX veka." *Sovetskaia bibliografiia*, no. 1 (59) (1960): 54–69.

Reiser, S. A., and Iu. A. Andreev, eds. *Vol´naia russkaia poeziia XVIII–XIX vekov.* 2 vols. Leningrad, 1988.

Reiser, S. A., and A. A. Shilov, eds. *Vol´naia russkaia poeziia vtoroi poloviny XIX veka.* Leningrad, 1959.

Retish, Aaron B. *Russia's Peasants in Revolution and Civil War: Citizenship, Identity, and the Creation of the Soviet State, 1914–1922.* Cambridge, 2008.

Riall, Lucy. *Garibaldi: Invention of a Hero.* New Haven, 2007.

Riasanovsky, Nicholas V., and Mark D. Steinberg. *A History of Russia.* 8th ed. New York, 2011.

Rice, Christopher. *Russian Workers and the Socialist-Revolutionary Party through the Revolution of 1906–07.* New York, 1988.

Rioux, Jean-Pierre. *Erckmann et Chatrian ou le trait d'union.* Paris, 1989.

Rolf, Malte. *Soviet Mass Festivals, 1917–1991.* Pittsburgh, PA, 2013.

Rose, Jonathan. *The Intellectual Life of the British Working Classes*. New Haven, 2001.

Rosemont, Franklin. "Bellamy's Radicalism Reclaimed." In *Looking Backward 1988–1888: Essays on Edward Bellamy*, edited by Daphne Patai, 147–209. Amherst, MA, 1988.

Rossman, Jeffrey J. *Worker Resistance under Stalin: Class and Revolution on the Shop Floor*. Cambridge, MA, 2005.

Rozanov, I. N., comp. *Russkie pesni XIX veka*. Moscow, 1944.

Rozanov, M. *Obukhovtsy*. Leningrad, 1938.

Rubach, A. M., ed. "Ubiistvo gen. Strel´nikova i kazn´ Khalturina i Zhelvakova." *Letopis´ revoliutsii*, no. 2 (7) (1924): 185–91.

Rubach, M. A., ed. *Istoriia ekaterinoslavskoi sotsial-demokraticheskoi organizatsii 1889–1903: Vospominaniia, dokumenty, literaturnye i khudozhestvennye materialy*. Ekaterinoslav, 1923.

Sablinsky, Walter. *The Road to Bloody Sunday*. Princeton, NJ, 1976.

Sacks, Oliver. *Musicophilia: Tales of Music and the Brain*. 2nd ed. New York, 2008.

Saikin, O. A. "Iz istorii narodovol´cheskogo dvizheniia." *Sovetskie arkhivy*, no. 3 (1969): 63–66.

Salova, N. [Neonila Salova]. "Pamiati Kokovskogo." *Byloe*, no. 2 (Rostov-na-Donu, 1906): 78–92.

Samoilov, F. N. *Po sledam minuvshego*. 2nd ed. foreword by Em. Iaroslavskii. [n.p.], 1948.

Sapir, Boris, ed. *Lavrov—gody emigratsii: Arkhivnye materialy v dvukh tomakh*. Dordrecht, Netherlands, 1974.

———. *"Vpered!" 1873–1877: Materialy iz arkhiva Valeriana Nikolaevicha Smirnova*. 2 vols. Dordrecht, Netherlands, 1970.

Schleifman, Nurit. *Undercover Agents in the Russian Revolutionary Movement: The SR Party, 1902–14*. New York, 1988.

Schneiderman, Jeremiah. *Sergei Zubatov and Revolutionary Marxism: The Struggle for the Working Class in Tsarist Russia*. Ithaca, NY, 1976.

Sedov, M. G. *Geroicheskii period revoliutsionnogo narodnichestva: Iz istorii politicheskoi bor´by*. Moscow, 1966.

Sergeevich, V. *Zavod—kuznitsa revoliutsii: Rabochii o starom i novom zhit´e byt´e*. Moscow, 1929.

Sergievskii, N. L. "'Chernyi Peredel' i narodniki 80-kh godov." *Katorga i ssylka,* no. 1 (74) (1931): 7–58.

———. "Narodnichestvo 80-kh godov." In *Istoriko-revoliutsionnyi sbornik,* edited by V. I. Nevskii, 3: 148–84. Moscow-Leningrad, 1926.

———. *Partiia russkikh sotsial-demokratov: Gruppa Blagoeva.* Moscow–Leningrad, 1929.

———, ed. *Rabochii: Gazeta partii russkikh sotsial-demokratov (blagoevtsev) 1885 g.* Leningrad, 1928.

Service, Robert. "Russian Populism and Russian Marxism: Two Skeins Entangled." In *Russian Thought and Society 1800–1917: Essays in Honour of Eugene Lampert,* edited by Rogert Bartlett, 220–42. Keele, UK, 1984.

Shanin, Teodor. *The Roots of Otherness: Russia's Turn of Century,* 2: *Russia 1905– 07.* New Haven, 1986.

———, ed. *Peasants and Peasant Society.* 2nd ed. Oxford, 1987.

Shapovalov, A. S. *Po doroge k marksizmu: Vospominaniia rabochego revoliutsionera.* Moscow, 1922.

———. *V podpol'e: Na puti k marksizmu.* Moscow–Leningrad, 1927.

Shapovalova, A. T., ed. *Biografii pesen.* Moscow, 1965.

Shaw, Brent D., ed. *Spartacus and the Slave Wars: A Brief History with Documents.* Boston, 2001.

Shelgunov, V. "Rabochie na puti k marksizmu." *Staryi bol'shevik,* no. 2 (5) (1933): 98–103.

Shesternin, S. P. *Perezhitoe: Iz istorii rabochego i revoliutsionnogo dvizhenii 1880– 1900 gg.* Ivanovo, 1940.

Shiriaeva, P. G. "Revoliutsionnaia pesnia v rabochei pechati 1905–1907 godov." In *Revoliutsiia 1905 goda i russkaia literatura,* edited by V. A. Desnitskii and K. D. Muratova, 384–403. Moscow–Leningrad, 1950.

Shirokova, V. V. "Vozniknovenie narodovol'cheskoi organizatsii v Khar'kove." In *Iz istorii obshchestvennoi mysli i obshchestvennogo dvizheniia v Rossii,* edited by M. S. Persov. 64–95. Saratov, 1964.

Shishko, L. E. *Obshchestvennoe dvizhenie v shestidesiatykh i pervoi polovine semidesiatykh godov.* Moscow, 1920.

———. *Sergei Mikhailovich Kravchinskii i kruzhok chaikovtsev: Iz vospominanii i zametok starogo narodnika.* St. Petersburg, 1906.

Shotman, A. V. *Zapiski starogo bol'shevika.* Leningrad, 1963.

Shukman, Harold, ed. *The Blackwell Encyclopedia of the Russian Revolution.* Oxford, 1988.

Shuster, U. A. *Peterburgskie rabochie v 1905–1907 gg.* Leningrad, 1976.

Siljak, Ana. *Angel of Vengeance: The Girl Who Shot the Governor of St. Petersburg and Sparked the Age of Assassination.* New York, 2008.

Sinegub, S. "Vospominaniia chaikovtsa." *Byloe,* no. 8 (1906): 39–80; no. 9 (1906): 90–128; no. 10 (1906): 31–77.

———. *Zapiski chaikovtsa.* Moscow, 1929.

Sistematicheskii ukazatel´ luchshikh knig i zhurnal´nykh statei (1856–1883 g.) [Cheliabinsk catalog]. Cheliabinsk, 1883.

Smirnov, N. E. "Cherty iz zhizni lakhtinskoi tipografii." In Iakimova-Dikovskaia et al., *Narodovol´tsy 80-kh i 90-kh godov,* 178–209.

Smith, Denis Mack. *Garibaldi: A Great Life in Brief.* New York, 1956.

Smith, S. A. *Red Petrograd: Revolution in the Factories, 1917–18.* Cambridge, 1983.

———. *Revolution and the People in Russia and China: A Comparative History.* Cambridge, 2008.

Snytko, T. G. *Russkoe narodnichestvo i pol´skoe obshchestvennoe dvizhenie 1865–1881 gg.* Moscow, 1969.

Sokolov, O. D. *Na zare rabochego dvizheniia v Rossii.* 2nd ed. Moscow, 1978.

Stasova, E. D., ed. *Iz istorii nelegal´nykh bibliotek revoliutsionnykh organizatsii v tsarskoi Rossii: Sbornik materialov.* Moscow, 1956.

Steinberg, Mark D. *Moral Communities: The Culture of Class Relations in the Russian Printing Industry, 1867–1907.* Berkeley, CA, 1992.

———. "'A Path of Thorns': The Spiritual Wounds and Wandering of Worker-Poets." In *Sacred Stories: Religion and Spirituality in Modern Russia,* ed. Steinberg and Heather J. Coleman, 304–29. Bloomington, IN, 2007.

———. *Proletarian Imagination: Self, Modernity, and the Sacred in Russia, 1910–1925.* Ithaca, NY, 2002.

———. "Worker-Authors and the Cult of the Person." In *Cultures in Flux: Lower-Class Values, Practices, and Resistance in Late Imperial Russia,* edited by Stephen P. Frank and Steinberg, 168–84. Princeton, NJ, 1994.

———, ed. *Voices of Revolution, 1917.* New Haven, 2001

Steinberg, Mark D., and Valeria Sobol, eds. *Interpreting Emotions in Russia and Eastern Europe.* DeKalb, IL, 2001.

Stepniak, S. [S. M. Kravchinskii]. *The Russian Peasantry: Their Agrarian Condition, Social Life and Religion.* London, 1905; reprint, Westport, CT, 1970.

———. *Underground Russia: Revolutionary Profiles and Sketches from Life.* With a preface by Peter Lavroff. New York, 1883.

Stites, Richard. *Passion and Perception: Essays on Russian Culture.* Edited by David Goldfrank. Washington, DC, 2010.

———. *Revolutionary Dreams: Utopian Vision and Experimental Life in the Russian Revolution.* Oxford, 1989.

Sukhomlin, V. I. "Iz epokhi upadka partii 'Narodnaia Volia.'" *Katorga i ssylka,* no. 3 (24) (1926): 75–89; no. 4 (25) (1926): 29–45; no. 6 (27) (1926): 65–87; no. 7–8 (28–29) (1926): 61–103.

———. "Narodovol'cheskaia rabochaia organizatsiia na st. Liubotin, Khar'kovo-Nikolaevskoi zh. d." *Puti revoliutsii,* no. 5–6 (8–9) (1927): 31–42.

Suny, Ronald Grigor. *The Soviet Experiment: Russia, the USSR, and the Successor States.* Oxford, 1998.

Surh, Gerald. *1905 in St. Petersburg: Labor, Society, and Revolution.* Stanford, CA, 1989.

———. "Petersburg's First Mass Labor Organization: The Assembly of Russian Workers and Father Gapon." *Russian Review* 40, 3 (July 1981): 241–62 (pt. 1); and 40, 4 (October 1981): 412–41 (pt. 2).

Sushkin, G. G. *Maevki proshlogo.* Moscow, 1926.

Sviatlovskii, V. V. "K istorii pervogo maia (1890–1893 g.)." *Byloe,* no. 16 (1921): 167–73.

———. "Na zare Rossiiskoi sotsial-demokratii." *Byloe,* no. 19 (1922): 139–60.

Takhtarev, K. M. *Rabochee dvizhenie v Peterburge (1893–1901).* Leningrad, 1924.

Taratuta, Evgeniia. *Etel' Lilian Voinich: Sud'ba pisatelia i sud'ba knigi.* Moscow, 1964.

———. *S. M. Stepniak-Kravchinskii—revoliutsioner i pisatel'.* Moscow, 1973.

———. "S. M. Stepniak-Kravchinskii v Italii." In *Rossiia i Italiia: Iz istorii russko-ital'ianskikh kul'turnykh i obshchestvennykh otnoshenii,* 227–58. Moscow, 1968.

Terras, Victor, ed. *Handbook of Russian Literature.* New Haven, 1985.

Tikhomirov, Lev. *Vospominaniia.* 1927; Moscow, 2003.

Travushkin, N. S. "Revoliutsionno-propagandistskaia zarubezhnaia belle-tristika v Rossii." In *Materialy nauchnoi konferentsii Astrakhanskogo pedagogi-cheskogo instituta im. S. M. Kirova,* 57–68. Volgograd, 1972.

Travushkin, N. S. "Zarubezhnaia belletristika v russkom revoliutsionnom obikhode." In *Iz istorii russkoi i zarubezhnoi literatury: Materialy IV zonal'noi konferentsii literaturovedov Povolzh'ia*, edited by V. N. Anoshkina and N. P. Elanskii, 79–98. Saratov, 1968.

———. "Zarubezhnaia khudozhestvennaia literatura v revoliutsionnoi Rossii (2-ia polovina XIX v.–nachalo XX v.)" Doctoral diss., Astrakhanskii gosudarstvennyi pedagogicheskii institut im. S. M. Kirova, 1973.

———. "Zarubezhnyi utopicheskii roman v russkom revoliutsionnom dvizhenii kontsa XIX–nachala XX veka." *Uchenye zapiski Astrakhanskogo gosudarstvennogo pedagogicheskogo instituta im. S. M. Kirova* 27, *Voprosy literatury i zhurnalistiki* (1969): 93–114.

Troitskii, N. A. *"Narodnaia volia" pered tsarskim sudom*. Saratov, 1971.

———. *Rossiia v XIX veke: Kurs lektsii*. Moscow, 1997.

———. *Tsarizm pod sudom progessivnoi obshchestvennosti 1866–1895 gg*. Moscow, 1979.

———. *Tsarskie sudy protiv revoliutsionnoi Rossii*. Saratov, 1976.

Trow, M. J. *Spartacus: The Myth and the Man*. Stroud, UK, 2006.

TSK KPSS, Vysshaia partiinaia shkola, Kafedra zhurnalistiki. *Bol'shevistskaia pechat': Sbornik materialov*, 1: *1895–1903 gg*. Moscow, 1959.

Tvardovskaia, V. A. *Sotsialisticheskaia mysl' Rossii na rubezhe 1870–1880 gg*. Moscow, 1969.

Ushakov, A. V. *Revoliutsionnoe dvizhenie demokraticheskoi intelligentsii v Rossii, 1895–1904*. Moscow, 1976.

Vakhrushev, I. S., and L. P. Roshchevskaia. "D. P. Klements—revoliutsionnyi publitsist i prosvetitel'." In *Ocherki istorii revoliutsionnogo dvizheniia v Rossii v 60–80-kh godakh XIX veka*, edited by E. I. Kiriukhina, 3–20. Kirov, 1979.

Valk, S. N. "Materialy k istorii pervogo maia v Rossii." *Krasnaia letopis'*, no. 4 (1922): 250–88.

———. "Molodaia partiia Narodnoi Voli." *Problemy marksizma*, no. 1 (3) (1930): 95–119.

———, ed. "P. L. Antonov v Petropavlovskoi kreposti." *Krasnyi arkhiv*, no. 31 (1928): 103–17.

Valk, S. N. et al., eds. *Revoliutsionnoe narodnichestvo 70-kh godov XIX veka: Sbornik dokumentov i materialov*. 2 vols. Moscow–Leningrad, 1964–65.

Varzar, V. E. "Vospominaniia starogo statistika." *Donskoi statisticheskii vestnik* 3, 7–9 (1924): 3–22.

Vasil'ev, G. A. *Iz revoliutsionnogo proshlogo: Vospominaniia*. Ulan-Ude, 1954.

Veden'ev, I. "V Khar'kovskikh revoliutsionnykh kruzhkakh 1882–1884 gg." *Letopis' revoliutsii*, no. 5 (1923): 98–111.

Venturi, Franco. *Roots of Revolution: A History of the Populist and Socialist Movements in Nineteenth Century Russia*. Translated by F. Haskell. New York, 1966.

Verhoeven, Claudia. *The Odd Man Karakozov: Imperial Russia, Modernity, and the Birth of Terrorism*. Ithaca, NY, 2009.

V.F.G. *Za Nevskoi zastavoi: Zapiski rabochego Alekseia Buzinova*. Moscow–Leningrad, 1930.

Vilenskii-Sibiriakov, Vl. et al., eds. *Deiateli revoliutsionnogo dvizheniia v Rossii: Bio-bibliograficheskii slovar'. Ot predshestvennikov dekabristov do padeniia tsarizma*. Moscow, 1927–34.

Vincent, David. *Literacy and Popular Culture: England 1750–1914* Cambridge, 1989.

Volk, S. S. *Narodnaia volia 1879–1882*. Moscow–Leningrad, 1966.

Volkov, N. [I. I. Mainov]. "Narodovol'cheskaia propaganda sredi moskovskikh rabochikh v 1881 g." *Byloe*, no. 2 (1906): 175–82.

Volkovicher, I. *Nachalo sotsialisticheskogo rabochego dvizheniia v byvshei russkoi Pol'she: Podgotovitel'nyi period partii "Proletariat." Opyt istoricheskogo issledovaniia*. Moscow–Leningrad, 1925.

Von Geldern, James. *Bolshevik Festivals, 1917–1920*. Berkeley, CA, 1993.

Voronin, Aleksandr. "Kruzhok na zavode Gretera-Krivanek." In *K dvadtstatipiatiletiiu pervogo s"ezda partii (1898–1923)*. Moscow–Petrograd, 1923.

Vpered!/Forward! 4 vols. Zurich and London, 1873–76. Reprinted as *Vpered! Neperiodicheskoe obozrenie*. The Hague, 1974.

Vpered! [newspaper]. London, 1874–76. Reprint, The Hague, 1969.

Wade, Rex A., and Scott J. Seregny, eds. *Politics and Society in Provincial Russia: Saratov, 1590–1917*. Columbus, OH, 1989.

Walicki, Andrzej. *The Controversy over Capitalism: Studies in the Social Philosophy of the Russian Populists*. Oxford, 1969.

———. *A History of Russian Thought from the Enlightenment to Marxism*. Stanford, CA, 1979.

Weinberg, Robert. *The Revolution of 1905 in Odessa: Blood on the Steps.* Bloomington, IN, 1993.

Weitz, Eric. *Creating German Communism, 1890-1990: From Popular Protests to Socialist State.* Princeton, NJ, 1997.

Wildman, Allan K. *The Making of a Workers' Revolution: Russian Social Democracy, 1891–1903.* Chicago, 1967.

Williams, Raymond. *Culture.* Cambridge, 1981.

———. *The Long Revolution.* Westport, CT, 1975.

Winter, Jay. *Dreams of Peace and Freedom: Utopian Moments in the Twentieth Century.* New Haven, 2006.

Wortman, Richard. *The Crisis of Russian Populism.* Cambridge, 1967.

Wynn, Charters. *Workers, Strikes, and Pogroms: The Donbass-Dnepr Bend in Late Imperial Russia.* Princeton, NJ, 1992.

Yarmolinsky, Avrahm. *Road to Revolution: A Century of Russian Radicalism.* New York, 1962.

Zaborov, M. A., ed. *Pervoe maia v dokumentakh i svidetel'stvakh sovremennikov, 1886–1918.* Moscow, 1989.

Zaborov, P. R. "Russkaia kritika kontsa 60-kh–nachala 70-kh godov XIX veka i frantsuzskii demokraticheskii roman." In *Problemy realizma russkoi literatury XIX veka,* ed. B. I. Bursov and I. Z. Serman, 368–78. Moscow–Leningrad, 1961.

Zakharina, V. G. *Golos revoliutsionnoi Rossii: Literatura revoliutsionnogo podpol'ia 70-kh godov XIX v. "Izdaniia dlia naroda."* Moscow, 1971.

———. "Roman Erkmana-Shatriana 'Istoriia krest'ianina' i ego peredelka v revoliutsionnoi narodnicheskoi propagande." *Russkaia literatura,* no. 2 (1964): 117–25.

Zalezhskii, V. *Na putiakh k revoliutsii: 1896–1906 gg.* Moscow–Leningrad, 1925.

Zalkind, L. S. "Vospominaniia narodovol'tsa." *Katorga i ssylka,* no. 3 (24) (1926): 90–94.

Zdobnov, N. V. *Istoriia russkoi bibliografii do nachala XX veka.* 3rd ed. Moscow, 1955.

———. "Iz istorii rekomendatel'noi bibliografii 80-kh godov: Odesskii i cheliabinskii ukazateli." *Sovetskaia bibliografiia,* no. 1 (19) (1941): 152–74.

———. "Konfiskovannye bibliograficheskie izdaniia 80-kh godov." *Katorga i ssylka,* no. 4 (113): 106–22.

Zelnik, Reginald E. *Labor and Society in Tsarist Russia: The Factory Workers of St. Petersburg, 1855–1870.* Stanford, CA, 1971.

———. *Law and Disorder on the Narova River: The Kreenholm Strike of 1872.* Berkeley, 1995.

———. "On the Eve: An Inquiry into the Life Histories and Self-Awareness of Some Worker-Revolutionaries." In *Making Workers Soviet,* edited by Lewis H. Siegelbaum and Ronald Grigor Suny, 17–65. Ithaca, NY, 1994.

———. "Populists and Workers: The First Encounter between Populist Students and Industrial Workers in St. Petersburg, 1871–74." *Soviet Studies* 24, 2 (October 1972): 251–69.

———. "Russian Bebels: An Introduction to the Memoirs of Semen Kanatchikov and Matvei Fisher," Parts 1 and 2. *Russian Review* 35, 3 (July 1976): 249–89; and 35, 4 (October 1976): 417–47.

———. "'To the Unaccustomed Eye': Religion and Irreligion in the Experience of St. Petersburg Workers in the 1870s." *Russian History* 16, 2–4 (1989): 297–326.

———. "*Weber* into *Tkachi*: On a Russian Reading of Gerhart Hauptmann's Play *The Weavers.*" In *Self and Story in Russian History,* edited by Laura Engelstein and Stephanie Sandler, 217–41. Ithaca, NY, 2000.

Zelnik, Reginald E., ed. *Workers and Intelligentsia in Late Imperial Russia: Realities, Representations, Reflections.* Berkeley, 1999.

———, ed. and trans. *A Radical Worker in Tsarist Russia: The Autobiography of Semen Ivanovich Kanatchikov.* Stanford, CA, 1986.

Zel'tser, V. "Iz istorii sektantstva v rabochei srede: Sektanty v g. Nikolaeve v 1890–1900 gg.—po neopublikovannym materialam." *Voinstvuiushchii ateizm,* no. 4 (1931): 29–46.

Zhabko, M. *Iz dalekogo proshlogo: Vospominaniia starogo rabochego.* Moscow–Leningrad, 1930.

Zhitomirskii, D. "Pesni na stikhi G. M. Krzhizhanovskogo." In Shapovalova, *Biografii pesen,* 90–100.

———. "Pesni revoliutsionnoi bor'by: Ocherk tretii—Pesni na stikhi A. N. Pleshcheeva." *Muzykal'naia zhizn',* no. 15 (1958): 8–9.

Zhuikov, G. S. *Peterburgskie marksisty i gruppa "osvobozhdenie truda."* Leningrad, 1975.

Index

The Allan K. Wildman Group Historical Series

1. Michael Melancon and Alice K. Pate, eds., *New Labor History: Worker Identity and Experience in Russia, 1840–1918* (2002)

2. Page Herrlinger, *Working Souls: Russian Orthodoxy and Factory Labor in St. Petersburg, 1881–1917* (2007)

3. Jeff Jones, *Everyday Life and the Reconstruction of Soviet Russia during and after the Great Patriotic War, 1943–48* (2008)

4. John W. Steinberg and Rex A. Wade, eds., *The Making of Russian History: Society, Culture, and the Politics of Modern Russia. Essays in Honor of Allan K. Wildman* (2009)

5. Rose Glickman, trans., *Agnessa: From Paradise to Purgatory. A Voice from Stalin's Russia,* by Agnessa Ivanovana Mironova-Korol', as told to Mira Yakovenko (2012)

6. Felicitas Fischer von Weikersthal, et al., eds., *The Russian Revolution of 1905 in Transcultural Perspective: Identities, Peripheries, and the Flow of Ideas* (2013)

7. Alice K. Pate, *Workers and Unity: A Study of Social Democracy, St. Petersburg Metalworkers, and the Labor Movement in Late Imperial Russia, 1906–14* (2015)

8. Deborah Pearl, *Creating a Culture of Revolution: Workers and the Revolutionary Movement in Late Imperial Russia* (2015)